World War II Reminiscences

Edited by Colonel John H. Roush

John H Roush

World War II Reminiscences
A Collection of Vivid Memories of Combat During World War II
by California Veterans for the most part
Second Edition, 1996, Revised and expanded
Third Printing, 2001

Sponsored by
The Reserve Officers Association of the United States
California Department
World War II Commemoration Committee
Colonel John H. Roush, Jr., AUS-Ret., Editor
Major General Sidney Novaresi, USAF-Ret., Committee Chairman
LTC Ronald Harris, USAFR,
California Department President 2000-2001
Major General James C. Wahleithner, USAF-Ret.,
California Department President, 1993-94
National President 1994-95

600 Deer Valley Rd. Apt. 2E
San Rafael, CA 94903

ISBN 0-9600830-4-9
Library of Congress Control Number 2001130120
Library of Congress Catalog Card Number 95-92808
The first edition carried LC 95-92230

Cover photo by Col. John H. Roush, Jr.
Design & page composition by Val Sherer
Printed by Thomson-Shore, Inc., Dexter, Michigan, U.S.A.

This book may be purchased from:
The Reserve Officers Association of the United States
California Department Chairman
esi, USAF-Ret.
Colonel John Roush
600 Deer Valley Rd. Apt. 2E
San Rafael, CA 94903
rg
Fax 916-482-2045

This volume is dedicated to those men and women who served in the United States Armed Forces during World War II, particularly those who carried the burdens of actual combat. The latter comprised but a small portion, perhaps ten percent, of the nearly eighteen million who served. They carried the major burden of efforts to preserve our cherished ideals of freedom in opposition to the forces of tyranny, aggression and oppression.

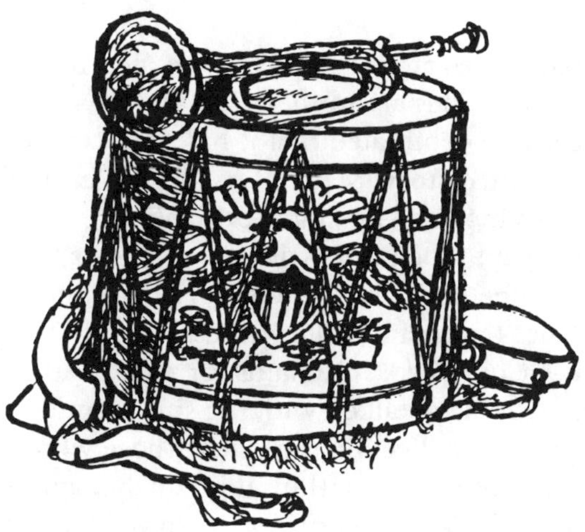

Acknowledgments

The editor wishes to thank the many contributors of personal World War II experiences who made this book possible. Because of the space and time limitations, it was necessary to re-phrase, edit and eliminate some of the material which was not necessarily pertinent to the stories. Every effort was made to not change any facts. In some cases it was necessary to expand the material to make the story clear for readers who might not understand "GI lingo" and might not understand the background or history of the incidents being related. For those not familiar with military abbreviations, which are many, a table is included in the appendix.

Some of the stories are incomplete. The men in this volume, and their living contemporaries are in their 70's and 80's. Many have health problems, some are so debilitated that it has not been possible to obtain more than a fragmented story. Many of us still suffer disabilities from wounds or illnesses incurred during World War II.

Many men spent much time with me in efforts to reconstruct their experiences. For some individuals their story has gone through many revisions. Several of the participants wished to retain their own wording, to which we have acquiesced. It remains for me to express to the many officers and men who have talked with me sincere gratitude for their help in assembling this collection, primarily those who labored with me in a mutual effort to put down within individual chapters their most vivid reminiscences of World War II. Many have loaned to us irreplaceable photographs that we have used in this volume, and for which we extend our thanks.

I would like to extend my most sincere appreciation to Major Abner D. Kuperstein and Mrs. Val Sherer, who have given many hours of valuable help to the development of this volume. Without their help we would never have met our deadlines on either edition.

Many of the subjects have allowed me to extract from their earlier writings portions that could be developed into a chapter of this book. The committee is grateful to them for their participation in this project.

Special thanks are extended to the editors of the following periodicals from which portions have been extracted with their permission:

McCall Corporation, The New York Time Co. Magazine Group, for use of the article by Charles Dickey, which appeared in the Blue Book Magazine in August 1945.

World War II Magazine, published by Cowles History Group, 741 Metler Drive, Suite D-2, Leesburg VA 22075, for use of portions of the article by Thomas Larson, that appeared in the November 1991 issue.

...and the editors and publishers of privately printed volumes mentioned within the chapters.

Many people have helped me locate persons who might contribute stories within this collection; I would like to thank them and those who pre-subscribed volumes thus facilitating the financing of the publication expenses. As you may know, the editors are volunteers, and the profits of this book will be devoted to the Publications Trust Fund, California Department, Reserve Officers Association of the United States, whose charter directs our support of an adequate national defense.

The copyright on this volume is not intended to inhibit the writings of participants in this collection in any way should they wish to develop their stories further. Out of courtesy to the participants in this collection their highest rank attained is shown. You must realize that most of us held a lesser rank during World War II. With some exceptions, the people whose stories are included were junior officers or enlisted men during that war.

The second edition picks up an additional eleven chapters, largely those of individuals whose first draft was received too late to be incorporated into the first edition. These additional stories add further dimension to the collection. However, much more information has been incorporated. Some participants found that there were errors to be corrected. Your editor was able to add more pertinent information, often with the help of others whose eyes were keener.

Special thanks are extended to artist Lou Varrone, whose sketches of an infantryman are included on pages 59 and 322.

Worthy of special recognition is Major Hal Geer, whose fine photographs are included in Appendix L. His Chapter 51 begins on page 84 and further details of his most interesting career are shown on page 370.

Many thanks also to the many other veterans who shared with us photographs to illustrate this volume.

Contents

List of Contributors of Stories

Foreword

It has been almost 50 years now since the ending of World War II. As a youngster of just eight years, I vividly remember Pearl Harbor and the seemingly unending, almost five years that followed. I well remember the departure from our little community of the young men as they traveled throughout the neighborhood saying their farewells. In those days it was appropriate for families to hang in their living room window, a small red flag with white star on it, signifying that a member of that family served in the Armed Forces of the United States. As the war progressed, I well remember the white stars that were replaced with gold stars, telling all that a family member had given the greatest sacrifice possible for their Nation. How sad it was to realize that these fine young people would not live to celebrate the victory that was surely to be ours. In the end, more than 16 million men and women would serve in the military forces of our Nation during that great war, and 295,225 gold stars would be displayed in the windows of grieving families. Another 78,700 soldiers, sailors and airmen would be listed as missing in action.

It is highly appropriate that Colonel Roush has put this book together during the year celebrating the 50th anniversary of the ending of that terrible conflict. In a sense, the book serves to honor the service of our fellow ROAers, but more than that it serves as a precious memory of our many friends who offered their lives to defend this nation during that great war.

More than 2300 years ago a great Philosopher, Plato, said, "Only the dead have seen the last of war, only the strong have avoided war." We in the Reserve Officers Association of the United States are dedicated to building and maintaining a military force in our Nation so strong that no potential enemy will challenge us, so that we will never again have to sacrifice on a field of battle the most precious resource our nation possesses, its young. So let us read of the contributions and sacrifices of our fellow Californians as they appear in this book, and let us learn from their experiences and work together to build a military force that will guarantee the precious freedom that we so enjoy today for many generations to come.

My most humble and sincere thanks to all who participated in the effort to bring this book to us.

James C. Wahleithner, Major General, USAF-Ret
1994-95 President, Department of California
Reserve Officers Association of the United States
1995-96 National President

Subsequent to the publication of the first edition, General Wahleithner was elected National President of the Reserve Officers Association for the term 1995-96 at the National Convention held in Des Moines, Iowa, in June, 1995.

General Wahleithner served as Commander of the Air Force Reserve's 4th Air Force, McClellan Air Force Base, California, where he was responsible for the supervision of more than 26,000 reservists in tactical and strategic airlift missions in the western United States, as well as all Reserve combat rescue, special operations, and weather-reconnaissance missions. He retired from the Reserve in February 1990.

Introduction

Some months ago a committee was formed within the California Department, Reserve Officers Association of the United States, pursuant to a mandate from the national headquarters, to develop and stimulate interest in the Fiftieth Anniversary of World War II.

Many of us gave talks to various groups of community leaders. Subsequently I was asked to edit a book containing the experiences of about fifty people who served in combat theaters during that war.

It has not been difficult for the individuals in this volume to recall vivid memories of World War II, even though fifty years have gone by. Those recollections persist after many years have elapsed because they include some of the most indelible episodes of our lives.

Relatively few of our present population are old enough to have had the experience of being in W.W.II, and, of those, not many served in the armed forces. Less than five or ten percent of those who served during the war had combat experience. Since it was such an important period of this century, the memories and lessons we might learn from that tragic decade should not be lost.

This book does not endeavor to tell the big picture; many histories have done so. These are individual experiences, and, I think, greatly more interesting.

You will find a modesty in the recitals contained here. These people are reluctant to tell you of their bravery and of the great risks most incurred. It wasn't easy to get these stories. Perhaps a good many were more receptive to talking to someone else who shared some of their experiences. Many more men were contacted, seeking their stories, but they were unwilling to bring back to the surface unpleasant memories of suffering and tragedy.

Some of the people in this volume were awarded high decorations, many more of them deserved such, yet, unfortunately, no one got around to writing the necessary paper work.

Abner Kuperstein and/or I were able to help with the editing of these stories, yet they are in the man's own words as much as possible. Some narratives went through half a dozen drafts. Wherever any question occurred, we deferred to the wishes of the participant, even though better form might have been achieved. We regret that we were unable to generate any stories from women, although we talked to many who served during the war. Many persons who had interesting stories felt they should defer to those men who had combat experience.

With a guide line allocation of only a thousand to fifteen hundred words, one cannot say much about four years, or more, of intense activity. However, you will get some vivid impressions from those memories most lucid after the elapse of fifty years. You will see instances of incredible courage and enormous suffering in the course of dangerous assignments. Some of the stories were so absorbing that we extended them to a greater length.

These stories are not just historical accounts with a nostalgic tear here or there. They are vivid experiences of real people, almost entirely Californians, not fanciful fiction; they are recitals of what combat was like. Truth may be stranger than fiction. Certainly these stories are truthfully recited, and thus their value is greater than fiction. Even those born after W.W.II can profit by the experiences of these men.

Most of the people in this book continued on to serve after the war ended, some in a regular career in the armed forces, but most were involved in the reserve sections of the various branches, advancing in due course to higher rank. Many retired after twenty or thirty years of commissioned service, not counting prior service as enlisted men.

All of the branches of service are represented in this collection, and all ranks. Episodes from all of the theaters of war are included. Some of the impressions in this book are those of enlisted men, for the broader range of images cannot but help to give the volume greater depth of meaning. Some who became high ranking officers were enlisted men for part of or entirely throughout the war.

Many of us believe that these memories should be preserved, in part, at least, that subsequent generations might realize what we went through. That might result in better preparation for national defense, which in turn, might reduce our chances of getting involved in another tragedy of such magnitude.

We wish to avoid villifying people of the nationalities who were once our enemies in W.W.II but are now our allies. We must forget our differences of the past and build together a better world.

The recent success of Brokaw's book indicates considerable interest still exists within the public about WWII. These stories are more succinct as to what it was like to have been deeply involved.

It is remarkable to me, as your editor, that many men have told me of the belief in miracles that they survived, something I share with them. Many have found greater faith, as you see in some almost incredible stories of survival.

The task of putting this book together has not been easy, for the aftermath of a severe concussion has created its handicaps, but it has been an indelible series of experiences collecting and editing these stories.

John H. Roush, Jr., Colonel AUS-Ret., Editor

1

Eye Witness to History Attack on Wheeler Field

Master Sergeant Carroll Walker

Carroll Walker entered the service before we were attacked, enlisting December 4, 1940 in the U.S. Army Air Corps. He and one man from each of the squadrons had received some infantry training. As a young soldier he was walking guard duty on December 7, 1941.

The man I relieved said that I could stand in front of the Base Engineering Building or I could stand on the post, over the underground supply of aviation gas. I started my tour of walking my post at 6:00 a.m., while the attack occurred at 7:50, well after sunrise.

I saw the formation of planes coming, however it was not unusual for us to have a mock attack by Naval planes, so I assumed that was what was happening. But I soon saw this one was different. I saw the lead plane dive toward us and the bomb coming, and I hit the deck. It landed right where the guard had stood that I had relieved. Since I was carrying only a sawed off riot gun, I half ran and half crawled, retreating to a banana grove nearby where I watched the action. Planes were strafing personnel who were running in the open. My mouth got dry and I was scared! That's where my friend I enlisted with was killed.

We were attacked seven minutes prior to the attack upon Pearl Harbor, about twenty miles away. We had about 220 fighter aircraft at Wheeler Field, and all but 10 were destroyed by the attack, which lasted about 20 minutes. The attacking fighters flew down the rows of our parked aircraft destroying most of our planes.

I walked through all that rubble, smoke and damage and reported back to the guard house, then tried to help people load guns and prepare for their return.

There was a lull of about twenty minutes before we were attacked again by straggler planes coming back from Pearl Harbor. We were ready then, and our guns were used against the Japanese, who strafed and bombed our field again.

Several of our pilots did race to Halfiva an outlying field and got airborne. Our pilots Welch and Taylor, between them, shot down 5 or 6 Japanese planes. Bellows Field was also hit by the Japanese, but the outlying base of Halfiva was not.

The Japanese came in from the north, using a radio homing beacon that was also being used by twelve B-17's coming in from the northeast, just arriving from Hamilton Field, Marin County, California. Our Radar at the N.E. corner of the island saw a big blip. The officer at Fort Shafter underground bunker thought it was the B-17's coming in and told his men to ignore the reading. The radar did not recognize the size of the attacking force.

One B-17 landed at Wheeler on the short end of the Y runway, Another was shot up at Bellows field.

The severe damage would not have occurred had we been on the full alert that existed during the week before the attack. We went off full alert at noon Saturday. Many people took off Saturday night and were sleeping late Sunday morning. Ironically, a message came in about the time of the attack ordering a resumption of the full alert. The message came in as a telegram, for the radio-telephone communications were not working. I believe the message could have been sent by a more rapid means of communication, which would have given us a hour or two warning time.

I should mention that we could not stay on full alert for long periods. At the time the authorities were more concerned with the potential threat of sabotage than with a potential attack from the sea by the Japanese fleet.

I became a communications person, working with radio and radar. For the next ten days we copied all the code from the Japanese. I recall that they put out a lot of propaganda, speaking of their formulating a "Greater East Asia Co-prosperity Sphere" The Philippines were attacked 7 or 8 hours later, since the attack was held up by fog, and while they had an alert, the Japanese knocked out most of the B-17s and P-40s parked on the runway.

After the attack our people worked feverishly to repair what planes we could. We only had about 10 left of 220. More planes, brought in by freighters, were shipped in crates containing component parts and assembled on the field. That same day of the attack we painted out the red circle that encompassed the star, the insignia on our planes, so that there would be no confusion with the enemy planes carrying a red circle. Our planes were dispersed out among many other temporary air fields on Oahu. We were apprehensive that the Japanese would make a landing of troops the afternoon of the attack. Since the Japanese wore blue, we were ordered out of our blue dungarees.

Assigned to a Pursuit Interceptor Squadron, later named a Fighter Squadron, my squadron went on to serve in the Marianas, Saipan, Guam, and an island off Okinawa, from which our fighters escorted B-29's on their bombing raids over Japan. We had lengthened runways for B-29's to use on Saipan, and later on Tinian, where the *Enola Gay* took off for its nuclear attack. I returned in December of 1944 from Saipan to the United States.

I served on active duty five years and in the Reserves 11 years, but had to withdraw with a back injury. Following the war I graduated from the University of California at Berkeley and have had a career in Life Insurance and Financial Services.

Code named Operation Z, the Japanese attack on Pearl Harbor on December 7, 1941, was planned by Admiral Isoruku Yamamoto (1884-1943), Chief of the Combined Fleet. He advocated carrier warfare and was opposed to initiating a war against the United States. However, if that was to be, he concluded Japan had to make a decisive first strike against the U.S. Pacific Fleet.

On January 2, 1941, Admiral Yamamoto ordered a study by his staff of possible attacks upon Pearl Harbor. The plan was based upon the success of the British torpedo attack upon the Italian fleet at Taranto in 1940. Admiral Yamamoto was killed on April 18, 1943, by U.S. Army Air Force P-38's near Bougainville. (*See page 184.*)

The question of who was to blame for the disaster has been a matter of vexing concern of all who have thought of the terrible losses we initially incurred. *(See page 359 for additional comments.)*

2

Witness to the Commencement of the War

Commander Warren L. Craig, USNR-Ret.

December 7, 1941, Pearl Harbor. It was a peaceful morning until about 7:55 a.m., when the sounds of bombs dropping out of the sky and the screech of General Quarters from our alarm system filled the air. I was aboard the *USS Montgomery*, Destroyer Mine-Layer #17, nested with other ships in Mine Division II, opposite Pearl City, Hawaii.

I had been planning to meet my twin brother, Ensign Wesley P. Craig, Jr., aboard his ship, the *USS Cassin*, which was in dry dock. At the sounding of General Quarters, I was in my stateroom dressing in my whites. I strapped on my .45 cal. pistol and started up the ladder. Emerging, I realized that Japanese planes were dropping bombs on Ford Island. They made a direct hit on the old battleship Utah, which turned over immediately. The signal tower at Hickham Field was flashing: "This is not a drill!"

Our first duty was to bring up ammunition for our three inch anti-aircraft guns and our two .30 caliber guns. Our five inch guns were useless, because of our ship being tied up parallel with two other old destroyers.

As the spotter for the three inch gun, following an enemy aircraft, I gave the gun crew corrections of burst and proper compensation to reach the target. At our mooring location we had close range shooting at the Japanese planes, which were just pulling up after dropping their torpedoes. Their planes were crashing in the harbor all around us. I am certain we contributed to the shooting down of many enemy planes.

After the first Japanese wave had departed, the OD (Officer of the Day) asked me to have the coxswain motor me ashore, to use the public phone at Pearl City. Without the proper change the operator gave me a hard time until she realized we were being attacked. While coming ashore we were strafed by Japanese torpedo planes after they had dropped their torpedoes destined for our battleships. The survivors of the *USS Utah* were coming ashore at Pearl City. Some of the personnel were badly wounded.

On one occasion we noticed a Japanese pilot still alive in his downed plane. We sent our coxswain out in the motor whale boat to pick up the downed pilot. Our man returned with only the Japanese helmet. He said he had to shoot the pilot in a struggle. CINPAC wanted a more detailed explanation why he was not taken prisoner; they wanted information from the flyer.

In retrospect, if we had taken him prisoner, and he had told us the location of the Japanese battle fleet, I am quite certain none of the U.S. Pacific Fleet would have been afloat after that day. All of our ships would likely have steamed right into range of Japanese 16 and 18 inch guns and would have been picked off like sitting ducks. The largest ships to get out of Pearl Harbor then were light and heavy cruisers with only six or eight inch guns, inadequate for a confrontation.

At about the time of the second wave of Japanese bombing, we saw a two-man Japanese submarine steaming up the channel with its conning towers exposed. Our outboard DM, the *USS Ramsey*, sent a five inch shell through the conning tower, and the sub sank in the channel. I will

Wesley Craig (left) and Warren Craig, 1941 graduates, University of California, Berkeley

always remember, in the heat of battle, the senior officer aboard the Mine Division, standing on the *Ramsey*'s forecastle raising his fist at the Japanese pilots, as they flew over us, repeating over and over, "You son of a bitch!"

Most of the other ships in the harbor were directed by a junior officer aboard. I witnessed many events: the destruction of the hangers on Ford Island, two PBY seaplanes shot down trying to land on the island, a gallant battleship trying to make a run out of the channel, while many brave men were incinerated from direct hits of bombs and fire. The most courageous scene I witnessed was the dog fight of two Army Air Force pilots, who took on the whole Japanese Air Force, and shot down two Zero fighter planes. There were black clouds billowing upward from battleship row.

After the last attack at about 10:45 a.m. we were steaming out to sea, with most of our crew aboard, including our Captain and Division Commander. Our first mission was to hunt enemy submarines and keep the channel open for our cruisers to steam out of Pearl Harbor. All destroyers turned on their sonar gear as soon as they cleared the channel. Depth charges were being dropped everywhere by the destroyers

Wesley Craig (left) and Warren Craig, retired in 1987.

searching out the enemy. However, it developed that most of the soundmen were pinging on coral reefs and other underwater marine obstructions.

Our next assignment was to herd all local Japanese fishing boats back to port in Honolulu. With all our guns trained on them, I have never seen such frightened people. Our third assignment that day was to patrol a sector of the western sea frontier off Honolulu and Pearl Harbor. That evening planes from our own carrier Enterprise tried to land on Ford Island, but they were shot down. It looked like a Roman Holiday with tracer bullets flying everywhere.

We stayed at sea for nine or ten days patrolling and guarding the outer sea frontier until we had to go in for refueling. At that time we saw the row of sunken battleships. Then I was happy to learn that my brother had survived. We shared my uniforms, since Wesley lost everything on the Cassin. His ship had taken a direct hit.

The day prior to December 7th I had been given guard mail duty. That required an officer to board every ship in Pearl Harbor to pick up all confidential and secret mail and deliver the packet to CINPAC. Thus I had a lasting impression of all our fleet the day before the sneak attack. I was left with a depressed feeling, knowing that a lot of my shipmates on other ships would never fight another battle.

Like so many Navy people, it bothered me to have seen how the Japanese penetrated our outer defenses and successfully completed a sneak attack without our having had any warning. In retrospect, I concluded there existed a lack of communication throughout the chain of command. Our flag and staff officers did not receive any warning of approaching enemy planes. Let us hope that such a disaster may never happen again to the American people. Next time, we may not have the privilege of time to rearm.

Another story of Commander Craig's adventures in the South Pacific Theater is included later in this collection.

3

Reporting in With a Bang!

Lieutenant Commander
Thomas J. Larson, USNR-Ret.

Fate, destiny, luck, and obedience to military orders can determine if one is to die or survive in a war. As a high school youth in my original home town at Aitkin, Minnesota, I'd served from age 15 to 18 as a private in Company B, 135th Minnesota National Guard Regiment. While cycling through Europe as a Rover Boy Scout in 1938 and 1939, I'd visited many of the World War I battlefields in northern France. World War II would come soon; and those still battered battlefields convinced me I must not let myself get drafted into the army. On my vagabond journey I'd worked as a seaman on one tanker and two freighters. I decided I'd join the Navy. After one semester at the University of California at Berkeley, I took midshipman training at Northwestern University in Chicago.

In late November of 1941, in that same great Pacific storm, while the Japanese Fleet was heading for Pearl Harbor, I was the Executive Officer on *YP 109* (Yacht Patrol), a large yacht converted to Naval use, which arrived on December 5th.

CINCPAC Staff Lt. J.G. Herb Fairchild, from Berkeley, California and I were leisurely walking toward the submarine base where CINCPAC had its headquarters, and where I would report for the first day of duty at my new post. Chirping noisily, the myna birds heralded a lovely sunny day. My sea legs were not yet used to solid ground. Breathing deeply, I enjoyed the wonderful fragrance of the balmy air.

It was about 7:45 a.m. We would relieve the night watch a bit early, as was polite naval custom. While we walked along in our tropical white uniforms, we saw low-flying, small, black single-winged planes above us and to our left.

"How interesting," I thought. "Maneuvers on Sunday."

Not far away, I heard anti-aircraft guns shooting.

Ahead of us was a large spreading tree. I waved nonchalantly up at the pilot in one of the black planes. I noticed a few leaves fluttering down from the tree. At the time I didn't think anything of it. Yet the wind wasn't blowing.

Then I saw men running for shelter. More planes flew low overhead—over the submarine base toward Ford Island and our battleships. Now, there were more scattered bursts of .50-caliber gunfire and anti-aircraft. Overhead, a dark plane with a red rising-sun insignia burst into flames. It plunged into the water nearby.

As we walked around the corner of the building, I saw more men running into the headquarters. I still thought I was seeing maneuvers, but wondered why they were being held on Sunday.

I followed Fairchild up to the second floor, headquarters for the senior officers, wondering how I had received the assignment to a great staff.

Rickshaw, October 1945, Tokyo

Yokasuka Harbor, 1945, from the carrier Lexington

Someone in the communications office told us we were at war. Unbelievable! The Japanese were bombing us! I was in a state of shock. I remember that I had no fear, just complete surprise.

No one had time to give me any training. Lt. East shoved a clipboard in my hand and said I was "officer messenger plugger." Freshly decoded messages were to be delivered by me to the various staff officers. All such messages were top secret and urgent.

I was in and out of Admiral Husband Kimmel's office many times. He was a lean middle-aged man with a fiery temper. Far from being cool and collected, Admiral Kimmel was cursing and ranting and raving whenever he read the dreadful messages I brought him about batttleships blowing up and sinking, the planes and hangers at Ford Island being demolished, and the Army's Schofield Barracks being bombed and staffed.

He was red-faced and completely flustered. My many appearances brought nothing but bad news. Of all the staff officers I delivered messages to that sad morning—and there were many—it was Admiral Kimmel I would remember most vividly. He had to take all the blame. He was relieved by Admiral Chester Nimitz, while the rest of his staff remained.

When not required to deliver messages and replies back to the communications office, I was up on the roof of the building watching the battle. While not feeling fear, I was shocked at the sight of battleships being destroyed. I saw the *Oklahoma* rolling over, the *Arizona* sinking, the other ships trying to get underway, the *Nevada* making it to a mud bank, and all hell exploding over at Ford Island.

Later that day our staff of ensigns was increased with survivors from sunken ships. One, a small man, had slipped through a porthole when the *Oklahoma* rolled over. He told me a broad-shouldered officer behind him was too big to slip through and was left in the ship to drown. Other junior officers had been rescued from the oily water. A few lucky ones had been on liberty and were ashore.

Still without fear, I went about my grim messenger duty and returned often to the roof to watch my first great naval battle. Flames and explosions were to be seen all over Pearl Harbor. Our guns were shooting at the enemy planes. Rescue boats were pulling men out of the water who were covered with thick, burning oil. A few enemy planes were being hit and exploding into the water.

By evening I fully realized we were in war, and we were restricted to base. Anti-aircraft shells were still exploding and machine guns rattled. Anything that moved that night was in danger of being shot.

In the middle of the night I heard shooting and shrapnel and machine-gun bullets flying around. The air-raid alarm was an awful, scary-sounding noise. Even my British roommate was uneasy—he had been in the Battle of Dunkirk. We learned later that it had been our own planes flying overhead that were shot at; everyone was jittery and trigger-happy.

No one in the communications office had any time to train me in communications. So, to kill time, I went up on the roof to talk with the machine-gun crews. The *Arizona* was still smoking, although most of her was under water.

I met many men of the ill-fated ships that were victims of the fury of the Japanese attacks. Yet morale was high, despite the many rumors. By the tenth we saw some of the battleships being salvaged. While off duty I was able to visit the *Elvida* (YP-109); the little ship had been repainted and the crew were fine, although a bomb had landed nearby. I visited Hickam Airfield, where scores of men had been killed in their barracks. The place was in ruins, with most of the planes destroyed.

Later, after seven months with CINCPAC, I served with the COMSOPAC (Commander, South Pacific) staff for four months in New Caledonia. From there I was sent to Naval Base Tulagi for 11 months in the Solomons. I was sent back to the states as a liaison officer on the damaged light cruiser *Leander* (a New Zealand ship). After a year at Naval Air Station Livermore in California, I finished the war serving on the second aircraft carrier *Lexington* when she steamed triumphantly into Tokyo Bay with the U.S. Seventh Fleet.

A Lieutenant Commander by war's end, Tom Larson returned to civilian life at Berkeley, California, traveled on several expeditions, and graduated with a BA degree in Anthropology from the Univ. of California. Subsequently he earned advanced degrees (M.Litt at Oxford, Ph.D. at Univ. of Virginia). He taught anthropology at various universities for twenty years and has been on many expeditions. He is an Emeritus Fellow of the Explorers Club.

This story is extracted from a larger article appearing in *World War II* magazine, in the November 1991 issue, with permission of the editors and Dr. Larson.

4

Japanese Attack California

MG Sidney Novaresi, USAF-Ret

With the unanticipated attack on Pearl Harbor on December 7, 1941, Californians were ill-prepared for war, and apprehensive of a Japanese landing along our coastline. The Japanese did accommodate that apprehension with a few token feints, but hardly deserving of the wide-spread fear among the population.

Considering the treachery of the circumstances involving this country in World War II, immediate mobilization was something desired, but not easily achieved. There was an enormous amount of confusion even among the National Guard troop units that had been mobilized earlier in the year, among which was mine.

I was hastily drafted into coast-line patrol in the vicinity of Morro Rock (about 100 miles northwest of Santa Barbara). Here I was, a lone soldier carrying a BAR (Browning Automatic Rifle) with 200 rounds of .30 caliber ammunition and a 60 pound radio. My orders were to patrol 5 miles northerly from Morro Rock and report any impending invasion. And there I was, desolate to be left alone for 13 hours, without relief, apprehensive and trigger-happy, guarding against invasion.

This is amusing now, but at the time the general public (to say nothing about the military services commands) were in a state of absolute panic.

The west coast became a dangerous place in which to roam, especially at night. Cows were turned into hamburger by machine gun fire, since they didn't know the password. People drove along the coastal highways without lights at night because lights would silhouette our tankers at sea, making them easy targets for Japanese submarines. Many ships were, indeed, sunk by Japanese subs.

In late February of 1942 the Japanese submarine I-17, (Commander Kozo Nishino, commanding) made landfall off San Diego, then moved northward up the California coast. I-17 was one of a new, long range class, copied from the latest German model, with some modifications. Launched in July 1939, it was 348 feet long, weighed 1,950 tons and had an impressive surface speed of 16 knots. With a cruising range of 16,000 nautical miles, it could remain at sea for 90 days without refueling. The sub carried 6 forward torpedo tubes and a 5.5 inch deck gun. It also mounted a hangar containing a reconnaissance plane.

In the late afternoon of 23 February 1942, Commander Nishino surfaced off Santa Barbara to repair a faulty engine. He ordered the gunnery officer to prepare to fire the deck gun. Taking the vessel to within a mile of the Bankline (Richfield) Oil Company installation on the coast, Nishino opened fire, putting 29 rounds into the oil field area. Commander Nishino then took the sub leisurely back out to sea, leaving unbelievable chaos in his wake. Everyone was trying to find out what had happened—communications systems were totally jammed, and the military defense commands were not able immediately to determine the true extent of the raid.

The skipper of I-17 radioed Tokyo that he had shelled Santa Barbara and had left it aflame, with panic in the streets. In reality, the attack had accomplished only about $500 worth of damage to the oil installation. By 2000 hours that night (8 PM) a blackout was enforced all the way from San Diego to Monterey, and all radio stations along the coast were silenced.

As a result of this incident, my unit, Battery A, 143rd Field Artillery, a part of the 40th Infantry Division was rushed 123 miles, under blackout conditions, to the Santa Barbara coast, with the mission to engage any surfacing submarines with artillery fire and to repulse any land assault.

At the oil installation we found a number of unexploded shells (duds) from the submarine gunfire. Captain Barney Hagen, our company commander, decided these were too dangerous to ignore, and ordered attempts to explode the duds with small-arms fire. Most were detonated, but one remained. Capt Hagen decided to do the last honors himself. Using a Colt .45 caliber handgun, he fired a number of times before detonating the shell. Unfortunately, standing too close, he received a fairly serious leg wound from a piece of shrapnel as the round exploded, requiring several months of hospitalization. Captain Hagen may be the only US serviceman to be awarded the Purple Heart Medal for wounds received in action within the contiguous United States during WWII.

We continued our mission, but no submarines were sunk by our regiment. The fear of invasion, however, was real and caused a lot of excitement along the California coast. In a few instances, death occurred for unwary travelers who encountered nervous soldiers demanding passwords the victims did not know.

One puzzle was why the submarine attack selected the particularly insignificant Richfield Oil Company site near Santa Barbara. The story came out only after I-17 was sunk near New Caledonia in August of 1943.

The six surviving members of the submarine crew revealed the reason.

In the early 1930's, Commander Nishino had taken on oil at the oil company installation and was treated to the usual company hospitality offered to visiting foreign shipping captains. During a stroll along a beach trail, Nishino stumbled and fell into a large patch of prickly-pear cactus. The painful removal of the needles marked one of the most excruciating moments of his career, making him suffer an unbearable loss of 'face' and generating a longing for revenge.

It is remarkable how little personal incidents such as this one had such substantial impacts on the lives of so many people during the war.

While this story arises out of an incident early in W.W. II, the young soldier went on to a distinguished career in the Air Force, retiring with the rank of Major General. Another story is included later in this collection telling of his exciting flying experiences.

5

Leadership of the Tokyo Raid

General James Harold "Jimmy" Doolittle, USAF (1896-1994)

Early after the attack at Pearl Harbor, President Roosevelt declared his desire to top military leaders that a substantial retaliatory attack on the main islands of Japan be mounted as soon as possible to increase home morale and instill a greater sense of "can do" attitude among our people.

The key to the success of the mission, our top military people agreed, was the selection of a highly experienced pilot and aeronautical engineer, who was also an inspiring, courageous leader. Doolittle was selected since, as Hap Arnold explained, "He was fearless, technically brilliant, a leader who not only could be counted upon to do a task himself if it were humanly possible, but could inspire that spirit within others." Doolittle had proven exceptional skill by winning an impressive array of air trophies. We was well renowned for his aeronautical knowledge and had proven superb flying ability.

America and its Allies desperately needed a morale booster, what with the devastatingly rapid success of the Japanese in moving throughout the Pacific on their plan of conquest.

It was decided to use Mitchell B-25 bombers, which could carry 2,000 pounds of bombs and make a two thousand mile flight, provided extra gas tanks were incorporated. The key question was whether they could be launched from an aircraft carrier. Doolittle's expertise and superb training of the group developed that capability. Since the Japanese knew the range of naval aircraft was 350 miles they planned to launch from the aircraft carrier when 400 miles out.

Carrying 500 lb. bombs and incendiary bombs, it was thought that great damage could be occasioned to the heartland of the predator nation. This was to be the beginning of the reversal of the tide of aggression. The planes were to land in that part of mainland China still held by our ally, with the planes to be donated to new aviation units being formed.

Lead by then Lieutenant Colonel Doolittle, each plane had a crew of five courageous men. Volunteers were requested for few thought they would soon return to the U.S.A. The 80 brave men were to be returned home as heroes adored by the nation.

One of the most dramatic events of World War II was planned by General Doolittle. On April 18, 1942, five months after we were attacked by Japan, a daring assault was launched from the aircraft carrier Hornet, the Navy's newest carrier.

Doolittle knew that if Admiral Halsey's ship were under fire and if they were not within reach of Japan the bombers would be dumped into the sea. Such would be necessary to bring up the Hornet's fighters from below deck to join the action. Refueling of all vessels of the armada was planned for 800 miles off the coast of Japan, but took place a thousand miles out. After launch of the bombers the flotilla was ordered to proceed eastward as rapidly as possible, for the group was outclassed by the naval power available then to the Japanese.

Doolittle was airborne at 8:20 a.m. He had the most difficult take off due to the shorter space caused by the crowding of planes. Upon being spotted by Japanese fishing vessels maintaining an outpost line, it was decided to launch prematurely. The 16 B-25 twin-engine medium bombers flew 650 miles west to Japan against specific industrial targets in the major cities of Tokyo, Yokohama, Kobe, Osaka, and Nagoya. The raid had caught the Japanese by surprise. Doolittle's plane dropped bombs at 12:20 on factories in Tokyo. Increased speed to avoid fighters, low level flight and bad weather made further demands on limited fuel.

In a rainy darkness Doolittle reached landfall over China at 8:45 p.m. Flak had shaken them up, his plane had sustained a few holes in the tail. His plane, like all of the others, except one that landed safely in Russia, ran out of fuel while over Japanese occupied territory of China, and the crew bailed out before the plane crashed.

Fortunately they were rescued by friendly Chinese. They met up with other fliers of the group in Chosin, went then to Chunking, and after passing through Calcutta, were returned home.

While the damage to Japan from the raid was not great, the

Japanese developed the realization that Japan was not invulnerable. It was a severe psychological shock to the nation that they had been attacked and their forces were unable to intercept the intruding force. The people had been inculcated with an emphasis of spiritual strength and an assurance that they were invincible. This then came in doubt. The effect was considerable. The Japanese press countered with an effort to increase morale: "We must rouse our warrior spirit and vow to defend our homeland to the death."

The Japanese launched a campaign of vicious retaliation, committing widespread atrocities to the Chinese communities that had given aid to the downed airmen. The Japanese military used vicious tactics to teach the Chinese a permanent lesson of the consequences of giving aid to Americans.

Eight airmen were captured and flown to Tokyo. They were tortured violently in an effort to learn the secrets of the attack. Two were executed, after a phony trial. Some did not get home until after the war ended.

Doolittle, a Californian, received the Medal of Honor on May 19, 1942, and was promoted to Brigadier General. The citation read: "For conspicuous leadership above the call of duty, involving personal valor and intrepidity at an extreme hazard to life. With the apparent certainty of being forced to land in enemy territory or perish at sea, Gen. Doolittle personally led a squadron of Army bombers, manned by volunteer crews, in a highly destructive raid on the Japanese mainland."

Four other officers of the flight group subsequently became generals of the Air Force. In 1989 Doolittle was the recipient of the Presidential Medal of Freedom.

As an Army man, most people of similar background would disagree with the quote of Gen. Doolittle, made in 1949: "The function of the Army and Navy in any future war will be to support the dominant air arm."

Tokyo Raid 1942

Kappeler, Birch and Lawson

Other Californian participants in the Tokyo Raid included Lt. Frank A. Kapperler, navigator (from San Francisco), who subsequently retired as a Lieutenant Colonel, and S/Sgt. William L. Birch, bombardier, who subsequently became a Second Lieutenant (from Calexico, CA), both on the plane named *"Hari Karier"* by their crew.

Major Ted W. Lawson (from Fresno, CA) was the pilot of another plane and sustained severe injuries. Unfortunately one of his legs had to be amputated. Together with Bob Considine, in 1943, he wrote the highly acclaimed book, *Thirty Seconds Over Tokyo.* He won the Distinguished Flying Cross.

All three officers mentioned above were able to link up with the other fliers, through the assistance of friendly Chinese, and were able to return home in due course.

In response to a questionnaire, Office of Air Force Information, March 27, 1957, Birch told of his experiences:

"The takeoff was surprisingly easy, and, believe me, from my bombardier's station in the nose I could see everything that was going on. Since the *Hornet* could swing directly into the wind, there was no drift as we started our roll down the carrier's deck. My biggest worry was that the pilot, Captain Greening, might catch the island of the carrier with the right wing tip as we went by.

"Our targets were the docks, oil refineries, and warehouses between Tokyo and Yokohama. When we arrived over the coastline, it reminded me of Southern California. People on the ground waved at us. We reached Tokyo northeast of the city when we were first attacked by enemy fighters. Four of them jumped us, and we ran into flak. Sergeant Gardner put two of them out of action, firing from the top turret. I released my bomb load of two incendiaries and two high explosives (500 pound bombs) on a large oil refinery and tank farm from about twelve hundred feet. There was an immediate explosion and fire broke out.

"With the bombs gone, we headed out to sea at about fifty feet. We sighted several small fishing craft about five miles off shore, so I machine-gunned them with the .30 caliber gun in the nose. The first one burst into flames, and the crew jumped overboard."

Most of the crews bailed out over China when their planes ran out of fuel. Birch's crew laughed about how the ship was aptly named, having committed *hari-kari* over China.

The story of Ted Lawson's rescue sounds as though it was a heroic tale of imaginative fiction. When Doolittle gave the pilots a choice, Lawson chose a steel smelter plant in Tokyo to target with his three 500-pound demolition bombs plus one 500-pound incendiary. Seventh in line of take-off for the 2,200 miles of non-stop flying, they flew in single file at a slow, gas-saving speed. Trying to land on the Chinese beach in a storm, a wave caught the wheel of the plane and it crashed near shore. All five men reached the beach, but they were all injured in the accident. The crew was moved repeatedly by friendly Chinese, narrowly escaping capture by Japanese patrols.

The Tokyo Raid was launched from the *U.S.S. Hornet* (CV-8) aircraft carrier, weighing 20,000 tons, commissioned in 1941. President Roosevelt referred to the ship as *Shangri-la* when he spoke of the origination of the raid. Its captain was Marc "Pete" Mitscher, who later became a Vice Admiral and commanded Carrier Task Force 58 in the Pacific Campaign. The *Hornet* was sunk in the Battle of Santa Cruz, October 16, 1942, after being struck by two Kamikaze planes and follow-up attacks of two Japanese destroyers *Makikumo* and *Akigumo*. A second carrier named *Hornet* (CV12) served later during the war and was only recently decommissioned. It was launched August 30, 1943, and it destroyed nearly 1500 Japanese aircraft and sunk 54 ships.

6

Bombers Over Java 1942

M/Sgt. Robert F. Graf, USAFR

Serving as the only radio man, as well as a tail and waist gunner, I flew as part of the crew in LB 30 Liberator and B-17E Flying Fortresses four engine bombers operating out of Java early in the war in an effort to hinder the rapid advance of Japanese aggressors. As a part of the 7th bomber Group, 5th bomber Command, we slowed their path of conquest and probably precluded the Japanese invasion of Australia.

On January 12, 1942, the first of our bombers landed on a soggy grass runway at Malang, Java during the monsoon season. Some of the crews went to Java by the established route westerly, but others came easterly the hard way by way of Brazil, the African Gold Coast, to the Mid-East, then through India.

On January 16, we took off at 0440, our first mission (3 LB 30's and 2 B-17's). We stopped enroute to refuel and load bombs at a short airstrip at Kendari in the Celebes, then went on to bomb the airdrome at Langoan, 20 miles south of Manado in the Celebes. I counted 24 fighters lined up on the runway and more in revetments, while several were coming up to meet our formation of four planes. One had to return because of engine trouble. Our Liberator lurched upward as 2 tons of bombs fell from our bomb bay. They dropped in trail from all three Liberators across runways, buildings and planes. The B-17E hit the ships in the harbor.

In the back, I watched a Zero slide gracefully into a position opposite the waist gun, the pilot deftly placing himself beyond the travel of the top turret and outside the arc of the tail guns. It was a beautifully executed maneuver intended to take out the top turret. But in his haste, the Japanese airman overlooked the Liberator's waist gun, a mistake I quickly brought to his attention.

Aiming at a triangle-shaped area formed by the Zero's cockpit, wing, and engine, I emptied a 250 round ammo can in the triangle, then watched as the Zero tipped up gracefully on a wing, started spinning down and exploded. I patted the gun affectionately and put in a new can of ammunition. It wasn't easy to handle the gun with gloves on, but they were a necessity at an altitude where the air temperature was twenty degrees below zero, where bare hands froze to metal.

Back in the tail, Skip Flanagan shot down two Zeros before they could get close enough to use their thirty caliber guns. With his guns empty more Zeros came in. I heard the machine gun bullets rattle against the armor plate behind me. Cannon shells exploded under my feet and heavy smoke boiled up from under the decking.

I looked down to find my flying suit shredded below the knee. I had shrapnel in my legs and two other men were wounded. Skip finished loading and blew two Zeros to small pieces. Upon seeing smoke, I tore up the deck to find blankets and luggage were on fire. I tossed them out as the pilot put the plane into a shallow dive to the protection of a huge cumulus cloud.

We crash landed on the runway at Makassar, for a tire blew and sparks flew when the body of the LB-30 hit the runway sliding through a mound of dirt, snapping off the wheels. The fuselage buckled, but to the surprise of everyone the plane did not catch fire. It had more than a hundred bullet holes, and dozens of cannon shells had hit the wings and fuselage. The two other Liberators had also been badly damaged by enemy fighters.

On another mission we replaced one of our wounded gunners with a new arrival, who proved to be a phenomenal shot, taking out two Zeros at 2,000 yards, using the compensating sight. He was awarded a citation and returned to the States to become an instructor of aerial gunnery.

Our prescribed tactics called for a forward formation on the bombing run without deviation although attacked by fighters. We found that the Zero pilots learned our vulnerable spot and approached us low and head-on. We of the crew figured out that if our plane suddenly dived, upon attack, the top turret could take out the fighters with ease, for our guns had longer range and were twin .50's as compared the Zero's .30 caliber machine-guns. We shot down a lot of Zeros, however we were reprimanded for deviating from direct orders.

We flew a number of missions seeking a Japanese aircraft carrier. We flew night flights over the Sundra Strait with the sea calm in bright moonlight. Upon sighting the ship, the pilot called Jokjakarta to give the carrier's location. All of our guns were manned. The carrier steamed east, spitting Zeros into the sky.

"We'll bomb from twenty-thousand, Roy," lst Lt. Bayse, our pilot, told the bombardier over the intercom.

"That's too high, Sir. She'll turn out of the way." replied S/Sgt. Bob Wilhite.

"I know it, but I've got orders."

A dozen Zeros climbed to the bomber's altitude and trailed along behind them, biding their time, waiting until the pilot settled into a committed bomb run and became vulnerable to their attack.

"My guess is she's headed for Lombok Strait, east of Bali," 2d Lt. Danny Skandera, the navigator, told the pilot over the intercom. "If she gets through the strait, she'll be able to get close enough to send those Zero's to Kendari and those already at Kendari can keep her covered until she gets out of our range."

When we moved into the bombing run it was the moment the Zeros had been waiting for. They came in fast. I fired a long burst at two fighters closing on our tail. My aim was high and the Zeros dived under our plane. Tony brought both down with a long going away shot. M/Sgt.Skip Flanagan, the flight engineer, got another one with the right waist gun.

Bullets rattled against the armor plate under me as a Zero slid by in a low quartering pass. A second one tried that while my incendiaries found the attacker's gas tank.

The Zero exploded in a cloud of smoke, fire and debris. I missed another as it tried a pass from above, while Danny finished him with a short burst from the top turret.

We were bounced around by flak, for the Zeros gave the ship our altitude. We dropped our bombs, but the carrier pulled hard right rudder and the explosions were in the water where the carrier should have been.

On February 20, 1942, we were on a mission performing bomb runs over a battle cruiser and landing ships, but the Zeros would not attack our B-17E's or LB-30's. We sank the Cruiser, which is still where we left it, deep in the Bali Trench, too deep for salvage. But after we had returned to our field near Malang (Singoseri) Java, the field was strafed by Zeros. The picture shows that occurring.

Six weeks later we had to evacuate Java. I went on to serve during the battle of Coral Sea in the summer of 1942 and later became a gunnery instructor. I earned the Silver Star, and the Air Medal, but did not wait around for a formation at the separation center to receive the Purple Heart. In civilian life I was an electronics engineer.

In 1988 my book, *Java 1942,* was published by Thousand Springs Press, after a great deal of research, that told the story in greater detail.

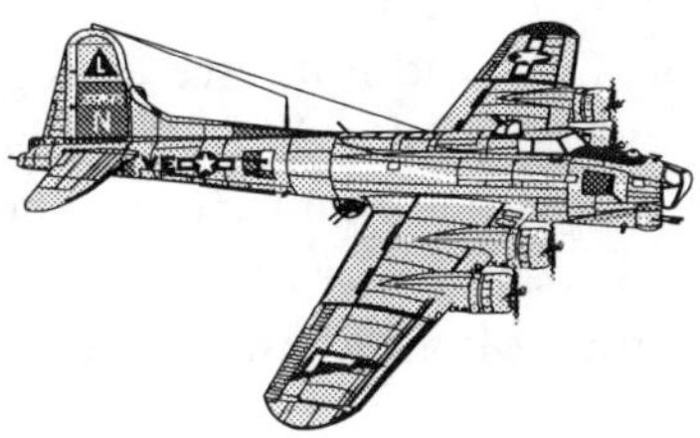

7

Coast Guard in Action

Rear Admiral Bennett S. Sparks, USCGR-Ret

Soon after my 17th birthday I entered the armed forces on December 14, 1942—one of the many millions who were caught up in a conflict that changed our lives forever.

My experiences in W.W.II initially were in the Pacific as a Coast Guard petty officer air crewman, qualified in aviation electronics, radio, radar and Loran, as well as aerial gunnery.

In the Pacific, the Japanese did not have enough submarines to occupy our efforts, so we were transferred to the North Atlantic. I was serving in a crew flying PBY seaplanes, a twin-engine patrol aircraft searching for enemy submarines. By present day standards that was not a sophisticated aircraft. We took off at 90 knots, climbed, cruised and landed at 90 knots.

PBM's were a much larger aircraft, called the Martin-Mariner, a twin-engine plane, more capable; it could fly for up to 23 hours without refueling. I served also on other amphibious aircraft. Many flights averaged 21 hours patrolling the Atlantic searching for subs. Our missions often took a week, with stops at Newfoundland, Greenland, Iceland, Liverpool, England and back to Elizabeth City, North Carolina via Bermuda. Our duties involved flying most of the time, with 3 days off between trips. Patrolling the oceans looking for a surfaced enemy submarine is tedious, boring duty, and your eyes get very weary. We would quickly attack German submarines that were surfaced; that was easy. Trying to find submarines below the surface in those days was more difficult. Our radar was primitive but effective. We had the first of very unsophisticated sonars. We would drop sonar buoys and could depth-charge submarines located below the surface.

In the Atlantic, in those early days of the war, German submarines were very active and kings of the seas. From the beaches of the southeastern States one could see our ships go up in flames every day;

sometimes two or three per day. They would get our oilers coming up from Aruba with fuel for the United States. They would get our freighters bringing cargo from the Gulf of Mexico. They would sink Allied military vessels as well. They would seldom attack convoys that were just leaving the States, but would wait to strike those deeper out to sea.

I have selected just a few incidents to reflect my flying experiences seeking enemy submarines. I can remember landing our PBM, a large aircraft, somewhere off Bermuda to pick up an American sailor with a ruptured appendix from a submarine at sea. We carried a doctor to see if he could operate in the plane on the way back to the States.

After meeting a life-raft off the submarine we picked up the sailor in ten foot swells, which is pretty rough for an aircraft. But, unfortunately, we dug a wing into the seas on take-off and found ourselves at the mercy of a very unfriendly Atlantic Ocean. Our plane sinking, we took to the life-rafts. The doctor was not hurt, got aboard the submarine and operated on the young lad, removing his appendix. We all came back to the States by submarine to Charleston, South Carolina—rescuers rescued by the submarine whose crewman we were sent to rescue.

Another incident involved a German submarine that had surfaced and managed to shoot down one of our Marine fighter aircraft about 150 miles off St. Simon Island, Georgia. We didn't have a large enough aircraft to rescue the Marine pilots, but we did have a Gruman Goose, a small twin-engine amphibian. We found the two pilots, landed in a moderately friendly Atlantic and took the two aboard. They were near freezing and were suffering from hypothermia so I took off my flight suit and put it on one of them. I was pretty wet and cold myself after going into the water to rescue them.

When we landed back at the Navy Base at St. Simon Island, we called for an ambulance and the medical people responded. Seeing me almost naked and shivering, they thought I was the victim and tried to take me to the hospital. I kept trying to tell them that I was not one of the downed pilots, but they insisted "He is delirious, too!"

A third incident was an attack on a German submarine off Myrtle Beach, South Carolina, where we assisted two Coast Guard cutters, a Navy destroyer and two or three other aircraft. We dropped depth charges from our plane and the sub was hit. I don't know whether it was the cutters, the aircraft, or the destroyer that was responsible for the kill, but after the others had left the scene, we continued to patrol the area. We found a few German sailors in the water on some floating debris, radioed Norfolk and were directed to land our seaplane, pick up the German survivors and bring them back for interrogation.

Landing in the Atlantic, even under the best conditions, is something you wouldn't want to do daily for a living. We did, however land safely, got out our sub-machine guns, and since this was our first encounter with Nazis we were really very guarded. Our crew members had to go into the water to rescue the German sailors, so we had to leave our weapons on the deck. In the confusion of the rescue operation some of the weapons were handed to the Germans as they came aboard. It was the sort of encounter you would anticipate in a comic war movie. However, the Germans were glad to be alive and we were glad to get them aboard without the need to fire our weapons. We did get them safely back to Norfolk for interrogation by Navy intelligence.

Admiral Sparks won his commission after the war, and went on to an illustrious career, becoming the Senior Reserve Officer of the Coast Guard. After his retirement from the Coast Guard he became the Deputy Executive Director, Reserve Officers Association of the United States. He was the first Coast Guard Admiral President of the Association during the term 1982-83.

8

Death March—Philippines

LTC Mariano Villarin, AUS-Ret

Nine hours after the Pearl Harbor raid on December 7, 1941, Japanese planes attacked Clark Field in the Philippines, destroying half of General Douglas MacArthur's Air Corps on the ground. That was followed by the devastation of Cavite Navy Yard and part of the US Asiatic Fleet in Manila Bay. Those raids left the United States Army forces in the Far East with hardly any air or naval support. The Japanese began landing at two places north and south of Manila in late December, intending to converge upon the capitol city. However, Gen. MacArthur and his troops had already begun a retrograde movement into the Bataan Peninsula where the "last ditch stand" was made.

The Battle of Bataan officially began on January 7, 1942. Opposing the Japanese was one US Army Division (The Philippine Division) consisting of three well-trained and seasoned regiments, namely, the American 31st Infantry, and the 45th and 57th Infantry regiments of the Philippine Scouts. In addition, there were 12,000 Philippine Scouts under 685 American officers who were a part of the Regular United States Army.

The Philippine Division bore the brunt of the battles on Bataan. The 26th Cavalry and tank units covered the withdrawal of the troops from the Lingayen landing area to Bataan. There also were nine Philippine Army divisions, seven of which consisted mainly of reservists who had been mobilized only a few weeks earlier and were inadequately trained and ill-equipped. The Battle of the Points and the Battle of the Pockets were the bloodiest in the defense of Bataan.

A conglomerate force of American Air Corps personnel (they had no planes) supported by tank units, Philippine Scouts and Philippine Army troops, along with some Navy personnel and a company of Marines inflicted heavy casualties on the enemy. These victories were only temporary, but they disrupted the Japanese Army timetable of conquest by four months. Without that resistance the enemy might have been able to mount an invasion of Australia.

The constant shelling and unopposed aerial bombardments, rampant disease, and inadequate food (mostly rice and gruel) were demoralizing. The reassurance on January 15 by Gen. MacArthur that "help was on the way" did not materialize. No ships arrived and all hope of getting reinforcements from the United States vanished. We got the impression that the Philippines had been written off. United Press correspondent Frank Hewlett referred to us as the "Battling Bastards of Bataan—no mama, no papa, no Uncle Sam."

We kept retreating from one main line of resistance to the next, suffering many casualties. Many members of my own unit were killed by shrapnel and strafing by low-flying Japanese dive-bombers. During Holy Week in April, the Japanese commander, Gen. Masaharu Homma, unleashed his catastrophic devastation of Bataan with a force of 15,000 fresh troops, 150 artillery pieces and 80 bombers. The Christian defenders observing the anniversary of the Crucifixion were crucified by Homma. Although the defenders fought with tenacity, the enemy

LTC Mariano Villarin, AUS, retired in QM Branch as Lt. Col. (left)

After the war, 1945. (below)

continued to advance and soon it was over—the most humiliating defeat in American military history. Major General Edward King, on April 9, 1942, surrendered his 78,000 Bataan troops, including 12,000 Americans, to avert further needless bloodshed.

The Japanese told us in no uncertain terms, "You surrendered. You deserve no mercy. You are not prisoners of war. You are captives."

That was their justification for the grossly inhumane treatment inflicted on us during the march from Bataan to a then-unknown destination. We were subjected to the most incredible and unimaginable atrocities.

During the infamous Bataan Death March some 7,000 to 10,000 prisoners died from starvation, disease, beatings, and decapitations. Estimates by US historians are that 650 to perhaps 2,330 Americans died on this march.

Japanese guards took our watches, rings and money. They would not allow us to obtain water from streams or artesian wells along the road, and warned us to stay away from those who could barely march. Only the fittest survived. Those who lagged behind or could not make the march were clubbed, shot or bayoneted. Thousands of putrefying, bloodied corpses littered the main road to San Fernando. There were headless corpses also, roughly one American to five Filipinos. Often a Japanese soldier would select a prisoner from among the marchers and toss him around for the barbaric amusement of his fellow soldiers. The Japanese preferred to pick on the Americans to impress upon their countrymen that the bigger the POWs were, the harder they fell.

Finally, we reached San Fernando after a six-day, 65 mile march under broiling sun. The kindly townsfolk who lined each side of the road often risked their lives to throw food to starving American and Filipino prisoners. Japanese guards would swing their rifles at the local people, sometimes shooting.

We were herded into boxcars for the trip to the Camp O'Donnell prison camp. Of the 78,000 who surrendered on Bataan, only 54,000 reached Camp O'Donnell, 9,300 of them being Americans. Some 2000 had escaped to Corregidor which fell on May 6, 1942, and several thousands, including several dozen American soldiers, had escaped along the Death March route with the help of the Barrio people.

Practically every prisoner became a living skeleton due to starvation, malaria and dysentery. In the Philippine sector the death rate reached a peak of 500 a day. The Americans lost 60 a day. To save face, the Japanese "paroled" Philippine POWs to the constabulary (the National police) and moved the American POWs to Cabanatuan prison camp. By the time Camp O'Donnell was deactivated 29,000 Philippine soldiers and 1,600 Americans had died. For these war crimes, General Homma was tried, convicted and executed in Manila after the war.

Lieutenant Colonel Mariano Villarin, AUS-Ret was a Second Lieutenant in the Philippine Army when war broke out. The Philippines, then being an American Colony, all PA units were sworn into the US Army Forces in the Far East. After the war LTC Villarin joined the United States Army. He is a life member of ROA and seven other veteran's organizations. He is the author of a book, *We Remember Bataan and Corregidor.*

9

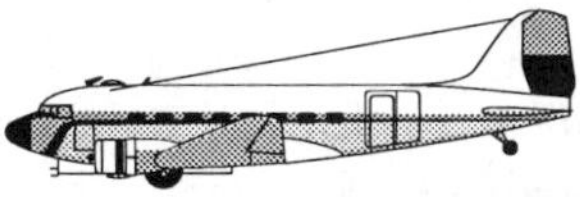

Early Air Support in the Pacific

Major George Wamsley, USAF-Ret.

A pilot in the early days of the war in the Pacific, flying a C-47 transport plane, Major Wamsley recalls that in October of 1942 there were many urgent missions to move badly needed supplies to ground troops and to evacuate wounded from minimal air strips. It was hazardous duty. They often had to fly over ground held by enemy infantry dug in near the landing sites.

Speaking of his operations out of Port Moresby (Papua New Guinea), "The Australian and US ground forces were locked in critical jungle combat with the Japanese. We flew every day attempting to supply our troops. The Japanese had moved rapidly throughout the entire theater early in the war, since they had been preparing for years to conduct an aggressive war. They had large, well-equipped ground forces and their objective seemed to be to control the entire Pacific, including Indonesia, China and Australia."

Port Moresby in 1942 was not much of a city. Military trucks were used on a main road from the port to the airport. Supplies were then taken forward in our planes, routed to those places most in need. Few cargo vessels arrived then, because the Japanese were within 30 miles of town. Many people on both sides presumed that Moresby would fall. It didn't. The Aussie infantry held the Japanese back around Kokoda, which was near the top of the Owen Stanley Mountains which divided the sea to the north from the sea to the south. Our troop carrier planes lifted the US 32nd and 41st Infantry Divisions over the heads of the advancing Japanese foot soldiers to port villages along the north coast of Papua.

We had begun the leapfrog tactical envelopment of the Japanese. We landed engineers and troops at such places as Waningela Mission, Buna, Pongani, and some open spaces that the engineers would pick from the window of the plane. The Kunai grass would be as much as five feet tall, but it wasn't thick, so we could tell from the air whether the ground was rocky, level and free of gullies crossing through it. We wanted to be assured that the landing site was long enough to be able to stop the plane. The dust would fly as we hit the ground; we would stop, open the cargo door and without delay the engineers would manhandle their jeep down the ramp, grab their rifles and radio gear and head for the jungle.

Some of these clearings actually became usable strips for follow-up deliveries of men and equipment. One long valley, half-way between Kokoda and Buna, became a major staging area while the battles for those points were still going on. Ultimately two long strips were built there and remain presently.

The Aussies had been administrators of Papua for years and because there were no roads they had developed a number of small landing strips. However, to expand operations our engineering battalions could not get any dirt-moving equipment in, so they had to hire native labor. We hauled a lot of steel runway, interlocking matting, that first had to come in to Moresby by ship. Somehow, the airstrips were lengthened and broadened.

When our half of the squadron arrived at Ward's Airdrome at Port Moresby the entire shoreline of Papua New Guinea was under entrenched Japanese control. Port Moresby was not secure. We all had dug slit trenches near our tents and along the revetment areas where the

The Natives came out of the hills of New Guinea for their first sight of the "big birds".

planes were parked or worked on when not in the sky. Enemy air attacks on our base were infrequent, but our flights over the other side of the mountains were subject to both air and ground attack.

We only got credit for a combat mission when we flew across the mountains. Because our planes were unarmed, our only defense was to "go like hell" when Zeros were spotted nearby. We would get down as low as possible and head for home. The Zero pilots did not like to dive low because it put them in jeopardy should there be P-39's or P-40's in the area. Our fighter pilots were much superior to the Japanese, so we felt quite secure when our fighters were covering for us.

One of the wildest dogfights I ever witnessed was over Milne Bay, at the extreme east end of New Guinea. About 60 to 80 Japanese bombers were escorted by 75 to 100 Zeros. It was surprising that we got as many as 40 or 50 fighters up to meet them. But our planes and pilots excelled—the lead P-40 picked up the large enemy formation only a few miles from Milne Bay harbor, and the fight was on. Planes began to fall out of the sky in every direction. Those crashing were nearly all enemy. So many of their bombers were knocked down in the first part of the attack that the remaining bombers did not complete their runs. They turned and headed back for Rabaul. Sitting on the ground, I saw at least 30 enemy planes go down. We lost only 4 fighters—score 30 to 4, which was not an uncommon ratio. Our guys were good, and the Japanese were beginning to learn that fact. The Japanese, however, were pushing hard on many fronts because they wanted to capture Port Moresby.

In January of 1943, the Japanese were reinforcing their ground troops approaching Wau. They brought in supplies and personnel over a mountain trail on foot, while we were flying our reinforcements in. Although the Japanese advance was heavily contested, by February 6 they were in control of one side of the creek at the foot of the airstrip and the Aussies had control of the other side, as well as about a third of a mile of land including the airstrip. Japanese fighters and bombers had been attacking Wau and Bulolo for some time and those distractions were frequent enough to make us approach as low as possible so as not to give enemy fighters an easy shot. The Japanese were after our cargo planes which were bringing in troops and supplies.

Leaving Port Moresby one morning with a load of ammunition and hand-grenades I had one passenger, an Australian Brigadier who wished to observe from the air. We were careful to approach Wau at low altitude and to be attentive that we used the right pass. If one was not familiar with the terrain one could find the route dead-ended in a wall of mountains. A turn-around was easy enough for one plane but there was not room enough to turn a formation.

Just before we reached the opening into the small Wau valley, two Zeros came out of the clouds directly in front of me. We had four P-40's as low fighter cover and four high. They had just passed overhead when I saw tracer bullets going by. With little clearance I went down as low as possible, looked left to see whether my companion plane (Schwensen) was still there, but he was gone.

The lead P-40 didn't get a shot, but his wingman, (Danacher) was trailing enough to get off a short burst, knocking down one Zero. I was so low, following a creek that I had to keep checking to see that a wing did not touch water when I had to make turns. My co-pilot, Sgt. Johnson, looking out the windows, hollered an exciting blow-by-blow report of the dogfights going on around us.

All this time our cargo was shifting about the cabin, giving the Brigadier a rough ride! We flew downstream about 5 miles, got behind a ridge, then over the mountains and headed home without being able to deliver our load.

I believe six Japanese planes were shot down in that action, while we lost one P-40 and my wingman (Schwensen's C-47), whose wreckage was not found until October 8, 1988. (Two of Lt. Schwensen's brothers also were killed during the war in the European theater.)

Terminating his service at the end of the war, Major Wamsley had earned five Distinguished Flying Crosses. He is a retired building contractor and real-estate developer now living in Prescott, Arizona. Nearly half of the planes of his squadron were lost in action.

George Wamsley beside trusty C-47 in New Guinea, 1942.

10

Greenland, North Atlantic and North Pacific

Carlton Skinner, Commander, USCGR

We all know, consciously or unconsciously, that war is the most universal of human experiences. It embraces every other human activity. To mention only a few, bravery, nobility, cowardice, learning, greed, self-sacrifice, destruction and construction.

Thus any reminiscence of war will recall several of these, but never all of them, and the experiences of any one person are the chance result of the course of the war and his chance duty assignments.

I was what was later called a premature anti-fascist. Maturing at the period of the Spanish Civil War and young enough to be an idealist, I was appalled at the cynicism, brutality and viciousness of Hitler and Mussolini and their lackey, Franco. I believed that if they were successful, western civilization would be set back a thousand years. I was tempted to go and fight for the Republican side in Spain. However, as that war progressed, the Communist control of the Republican forces and the equal atrocities which they committed became clear.

So, I was determined to get into the war to defend my country and in a combat capacity. As a sailor and boat racer, the Navy and Coast Guard were my preference. At that time, the Navy did not send glasses-wearing officers to sea. However, in early 1941 the Coast Guard established a Reserve Officers program. So, by organizing and, finally, teaching a class of my fellow sailing members of the Capital Yacht Club in Washington D.C., I qualified to pass the examination and in June, 1941, was commissioned Lieutenant, j.g., U.S. Coast Guard Reserve. Reporting for duty in early July, I was sent to the *USS Northland*, CG, the flagship of the Greenland Patrol, then at the Boston Navy Yard.

With the Nazi invasion of Denmark, the Danish Ambassador to Washington had stayed on the side of freedom and executed an agreement under which Greenland was placed under the protection of the United States, and a Greenland Patrol was created by the U.S. Navy to protect that remote island in the frozen north from being used as an axis base. Two months later, in September 1941, while patrolling east Greenland, the *Northland* received a message from British Intelligence that the Luftwaffe had dispatched a trawler from Tromsoe in Occupied Norway, carrying equipment for a weather station and four men to operate it—one German and three Norwegian Quislings. Several days later on the morning watch, we spotted the trawler, came alongside with our crew at General Quarters, and ordered it into the nearest Greenland port. When both ships had anchored and we had put a prize crew aboard the *S.S. Buskoe*, our Force Commander, Commander Edward Smith (later Admiral), seized the vessel for having entered Greenland waters without the permission of the Greenland Government, which was, of course, the Danish Ambassador in Washington.

Put in charge of interrogation with my schoolboy German, I soon identified the shore location of the enemy weather station. The *Northland* then proceeded to the fjord chosen. That evening, the Captain, Carl C. von Paulsen, came to the wardroom and designated Lieutenant McCloskey, USCGR, and myself to lead the landing party, saying ironically, "I'll put a couple of reserves in charge of this, as I can spare them better." At 2 a.m. the *Northland*'s motor surfboat put-putted up the fjord and in the Arctic dawn, landed 12 Coastguardsmen and two officers, armed with six tommyguns, six rifles, and two .45 Colts. We must have been properly quiet because we surrounded the small shack they had built without any response. Then, what to do? Ridiculous to shoot, the occupants were obviously asleep. Finally, I went and knocked on the door. Four astonished and sleepy young enemy filed out in their long underwear. We put the safety catches back on our weapons, took the captives, sent them back to the ship under guard and four Luftwaffe auxiliaries proceeded to dismantle the weather and radio equipment and burn the buildings. They had just finished setting up and had not yet sent their first weather report to the Luftwaffe in Oslo.

Thus, quickly and efficiently, was accomplished the first U.S. land combat with the enemy in World War II. Later, the *Northland* crew were authorized to put a letter "A" on their service ribbons for "combat with the enemy before Pearl Harbor," but since the U.S. had not yet declared war and Greenland was a technically neutral area, there was no publicity and the capture of the *Buskoe* went unnoticed.

The *Northland* continued its patrol of Greenland waters, helping to set up three major U.S. air bases for ferrying of aircraft to England, rescuing downed U.S. and Canadian aviators from the Greenland ice cap, and conducting anti-submarine patrols in Denmark Strait.

Responsibilities in the Armed Forces expanded rapidly in the early years of America's involvement, and in the fall of 1942, less than a year after first going to sea, I became Executive Officer of the ship. This duty imposed other functions, different but no less useful for the war. Among his many duties, an Executive Officer supervises the promotion of enlisted men. At that time, Negroes served in the Navy and Coast Guard only as Stewards and Stewards' Mates—officers' servants. In the *Northland* crew, there was a stewards' mate who was also a highly competent mechanic. By preference, this sailor spent his spare time in the engine room helping with even the most complicated repairs. The Engineer Officer recommended him for examination as a Motor Machinist's Mate and he passed with a very high score. I sent his papers to Headquarters, recommending the mechanic's rating. The rating was refused for the reason that he was a Negro and that Negroes were not accepted for general ratings. I felt this was wrong—for the man, for the service and for the war effort—and appealed. The appeal was granted and the man was rated.

In the late spring of 1943, after commanding an LST crew in training and briefly helping to commission a ship, I was transferred to Headquarters as Executive Officer of Public Relations, not my choice. In the meantime, the experience with the Negro stewards' mate had been festering in the back of my mind. The denial of a rating because of his race was unjust, but that was not what troubled me. By this time in the war, all services were getting their men from the draft. Officers' servants aboard ship, Navy and Coast Guard, were about three percent of a ships' company. Negroes were 11% of the population. Thus, as the war progressed, eight percent of the Negroes in the sea services would have to be kept ashore. This would deprive the ships of the qualified and skilled Negroes who could increase the efficiency of a ship and, more, would keep a disproportionate number ashore. Also, I had read about disturbances in World War I, when able-bodied men who stayed in the U.S. instead of serving in France were the subject of bitter recriminations. Nor did the situation mesh with President Roosevelt's call for equal sharing of the war burden. I put all this in a memorandum to the Commandant.

Six weeks later, I received orders to the *USS Sea Cloud*, part of Atlantic Fleet's Task Force 24, responsible for weather reports from four mid-Atlantic locations used to provide weather forecasts for the bombing of Europe. The *Sea Cloud*, built in Kiel, Germany, in 1929, for Mrs. Marjorie Post Hutton Davies, had been the world's most luxurious yacht—316 feet overall, 3600 tons. Stripped of sails and all masts but the mainmast, it had been equipped with two 3 inch 50's, depth charges and

40 millimeter guns. Beautifully designed by William Francis Gibbs, it had a hull form like a clipper ship, and its twin screws made it highly maneuverable. On its four Krupp Diesel engines, it made 14 knots. It had 175 men in its crew.

In my memorandum to the Commandant, I had urged an experimental ship with Negroes in general ratings, recommended that they be trained and qualified aboard ship in the normal way at sea with experienced crew members and said I would be glad to serve aboard such a ship. Returning from my first patrol as a watch officer, orders were received by radio assigning me to command. While in port in Boston just before proceeding to the next weather station, a draft of 20 Negro seamen arrived from the receiving station. Even though I had suspected my recommendation was accepted, this was the first formal notice that the experiment was on. It was the beginning of the first completely racially integrated ship in the history of the Navy and the Coast Guard. The Navy had tried manning a destroyer escort with an all-Negro crew, trained totally ashore, and all white officers. It had not worked, I was told, largely because of seamanship problems and, perhaps, because of officer attitudes. This was 1943 and even though some progress had been made in equal opportunity, there was still a strong residue of racial prejudice in the population generally and among southerners in particular, and many officers as well as enlisted men were from the South.

With Boston and later Argentia, Newfoundland, as home ports, our assignment was to proceed to designated points in the Atlantic, one between Greenland and Iceland, one between Newfoundland and Greenland, one off Bermuda, and one 400 miles off the coast of France. We stayed 21 days on each station, remaining within 50 miles of the fixed point, then were relieved, returned to port, provisioned and on to the next station. Each time in port, a new draft of Negro seamen would come aboard to be trained, including four Negro officers, the first for sea duty in the Navy or Coast Guard. They learned their jobs well, were promoted when they qualified. There was no segregation. There were no racial incidents. When the proportion of Negroes in the total crew of 175 reached about 50%, I suspended the special recruitment in order to keep a reasonable number of long service men and to avoid the possibility that due to past discrimination, some Negroes might try to dominate or be arrogant. In summary, it worked well. The ship went through two Atlantic Fleet inspections with high marks.

After my first voyage in command, I called on the Navy Intelligence Officer of the Boston Navy Yard and asked why, when we stayed 21 days within 50 miles of a fixed point in the ocean, sending radioed weather reports four times a day to Arlington, VA, one or more German submarines did not attack. He responded that the first weather patrol ship sent out had been sunk with all hands. Thereafter, the Navy simplified the code used for the weather messages so that the Germans were copying the weather reports too. We had one major encounter with a submarine, lasting eight hours, without forcing it to the surface. However, a task force of two destroyer escorts and a sea plane, relieved us and destroyed it, the captain of one of the DE's being killed by gunfire from the surfaced submarine. On June 2, 1944, the *Sea Cloud* was on station 400 miles off the coast of France. On the morning watch, 5,000 ships came on us; the horizon was blocked out. It was, of course, the invasion fleet arriving from the U.S. to make the Normandy landing. A plane flew over and ordered us to fall in astern of the carrier. Excited and exhilarated, we thought we would participate in the landing. After 24 hours, we were ordered to return to station as the admiral thought we could have interfered with his submarine search.

In November 1944, the *Sea Cloud* was decommissioned because it had problems affecting repairs, since it was equipped with foreign manufactured engines. Enough U.S. built ships had become available. The Negroes of the crew entered the general stream of personnel and went on to other seagoing units with their general ratings of boatswain's mate, gunner's mate, etc. Early in 1945, I was assigned to command the *USS Hoquiam*, PF-5, a frigate on escort duty in the Aleutians and earmarked for the invasion of the Northern Japanese islands. Two of the Negro officers were also assigned, as well as some of the crew and some new Negro seamen. The ship functioned well—in fact, better than under my predecessor, as he had dropped morning quarters because of the abominable Aleutian weather, and the ship was not as clean and shipshape as it should have been. Our crew rose to the challenge and the *Hoquiam* became a proper unit of the U.S. Navy.

In June, 1945, the *Hoquiam* was scheduled for transfer to the Soviets and assigned to train Russian crews for the invasion of the Japanese home islands, pursuant to a promise made by President Roosevelt to Stalin at Yalta. After being re-outfitted in Seattle, we proceeded to Cold Bay, Alaska, where the training was conducted. The Russians came aboard in drafts for crew replacement, much as we had done on the *Sea Cloud* for the new Negro crew. We had the Russians for 12 weeks, training them in navigation, seamanship, gunnery, and engine operation by American standards. They were marvelous gunners, literally loved their guns and fired skillfully but poor navigators and lousy seamen. They were suspicious of our every move and even could think they were being kidnapped, as once when we needed to shift anchorage in the middle of the night to avoid two anchor-dragging Liberty ships, I had to threaten the Russian engineer officer with arrest and the brig to make him get up steam to move the ship, a somewhat empty threat with 200 Russians aboard. The war ended while the Russians were operating the ship, although I was still in command with two Negro officers, functioning well, three U.S. enlisted men and the 200 Russians. The Russians were a little surprised when, after hearing the surrender ceremonies of the *USS Missouri* on the radio, I held the whistle lever down for one hour on our return from a training exercise. The Russians were rigid and did not do such unauthorized and undisciplined things.

In summary, the experiment which had lasted a little less than two years had worked as I had predicted. The Negroes made acceptable wartime sailors, learned quickly, performed well, were not a disciplinary problem and cooperated aboard ship. Some of our experiences with other ships in port were less agreeable and, particularly with Navy yard civilian workmen, many of whom were "rednecks." But aboard ship, the experiment was successful. It was copied by the Navy. After decommissioning the *Sea Cloud* in Boston in November 1944, I passed through Washington en route to a Navy refresher command school. I looked up a pre-war colleague of mine on the Wall Street Journal—Eugene Duffield. He had become Special Assistant to Secretary of the Navy James Forrestal. I gave him a full account of the experiment. Three months later, in February, 1945, the Navy issued a General Order, authorizing Negroes to fill 10% of the general duty billets in fleet auxiliaries. Prior to that they had been acceptable, except as officers' servants, only on yardcraft. Thus, with a strange twist, a program for naval personnel efficiency, equal opportunity, and perhaps, social justice was finally accomplished through the medium of the Wall Street Journal. Of course, the subsequent progress in this field has been colossal, to the point that there has been at least one black admiral and a black Chairman of the Joint Chiefs of Staff and a more efficient use of American manpower in the armed services.

Thus, a minuscule armed capture of an enemy force before the U.S. was in the war, then through a significant experiment in efficient use of manpower and social justice, to an exercise in foreign relations by commanding foreign troops, one U.S. Naval Officer experienced several of the odd facets of the universality of war.

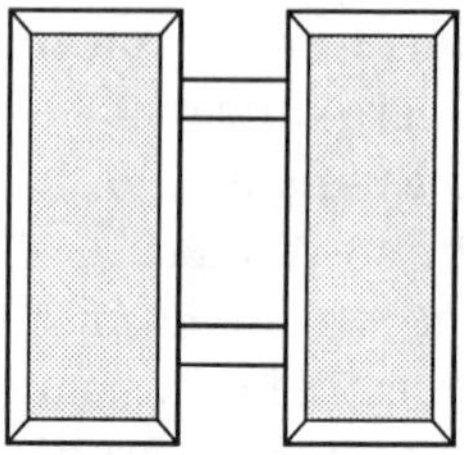

11

Resisting the Conquest of the Philippines

Captain Kermit R. Lay

General Sinforoso Dugue, Adjutant General of the Philippine Army presented the Gold Cross to Captain Lay on January 10, 1985 at the Philippine Consulate in San Francisco. The award was presented for gallantry in action while he was a 2d Lt. on the Batan Peninsula on April 4, 1942. The gold cross is equivalent to the U.S. Silver Star.

Two Filipino guards at the forward post of the First Provisional Military Police Company were in danger of being killed or captured. Lay voluntarily rescued them through intense fire, unconcerned for his own safety, even though he was weak from fresh wounds.

Consul General Romeo Arguelles cited such gallantry as the force upsetting the Japanese conquest of Bataan and Corregidor. He added that "the men in Bataan hung on—and they waged four months of heroic struggle against men, arms, disease, hunger and fatigue." An example of the resourcefulness of Capt. Lay is in the following account: "At Aglaloma Point, the Japanese made a landing of six hundred men on 23 Jan 42 and holed up in the caves and ledges. Because the Air Corps provisional infantry was having a hard time getting rid of them, they called on the 724th Ord. Co. for assistance. Twenty men with a load of 30 pound fragment bombs were used to make cluster bombs, with an electric charge in the middle. These were swung over the cliff edge and other fused single bombs were rolled over. The two and a half day mission resulting in eliminating the threat to the aviation units.

"Outnumbered and battered into bloody defeat, Maj. Gen. Edward King, Jr., senior American officer surrendered Bataan on April 9, 1942. Then began the most horrifying episode in World War II, the infamous "Death March". A victim of the "Death March", Lay has many stories of his three and a half years as a prisoner-of-war (POW).

"We were not in any condition for any marches. Malaria, dysentery, yellow jaundice, beriberi and diphtheria were common. When the Death March started, if you fell out to relieve yourself or if you fell out for water, they would shoot you or bayonet you to death," Lay said.

The officers had been told that they would have orderlies and bed rolls. "We thought we would live high on the hog," he said. "But it was all lies."

Lay commented that many Death March POWs cry when they discuss their experiences.

Tears came to his own eyes as he told the story of a Lieutenant Colonel who rode in the same recon car before they were all confined into ranks for the march. "The car stopped and a Japanese soldier came up and touched the colonel's rank insignia. The Colonel pulled away, angering the Japanese. The Colonel was jerked from the car, at which time the Japanese bayoneted him, cut off his private parts and stuffed them in the colonel's face as he died," he said with great difficulty.

According to Lay, there were more than just one Death March, there were many Death Marches, as the Japanese would assemble 100 to 150 POW's and lead them off on a march to a prison camp.

Lay said that at one point, "we were put in box cars with 100 POW's in each. We stood up like sardines in a can. It is a miracle any got out alive. There were probably 20 dead in the boxcar I was in. When we got out, they all fell to the floor."

Lay helped in the burial of approximately 1,900 POWs. "We would take off their clothes and sterilize them for those who were alive to wear. I sought out the first chaplain for the burials when I saw it wasn't being done. The Japanese didn't want a chaplain or a prayer, so they would slap or hit you with their rifle butt. Sometimes I got away with it; I took a chance in getting a chaplain. I would give orders to the burial detail to render a hand salute if I couldn't get a chaplain."

Captain Lay retired in 1951 after 19 years of service. His U. S. Army awards include the Silver Star, Bronze Star and Purple Heart with oak leaf clusters. He was a POW for 3½ years and survived the Bataan Death March. Formerly a private in the 724th Ordnance Co, AVN;, he was given a field commission to 2d Lt., Inf., in Jan. of 1942, during the four months battle on Bataan.

From left: Major William Adair, Major Felix Porter, Captain Paul Geer, Captain Wayne Hightower (deceased), and Captain Kermit Lay

His citation for the Silver Star read: “Second Lieutenant Kermit R. Lay is awarded a Silver Star for gallantry in action on Bataan Peninsula, Philippine Islands, on 4 April 1942. When the Japanese were making their final thrust to Bataan Peninsula, pressing along the whole front and blasting communications with artillery fire, the two guards at the forward post of the First Provisional Military Police Company were isolated and in danger of being killed or captured. Lt. Lay proceeded in a weapons carrier with several others to a point where artillery fire prevented their forward movement, and then volunteered to continue on foot alone in an attempt to rescue the two men. Heedless of his own safety, and despite being weakened by recently incurred wounds, he made his way through the intense shell fire, reached the post, and led the men back to safety. By his courageous and unselfish act, Lt. Lay set an inspiring example of heroism to the members of his command.”

The memories of those bitter days are indelible in his mind. “I could live to be 200 years old, and I would never forget what happened,” he said feverishly, “The Japanese came in, and they were killing everybody. We were carrying white flags—torn up white sheets. But they didn't care. My commanding officer was beheaded. They killed a fellow soldier in our arms. The man had malaria and dysentery. He was exhausted. So they ran a bayonet through him. If you fell out to get a drink of water, they would kill you. They would shoot men, bayonet them and behead them. We had to relieve ourselves as we walked. We had to keep walking.” About seven to ten thousand soldiers died during the death march to San Fernando.

After the conclusion of W.W.II, Lay served as an ROTC instructor at the University of California, Berkeley, and later in Germany in 1948 and 1949 as a Captain, MPC Corps, commanding a food train that carried supplies to beleaguered Berlin.

More recently Lieutenant General Glynn Mallory, Commander of the Sixth U.S.. Army presented Capt. Lay with a Humane Action Award, on September 8, 1993, stating: "We are gathered this morning to recognize the matchless actions of a man who clearly meets the traits of a heroic figure. He truly symbolizes the strength of America."

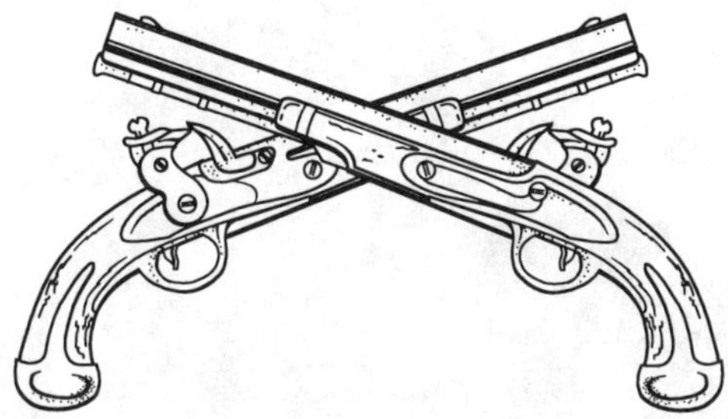

U.S.

12

North Africa to Italy

Sgt Harry W. Fox, AUS-Ret.

Harry Fox entered the war early with the 1st Armored Division, one of the first of our divisions to enter the combat zone in Europe, and stayed with that division throughout the war.

He says: "We arrived in Northern Ireland May 1, 1942, moved to England, and landed in North Africa in November of 1942, taking part in the Tunisian Campaign of II Corps against Romel's Afrika Korps that ended in May of 1943. Our division took 40,000 German POWs as that campaign ended with our division overlooking the Mediterranean from high ground. This Afrika Korps consisted of first rate soldiers of the German Army, not the young kids we saw in uniform in Italy later. Their tanks were much bigger than ours and much more difficult to take out."

One regiment of the division went in first, and our 13th Armored Regiment followed later. I drove a tank during that campaign, was a half-track driver in the assault gun platoon, during the Tunisian campaign, and subsequently took over the ammunitions section of the assault gun platoon.

In the early days of the war in Tunisia the Germans controlled the air, and we were strafed frequently by ME-109's and attacked by Stuka dive bombers. Sometimes three or four at a time would come at us. They screeched awfully loud as they dove to attack. They would scream down upon us with the fury of a messenger of death straight from hell. Those dive bombers certainly got our attention. Our reaction was immediate.

I remember there were about twenty to thirty attacks upon us by Stukas. There were many occasions when their bombs narrowly missed my vehicle. In one of those attacks my sergeant was wounded and I replaced him in that position.

Once or twice we were strafed by our own American planes. The P-40's came back and wiggled their wings, as if to apologize. We never saw more than six P-40's, while the Germans had more aircraft in the sky.

After taking part in the Tunisian Campaign, which ended in May of 1943, we were sent back to Morocco, took part in a lot of training near Oran, before landing in Salerno, Italy. We moved up through Italy, but the advance was held up by the fortress of Monte Cassino, heavily defended by the Germans on a high hill. So the 1st Armd. Div. took part in an end-run-around Cassino. The landing at Anzio was only about 25 miles from Rome. Initially, there was no resistance, and the Americans controlled the high ground above the landing, but the General in charge, fearful of attacks upon his flanks, pulled back to the lower plain. Within ten or twelve days the Germans had pulled in over a hundred thousand troops, some from far away, occupied the high ground and encircled the Allied forces. While we had about 125,000 troops at Anzio, including a British Division, we couldn't move. The firing on both sides was intense.

We had a lot of anti-aircraft artillery and controlled the air during the day, but at night the Germans flew over and bombed us, trying to hit our ammunition dumps. The sky lit up like Times Square with so many tracer bullets, spotlights, flares and so much ammunition going up.

Space was limited in the pocket we occupied. I was then an intelligence sergeant in G-2 Section, of Division headquarters, but we in the division headquarters were still close to the action. There was an artillery battalion only three hundred yards away that remained in place, firing often, and, of course, there were counter-battery shells coming in on us.

German Junkers Ju 87 dive bomber

We had to sleep in trenches, built up with ammunition crates and covered with shelter halves, in an attempt to keep ourselves dry in the rain. The large cemetery at Anzio holds thousands of American and Allied soldiers that were killed during this period.

Harry W. Fox operated a successful real estate firm in Denver before retiring to California to be closer to his married children.

Editor's note: We all, who were in W.W.II, recall the newsreels showing the Stukas attacking Poland at the inception of the war. Few of us actually saw them in action. Most of the Stukas were casualties by time we got in the action in mainland Europe, yet about forty were used against our rear echelons during the rapidly moving Battle of the Bulge. Most were replaced by the faster ME-109's, the enemy plane that ground troops saw more often.

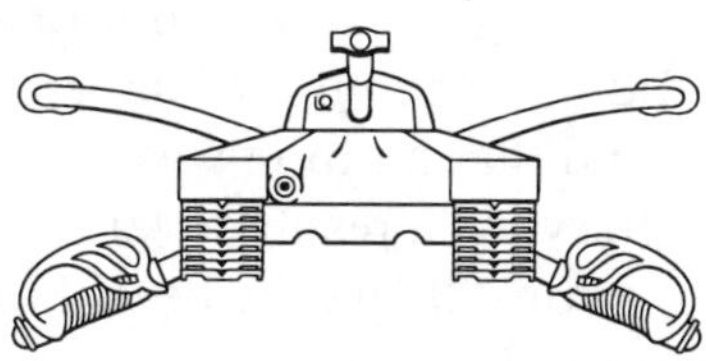

13

The Sicilian Campaign Phase I – The Landings at Licata

A.D. Kuperstein

Above the beachhead on a wooded hillside dirt trail the German soldier's body lay face down across his rifle, a pool of drying blood under his head. The flashing on his shoulder bars indicated he was a signalman. A short distance away was a small wooden hut in which two or three bunks marked the quarters of a small signal detachment. Since this was Italian Army territory, the presence of Germans could indicate there was a danger of counterattack.

Fortunately, after the assault troops had passed across the beach a newspaper reporter (Mike Chinigo, it turned out to be) picked up a ringing telephone in a building and in fluent Italian assured the Italian Army officer on the other end that nothing was going on down here in spite of rumors to the contrary. As a result, a dangerous counterattack was avoided, allowing us to consolidate the beachhead.

Following the end of the Tunisian Campaign, the regiment to which I belonged began to assemble in its landing craft in the harbor at Bizerte on 6 July 43. I was assigned to the regimental headquarters craft which was one of the newer type landing craft infantry (LCI) having a gang-plank arrangement at its bow which infantrymen would descend to the beach. (Vehicular craft (LCTs and LSTs) had flat bows which could be let down on the beaches to allow vehicles to run off on their own power.) Exhausted after several days of training and loading activities I fell asleep in the small 4-man compartment below just behind the engine room and completely missed the 0400 enemy bombing raid on the huge fleet in the harbor.

After a diversionary sail southward to Sousse harbor (where we were allowed to leave the ships and take a speed hike inland for exercise) we re-embarked and set sail for Sicily. The stunning view of the huge fleet heading to sea behind us was unforgettable. Three columns of craft in perfect alignment on the mirror-like harbor waters seemed like a formal pass-in-review exercise.

As we passed into the ocean and headed for Sicily, the weather changed into a violent windstorm which created high surf and rocked our boats unmercifully. Even though I was not normally seasick-prone I found it difficult to stay on deck for long, and found it equally difficult in our small quarters into which leaked gasoline and oil fumes from the noisy engine in the next compartment. On one foray to the deck to get some fresh air I noticed one of my friends sitting casually on the stern

Col. John H. Roush, Jr. and Major A.D. Kuperstein, editors of this collection

rail, going up and down as if he were enjoying a thrill ride at an amusement park. After cautioning him to get off I started down the hatchway but flew back up to the deck at the cry "man overboard!" Sure enough, my friend had fallen off and we could see his head bobbing in the surf behind us.

At that time, the fleet had been given strict orders that no boat was to leave its column because of the danger of mines, and we had been told that anyone overboard was on his own. Fortunately, I found out years later, my friend had floated closely enough to a following boat for it to pick him up.

Thus, as we reached the beaches of the south coast of Sicily, some few miles west of the small town of Licata, most of the troops were the worse for the wear of several days of seasickness.

Almost precisely at 0600 (the assault troops had landed about 0430) my ship struck the beach some 50 yards out in the water. On the starboard side between us and another landing craft floated the body of an unfortunate GI who undoubtedly had been drowned in the heavy surf. Farther out, a huge column of smoke marked an ammunition ship bombed by enemy aircraft. Responding to a commotion on the port bow (port = left) I felt myself impelled to go over the side onto a small raft to help a lone radio man who was desperately trying to hold on to both the raft and his precious radio. When I got down to his raft the swells were so strong as to tear me away and I found myself walking chest high toward the beach. Suddenly my footing disappeared and I realized the ship had stopped on a shoal with deep water between it and the beach making it impossible to unload the ship. Fortunately, being a good swimmer I headed toward the beach, confronted immediately by another waterlogged sergeant struggling in panic to get back to the ship. Realizing he couldn't make it in the surf, I treaded water in his path shouting for him to turn back to the beach. He finally managed to struggle to a rope thrown out from the beach and was pulled in. As I grabbed the rope and pulled myself onto the sand I found that while I still had my carbine, my helmet had been swept away in the surf along with my badly needed eyeglasses!

I stepped onto the beach, exhausted, realizing that at first, the pack on my back had had enough air in it to act as a float, but by the time I had reached the beach it was 50 pounds heavier with seawater. My wrist watch (stupidly left un-waterproofed) had stopped a few minutes after 0600 and then I remembered to drop the safety belt around my waist. (These

were tubes made to act as life preservers by squeezing the buckle and puncturing two soda gas cartridges that would inflate it. Of course, I had forgotten to inflate it!) Emptying my pack of water on the beach near a group of amused Italian prisoners huddled under the overhang above the beach I became suddenly aware of bullets and firing from a concrete pillbox above the left edge of the beach on a high cliff.

By that time, the landing craft I had left had managed to back off its reef and charge over it to get to the beach where the surf managed to push it broadside, its stern toward the enemy pillbox. As troops began to unload over the side, a brave Navy stern gunner managed to get to his 50 caliber machine gun and he quickly fired a burst right through the gun slit in the pillbox.

Leaving the beach by a dry creek bed I found the command post a short distance inland and discovered I had left my dispatch case on the beach.

Because it had both a classified codex instrument in it and a prized picture of my wife, I quickly returned to the beach and luckily found it still lying on the sand in front of the even more amused Italian prisoners. I wasn't even aware at the time that the beach was still being fired upon by a few leftover enemy (who were shortly silenced).

In the midst of the initial confusion a peasant farmer and his mule passed by bringing two huge jugs of water to his home. As we were desperately in need of any kind of transport for the headquarters heavy equipment and radios someone ordered him to take off the jugs and give us the mule. He remonstrated but to no avail. I felt badly at his plight and when I too suggested we give him back his mule one of our group who must have been a farm boy assured me that any mule would know his way home and we would let him go as soon as we located our command post.

Oh, yes! The helmet I lost was a more serious problem than I thought. General PATTON had ordered that EVERYONE must wear his helmet at ALL times and have his weapon handy or be subject to dire punishment. (He once, in Tunisia, fined a platoon leader three-quarters of a months pay because one of his men had lost a legging and was marching along with one pant leg flapping in the breeze.) Accordingly, because there were no supplies available for several days, I was ordered by my commanding officer to remain in hiding to make sure that PATTON wouldn't see me in his visits to command posts. (A few days later we heard enemy firing from a road below our command post, I started downhill where I could see two Italian soldiers, surrounded by 20 or 30 members of the nearby village, firing at something to our front. As I started to aim my carbine, my commander yelled at me to get back into hiding and RIGHT NOW!! Only a few minutes later I understood why—Gen PATTON was on his way to congratulate some of us who at that moment were given battlefield promotions. Someone handed me a brand new helmet and a set of Captains bars. I put two strips of adhesive bandage tape on the front to make myself presentable. (Someone else got the two Italians to surrender—shooting at them was not possible because of the crowd of civilians calmly surrounding them and watching them firing as if on a Sunday outing.)

As for the eyeglasses—because of the heat and the obvious inability of the rapidly retreating enemy to use gas, we were able to discard our gas masks, and fortunately I remembered the set of gas-mask glasses (tiny lenses and flat ear pieces that could be worn inside the mask) which I was forced to use for the rest of the Sicilian campaign. That they made me look like a cartoon character didn't help much.

And the wrist watch. Because I desperately needed a timepiece, I managed to talk an Italian soldier prisoner out of one he was wearing. He gave it to me seemingly happy to part with it. I found out why later when I discovered it had a tendency to stop whenever it felt tired, and I had constantly to keep resetting it for the rest of the campaign.

14

The Sicilian Campaign Phase II – Agrigento to Palermo

A.D. Kuperstein

During medieval times Sicilian towns were built as fortified enclaves on the tops of the hills and volcanic cones that make up the Island of Sicily. To stand on one of these hilltops and see the white stone buildings covering every hilltop all along the horizon is an unforgettable sight. Agrigento is perched on just such a low hill mass commanding the junctions of several major highways leading westward and northward, thus being the key objective of my division in its mission to protect the left flank of the British Army fighting south of Messina and Mt. Etna. Agrigento boasts a number of ancient Roman temple ruins, one of which I passed having an incongruous abandoned light machine gun sitting on the floor in the midst of the beautifully constructed marble columns.

As my regiment (of which I was the staff Intelligence Officer) was moving eastward on the highway south of the city I contacted one of the Artillery fire control officers sitting on a high cliff above a large flat plain across which troops were moving in assault against a hill mass to the front. Through my field glasses I could see shells bursting on the now-blasted-bare hills. To the right (north) side I could see a company of Italian soldiers organizing into ranks, having been driven off the hillsides. Immediately to the right was an orchard. I contacted the artillery battery and had their fire shifted off the hill to the orchard area. As the first shells began to drop there, the Italian group broke up and even today I can see that tall, skinny, long-legged soldier running away through the trees in tremendous strides, just like an antelope fleeing from a lion.

Because British General MONTGOMERY (who had a low opinion of American troops after the unhappy experiences in Tunisia) had ordered General George PATTON not to get into any pitched battles, our Division Commander, MG TRUSCOTT, conceived the idea of capturing

Agrigento by what he called a "reconnaissance in force". My regiment (7th Infantry) managed to get one battalion clear around the north and west of Agrigento, while the others attacked along the road nets south and east of the city. After some rather hard fighting, the city was captured on 17 July 43, with some 3000 to 4000 Italian troops as prisoners of war.

During the night, the Division Military Police commander came to our Command Post asking for a guide to take his battalion and a huge convoy of trucks into Agrigento to get the POW's off the hands of the fighting troops. It was my misfortune to be standing close by, and my regimental commander simply pointed at me. Since I had not had a chance to get into the city and was totally unaware of the road net, choosing me as a guide was like having the blind leading the blind. To avoid the obvious problem, I got my driver and a jeep and we headed westward on the main highway so I could find my way in the morning. Fortunately, it was a pleasant moonlit night and we easily found the road junction where the road to the city led sharply uphill, curving back toward the east. Visible in the moonlight was the ruins of another Roman temple. Noting a rather black mass ahead of us above the junction, I had the jeep driver stop so that I could get out and reconnoiter on foot. We moved the jeep back under some trees and I stepped forward almost on top of some rectangular box-like objects across the roadway. They were mines! The jeep tire track had stopped no more than 6 inches in front of one of them. Evidently the mine layers had not had time to camouflage them. Beyond the mine field the black mass I had noted turned out to be a huge, deep tank trap completely destroying the road. Upon my return to the CP and reporting that it was impossible to get the MP trucks up that road, I was relieved of the problem. The next morning I got to see the huge formation of Italian POW's streaming down the hill guarded by a lot of cursing MP's who had been forced to hike a couple of miles uphill instead of riding up there in their trucks. I can still see the line of box mines in the road and the tire track leading right up to it.

A day or so later, from the heights of Agrigento I could see, through my field glasses, another hill mass to the north where our troops were beginning the 75 mile push toward Palermo, a dirt mountain road along which an Italian Army truck was heading down around a curve. Unseen was an American Army truck heading uphill toward the same blind curve. The Italians quickly surrendered, which was characteristic of the entire western Sicily Italian defense forces. (MUSSOLINI, in the theory that good Sicilian-born soldiers would fight to the death for their own homeland, had shifted all such troops into Sicily. To his dismay and our gratitude, as we advanced, Sicilian-born soldiers quickly shed their uniforms for civvies and disappeared into their home towns. I was often accosted by townspeople who would point out where some of these soldiers lived, but we knew it was pointless to take them prisoner and have to feed them because for them the war was over.) On one road patrol north of Agrigento, I passed through a small town only to be stopped by a crowd standing in the roadway. Someone pointed up a side street and there were two Italian soldiers, rifles slung on their shoulders, coming down toward my jeep with hands raised. They were happy to be transported to the POW camp at Prizzi, nearby.

Summers in Sicily are HOT! Still dressed in our woolen uniforms, our troops on the 3-day forced march northward to capture PALERMO suffered greatly—I had never seen men so tired and exhausted as they tried to keep up the "Truscott Trot" 5-miles an hour march with full packs. As I patrolled northward, I often picked up exhausted stragglers and got them up to their units. (Our Division Commander, Gen Lucien TRUSCOTT, had instituted in North Africa a physical training regime requiring all men and officers to make a 5-mile in one hour speed march every day to get us in shape for just this kind of operation—to say it paid off is an understatement.) Suffering from the heat and dense cover of flies that would ride our food right into our mouths, a chance to take a bath was a first priority. On one mission to get an urgent message to some troops, it was necessary for me to swim across a small river, leaving my jeep and driver on the road. On the way back I took time to really soak in the cool water, fully dressed. Then my driver got to go. We drove back along the highway joyous in the warm breeze that quickly dried us off before anyone could notice our bedraggled appearance. On another occasion below PALERMO we stopped at a roadside stone farm building from the roof of which poured a diverted stream of beautiful cold water. Seeing no one around I stripped and stepped into the stream, reveling in the chance to get rid of several days of dust and sweat. Suddenly I heard girlish voices in excited tones—two farm girls had just walked around the corner of the building and prudently ran back up the road, giggling all the way.

As we neared PALERMO signs of battle increased. Checking on the status of a railroad line paralleling the highway I walked along it for about a mile past the huge air-bomb craters that resulted from multiple air-strikes. I noted that out of the many hundred such craters not a single one had hit or disabled the tracks! This was just one more experience that made me forever discount the effectiveness of our air power during the War. (Earlier, in the first few days of the Sicilian Campaign, when very little transportation had been landed, every wheeled vehicle was precious. One day I was tasked to act as a body-guard for our Division Deputy Commander on a jeep trip to find the CP of a unit located in the hills inland. As we approached the forested area in which the CP was located, we heard an airplane engine roaring behind us and some dirt kicking up behind us in the roadway. All of us scattered in split seconds and from the sides of the road watched one of our P-51 fighters drill 50 caliber holes into our precious jeep!)

Unknown to one of our battalion commanders, General PATTON had ordered that no units were to enter Palermo after its surrender until he and his tanks could make their usual publicity foray into the city. When the General entered the city he was somewhat put out to find troops already there rounding up thousands of Italian soldier prisoners. Shortly I found myself on one of the main streets near the harbor watching long columns of Italian Mountain troops in their feathered alpine hats marching happily toward prisoner of war enclosures south of Palermo. Riding in a jeep was an Italian General Officer of immense belly size, wearing one of the smallest pistol holsters I have ever seen. Ludicrous as it was, it was the Italian Army custom that the higher the rank, the smaller the sidearm! With its capture, Palermo afforded us a day or so of rest and recreation. Outside our Division Headquarters, established in a huge stone palace in the city, someone had placed a huge wheel of Parmesan cheese, with bayonet attached for use by anyone entering or leaving the building. From that day I have been a lover of Parmesan cheese—especially after several weeks of K and C ration diet.

After a few days of refitting and retraining near Palermo, my unit was ordered to start marching along the north coast highway to Messina. From that point on we began to meet more severe resistance as we entered territory defended by crack German veteran troops who had escaped from Tunisia before its fall. The easy days were over!

Maj A.D.KUPERSTEIN, USAR-Ret received his reserve commission on 17 Nov 39 as a graduate of the Citizen's Military Training Camp at the Presidio of Monterey, CA. Following graduation from the University of California in Dec 39, he was placed on extended active duty beginning on 17 Mar 40 with the 7th Infantry Regiment, Third Infantry Division, then stationed at Vancouver Barracks, WA. Maj KUPERSTEIN served continuously with the 7th Infantry Regiment, taking part in the North African landings at Fedala, Morocco, and the Tunisian and Sicilian Campaigns. Hospitalized for a year after the Sicilian action for a fractured leg received in a patrolling action, he was returned to the States and was assigned as company commander at Camp Fannin Basic Training Camp in Texas until discharged on 19 Nov 45. Subsequently he was appointed Major, Officers Reserve Corps (Inactive) on 15 Dec 52. As a civilian employee he served from 1946 through 1970 in Headquarters, Sixth US Army at the Presidio of San Francisco.

The island of Sicily was assaulted on July 10, 1943 in operation Husky. Over 467,000 Allied troops were opposed by 60,000 Germans, two-thirds of whom escaped to Italy with their equipment.

15

The Sicilian Campaign Phase III – Palermo To Messina

A. D. Kuperstein

The 100-mile-long north coast road from Palermo to Messina is much like the California coast highway—narrow, curvy, at beach level in some places and high up the hanging cliffs in others. It crosses innumerable rivers (all dry in summer) with only a few bridges left intact by the retreating Germans. Unlike the Italian Army retreat from Agrigento to Palermo, the German resistance along the coast highway was fierce because it allowed small enemy units to carry out effective delaying actions requiring mule-supported supply trains up and around the cliffs in order to outflank resistance points. The major problem was the German propensity to lay mines and mine-fields and booby traps (even to booby-trapping dead soldiers) wherever they could. Thus, wheeled vehicles, like the small amphibious jeep that was assigned to me for the eastward push, were never allowed to use road shoulders or get off solid pavement except in emergency. During the 3 weeks it took us to reach Messina, I never had a moment that I didn't worry about mines and booby traps.

The mine dangers were so prevalent that Bill Mauldin published a cartoon in the Army Times showing a long line of tanks and troops winding down a curved mountain road, all preceded by one single poor GI holding a mine-sweeper. As a matter of fact, the few tanks we had were forbidden to move along the roads until they had been mine-swept.

One incident illustrates. At a rather wider-than-usual river crossing at which the concrete bridge was still intact, I recall passing along the stone wall of a doctor's large home which had one narrow wrought iron gate, open and protruding into the narrow curved roadway leading to the bridge abutment a short distance away. (In Sicily countryside there are no sidewalks. Generally, buildings and walls line the roads with barely room for vehicular traffic.) As my jeep drove by the gate one of my

friends, a company commander, was standing on the abutment watching his company cross the bridge. I waved at him and drove ahead. A few hours later I learned that an exhausted soldier marching along the wall angrily kicked the protruding gate out of his path—at which moment the abutments and bridge exploded and fell into the dry river bed below. Only a small skull fragment was all they could find of my friend.

At a major road intersection we were held up by a protracted mortar and artillery interdiction. One poor MP had been hit and was lying on top of a stone wall alongside the road as our Regimental Surgeon was probing for shell fragments. Because it was getting dark, we established our Command Post off the road amidst some stone farm buildings. As mortar shells began to fall into our area I ducked behind a small stone shed, sheltered by a large dirt mound. A shell exploded just behind me and fragments shattered the stone on the wall in front of me. One small very sharp fragment literally fell off the wall into my hand - it was red hot and I dropped it quickly, retrieving it as a souvenir after it had cooled. (I threw it away later because the razor-sharp edges from the nose cone kept ripping up things in my pack.)

A day or so later we had to plan a massive coordinated artillery supported attack across a river bed, and I was sent to reconnoiter the near river bank and report the progress of the attack in the morning.

About midnight, I and a telephone wire-man crept down toward the river through a grape-vine field (trusting only to luck that the Germans hadn't booby trapped the vines as they normally did). At the edge of the vine field overlooking the dry bed of the river I found what appeared to be an old fox-hole, partly filled in, that would provide some shelter. As I started to dig a little deeper I suddenly realized that most foxholes we and the Germans dug were not as large as this one.

The thought arrived that if I dug any deeper someone might be down there, and I decided to just use it as is. Meanwhile, because we were so close to the river I had instructed the CP operator not to ring us on the telephone, but that if we had anything to report we would call them.

I observed across the river the dim shape of a one-slit round concrete pill-box (of which there were many in Sicily at strategic defense points). Since nothing had fired at us, I began to think that there was no one in there, particularly as the stillness was shattered by the shrill ringing of the field telephone. In shock and horror I ripped the line off one terminal

to stop the ringing. Nothing happened! Gingerly, we reattached the wire lines and rang the CP operator whom I chewed out in hoarse whispers. "We didn't call you, Captain," he said, "Some other unit must have found your wire and patched in." I then was able to report that there seemed to be no one across the river or we would, by now, have been punched full of holes. This was confirmed a while later when some dumb young lieutenant drove his jeep up and down the dry river bed trying to draw fire, which didn't happen, fortunately for him. As dawn broke, the artillery was called off and troops and vehicles began to move across the river bed (the bridge was long gone). As I stood up to look across the river, there was a tremendous explosion from the river bed crossing and I could see the entire right rear wheel and fender of a jeep rise some 30 feet straight up into the air, wheel over and fall down again. The Germans had double-mined the dirt roadway, putting the mines deep enough to let the first few vehicles pass over until the ruts got deeper and allowed some following vehicle to set off the mines.

The stresses of being in a combat zone for lengthy periods are often relieved by comic incidents. One evening my jeep (now exchanged after bitter pleas to our supply officer that the amphibious body was so low as to keep hanging us up on deeply rutted roads or even on small rocks in the roadway) was chasing our rapidly moving front lines when darkness began to fall. Realizing we could go no farther we looked for an off-road place where we could spend the night with some safety. In one ravine we explored, we found a Sicilian farmer still trying to sell small bags of apricots to passing GI's, so I purchased two bags, one for me and one for my driver to ease the monotony of the K-ration diet. Finally, we found a grapevine farm with a dirt road climbing uphill in a series of steps, each step being a line of vines. We found a suitable place in which to park the jeep and to stretch out. As it got dark, we each feasted hungrily on about half of each bag of delicious apricots, leaving the rest for breakfast. We fell into exhausted sleep.

BOOM! BOOM! BOOM! BOOM! In heart-stopping fright we jumped to our feet thinking we were being shelled by the enemy. On the step above us a GI helmet appeared and the order "CEASE FIRE, CEASE FIRE" emitted therefrom. The helmet then spoke to us, or rather, shouted "What the ____ are you dumb _______s doing down there?" We learned that during the night, our battery of "LONG TOMS" (155 mm artillery) had moved into position behind us and were firing a morning attack mission. We departed quickly, of course, and went down the road a piece, stopping to finish off our apricot breakfast while we settled our nerves. As I picked up the first apricot, and bit into it I noted it had some tiny little worms crawling around inside. To make it short, we picked out every apricot one by one, not one of which was not being used as growing space by a host of little worms. Later, one day, I met the artillery commander who told me that if we had been a little further forward and higher in the grapevine field, the muzzle blast from the 155's would have killed us!

Following a short attack, I walked up a sharp bend in the narrow road, steep cliffs above us, and there in the center of the road, as if in firing position was a dead German automatic rifleman. As the Germans retreated, they often had to leave their dead behind, and passing along the roads you always could tell where they lay by the horrendous stench that one never forgets.

One day, someone brought me, for interrogation (using an interpreter) a German soldier who had suddenly appeared, unarmed and helmetless, right in the middle of the command post. He and a friend had decided to desert, and when their unit retreated they waited until they saw some American troops advancing. This soldier's friend stood up from their hiding place and raised his arms in a signal of surrender when he was cut in half by a machine gun blast. Our prisoner wisely stayed hidden until he had been bypassed and could surrender to less trigger-happy rear area units. Unknown to him, the reason for his friend's demise was that several days before, a German unit held up a white flag at the edge of a field upon which we were advancing. The young lieutenant, trusting in the Geneva Rules stood up and went forward to accept the surrender, only to be shot down. Thereafter, it was difficult for German soldiers to surrender.

Approaching closer to Messina, the terrain flattens and allows the railroad to parallel the highway. At a place called Rometta Station, some German mortar fire had ignited a very long train of ammunition cars. As these exploded, one by one, fragmented hardware made it necessary to close the highway to all troop movement. It so happened that Mike Chinigo, the newspaper reporter who followed us through Sicily, thought it was such an interesting event he wanted to take a look. I was assigned as his guide and his safety was my responsibility.

With much misgiving, I allowed him to persuade me that we could maneuver between some of the nearby buildings and get into the little stone shed which housed the tiny steam locomotive. As we climbed into the cab, Mike wanted to see if it could be operated so as to push the rest of the train back along the track which would take it away from the roadside. With no steam in the boiler he gave up and started walking back along the line of burned out railcars. I was still inside the shed when I heard German machine gun fire to our front somewhere, and then a huge explosion from another railcar sent one-half of one of its steel wheels (about 10 inches in diameter) whooshing over our heads. In a panic to get Mike out of there safely, I persuaded him that the machine gun fire might prove to be a more serious problem and to my relief, we departed.

The most serious hold-up to our advance was at Cape Calava, about half way to Messina. There, the road enters a short tunnel in solid lava rock and emerges along a perpendicular cliff. The Germans had very cleverly blown up the inside of the tunnel, leaving huge boulders on the roadway, and blown away the road at the exit. The 10th Engineer battalion in about two days managed in a remarkable feat of engineering, to build a timber-supported roadway bridging the gap over a frighteningly high point on the cliffside. My jeep driver turned white as he slowly crept over the bending timber tracks, and I tried not to show him my white knuckles, but we were reassured that it was built to take our heavy trucks as well. The night before, I had wandered into the dark tunnel as jackhammer drivers were reducing large boulders to allow them to be removed from the roadway. Also wandering through the dark tunnel was our Division Commander, anxiously trying to spur faster and faster work so we could get moving again. As he kept tripping over the jackhammer lines and bumping into the exhausted engineer troops trying to do the impossible, one of them said something to the effect that "If your not going to help why don't you get the hell out of here!"

Of course he didn't know who the dark figure was, and I often wonder if he ever found out. The General quickly departed without a word, satisfied that all that could be done was being done.

On 17 August 43 our first patrols got down into the city of Messina. Although there was still some minor sniper firing I thought it my duty to reconnoiter down the road from the hilltop overlooking the Straits of Messina. The few of us there that early morning could see the fleet of boats taking retreating enemy troops to the Italian shores a mile or so away, and quite visible. A sentry informed us that no one was to go down into Messina until Gen. Patton and his convoy led the way in the usual conqueror publicity effort. As we were waiting there, our Division Artillery commander came up and I asked if we could give the fleet down there a parting shot just for the fun of it. With a bright smile he reached for his radio and ordered a salvo at maximum range, since the battery had not yet had time to displace forward. We watched as the 4 shells burst in the water just behind the last group of boats.

Shortly thereafter, Gen. Patton in his trademark scout car and entourage grouped themselves at the roadstead and proceeded down the hill into the city. A while later I was allowed to follow, down past a huge concrete wall several stories high on which the word DUCE had been painted in huge letters so that they could be read from the mainland. Strangely enough, there was no one to be seen on the main street along the water. We passed along the street car tracks and past some bombed out streetcars. My driver and I stopped at a concrete balustrade overlooking the Straits. Using our field glasses we took a look across the Straits to the other side. Suddenly, with a whoosh and whistle a huge artillery shell whizzed over our heads and exploded against the side of a high-rise office building to our rear. Hopping into the jeep, realizing someone over there had spotted us, and explaining why we saw no one else in the area, we ducked into a street sheltered by other tall buildings. As another shell hit a wall high above our heads a British Army officer came out of a door, calmly asking, "What are you chaps doing here?" He suggested that we quit drawing fire and showed us a sheltered route back to our area.

Soon, I was sent back the entire length of Sicily to the area around Trapani on the west coast to find a bivouac area for our regiment which was to travel the 150 miles to the rear for rest and retraining.

Near Trapani I found an ideal area under some trees and next to a small farm. The area had been used as a German Engineer bivouac and was reasonably accessible. Having claimed it for my unit, further exploration revealed a huge open pit bulldozed into the ground, completely filled with explosives, ammunition, stacks of mines and related hazardous equipment. I had to get our Engineers to clear it away. Relieved that all was well, I strolled down a path toward the farm to see an old man waiting at the gate for me. As I approached he bent down and picked up two huge items to hand to me—they were tank mines. He sign-languaged that he had secretly watched the Germans plant these two mines in the pathway, and after they left he had dug them up himself. Another mine-sweep, however, failed to find any more. The next days were filled with more exhausting training exercises, including a continuation of the "Truscott Trot" for which I had to get up early every morning, put on my pack and rifle and hike the designated 5 miles an hour before breakfast. Combat was easier!

16

Missing the Action

Brigadier General Robert D. Upp,
AUS-Ret.

General Patton was sweeping Sicily, troops were preparing for the invasion of Italy and building up for D-Day, but I was sitting on Shagak Pass on Adak island in the Aleutian islands. We were waiting for the Japanese to return, but they never came. We were to launch the great conquest of Japan from the north, but it never happened. All of this was particularly ironic, because after more than a year in CONUS training camps, I had submitted a written request to be assigned to combat. Instead of going to North Africa, I was sent to Fort Lawton in Seattle under "top secret" orders, embarking on an unescorted World War I vintage ship listing slightly to starboard, headed for a destination unknown. While boarding the vessel, we noted "ADAK" stenciled on the crates being shipped with us.

The lonely voyage across the wild Gulf of Alaska was an adventure. The sea was so rough and the waves so high that the ship's propeller was clear of the water at times. This required a slow trip and we were a week late arriving in Adak. Since there was no convoy, we had to maintain radio silence and were given up as lost. Despite the fact that most of the passengers were seasick, the trip was pleasant because there were 20 Navy nurses making the "cruise", the first to be stationed in the Aleutians.

Upon arrival, we army replacements aboard were assigned to the backup reserve for the pending invasion of Kiska. That invasion was an historical debacle. The task force deployed 34,000 men. Although the island was deserted, 313 men became casualties. The navy said the enemy had to be there, but the air force reported there was no activity, not even any evidence of attempts to repair runway bomb craters. But the operation took place. Twenty-four men were shot to death by friendly fire. Booby traps and mines killed four more. Trenchfoot claimed another 134 victims. The *Abner Read,* a patrolling destroyer hit a mine in Kiska cove with a loss of 71 dead and 34 injured. Only a few abandoned dogs remained on the island. But the Japanese had scrawled a message in an underground barracks: *"We shall come again and kill Yanki-joker."* Those of us in the reserve force never disembarked.

While most of the force sailed south to retake Pacific islands, I was assigned to the 4th Infantry Regiment on Adak as adjutant of the 2nd Battalion. The commander was Major Brower, whose father was governor of Point Barrow and whose mother was a native American. It was Brower's father that Will Rogers and Wiley Post were going to visit when they had their fatal crash in Alaska.

Most of the members of the 4th Infantry were Alaskans, Aleuts, and Indians. It was an exceptional and talented group. Although the Aleutian campaign was over, the command was not confident that the Japanese would not return. As a parting shot, General Simon Bolivar Buckner, army commander, had the Eleventh Air Force undertake a bombing mission on Paramashiro, a Japanese base in the Kuriles. They dropped 12 tons of bombs and shot down thirteen enemy planes, but only nine of the 19 bombers returned to base.

Tokyo Rose announced that the Japanese were on their way back to the Aleutians. To guard against any surprise, our unit established outpost lookout stations around the perimeter of the island. These could be reached or supplied only by flat bottom barges on a rough sea, or overland on snowshoes.

The Aleutians have a rough terrain. There are no trees, only tundra, muskegs, mountains, volcanic gorges, and small streams. The weather is the world's worst, with temperatures usually in the thirties, almost constant rain, fog, sleet, or snow, and "williwaws", freak gale force winds that constantly change directions.

Shagak Pass, our location, was centrally located on a flat area between two mountain peaks. The Navy had erected Quonset huts which were used for housing, latrines, and kitchens. However, they had never put in any plumbing. To reach this area, one had to cross a deep crevice, about 50 feet deep and 20 feet wide. We had cut a path down and up, but to get supplies across, the Sea-bees had built a cable car trolley operated by a hand winch. The road ended on the other side of this small canyon, and after the supplies were winched across, we used makeshift sleds from corrugated roof tins with ropes attached to move items around the area.

One day Major Brower called me in and said, "Upp, you're a college graduate so you ought to be able to do anything. Heavy snow will start soon and we need to get some plumbing into these quonsets. The Navy has the plans and materials, but we're low on their priority list. So, you go down, get their plans, draw the equipment, and put in our waterworks."

Our personnel included many qualified construction men, so on a stream some 500 feet above our site we built a concrete dam with an imbedded 10 inch gate valve. We dug trenches down to permafrost to reach our two messhalls, four latrines, and the headquarters quonsets. The pipes were made of wood, barrel-like staves, tarred, and wrapped with wire. This construction was to keep them from freezing. They were graduated into smaller sizes as they came down the slope and finally into the regular metal pipe fixtures in the huts. We completed the job within a few days, leaving the pipe uncovered in order to check for leaks. Then came my big moment. I stood upon the dam, waved a signal that I was going to open the big gate valve and then spun it wide open. In a few minutes, we heard the loudest explosion of the war. We had failed to open the faucets in the sinks and as the water rushed down with no way for the air to escape, the huge pipes burst apart and flew into the air.

Major Brower laughed and said, "Upp, that was one hell of a show. Now you take your crew and go down and moonlight requisition enough pipe to do the job over and do it right this time." We carried out his order. However, when we made our night visit to the naval stores, my sergeant said, "Captain, there's a small snow cat and trailer sitting here, and if you'll let me, I can take a couple of days and run it around the mountain. Then we'll have it to haul supplies with instead of that cold tin roof piece." I gave consent, Sarge managed to complete the mission, and the vehicle made our hauling jobs much easier.

(from left) Brigadier General Robert D. Upp, Mrs. Robert Upp, RADM Bennett Sparks, and Betty Sparks, Washington, D.C., 1993

The Navy was getting ready to move most of its remaining Alaskan fleet to the Central Pacific when our unit got a phone call from the Admiral's aide saying that he wanted to requisition from us a competent work detail. The job was to scour the headquarters aboard the flagship. I had my versatile Sarge pick his men and sent them on this mission. The next day I got a call from the aide saying that the detail had stolen some of the Admiral's property and he wanted them courts-martialed. When I asked him to itemize the items, he said the value was in excess of $400. I told him that in order to file proper charges, it required a detailed listing of the missing items together with the value of each. He replied that he would get back to me. He called again and said the Admiral did not want to get involved, so I was to drop the matter. When I went into my office the next morning, a pinch bottle of Haig & Haig scotch was on my desk. Later, I found out that it was against regulations to have liquor on board ships in the task force.

When General Buckner left Alaska to go to Okinawa (where he was killed by shrapnel from a Japanese artillery shell), he was succeeded in the Aleutians by Major General Davenport Johnson. General Johnson found out that practically all of the men in the 4th Regiment had been there more than two years, so he released them to go home.

Those with less that two years were transferred. I was then assigned to the 138th Infantry on Unmak Island. We were given 48 hours to gather our gear and abandon Shagak Pass. On the way out, I stopped by the Navy warehouse and told the CPO in charge that there was a snow cat and trailer on the place we had just left. He asked for the serial number, and when I gave it to him, his reply was: "That's impossible, that tractor was lost in action on Kiska." I'd like to return to Adak and see if it's still there.

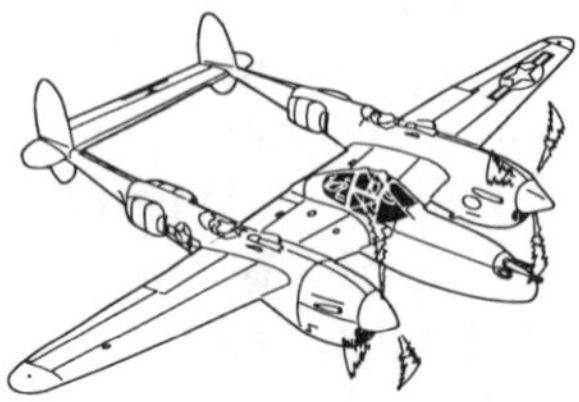

17

Intelligence Puzzle in Italy

Lt. Col. Earl M. Amundsen, USAF-Ret.

Col. Amundsen graduated from cadet training September 8, 1944 and flew 22 combat missions over Italy before the war ended. Like many other officers, he was initially trained in one type of aircraft (B-25 bombers) but transferred to another type, due to the exigencies of the war situation. His entire class went to P-38 Lockheed Lightning aircraft converted to photographic recon, stripped of guns and armor plating to reduce the weight of the aircraft and to give it added speed.

As a part of the 5th Photographic Sqdn. of the 3rd Group, his fliers shared the Peretola Airdrome with a British Spitfire Tactical Recon. Sqdn, primarily pilots from South Africa. They had priority for landing, since it was a short runway, and the spitfires had lesser endurance.

"The Peretola Airdrome was located only a few miles behind enemy lines in the Apennine Mountains of Italy. We were instructed to circle back after take-off and climb to altitude behind enemy lines to avoid small-arms and antiaircraft fire from the German side of the Gothic Line. I was amazed, as I would climb to altitude, to see farmers plowing fields along the foothills of the Apennine Mountains. The majority of those fields, away from main and secondary roads, had not yet been cleared of enemy mines. Each farmer who plowed was at risk to touch off a land mine. But it was spring, and no planting meant no crops. At age 21, I was learning quickly that life goes on despite perils.

Since we were so close to the Gothic Line, the daylight mission assignments were diversified, and often complex. From routine surveillance missions along the Po River and through the Brenner Pass, from Italy to Austria and Germany, to target photographs for fighter bombers, medium bombers, and front line artillery, we fulfilled all mission requests. We also flew missions to obtain location photographs for airborne supply drops to partisans, and to obtain bomb damage assessment photographs following bombing raids.

Captain Amundsen (above left); Lt. Amundsen receiving Air Medal from BG Meyers (above right); Lt. Amundsen on wing of his plane—P38 Lockheed Lightning (below)

From an intelligence standpoint, the Mediterranean Theatre activity had become a "forgotten war", since the Normandy invasion and that through Southern France had priority. However, it was an extremely bitter and costly "forgotten war". Costly for both the Allies and the Axis. The Gothic Line had been almost static during the hard winter of 1944-45, while the ground and air fighting remained fierce, with many casualties on both sides.

There was cause for concern to Allied intelligence. The final and complete defeat of the Axis forces in Italy was thwarted time and time again, since the Axis forces were being resupplied and reinforced repeatedly by some means that our intelligence personnel could not understand. Our daytime photo coverage verified that every bridge across the Po River was destroyed, and that the only major railroad and highway lines through the Brenner Pass were impassible in many, many locations. The Axis airborne cargo capability was virtually non-existent, since we had almost total air superiority. There was no logical explanation for the Axis ability to continually resupply their front line troops

There was some unofficial speculation that the Axis Powers had made a secret agreement with Switzerland to move supplies through the major passes in the Alps that were in neutral Swiss territory. Such would be one way to explain the steady movement of enemy supplies into the Po Valley. Interestingly, one of the photo interpreters spent many hours of his own time comparing the vast accumulation of photographs covering the Verona Marshalling Yards, at the Italian end of the Brenner Pass. He insisted there was often a two or three inch difference in the rail car positions on different days.

After the war in Italy ended, the truth finally became known. Axis engineering ingenuity brought about the fabrication of portable railroad track spans and portable bridge spans that were hidden during daylight hours. At dusk, those spans were lifted with giant cranes to drop into the "impassible" segments of the Brenner Pass rail line. With night-to-night repetition of the task, the rail line was restored in amazingly short time. Within a few hours after darkness, trainloads of enemy supplies would roll through the Brenner Pass into the Verona Marshalling Yards.

Just before dawn each day, the enemy would remove the temporary spans and replace rail cars in the marshalling yards, so that the next daylight photographs would look the same as those of the day before. Continuing repair work was an enemy ruse to convince our intelligence that they did not have the ability to make quick repairs.

The Axis ability to move supplies through the Brenner Pass was only part of the story. The supplies had to be transported through the Po

Valley to the front. The straight distance from Verona to Axis Headquarters at Bologna, Italy was less than 75 miles, but the supplies had to cross the 260 mile long Po River and there were no bridges left on the river. My squadron was a pioneer in night time reconnaissance. We had two B-25/F-10 medium bombers that were equipped for night photography. We patrolled the Po River night after night to try to photograph assembled pontoon bridges, but we seldom found them. It was a mystery as to how those supplies were getting across the Po River.

After the war ended, the truth finally became known. Axis engineering personnel had devised ways to quickly assemble and disassemble pontoon bridges in a repeatable manner, which they did in many locations along the Po River. By linking pontoon sections with long lengths of cable, attached to steam winches, they were able to float sections downstream and camouflage them during daylight hours. At twilight, they were winched back into position in less than an hour. They also had pontoon bridges assembled but submerged a foot or so under the water level, so that they could not be easily detected by photography.

Reaching the final days of the war in Italy, all of that ingenuity was useless, since the Axis had just run out of supplies and ammunition. While we felt that the grounded Axis aircraft were as a result of their lack of fuel, we also found that the reason was more so a lack of pilots; their pool of trained people had been expended.

Col. Amundsen became a commander of Flight A, 3566th Support Squadron, James Connally AFB, Waco Texas. He flew B-25 aircraft with state-of-the-art radar equipment to train radar observer cadets during the Korean conflict. He continued in the reserve until qualified for retirement. In civilian life he worked for General Dynamic Corporation on such interesting projects as Atlas Missile Systems, Convair commercial aircraft, Convair F111 Fighter/Bomber, the C-5A and C141.

18

Deadly Enemy Fire

Robert K Palassou, USA-Disch

I served in Co. "L", 363rd Regimental Combat Team, 91st Infantry Division in Italy, going into combat early in July of 1944, north of Rome and against the German Gothic Line manned by their 12th Parachute Regiment entrenched on high ground.

The initial battle to seize Mt.Vaso, not quite 400-500 feet high, proved to be one of the toughest of the campaign. Few of "L" Company remained after the third day on the line. My memory of those events is remarkably vivid!

After we took Mt. Vaso,Captain Tom Draney was the only officer left in the company. Our First Sergeant was the only non-commissioned officer, and only nine other men could be located. At that time we believed we were the only survivors. Such a calamity would have been a terrible enough experience for veterans, but this was only our third day of combat and the dreadful experience was devastating.

Company "L" had advanced three miles ahead of flanking units, thus our heavy casualties. We were reorganized, filled with replacements, and I became Platoon Sergeant. We went on to capture Leghorn, Pisa and positions along the south bank of the Arno River. On one patrol I was a half-mile behind the German lines when I came face to face with a German armed with a machine pistol. I fired first, but the bullet went between his legs, and my gun jammed! We were on the side of a steep hill, so I jumped down the bank as the German fired. My buddy protected me with his M-1 rifle while I was in the air! I never carried a Thompson submachine gun again!

Following that I had a problem with the 2nd Lieutenant, a former police officer from New Jersey, the only officer I ever had a problem with. He was briefing us about a forthcoming attack on the Gothic Line. We were all sitting on our helmets being shown aerial photos of the German positions that had been marked in red to show fields of fire.

They appeared so formidable that at the time I didn't think any of us would survive the assault.

When the Lieutenant said, "I want to change some assignments in the platoon," I became apprehensive. He knew I hated the Thompson gun, and was now armed with a sniper rifle. He said, "I want the best man possible as the platoon first scout," and of course he designated me!

He had the right to assign me to this position but when he said, "I don't want our sniper rifle to fall into the hands of the Germans.," I knew for sure he wanted me eliminated because I had embarrassed him earlier in the patrol action. He told me I was to carry a Thompson and wanted to take away my sniper rifle. I got up off my helmet, jacked a shell out of the rifle and said, "Lieutenant, if you want this rifle take it." I heard the men behind me scramble out of the way.

I was called to report to the Captain and asked to tell him what had happened. He told me he could not leave me in the same platoon.

February 1945, Rome

June 19, 1945, Venice

Sergeant Bill Montooth, who had overheard the altercation said he would take me into his platoon. I turned in my sniper rifle and took an M-1.

(The Lieutenant later cracked under pressure of the attack and was killed in action.)

Deciding that I didn't want the responsibility of being a Platoon Sergeant after six weeks of fighting the 16th SS Panzer Grenadier Division, I became, instead, a runner for the Platoon Leader.

On the morning of September 16, two Battalions of the 363rd were to cross the Sieve River and attack toward Monticelli. Our Battalion was to follow in reserve. We crossed the river, turning south along its bank to our assigned area. The cold water soaked us up to our chests, and one could hear our boots squish as we walked. I was able to drain some of the water from my boots, but it seemed our men were making far too much noise, causing me to become jittery. We slowed down as we came to a small creek where the Germans had blown a bridge. The embankment to my left was about twenty feet high and covered with trees.

As I waited my turn to go down into the draw ahead of us, just behind me and to my left I heard the bolt being drawn on a machine gun. My mind raced as I tried to picture the possibilities. I thought perhaps a German had been awakened by our noise, but afraid to fire for there were 200 of us. None of the other men had heard the bolt, so I became apprehensive that the men of the 2nd Platoon were not on their toes.

We advanced about a quarter of a mile, then turned east and proceeded through a field of knee-high grass. Dawn was approaching and the ground fog lay ahead of us, causing more worry. I came across a fresh pile of human waste with scraps of paper holding German script. I ran back to our Lieutenant reporting what I had found, but he was not impressed. The platoon seemed to be suffering from a false sense of security, since we were in reserve with units ahead of us. But I was nervous, sensing trouble.

I continued to move from man to man, urging them in a whisper to be alert. The fog seemed to thicken but I could see we were about to descend into a large draw. Within a few minutes the sun would rise over the hill in front of us and most of our cover would be eliminated.

As we started dropping down into the draw, shots were heard behind us. Spotting a ditch about five feet wide, about 20 men, the Lieutenant, and the Platoon Sergeant assembled in it, some relaxed, sitting down, some smoking. Being nervous, I paced back and forth with my "walkie-talkie" held to one ear. With the sun rising over the hill I saw one of my comrades (Stewart) from the platoon from which I had been reassigned approaching a haystack near the crest. A few moments later I looked back at him. He was relieving himself. Then I saw three men approaching his position—they were wearing raincoats with loops on their shoulders, and below their raincoats their sun-tan pants were visible—the uniform worn by German Paratroopers!

I grabbed my rifle and climbed out of the ditch, pointing it at the three Germans. All the while our Lieutenant cautioned me that they were Americans. I caught Stewart's eye and he quickly arose, grabbed his Thompson, yelling at the Germans to put their hands up. This was one of the funniest sights I have ever seen as Stewart stood there with his pants around his ankles and his Thompson pointed at the enemy.

Two of the Germans dropped their guns and put their hands in the air. The third dropped to the ground and positioned himself as if to commence firing. I pointed my rifle at him and yelled, "Drop it, Kraut!" He swung his head around to look with his burp gun still in hand. I yelled at him again to drop it, and I knew he was measuring me. All the slack was out of my trigger finger, but after a long ten seconds he capitulated and dropped his gun.

We discovered we had captured an officer with a map case and two highly decorated sergeants from the 4th German Paratroop Division. Puzzled as to where they had come from (they, like us, were apparently confused and did not recognize us as their enemy) I looked to the right and saw over fifty men with their backs to us, walking away. I focused on the lead man. He was carrying his weapon over the back of his neck with each arm raised to balance it. He turned to speak to another. After spotting me he reacted quickly, swinging his MG42 with bipod off his shoulders to the ground. A belt of ammunition was already inserted in the gun. I threw my radio and cigarette into the air, shouting "Germans!", and dove into the ditch to retrieve my rifle.

I whirled around to face the enemy, and although off balance, fired at the machine gunner. He slumped over his gun. The Lieutenant yelled at me, "You're shooting Americans!" I ignored him and continued firing at the men on the hill who were now 300 yards from us. I fired three clips (24 rounds) before the Platoon Sergeant opened fire also. The Lieutenant continued to yell, "You're killing Americans!" I continued to urge the other men to shoot because the Germans were nearing the top of the hill and would soon be gone.

When the last German disappeared over the hill, all was quiet except for the moaning of the wounded. I was cautioned to remain in place, but soon saw a man from one of the forward attack platoons make his way back down the hill and stop where the dead and wounded Germans were. The Platoon Sergeant and I led some of our men up the hill to join him. The grass was high so we were cautious. I found that I had killed 6 Germans and wounded 6 more; one had crawled away.

I wondered how I would sleep that night after my mind had a chance to absorb the happenings of that violent morning. The dirty work had fallen on my shoulders, yet if my initial shot had missed, that machine gunner could have made mince-meat of our platoon.

The trauma of the incident really had an effect on me. A few days later in a terrific mortar barrage, the worst I was ever in, I thought for certain that I was living my last day on earth. Lying on the ground as close as I could hug it, I had my M-1 in one hand and my 536 "walkie-talkie" in the other. I suspected even a fly could not live with all the fragments and bullets in the air. The German paratroopers had plunging fire upon us, and we were completely at their mercy—which was non-existent.

I made up my mind that no one was going to get me up and moving again. I concluded if I had to I was going to play dead until it got dark. Then, for some reason (I never questioned my instincts) I believed that by holding my arms out with my rifle and radio I was going to lose my arms. I let go of both, placing my arms under my body. The man in front of me had his feet near my head, and the fellow behind me had his head near my feet. I felt a number of times the blast of the shells near me, giving me a throbbing headache. During breaks in the shelling I would raise my head to see what was going on only to have the German riflemen fire at me, having seen the movement.

One time I raised my head and saw that my rifle was missing. When I raised up again to look for it they fired at me again. I never did find my rifle!

During a break in the shelling the man in front of me commenced screaming, and the man behind me complained of a wound in the shoulder. I wasn't aware at the time that I too had been hit by a fragment of shrapnel the size of a quarter in my right calf. I was lucky as it hit me flat, yet hot enough to burn the flesh. Rising up again I saw one of my best buddies, a medic, about a hundred yards up the mountain, rolling around in much pain. Without giving it a second thought, I went to his aid. I took him to the shelter of a building. Our Lieutenant came in with a shattered knee. He gave me his carbine, which I carried for the rest of the action. Although I thought by carrying a lesser weapon I would be relieved from the agony of killing, I was obliged to use it in another action for which I received the Bronze Star.

Most of the time I carried the carbine. In fire fights I gave more attention to caring for the wounded when I could. Saving a life was more important to me, I reflected, after having killed many men. I should have been a medic, I guess, for the wounded all trusted in me and believed me when I encouraged them that their wounds were not so bad.

Since the war ended many people have found that I was an infantryman have asked me my feelings about combat. I always tell them the same story:

I would never wish for my worst enemy to have to go through what I did. But, on the other hand, for myself I have considered what I went through an honor, as I had the opportunity to know those men that fought our war. To witness their bravery under fire was uplifting. For me to see friends in trouble and go to their aid gave me a feeling of justification. Many were to give up their lives in the process of this campaign. I knew many heroes first hand—they all were 1st class heroes in my mind.

Bob Palassou had many more fascinating stories to tell, and it was uncanny how well he could remember the details. From these recitals the reader must realize that Bob was an outstanding Infantryman, and a great credit to the Service. He probably deserved a more appropriate decoration, such as the Distinguished Service Cross, in addition to his Bronze Star, for his courage and leadership. Some of his adventures are recited in the Powder River Journal, published by the 91st Infantry Division Association. Like most of the people in his Company he was wounded (in his case, twice) and carries many scars to remind him of the Italian Campaign. Worth comment is the fact that he saved many lives by rendering prompt first aid to wounded men of his unit.

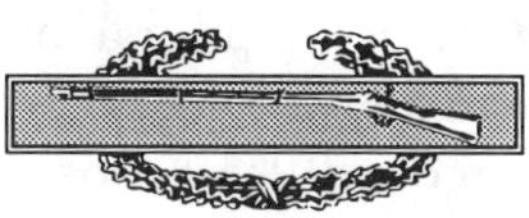

19

Wounded and Alone — Italy

Lawrence S. Ayers, AUS

People ask me, "Why are you wearing a large brace on your leg?" I explain that this device was made to strengthen my ankle which was shattered while serving with Co. "L", 363rd Infantry in Italy during World War II.

Early in 1944, the 91st Infantry Division moved to the Port of Oran, Algeria for amphibious training. This was followed by a cruise across the Mediterranean to the nearly devastated Port of Naples. Trucked to an assembly area near Riparbella, we made up our combat packs, put the balance of our belongings into duffel bags and moved forward. That was on July 3, 1944. I never saw my duffel bag again!

The next day we entered combat as a part of "Task Force Ramey" in an attack toward Mt. Vaso. Two days were uneventful, but on July 6, as we moved ahead, protected by a rolling barrage up the rocky slopes, I knew this day would be different.

I was contact man or first scout, charged with the duty of maintaining contact between our platoon and the 2d Platoon on our right. At one point during the advance we were held up for a long time and our Platoon Sergeant kept calling to me in a low voice, "Are they moving yet?" Somehow, during the confusion of battle, we lost contact with the 2d Platoon. When we finally reached the crest of Mt. Vaso I found myself with Lt. Aherabie and took cover near an abandoned enemy concrete-lined dugout. At dusk I rejoined my platoon and was glad to find my good friend Duke, who had survived the assault. I was distressed to hear him say that he knew he would not make it home. (Some time later his premonition proved correct.)

We were ordered to dig in, but the ground was so rocky we were forced to improvise by piling rocks around us to form a makeshift shelter. We were exhausted and sleep came easily.

I was awakened at 0300 and ordered to relieve our outpost some 75 to 100 yards ahead on the forward slope. I approached with extreme care, as we were all tense. Soon I was challenged and exchanged passwords. After settling down for my four-hour watch a feeling of loneliness swept over me. I wondered how far away the enemy was. What will this day bring?

Watching the sun rise on a beautiful morning, I was thankful my watch had been uneventful and was eager to be relieved. By 0800 there was no relief; I was ordered to stay in place. Occasionally I heard small arms fire behind me and calls for a medic. The action seemed to be back of me and I felt very insecure about this situation. I continued to watch and listen to the incoming and outgoing shells passing over my position.

At 0900 I changed my position slightly and propped up my legs on the rock that I had been sitting on and lit a cigarette. This proved unwise. The sound of shells passing over me suddenly changed, with incoming rounds kicking up dust in front of my position. I felt the rush of one round before it hit and exploded, but the next round gave me no

warning. It exploded and immediately I felt a searing pain in my right ankle, hit by shrapnel. My ankle was shattered.

After the artillery barrage many men called for medics. With none available, two buddies carried me back to our command post. As time passed I wondered where the medics were. Soon First Sergeant Weldon passed an order down the line, “If you can walk, move out. If you can't walk, we will be back for you later.” I was distressed to be forced to stay, but one of the largest squad members came to my aid. “I can't leave you here,” Joe said, despite a bloody flesh wound to his shoulder. He managed to stand me up on my left foot, and we moved out. As we stumbled down the mountainside I inadvertently put some weight on my right foot, causing a compound fracture, as a sharp bone protruded through the flesh. The pain was excruciating, so I asked my buddy to put me down and go on.

I have no ample way of describing the feeling of being left alone in “no man's land.” The thought that I was so helpless and that the enemy might soon reclaim the area was frightening.

I had been without food or water for two days. By mid-afternoon, the combination of thirst and pain became unbearable. Without a rifle, I contemplated a slow death. I wrote a note to my mother telling her of my desperate situation and of my intent to take my own life.

I cried out “God, there must be more to life than this!” Almost immediately I heard an inner voice, “Follow this trail and you will find water.” Somehow, I managed to crawl about 200 feet down the trail and spotted a trickle of water seeping slowly from the cliff above me.

Greatly refreshed, I started my slow, painful journey down the trail when I heard advice, “Stay here and you will be picked up in the morning.” Surprisingly, I spent a reasonably comfortable night.

At dawn I crawled up a small rise, saw some men, called out, and medics came to my aid. The roads below had not been cleared of mines, so I had to ride down on a mule, tended by an Italian native. He got separated from the column on the way down, but after a rough ride I was transferred to an ambulance.

It took a great deal of medical attention to take care of my injury. It was doubtful at times whether it would be possible to save my foot, but eventually I was released. A small piece of shrapnel is still lodged in my ankle. While working in the construction industry for 45 years the pain in my right leg has been a constant reminder of my personal ordeal on Mt. Vaso.

Despite the guidance from “an inner voice”,

it took me quite some time to resolve questions about one's faith in God. Now I can closely identify with David, who wrote in Psalm 23, Verse 4, "Yea, though I walk through the valley of the shadow of death, I will fear no evil, for thou art with me." He was correct, because I have walked there also!

Lawrence S. Ayers received a medical discharge in November of 1944, and returned to his home. He grew up in a farming family in Idaho, now lives in Arizona. He has had a career in the construction industry, been a Boy Scoutmaster, served on the Church Council and as an adult Bible Teacher. He had an interesting return trip to Riperbella, Italy, some fifty years later, and to the area in which he fought. He was warmly greeted by local citizens.

20

Taking a Hill

Lieutenant General William B. Fulton, USA-Ret.

This is Captain William B. Fulton. I am on top of the God Damned hill with only ten men. Now that I have it, just what in the hell do you want me to do with it?"

That was Monticelli Ridge, Italy, 1800 hours, September 17, 1944.

This action originally was published in the *Powder River Journal*, of the 91st Infantry Division Association, Inc., June 1992, titled "Attack of a Fortified Position". It describes in detail how the Germans had heavily fortified the ridges in the Gothic Line of the Appennines mountains in Northern Italy. The Appennines (the spine of Italy), some 870 miles long and from 25 to 125 miles in width, provided the German forces the classic defense terrain in which small forces could decimate larger numbers of attackers.

My regiment, the 363rd Infantry, was selected to storm the bastion of Monticelli, a strongly prepared defensive site on a steep, rocky and rugged mountain area. Guarding this area, the entryway into the Po Valley, was the German 4th Parachute Division. In many cases, the Germans had heavily fortified the ridges by tunneling in from the opposite side so that approaching attacking forces could not see those impressive defenses.

Supported by air bombing and intense artillery concentrations, two of our battalions struck initially without dislodging the enemy from their deeply dug, fortified positions. Small units began the slow, tedious process of working around one enemy position after another to gain a foothold.

The 1st Battalion made the initial penetration and held out against strong counter-attacks. Despite the fanatical defense, the enemy was driven back as elements of the 91st Division maintained constant pressure and cracked one strong point after another. With all battalions in the line, the 363rd withstood the intense enemy fires and counter-attacks. As the mountain mass of Monticelli fell to the 363rd, and the companion Mt. Altuzzo capitulated to units of a neighboring regiment, all enemy resistance in this position of the Gothic Line collapsed, opening the road to the north.

Because so many front-line officers had been made casualties in the earlier unsuccessful assault, I was given command of "K" Company, transferred from my position as battalion Personnel Officer (S-1). K Company moved up in darkness, but was detected by illuminating flares as the men made their steep ascent. We reached a barbed wire apron, but interlocking machine-gun fire protected the gap which we intended to use to move upward after firing a bangalore torpedo to breach the wire.

Determining that any attempt to breach the wire obstacle would be suicidal, the battalion commander (Lt. Colonel Glen C. Long) ordered me to withdraw, but that would endanger us to the automatic fires. Attempting to find another route, we found a little defilade and bedded down for a few hours of sleep.

Lt. Colonel Long, however, was ordered to take the ridge at all costs. He, in turn, ordered me to take the lead platoon and not to stop until we reached the crest of Monticelli. Reaching the protective wire, some scouts found a gap, and as a scheduled artillery barrage commenced I yelled "follow me" and headed through the pathway. While the enemy had taken cover during the heavy artillery barrage, the din, dust and dirt, and the heavy explosions may have demoralized them. I ordered the barrage to be lifted, but our forward observer had fled, and it was just fortunate that my radio operator was able to contact the Field Artillery Liaison Officer at Battalion Headquarters who relayed the order. The artillery barrage was marched in increments of 25 yards almost up to the top of the mountain. Even with that action, the enemy were able to come out and hit us with intensive fire.

We managed to take advantage of the curvature of the mountain and worked our way rapidly to the top. From that point, I was able to direct artillery fire to thwart counter-attacks, and shortly thereafter we were reinforced by other units of I and L companies, in time to repel repeated German counter-attacks.

For this action, the 363rd Infantry Regiment received the Distinguished Unit Citation "for outstanding performance of duty in action from 12 to 19 September 1944 in the assault upon the German Gothic Line near Monticelli, Italy. Chosen to make the main effort to penetrate the Gothic Line in the area of Il Giorgo Pass, in order that the divisions of the American II Corps could debauch into the Po Valley and outflank the vaunted Futa Pass position along the Florence-Bologna highway, the 363rd Infantry Regiment stormed the bastion of

Monticelli." Captain Fulton received the Distinguished Service Cross for gallantry in action.

General Fulton relates that "I would later command an Infantry Brigade in the Vietnam conflict. Many times in that war, when the going got rough, I would tell my staff, 'You people complain to me about battle conditions, when you really don't know just how tough they can get.' To really know the true answer to my comments you should have served with me in Italy in the autumn and winter of 1944.'"

General Fulton recently served as chairman for the Monument Committee that set out to refurbish the Monticelli Ridge Battle Monument in Italy. He stated: "My reason (for taking on this project) was much more than the thought that I had participated in the battle. It was because that battle represented to me an overall classic example of the most severe fighting, under the worst human conditions the 91st Division had experienced in Italy. Now the Apennines Campaign had put all the men in every unit to perhaps their most severe test of human endurance and fighting stamina any commander could ever expect from his men."

21

Blown up by a Mine

Major William Stanley Wood, AUS-Ret.

As a part of 40th Infantry Division CNG, I volunteered for AD before we entered the war, was commissioned in August 1942, entered action July 4, 1944 in Italy, and saw 9½ months of combat.

Perhaps one of the most memorable incidents was when I was blown up by a mine on the evening of July 17, 1944. I was a First Lieutenant, Liaison Officer in the operations section of regimental headquarters, 363rd Infantry, 91st Infantry Division. We were bivouacked that evening on the outskirts of the little town of Bagni di Cassiani, a few miles west of Florence, Italy, the thirteenth day of the regiment's combat as a part of General Mark W. Clark's Fifth Army.

A few minutes after we had finished eating, the Germans threw a few artillery shells at us. As the first rounds came whistling in, I distinctly remember bouncing off another officer as we both tried to go through the nearest doorway at the same time. While we weren't injured, we certainly were "nervous in the service".

My immediate superior, Major Floyd V. Pinnick, Regimental Operations Officer, asked me to be the I.P. (initial point) officer for our next move north scheduled to start at 1917 hours. We were to move into position for an all out attack on the city of Leghorn at 0300 hours the following morning.

My task was to see that units moved forward on a schedule that kept the portions of the convoy separated and allowed faster moving vehicles to deliver messages up and down the line. It was a long column of large trucks carrying troops, jeeps, weapons carriers, our Anti-Tank and Cannon Companies, Combat Engineers, a portion of the 91st Reconnaissance Platoon, and various other units.

Our route wound through a heavily wooded area for several miles, with no opportunity to see ahead for any distance. The road bed was in good condition, and the area had been secured; we didn't expect any opposition to our passage. Suddenly the column stopped and remained stopped for forty minutes.

I consulted with Major George C. Kotchik, Second Battalion Executive Officer, in charge of the next unit to move out. Recalling Major Pinnick's admonition that if a problem arose, "Don't just stand there, do something." I decided to drive down that road to see if there was anything I could do to get the convoy moving again.

I had been assigned a jeep and driver from D Company for the move. I soon found the driver, however he was holding a bottle of wine and socializing with a pretty Italian girl. I thought, "Why don't I just leave him here?" He was quite young, so why spoil a pleasant interlude when in a few days he might be wounded or dead. So I drove off without him against the rules; an officer was not supposed to drive a military vehicle. I rationalized that this was an emergency.

Driving down the left side of the road, passing the stalled convoy, including the vehicles occupied by a number of officers with whom I was acquainted, I wondered about mines, having heard several gruesome stories of men in jeeps being killed, losing limbs, being severely injured. I drove a mile or two without learning the reason for the stalled column. No one along the way knew why. Uneasy, I decided to return to my assigned post, and backing up, reversed my route. I had been thinking all the way about mines, but sighed with relief as I drove back for several minutes, and then...

When my mind slowly came back into focus I found myself lying on my back on a stretcher with an army blanket thrown loosely over me. I recall turning my head slightly to the left and realizing that someone was putting a shot into my arm, morphine, I supposed. Looking up I saw several people in a circle bent over looking down at me. I recognized Capt. Whitesel saying, "It's Woody". When he realized there were enlisted men present, he corrected his language, "It is Lieutenant Wood."

Someone asked, "What happened?" Whitesel replied, "He ran over a mine." I didn't feel a thing but looked to see whether my limbs were still there. Wiggling my left foot, then my right, I relaxed, finding everything O.K.

An ambulance was only fifty feet away. How fortunate, I thought. Someone remarked I was the calmest person there.

Perhaps it was because I thought I might have a free trip back to the States, or perhaps because I was in shock and couldn't move much even if I wanted to. Apparently I was not capable of saying a word.

Within a few minutes I was in the ambulance and taken to the rear C.P. Two dentists took a quick look at me, and then I was taken to a mobile medical facility. In the middle of the night I found myself in pain with the right side of my face swollen out of proportion.

Fortunately the jeep hit the mine with the right front wheel, the explosion mangling that portion of the vehicle. Had I been riding on the right seat I would probably have been killed.

I WAS JUST MINING MY OWN BUSINESS.

When I arrived at the Sixth General Hospital in Rome the side of my face was still extremely swollen. I found an acquaintance in the next bed, 1st Lt. Donald B. Phillips, of 2nd Bn. Hq. He didn't recognize me because of my disfigurement. Looking in a mirror, I didn't recognize myself either.

A few months after returning to the regiment I ran into a man from Cannon Company who informed me that he had been in the back of the mess truck that evening which was alongside my jeep when it hit the mine.

"Did you know I was in the ambulance with you that night when they took you back to the hospital, Lieutenant?"

"Gosh, no."

"When the mine blew, we in the truck thought it was incoming artillery fire. We went right out over the tailgate to get into the ditch along the road. I broke my big toe, so they put me in the ambulance also."

It is remarkable that my little thoughtfulness for the assigned driver probably saved my life.

Major Wood continued to serve in the Army Reserve for twenty-one years and won a number of awards, including the Purple Heart, and Bronze Star medals.

Stan Wood retired from the California Department of Motor Vehicles after twenty-eight years of service as a motor vehicle representative. He has a keen sense of humor and has a number of amusing tales of camp life before going overseas.

22

D-Day, Dog Beach
29th Infantry Division

Colonel Douglas A. Riach, AUS-Ret.

I landed on Omaha Beach on D-Day, 6 June 1944. Our outfit and others initiated *Operation Overlord*, the invasion of Europe by the Allies, which was the most massive operation of the war. Broken into segments, the landing of our 29th Division and the 1st Infantry Division was part of what was called *Operation Neptune.*

Overlord was the largest amphibious operation in history. 176,000 troops of all services were involved. They were brought in by 4,000 ships, protected by 600 warships and 9,500 aircraft. General Omar Bradley commanded the American Sector, which comprised landings at Omaha Beach and Utah Beach. We were within V Corps, commanded by Gen. Gerow, later by Gen. Hodges.

Visualize Omaha Beach as a five mile long tidal flat with a rolling countryside in the background. The beach extends only a short way to bluffs and cliffs, which had to be scaled. Only about 7,000 yards of the five miles are suitable for landings, and only three hundred yards of that remain dry sand at high tide. We knew the landings and ascent of the cliffs would be difficult.

I was a First Lieutenant in the 116th Infantry Regiment. The 116th was called *the Stone Wallers* because it was commanded during the Civil War by Gen. Stonewall Jackson. The *Big Red One*, the 1st Division was on our left. The Second and Fifth Ranger Battalions on our right assaulted Pointe Du Hoc. Huge concrete gun emplacements looked down the throat of Omaha Beach from the big rock on our right flank.

The beach was divided into eight sectors. The sector assigned to the 116th was designated Dog Green. Our objective required us to go ashore, secure the beach in our sector, proceed inland for about five kilometers to the little village of Vierville, establish a perimeter defense, and set up an assembly area by the end of day one. On our flank was the Vierville Ravine, known as exit D-1 in our plans. Only a few ravines

Troops in landing craft approaching the landing beach

allowed entry inland from the beach, and this was the only one in our sector available for our use to get off the beach and proceed inland.

The RCT came in the early morning at 0600, and landed at 0630. We went in on successive waves. The initial force consisted of an Engineers special task force called *Force O*. Their task was to clear gaps in the obstructions, make approach channels, and clear obstacles on the beach. The Germans had emplaced a lot of iron works in the form of crosses, and other obstacles to impede an invasion. The Engineer task force had about 1,600 men and 16 tanks. Their job was to blast holes in the obstructions and make eight gaps in Dog Beach as avenues of approach. But they were able to blow only six, and of the six only three were passable. So we had a big problem getting ashore right from the start. Our tasks had all been rehearsed prior to the invasion.

We off-loaded from the transport ship about twelve miles offshore, climbed down cargo nets into the small landing craft (LCVP's), a small boat with a ramp on the front to go ashore from. The sea was choppy and mean. As we moved toward the beach the small boats tossed so much that many of the soldiers became terribly seasick. The landing craft was designed to cruise right up to the beach and drop its ramp, permitting the troops to walk off. But, unexpectedly, we grounded on a sandbar quite a ways from the beach. As a result we had to prematurely off-load into rough waves four to five feet high. With men carrying so much gear it was disastrous. Many men drowned. Many never got as far as the shoreline.

We expected a barrage of enemy fire, but it was eerily quiet initially. We were given a false sense of elation, as if the landing was to be a "piece of cake". The enemy held their fire to the last moment. Then all Hell broke loose from what we learned later was the 916th Infantry of the 352nd German Army Division that was in the area on exercise.

As we scrambled ashore we were hit by a hail of gunfire from the German artillery, mortars, machine-guns, and small arms. That combination rained death and confusion. The enemy fire was devastating; dead and wounded were everywhere. It was so bad initially that my outfit Able Company was literally destroyed. All the initially assigned officers and most of the NCO's became casualties. Chaos and confusion were rampant. As I recall, nearly a hundred men in A Company alone were casualties that morning, nearly all from the town of Bedford, Virginia, where the National Guard Company unit originated.

We had expected assistance of several kinds that did not develop. Coastal defenses were scheduled to be pulverized by the huge air bombardment. However since the weather was overcast all the bombs were dropped inland (of great help later), but we had no craters on the beach to use as temporary shelters. Air commanders had been afraid of possibly hitting our own troops. Of the 29 amphibious tanks off-loaded from the initial landing craft, only two made it to the beach. We had literally no tanks or heavy weapons support initially. We were led to believe only coastal defense forces were opposing us. Instead we were faced with seasoned combat forces who delivered devastatingly fierce firepower. All of that contributed to a terrible day of combat, chaos, and confusion.

We finally reorganized and managed to get up those bluffs to the Vierville area by skirting the ravine assigned. We had literally no communications due to the loss of equipment.

We still had the big problem with the enemy entrenched in the ravine which impeded the forward movement of reinforcements. Our follow-on force was not able to reach us in a timely fashion. We had a Naval Liaison man with us, and he called for fire support. Four salvos from the battleship *USS Texas* eliminated resistance from that ravine. We then took some of the first POWs captured in Normandy.

Able Company, which I commanded shortly after we got ashore, took a terrible casualty rate. A number of the men still rest in the cemetery at Colville, near the beach, I am told.

Units were intermingled when we reached Vierville. By early afternoon we finally resolved the difficulties by shifting men back and forth to their proper units. By evening we had consolidated our forces, and were preparing to move out. The battle of St. Lo would rage farther down the road. On the advance toward St. Lo, I was wounded by a "Bouncing Betty", which was a wicked anti-personnel mine that bounced

up three or four feet before detonation. I was evacuated to the beach on a stretcher atop the hood of a jeep. We had no ambulances at that time. Mine was not a comfortable ride. Then I was air evacuated to a hospital in England. I still have fragments of shrapnel in my body to remind me of the war.

However our troops did move on forward. I was able to return to my Division months later, just in time to take part in the southern sector of the Battle of The Bulge. I crossed the Rhine at a town called Aachen, which was totally destroyed and finally ended up near Bremen at the end of the war in Europe.

The Longest Day was a hell of a long day, and one that I will never forget. For the record, approximately four thousand lives were lost on 6 June on all of the invasion beaches, of which approximately 2,500 American casualties were suffered on Omaha Beach. The Normandy Campaign has been officially described as the period between 6 June and 21 August 1944. During that time our forces sustained casualties totaling 37,000 KIA and 153,000 wounded, of which I was one.

I would like to add an interesting additional note. Have you seen the movie, "The Longest Day"? That film told the story of my regiment, the 116th Infantry, their tragedy and bravery on D-Day. Brigadier General Frank Cota, who was the Division Deputy Commanding General was in our area on D-Day; his part was played by Robert Mitchum in the movie. BG Cota received the DSC and was later promoted to Major General. The story told by the movie is essentially true.

Colonel Riach continued to serve in the Army Reserves for thirty-one years of commissioned service, retiring as a Colonel, and received the Legion of Merit at that time. Subsequently he served in the California State Military Reserve, commanding a Brigade, and was promoted to Brigadier General. He is listed in Who's Who in The West. He has a continuing career as a sales and marketing executive in the food distribution business. He was inducted into the Infantry OCS Hall of Fame at Fort Benning, Georgia in 1983.

General Eisenhower reviewing 29th Division troops; BG Norman D. Cota, Asst. Div. Comdr., on left

23

D-Day + 1, Omaha Beach

Captain Horace Edward Henderson,
AUS-Ret.

I served as a Lieutenant in command of a small intelligence unit attached to the Sixth Engineer Special Brigade, which included the amphibious engineer assault forces for the invasion of Omaha Beach in Normandy in June of 1944. My unit, with one officer and twelve enlisted men, had an important assignment, the responsibility for the receipt and distribution of all topographic maps to be used for the combat operations of the First Army in Normandy.

In England, prior to the invasion, we received the maps which not only revealed the Top Secret location of OVERLORD but also indicated the topographic features of the area. These would determine to a considerable extent the tactics to be used in operations destined to accomplish the successful conquest of Germany. At our United Kingdom depot, under the highest security precautions, appropriate strategical and tactical maps were selected, coded, sealed and packed in large wooden cases for shipment to Normandy.

After completing invasion exercises at Land's End and Woolacombe Beach, for security purposes my unit was placed in an isolation camp at Abergravenny, Wales. For two weeks we had nothing to do except to think about what lay ahead. Although we had complete confidence in the righteousness of our cause, we knew there would likely be a great loss of life in the assault and had to face the possibility that we might also die. As for me, I did what I am sure thousands of other young men did. I sought the comfort of the small Bible that all GI's were given, and I prayed and placed myself in God's care.

Two days before the invasion we were loaded with the 2nd Infantry Division on a former Caribbean cruise ship at Swansea, Wales. After feasting on the best food we had eaten for months, we joked that we were being served the last meal before we died. But having seen the channel literally covered with ships and the sky filled with planes we were confident that everything would go well. We were further reassured that the beaches would be under Allied control by the time we landed when we heard Ike's announcement of the invasion.

Early on June 7 we were awakened by an emergency alarm. When we got on deck we saw that a nearby ship had struck a mine and was sinking. Then, hearing loud explosions and seeing huge shells rising towards shore from a naval ship, we got our first look at Normandy and knew our time had come. Fortunately, the roughest weather had passed. After climbing down the rope ladders to our landing craft I was glad to find that none of my men appeared to be seasick or unduly scared. We assumed as we moved towards land that the overwhelming force of our initial assault had obtained surprise and that the inland objectives had been secured.

Once in sight of shore, however, I noticed that nothing moved on Omaha Beach except one bulldozer. The beach was covered with debris, sunken craft and wrecked vehicles. We soon saw many bodies in the water. But before we reached the beach our landing craft was stopped by an underwater obstacle, which fortunately was not mined. We jumped into chest-high water and waded ashore. Then we saw that the beach was literally covered with the bodies of American soldiers wearing the blue and gray patches of the 29th Infantry Division. Later we learned that we had landed on DOG GREEN beach opposite the Vierville exit, which was the bloodiest sector of Omaha.

Intermittent shelling and sniper fire from tunnels in the cliff continued at Omaha throughout D+l, and my men had quickly sprawled out on the sand for safety. Since our objective was located inland, I began to prod them off the beach. One of them suddenly pointed his rifle at me and shouted, "Don't touch me, you Son-of-a-Bitch or I'll kill you." I was scared too, but we were trained to think of our job first, so I took the gun away from him, kicked him in the butt and led the men off the beach.

After joining a column moving slowly up the D-l exit towards Vierville, we saw our first group of German prisoners and wondered why so many of them appeared to be Asiatic. Then I saw a Brigadier General looking dazed walking towards the beach without a helmet, and I knew all was not well ahead of us. Suddenly an airman behind me accidentally fired his sub-machine gun and the bullets missed me by inches. Shortly afterwards an 88 mm shell hit the column just ahead of us and splattered body parts everywhere. When we finally reached Vierville, less than a mile from the beach, it was dark. There we found that a truckload of ammunition had been abandoned near some burning buildings. It seemed the whole American army was being held up by this danger. However a young Captain took a bazooka and blew up the truck, enabling us to run one-by-one past the fire so as to not be picked off by snipers, allowing the column to move ahead.

Once we got through the village, the airmen went their way to build the first airstrip at Normandy, and we soon found ourselves alone on the road toward our assigned area. Suddenly an American Ranger came out of the darkness and informed us, "There is nothing in front of you but Germans!" Actually we learned they were about a half mile ahead of us just beyond the Chateau de Vaumicel.

I sent two men to the rear to find the Sixth Engineers and seek advice. Just as they asked a Captain for directions, he was killed by a sniper. Upon their return, learning our headquarters was still behind the seawall, we returned to the beach about 9 p.m. and dug in at the foot of the cliff opposite the Vierville exit. Just as we laid down an air raid commenced. A sea of ships began to fire hundreds of anti-aircraft guns, and it seemed they were firing at me with a noise that was terrifying. I was exhausted, wet, cold and scared. My teeth were chattering and my body was shaking. It was the most horrible nightmare of the war!

Since the situation at Omaha was critical, only men, ammunition and gasoline were brought ashore. So we unloaded Jerry cans of gasoline by day and slept on the beach, knowing that just beyond the cliff the three U.S. infantry divisions had few big guns and tanks with which to oppose the expected counterattack by Rommel's vaunted Panzers. Meanwhile, before the bodies and the debris could be removed, the first religious service was held on Omaha Beach. We prayed for those who had been lost and thanked the Lord for our survival. I promised God that I would do all in my power to help prevent such a terrible event ever happening again.

Soon we were told to get off the beach and move into foxholes at the top of the cliff. Following another air raid, we received a terrifying alert for poison "Gas!" As we lay in our foxholes we were paralyzed with fear. For all we knew it might be a new gas for which there was no detection or protection. Believe me, when the "all clear" came, I felt that I had been truly "born again."

Finally our huge map cases began to arrive at our initial objective, in an apple orchard. Orders arrived from First Army to "get those maps under cover immediately." So I found a vacant chateau near Normanville about three miles from the beach, a building other units had avoided since it was prominently within enemy artillery range. Thus, with colonels and generals sleeping nearby in foxholes, my little group occupied a grand chateau, complete with wine glasses and flowers left by the hastily retreating enemy. Several large barns and stables provided ideal storage for our maps. We soon did so much business we had to engage the help of German prisoners. They repeatedly asked why the Americans had not joined their fight against Soviet Communism?

As the brutal and costly Battle of the Hedgerows raged, our maps were heavily consumed. Platoon leaders and company commanders with maps were the first to fall. According to the Chief of Engineer Intelligence, thirty tons of maps per day were required to keep U. S. troops in action on the continent. In the first three months of the Normandy campaign, 125 million maps (6,000 tons) were distributed to our forces. We surely passed out our share.

While we complained about Montgomery being bogged down at Caen, we cheered when hundreds of our bombers flew overhead towards the breakout at St. Lo. Soon we were ordered to rush our convoy of map-laden trucks in pursuit of First Army rapidly moving across France. We passed the battered debris of the German Army in the Falaise pocket. First, we stopped momentarily at Alencon, then Chartres, slept under our trucks in a Paris still celebrating liberation, paused at Meaux, and ended up at Liege, Belgium. Within days, however we were driven out of the city by the V-1 and V-2 rockets. I searched in Malmedy, St. Vith and Bastogne for a safer location closer to the front but fortunately without success. We had barely unloaded our maps in an abandoned factory between Liege and Spa when German parachutists were reported in the area. Then, as the Battle of the Bulge developed, we safely evacuated our map depot behind the Meuse River. Shortly afterwards, I was transferred to Paris and volunteered to serve with the First Allied Airborne Army.

Following VE Day, I was with the First U.S. Airborne Army as we entered Berlin. There, secretly and under the very noses of the Soviets, I managed our removal from the German Foreign Ministry, located within the Soviet Zone, of great quantities of maps of Russia which had been captured by the Germans. Thus the United States gained possession of highly important strategic and tactical maps of the Soviet Union, data which would become essential should the Cold War have become a hot war. Our accomplishment was so outstanding that my superiors were decorated.

Horace Edward Henderson has an extensive background in war and peace affairs.

After the war he was elected Vice President of Junior Chamber International, and as National President of the United States Junior Chamber of Commerce he was named the Outstanding Jaycee of the World. He later served as Deputy Assistant Secretary of State for International Organizations at Washington and was appointed by President Eisenhower as United States delegate to numerous international conferences and as a member of the U.S. Delegation to the United Nations. He is the former Director General of the World Peace Through Law Center at Geneva, Switzerland, which was originally sponsored by the American Bar association and funded by the Ford Foundation. He is currently active as Chairman of the World Campaign for a Convention (Treaty) for the Peaceful Settlement of International Disputes.

He has been the editor of a legal journal, the author of numerous articles on international affairs and is now developing the manuscript of a book on political and strategical blunders of World War II.

August, 1994 (above)
October, 1944 (left)

24

OSS in Normandy

Major Rene Alexander Dussaq, AUS-Ret.

Rene A. Dussaq was among a small group of French-speaking Americans who parachuted into Normandy on D-Day June 5-6, 1944. He jumped there again on June 5, 1994, as a part of the commemoration event. They partook in this celebration, as he says, to "commemorate the thousands who died for the freedom of millions."

He says, "A few of us, who jumped again on the D-Day Commemoration on June 5, 1944, were invited to the White House on Veteran's Day, November 11, 1994, and I must admit I was impressed when the President seemed to know my war record. I said to him that as a former illegal immigrant (I was born in Buenos Aires, Argentina), I was honored to meet the President of the U.S.A. and the Commander in Chief of the U.S.A. Armed Forces. His gracious answer was: 'The honor is mine, in meeting you and your comrades.'"

While he was reluctant to go further into details of his impressive service, the citation awarding then 1st Lt. Dussaq the Distinguished Service Cross tells vividly in a few words of his courage and dedication within our efforts to liberate western Europe from tyranny.

"The Distinguished Service Cross is awarded to First Lieutenant Rene A. Dussaq, Infantry, United States Army, for extraordinary heroism in connection with military operations against an armed enemy as a member of the Special Operations Branch, Office of Strategic Services Detachment, European Theater of Operations, United States Army, from 22 May 1944 to 22 September 1944. Lt. Dussaq, having been parachuted into France in civilian clothes, organized and trained resistance forces for sabotage and guerrilla warfare activities against enemy installations and troops. The courage and skill with which he planned and executed his operations against the enemy and the success of his mission contributed to the demoralization of enemy troops, and to the subsequent liberation of the country. His personality was a strong incentive to all who worked with him. The courageous actions of Lt. Dussaq reflect great credit upon himself and the armed forces of the United States."

While he wishes to forget the circumstances, we should not forget the extraordinary courage of such men who contributed so significantly to our prevailing in a precarious landing against massive defense preparations by a cruel and barbaric totalitarian regime.

Subsequent to writing the above, Major Dussaq gave additional information regarding his extraordinary service in Continental Europe. Besides the DSC, he received the Croix de Guerre with palm, the Purple Heart, the Silver Star, the Bronze Star, and the Combat Infantryman's Badge.

From reading a report of his superiors in the OSS, one can draw conclusions of the perilous, challenging leadership role this brave officer was called upon to perform with the French underground:

I contacted Colonel Prince, *Intendant de Police pour l'Auvergne*, at his office in the Carleton Hotel at Clermont-Ferrand, Puy de Dome; and asked him for information about Lt. Dussaq, particularly with regard to the engagements of Chaudessiagnes, Le Puy, and Thiers. Colonel Prince (real name Huguet) said that he would have to consult his files and his fellow officers of the Maquis in order to do justice to Lt. Dussaq, and asked me to return the following day. Col. Prince spoke very highly of "Captain Bazooka" as did everyone who had been in contact with him. Col. Prince gave me the following statement.

"The Secretary General of the Police of the region of Clermont-Ferrand possesses the following information on the American Lieutenant Bazooka. Lt. Bazooka lived for a month and a half in the Maquis of Champetiere (Puy de Dome) in July and August 1944, where he had been taken by Colonel Gaspard. He visited various Maquis and trained the men. He commanded an attack against a German post at Escauteux (Puy de Dome) during the course of which five Germans were killed (August 1944). He participated besides in the taking of the city of Thiers, particularly by seeing that an ultimatum got to the German forces in the name of the American Army and a group of parachutists which were with him, although he was alone. The ruse succeeded completely (August 1944). He also took part in the taking of Issoire (Puy de Dome) under the same conditions and the German garrison of that town (about 500 soldiers) surrendered as a result of his ultimatum. Lt. Bazooka acted with considerable "bluff" by which the Germans let themselves be taken in. This American officer enjoyed a great popularity in the Resistance Groups in the Auvergne.

Commandant Bengali, styled as "Chief of Police, Maquis" wrote: "I knew Captain Bazooka during the campaign of the Auvergne Maquis after the 6th of June 1944. According to my way of thinking, he has all the qualities of the perfect officer. I am in a position to state that Captain Bazooka never ceased to participate in the struggle against the common enemy using the elements of the Maquis which came under his orders. Harassing the Boches, bearding him in his cantonments (Thiers), he was an example of fighting spirit. He was confident and a trainer of men. He knew how to give the irresistible impulse of the American troops to our boys (resistance). I had the opportunity to meet several of the men, who had esteem for him, some quite extravagant. (They said:) "He may be a lieutenant to you but to us he is Commandant Bazooka." Major Dussaq adds that "there was a great comradeship between us."

More than a quarter million men and women in France were lending active support to the Allies by V.E. Day. Nearly 200,000 lost their lives through executions or in other ways related to challenging the Germans during the occupation. The Maquisards, (members of the Maquis elite group similar to the U.S. Army Special Forces) with which Dussaq worked, accomplished a great deal of work that facilitated the invasion.

After his service in France, Major Dussaq worked in Germany as a part of SAARF (Special Allied Airborne Recon Forces) His mission was to jump inside concentration camps in Germany and liberate them. He served also as an Intelligence Officer.

While he left active duty after the war ended, he was recalled by the Air Force to participate in the Bikini Atomic bomb tests. He again returned to civilian life, but was recalled the third time to serve more than three years during the Korean War. In those years he was professor of military science at the University of California, Berkeley.

In civilian life Rene A. Dussaq, C.L.U., was the manager of the San Fernando Valley Agency of the Prudential Insurance Company prior to retirement in 1976.

He recently took part in the commemorative jump in Normandy honoring the fiftieth anniversary.

25

South Pacific Battles

Captain Kenneth Clark Holm, USN-Ret.

Immediately after the Pearl Harbor attack I enlisted in the Navy. To get off to the war, I turned down flight training and was soon assigned to the newly built cruiser *U.S.S. Denver (CL-58)* in Camden, New Jersey, commissioned in October 1942. Our crew, made up mostly of reservists, worked hard to get her ready for war. One night, without warning, we left heading south and steamed at top speed. After passing through the Panama Canal the next stop was Bora Bora, a tiny Mid-Pacific island, where an oil tanker refueled the ship. Our skipper gave us a swim call over the side, but a crowd of threatening barracuda chased us back aboard before we had much of a swim.

Every day we fired the guns and catapulted off the two small planes to reconnoiter. Soon we arrived in the New Hebrides, near Quadalcanal, and joined the other three ships of our cruiser division. Most of us carried hunting knives to fight off the Japs or sharks in the water if our ship went down. Being the log room (engineering) yeoman, at battle stations I was in direct communication by phone with the Captain's talker on the bridge. When you are below decks it is nice to know what's going on.

We entered action immediately upon arrival, becoming a part of Admiral A. S. Merrill's task force of cruisers and destroyers going up the "Solomon's Slot" and blowing up Jap bases and ships along the way. Our skipper, Capt. Robert B. Carney, was a man I respected more than any I have ever known during the war. He couldn't wait to get into action. The *Denver* was the first ship to arrive equipped with radar. We also had new proximity fuses on our five inch shells and special fragmentation projectiles for our six inch guns.

Denver always led the division into action and got off the first shots. We would steam up the slot in line, with a "V" of destroyers ahead looking for subs, and another destroyer astern to guard our wake. Our wake was a special concern because the South Pacific waters were so phosphorescent that a ship would leave a long, lighted trail at night in the waters churned up by the screws.

I remember well one night shortly after we arrived near Guadalcanal. A lone "Betty" Japanese bomber followed up our wake, and our trailing destroyer fired a single five inch shell. A brilliant fireball in the sky marked our first success against the enemy.

The battle of Kula Gulf was another recollection. An enemy detachment there on one side of the New Georgia Islands was to be bombarded by our group. At the same time Arleigh Burke's famous "Little Beaver" destroyers were to shoot up a detachment of "camp followers" on the other side of the island. In the dark our radar found two enemy frigates anchored close ashore, unlighted and unaware of our arrival. Although our guns and handling rooms were filled with H.C. bombardment ammo, we fired at point blank range. Not a shot was fired in return. Since I had been promoted to Captain's talker on the bridge I saw the scene and will never forget the awful devastation rendered to those two ships. Sailors ran topside through the flames and dove over the side. In minutes the ships went down and our guns were trained towards shore to do the job assigned.

Yeoman Ken Holm, San Diego, January, 1942

Years later, as a Commander at the Naval War College, I was staff member for a strategy and tactics course given to senior allied naval officers. One of my tasks was to act as a consultant and host for three of those officers. At our home one evening I heard the Japanese officer's story of surviving his ship's sinking in the Solomons. We learned that it had happened at Kula Gulf, the incident mentioned above. The Japanese Captain and I soon became fast friends even though we had been in direct combat many years earlier; we still communicate.

Captain K. C. Holm, the CO of the U.S.S. Pyro *during the Vietnam conflict.*

Returning to my wartime experiences, I remember that after sorties we always returned to Espiritu Santo, a tiny island in the New Hebrides with a large sheltered harbor. That harbor in mid-1943 was filled with U.S. warships of every type. While there for any length of time we became bored with the lack of activity. Every night an enemy plane came over at midnight, regular as clockwork, and dropped one bomb. He became known as "piss call Charlie". To my knowledge, he never actually hit any of the darkened ships in the harbor or caused any casualties on shore.

Boredom produced big fights at the "OK Corral". The crews of various ships would challenge others. As a former boxer in high school, I enjoyed the action, but frequently returned to my ship bruised, battered and bloody. Fortunately Captain Carney recommended me for OCS before I became a casualty. While the mighty Denver made her way up the slot one more time, I was transferred to another ship and eventually found my way back to the University of Southern California in Los Angeles.

Upon transfer to the NROTC as a midshipman, my WWII experiences ended, yet those incredible memories will never go away. I recall: the seaman who left his turret for a life jacket at the wrong time and was lost to concussion under our guns; the thousands of shell cases jamming up our deck; diving into a slit trench as "Charlie" unloaded bombs from overhead; the dash to save the cruiser *Helena* (my home town) to no avail; Admiral Halsey's huge sign reading "Kill Japs" painted on the cliff at Tulagi; hundreds of "bogies" coming down in flames at Purvis Bay as we watched from the foc'sle while sunbathing; and many more incidents.

Only days after I left it, my ship, the *Denver*, was hit by enemy shells and an aerial torpedo at Bougainville. The twenty shipmates lost were all engineers at my former battle station. During three years of action the *Denver* was credited with the destruction or "assist" of seven Japanese warships, downing 14 aircraft, and took part in 14 shore bombardments, most of which covered amphibious landings. On the other side of the ledger, she had her share of hits and near misses, having had three Nip eight-inch projectiles pass completely through her without exploding, but getting hit by an aerial torpedo within the next ten days in November 1943. I am very proud of my warship and now frequently attend her annual reunions.

Captain Kenneth "KC" Holm retired from the Navy after thirty years of continuous service. He now resides in Danville, California with his wife Zayna. During the Korean War he served in the submarines *Carp* and *Bream*, and in Vietnam commanded the ammunition ship *Pyro*. Captain Robert Carney, "KC's" skipper on *Denver* became Chief of Naval Operations, the Navy's most prestigious position. Three of the Captains of the *U.S.S. Denver* (CL-58) went on to become Admirals (R. B. Carney, R. P. Briscoe and A. M. Bledsoe.)

26

Keeping Up the Momentum

Colonel Joseph H. Stewart, USAF-Ret

Joe Stewart was a First Lieutenant in the Army Reserve, Cavalry Branch, when called to active duty, March of 1941, yet was assigned to the then U.S. Army Air Corps. Within six months he had the assignment of taking over a service group and building it to combat readiness. Before moving to England in September of 1942, he had become a Lieutenant Colonel in command of a unit consisting of 80 officers and 2,000 enlisted men.

Located at a former RAF base at Shrewsbury, we sharpened our skills and also serviced that base. The base was a CCRC (Combat crew replacement center), where all the combat pilots were sent from training schools in the United States to be indoctrinated with the flying conditions in the European Theater.

During that early part of our time overseas Air Force Headquarters in London sent me on a continuous circuit of all the air force units in England to establish their supply facilities and to do what I could to improve the efficiency of the flow of supplies and equipment moving to them. With an assigned driver and car, I probably covered over ten thousand miles driving throughout England.

A Service Group has a QM Company, a Trucking Company, an Air Force Supply Company and an Aircraft Maintenance Company. Our Group was divided into two teams, and most of the integral subordinate units were divided between the two teams. Each team was assigned to a Fighter Group, concentrating on its objective, that of facilitating maximum flight availability of the planes.

I kept my headquarters with Team A, which was assigned to the Fighter Group supporting General Patton's Third Army. Team B was assigned to a Group that took care of the northern sector of the front (First and Ninth Armies) and would end up in Liege, right under 'Buzz-Bomb Alley'.

Team A of our Service Group was soon relocated to the Normandy Peninsula after a hastily built airstrip became operational. Our logistical forces had already stockpiled a huge amount of supplies and equipment. The great accumulation of material became a stack 15 to 20 feet high, extending for fifteen miles in length. While this collection would have made an incredibly attractive target, our mastery of the skies there was absolute at the time. Enemy planes did not destroy any of that stockpile.

As our forces advanced so too did our teams. We had a severe problem with theft from our supply trucks which required that I order an armed guard posted at each end of the convoy at any halt to protect our drivers and the supplies being transported.

Toward the end of the war, in December of 1944, we were located about a hundred yards away from the Maginot Line. On one inspection tour, in December of 1944, I left to go to Liege to visit Team B. My driver and I stopped for lunch about halfway. When we arrived I learned that the last break-through effort by the German Army occurred shortly after we went on our way. Had there been an hour's difference in our timing we would probably have become casualties of the Battle of the Bulge.

After VE-Day we reassembled in the Liege, Belgium area, where a processing plant prepared all our equipment and assisted us in moving to Marseille, from which port we were to ship out to the Pacific Theater.

We arrived at Marseille to find that two things had occurred: (l) all of our equipment had arrived and was loaded on a large troop ship. (2) VJ-Day had happened that day.

Our equipment was off-loaded at the docks and within 48 hours we sailed for New York. We arrived there on September 4, 1945, exactly three years from the date we had sailed for Europe.

Incidentally, General Eisenhower's headquarters disseminated an order requiring that all officers be promoted to the rank called for their position in their unit's table of organization. My position called for a full Colonel, so I received my promotion somewhere between Marseille and New York.

Editor's Note: I believe what Colonel Stewart was doing was what General of the Army Omar N. Bradley (1893-1981) advocated:

"You must get around and show interest in what your subordinates are doing even if you don't know much about the technique of their work. And when you are making these visits, try to pass out praise then due, as well as corrections and criticisms." Speech to the U. S. Army Command and General Staff College, 16 May 1967.

I recall talking with General Bradley one fall afternoon in Washington, D.C. in the 1970's and was surprised to learn that he recalled speaking with a young Lieutenant during the war years. He was a gracious man and a highly respected leader.

27

My D-Day in Normandy

Rev. Carl Dodrill (CWO-AUS-Ret.)

I observed and experienced D-Day 5-6 June 1944. I was there, landing in the darkness of the previous night and on D-Day itself. As I recall the horror, I am amazed that I escaped death.

It is hard to resurrect and describe the feelings which I buried during that 'longest day in history.' Perhaps the lengthened day that God gave Joshua in the Valley of Ajalon so that the Israelites would have enough daylight hours to kill all the Amorites comes closest to describing D-Day in Normandy.

As a member of the 82nd Airborne Division, I rode into Normandy during the night of 5 June 1944 on a British wooden glider. The French village of Ste. Mère-Eglise, about 4½ miles inland from Omaha and Utah beaches, was our objective. We were tasked to destroy bridges, roads and communications and prevent German reinforcements from reaching their beach garrisons.

There were eight of us, a 105 mm Howitzer, ammunition and other weapons in our glider, which was being towed by a C-47 Army plane. We were flying low to avoid German ground fire when the green light came on. That was our signal for the glider pilot to cut us loose from the tow plane, a position which glider troops called, 'Down and Go.' We glided just above hedgerows at about 120 miles an hour looking for an open field between them.

Hazards awaited us, and one of them we feared was landing in a swamp. With our heavy equipment, we would not be able to swim out. Previous briefings had also alerted us to the danger of cables strung out by the Germans that were strong enough to slice a glider in half. Some were strung out across French farm fields, and machine-gun nests were known to be hidden in the hedgerows.

However, our primary concern was finding a place to land. The pilot saw a clearing surrounded by trees. We barely made it over them, for the bottom of the glider scraped branches before we hit the ground with a resounding crash.

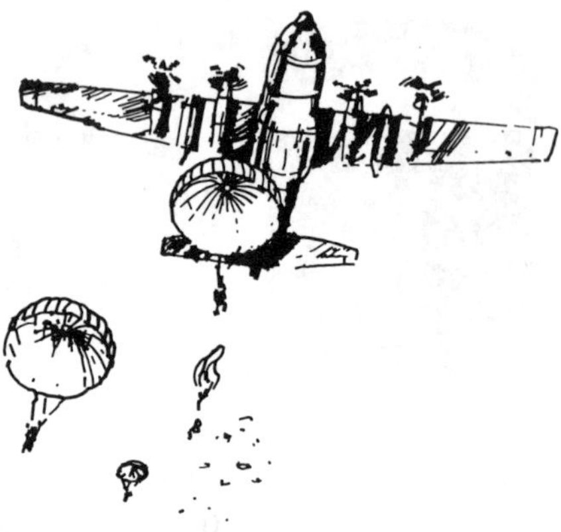

A barrage of machine-gun fire killed the pilot and two of my buddies. The glider changed ends as we hit a horse and skidded the length of the field. Men were thrown clear while the glider splintered and broke up. The howitzer broke loose, rolled over and killed a man. I was thrown into the branches of an apple tree and then hit the ground stunned.

As I lay there and slowly regained my breath, I clicked my bug in an endeavor to locate my comrades. That noise drew more machine-gun fire, while I crawled along the edge of the field looking for other American soldiers.

Suddenly I froze, since I felt the cold muzzle of a gun against my cheek. The night was warm, but I broke out into a cold sweat and thought I was about to die.

A miracle happened. I heard a loud click and someone cursing in German. Before he could get another round in the chamber, I brought my Thompson M-3 around and let a burst go that put him away. I have always wondered who he was and why his life instead of mine had to end that night.

I sat back against a tree and looked around. I saw lights and heard noises which told me I was not far from our objective, the town of Ste. Mère-Eglise. I decided to hole up until daylight, while my mind was a jumble of thoughts. I was bleeding, hurting, angry and scared. I became angrier, as I thought that no one cared if the whole 82nd was wiped out just as long as we confused the Germans and held them back from the beach. We were expendable. Then I cursed the German, Japanese, French and American leaders. It was not their blood but ours being shed. I recalled a Berlin radio broadcast by the Berlin Bitch, who told American soldiers that while we were fighting and dying, the 4-F's and our wives were living high on our allotments.

While I waited for daylight my mind wandered over my past life. I knew God didn't make human beings just so that they could destroy each other in war, however there seemed to be a lot of killing going on around me.

I tried to pray, but my pain and anger kept me from saying much. After all, what could I pray about? I had already killed a man, and unless I was killed, I would do it again many times before this war was over.

I mused about being a West Virginia farm boy sitting in the dark outside a little French village trying to be a good soldier. In that war-torn world my only concern was who was hiding in those shadows just an apple tree away.

I thought of home and family, my wife and my year-old son whom I had never seen. However, I put those thoughts from my mind and concentrated upon staying alive and carrying out our mission. Finally, I yielded to pain and an exhausted body and dozed off.

Intuition alerted me that someone was beside me as I awoke to morning light streaming through the apple trees. I reached for my weapon, and a soft, feminine voice spoke, "Don't be alarmed, just lie back while I bandage your wounds. I am a member of the French Resistance, and we were told to help all we could." Then she noticed me looking around and said, "I put your gun over there."

I thanked her and asked the way to Ste. Mère-Eglise. She replied, "The Americans, who wear your uniform, are there now. You go through this orchard and you will see the steeple in the village."

I started to hobble away, then turned and asked her if she had any food. When I found she had none, I gave her my rations. She thanked

Col. (then Capt.) Robert J. Greeenwald (Ch.72) in front of massive German fortification that faced D-Day invasion of France

me then ran the other way. I found what was left of my outfit. I sat down near a crashed glider and held a friend's head in my arms while he died.

As more men joined us, we methodically destroyed bridges, cut all lines of communications and blocked the advance of German reserves—all before noon.

I learned later that Senator Strom Thurmond, of South Carolina, had also glided in and landed in the same orchard, just an apple tree away from me.

Later, I was in the invasion of Holland, the Battle of the Bulge, and the final battle of the Rhineland, however, they can't compare with the night and day of Hell in Normandy. I try to forget, but when I am feeling bad, memories of all that time spent in war comes back to haunt me, to disturb my dreams.

Most of my service was as a Tech Sergeant (five striper), however I did become a CWO for the Normandy and Holland invasions so that I could be the glider co-pilot.

Carl Dodrill became a Methodist Minister after the war and subsequently established an independent church. He also is the president of Double G., Inc. of Ohio, a firm that represents inventors and is involved in the marketing thereof.

He served in the Army from March 1942 through September 1945 through six campaigns, with four spearheads for airborne invasions of Sicily, Italy, Normandy and Holland.

28

Pre-invasion Speech to Troops in England, May 29, 1944

General George Smith Patton, USA
(1885-1945)

Noted for fiery pre-battle speeches, this one prior to the Normandy Invasion (D-Day, June 6, 1944) is typical. We must warn the reader that there is some rough language without which the flavor of General Patton's leadership style would be lost. However, on consideration of the potential audiences, we have deleted portions.

"Men, this story we hear about America wanting to stay out of this war, not wanting to fight, is a lot of bullshit. Americans love to fight —traditionally. All real Americans love the sting and clash of battle. When you were kids you all admired the champion marble player, the fastest runner, the big-league ball players, the toughest boxer. Americans love a winner, and will not tolerate a loser. Americans despise cowards. Americans play to win—all the time. I wouldn't give a hoot in hell for a man who lost and laughed. That's why Americans have never lost, nor ever will lose a war, for the very thought of losing is hateful to an American.

"You are not all going to die. Only two percent of you here, in a major battle, would die. Death must not be feared. Every man is frightened, at first, in battle. If he says he isn't, he is a damn liar. Some men are cowards, yes, but they fight just the same, or get the hell shamed out of them, watching men who do, who are just as scared. The real hero is the man who fights even though he is scared. Some men get over their fright in a few minutes under fire, some take hours. For some it takes days. But the real man never lets his fear of death overpower his honor, his sense of duty to his country, and his innate manhood.

"All through your Army career, you men have bitched about what you call 'This chicken-shit drilling.' That is all for a purpose. Drilling and discipline must be maintained in an Army, if only for one reason: **instant obedience to orders and to create constant alertness**. I don't give a damn for a man who is not always on his toes. You men are veterans or you wouldn't be here. You are ready. A man, to continue breathing, must be alert at all times. If not, sometime a German will sneak up behind him and beat him to death...

"There are four hundred neatly marked graves somewhere in Sicily, all because one man went to sleep on his job. But they are German graves, for we caught the bastards asleep before they (knew what was happening).

"An Army is a team. Lives, sleeps, eats, fights as a team. This individual heroic stuff is a lot of crap. The bilious bastard who wrote that kind of stuff for the Saturday Evening Post don't know (anything) about real battle...

"We have the finest food, the finest equipment, best spirit, and the best men in the world. Why, by God, I actually pity those sons-of-bitches we are going up against. By God, I do!

"My men don't surrender. I don't want to hear of a soldier under my command being captured, unless he is hit. Even if you are hit, you can still fight. That's not just bullshit either. The kind of men I want is like a Lieutenant in Libya, who, with a Luger against his chest, jerked off his helmet, swept the gun aside with his hand, and busted hell out of the Boche with his helmet. Then he jumped on the gun and went out and killed another German. By this time, the man had a bullet through his lung. That's a man for you!

"All the real heroes are not story-book combat fighters, either. Every man in the Army plays a vital part. Every little job is essential to the whole scheme. What if every truck driver suddenly decided that he didn't like the whine of those shells, turned yellow, and jumped head-long into the ditch? He could say to himself, 'They won't miss me, just one guy in thousands.' What if every man said that? Where in hell would we be now? No, thank God, Americans don't say that. Every man does his job. Every man serves the whole. Every department, every unit, is very important in the vast scheme of things. The Ordnance men are needed to supply the guns, the Quartermaster to bring up the food and clothes for us. Where we are going there isn't a hell of a lot to steal. Every damn last man in the mess hall, even the one who heats the water to keep us from getting diarrhea has his job to do. Even the Chaplain is important, for if we get killed, and he was not there to bury us, we would all go to hell.

"Each man must not only think of himself, but think of his buddy fighting beside him. We don't want yellow cowards in this army. They should be killed off like flies. If not, they will go back home after the war and breed more cowards...

"One of the bravest men I saw in the African Campaign was one of the fellows I saw on top of a telegraph pole in the midst of furious fire, while we were plowing toward Tunis. I stopped and asked him what the hell he was doing up there at that time. He answered, 'Fixing the wire, sir.'

'Isn't it a little unhealthy, right now?,' I asked.

'Yes sir, but this damn wire has to be fixed.'

"There was one real soldier. There was a man who devoted all to his duty, no matter how great the odds, no matter how seemingly insignificant his duty may have seemed at that time. You should have seen those trucks on the road to Gabes. The drivers were magnificent. All the day they crawled along those roads, never deviating from their course, with shells bursting all around them. We got through on good old American guts. Many of the men drove over forty consecutive hours.

"Don't forget, you don't know I am here at all. No word of the fact is to be mentioned in any letters. The world is not supposed to know what the hell they did with me. I'm not supposed to be commanding this Army.

"I'm not even supposed to be in England. Let the first bastards to find out be the Germans. Someday, I want them to raise up on their hind legs and howl, 'Jesus Christ, it's the God-damn Third Army and the son-of-a-bitch Patton, again!'

"We want to get the hell over there. We want to get over there and clean the damn thing up. And then we'll have to take a little jaunt against the Japanese and clean their nest out too, before the Marines get all the credit.

"Sure, we will all want to go home. We want to get this thing over with, but you can't win a war lying down. The quickest way to get it over is to go get the bastards. The quicker they are whipped, the quicker we go home. The shortest way home is through Berlin. When a soldier is lying in a shell-hole, if he just stays there all day, the Boche will get him eventually, and will probably get him first. The hell with taking it! Get to them first! There is no such thing as a foxhole war any more. Foxholes only slow up an offensive. Keep moving! We will win this war! But we will win it only by fighting and showing our guts.

"There's another great thing you men will be able to say when you go home. You may all thank God for it. Thank God that, at least, thirty years from now, when you are sitting around the fireside, with your grandson on your knee, and he asks you, 'What did you do in the Great World War II,' you won't have to say, 'I only cleaned out the barracks.'"

Everyone agrees, even the Germans, that Patton was one of our best Generals. He pushed his men hard, but he accomplished a great deal. The casualty rate within his command was half that sustained by other units of comparable size. That record was attributable to his drive, keeping the enemy off balance, pushing them hard, through the maximum effort of all within his command. He used salty language; the editor hopes no one is offended by this account or distressed that I toned down some of the language. The more salty version got the attention of his men. He was seen up forward. Some of us, whose stories are included in this volume, saw him, some of us spoke briefly with him; he was unforgettable. He was an outstanding leader, and a Californian.

It was a stroke of brilliance, and an intelligence coup, that set him up with a phony Army Group in operation "Fortitude". That deception required the enemy to hold many Panzer divisions in reserve at Pas Des Calais, to counter an expected second landing, giving our vulnerable beachhead in Normandy an opportunity to consolidate and bring in necessary replacements and supplies.

No one doubts that General Patton was one of the most significant players in W.W.II. He was also far ahead of his contemporaries in visualizing the inception of the Cold War with the Soviets that followed the end of W.W.II.

29

Patton's Lesson on Leadership

Colonel Thomas D. Gillis, USA-Ret.

I played a key role in the Fourth Armored Division, which led Gen. Patton's Third Army all the way from the breakout in Normandy, through the Battle of the Bulge, and to the very end on V.E. Day in May of 1945.

When I was but a wee toddler in Nogales, Arizona, down on the Mexican border my dad, George S. Gillis, and George S. Patton, Jr., were both lieutenants in Gen. Pershing's Expeditionary Force chasing after Pancho Villa. Patton, as you know was Pershing's Aide de Camp.

I first met Gen. Patton during the Tennessee maneuvers, before we entered the war, when I was assigned to the Sixth U.S. Cavalry. I enjoyed immensely his frustration when, due to the incessant rain and pervasive mud, a troop of horse cavalry was the only unit able to wind up on the objective atop a hill. Georgie's tanks were all mired in the Tennessee mud!

The next time I saw Patton was just following his taking over command of Third Army in Normandy prior to the breakout. The Fourth Armored Division had just relieved the 4th Infantry Division and taken over a pie-shaped sector of the front, preparatory to leading the breakout of the Normandy Peninsula. Early on the morning of August 1st, when we had just come under the command of Third Army, General Patton's jeep, stars blazing from the front bumper, charged into our C.P. area. As I double timed over to greet General Patton, I noticed that his boots, normally bright and shiney, were covered with mud.

"Gillis," (I would like to think that General Patton knew me well enough, even in this early stage of the war, to call me by name. My experience has been that generals have a good memory of names.) "Where is 'P'?"

"Right this way, general", as I led him to the briefing room.

General Patton and 'P' Wood were old buddies and each admired the other very much. But there was one big difference—Gen. Patton had led his troops through Africa and Sicily while General Wood had never heard a shot fired in anger.

As he embraced 'P' Wood, Gen. Patton said, "P, How are you doing?"

"General, we're up against this un-fordable river and drawing fire from the opposite shore."

"That's strange, I just waded across that damn stream!" And, with that, Gen. Patton turned on his heel and strode out of the C.P.

'P' Wood had been content to remain in his C.P. and rely upon reports he received from his front line commanders. But Georgie Patton had toured the front himself, waded across the stream, drawn no fire, and made his own estimate of the situation.

Never again, throughout the entire war, did he ever have to prod 'P' Wood again or kick him in the butt to get him moving.

Major General John S. ('Tiger Jack') Wood, C.G. of the 4th Armored Division, won the sobriquet 'P' during a tour at West Point when he was a professor.

At Remereville, Belgium, on November 8, 1944, just prior to The Battle of the Bulge, Gen. George S. Patton wrote: "There has never been such a superb fighting organization as the Fourth Armored Division."

In ten months, the division took 90,354 prisoners in combat, killed an estimated 13,640 of the enemy, wounded an estimated thirty thousand more, destroyed or captured 579 German tanks, 3,668 other vehicles, 603 artillery and anti-tank guns, 1,172 horse-drawn wagons, 103 locomotives, shot down 128 Nazi planes, took a score of cities and hundreds of towns and villages. Men and officers of the Fourth won more than four thousand individual decorations. Three were Congressional Medals of Honor. There were granted 34 Distinguished Service Crosses, 14 Legions of Merit, 802 Silver Stars, 1 Distinguished Flying Cross, 3,031 Bronze Stars, 88 air Medals, 11. Soldier Medals, 72 Croix de Guerre, 12 Russian Medals for Bravery. Forty men received battlefield commissions as officers. In addition, there were more than six thousand Purple Hearts, grimly known as the "German Marksmanship Medal".

Stars and Stripes of March 29, 1945, reported, "FDR Citation to Fourth Armored Division. SHAEF, March 28, 1945—The War Department, by direction of the President, has cited the entire 4th Armored Division for 'extraordinary tactical accomplishment during the period from December 22 to March 27, inclusive,' it was announced here today."

Referred to by the Nazis as "America's elite 4th Panzer Division", the infantry and tank teams of the 4th spearheaded the Third Army's race across France.

The paper continued to speak of the 4th Armored's most significant accomplishments to include its move from Sarraguemines to Arlon. I remember well its great drive to relieve the 101st Airborne Division surrounded at Bastogne.

The 4th Armored Division made history in its sixty mile dash to the Rhine River; the move to Mainz, and the final drive on into Germany. One incident I remember vividly was our taking the Ohrdruf concentration camp. They had incinerated bodies, but there was also a great stack that hadn't yet been burned. We found 2l bodies of American prisoners who had been too frail to march, executed by the guards with a shot to the head. One was a pilot still in uniform. They had held American prisoners there as well as political prisoners. We took the Mayor of the town and his wife to see the horror of the camp. They professed ignorance of the activity, but both committed suicide the next day.

Time Magazine on March 19, 1945, had a note: "German soldiers facing the 4th Armored were told (according to a captured document): Each American had been qualified for the Division by proving that (1) he had been born a bastard, and (2) he had murdered his mother."

"To refute the above statement is unnecessary; our Division consisted of well-trained and disciplined American soldiers. Needless to add, our Division accomplished a great deal in the campaign across Europe that brought about the defeat of Nazi Germany."

Colonel Gillis is a distinguished retired career Army officer who won two Silver Stars for his bravery, the Legion of Merit, Purple Heart, Bronze Star, Air Medal, and the Combat Infantryman's Badge (unusual for an officer of the Armored Branch). In 1958 he was in command of a Missile Command in Italy equipped with the Honest John and Corporal missiles. He is in the process of writing a remarkable book entitled *Sabers and Spur—Vignettes in the Life of a Cavalryman,* which he has been working on for the past two years. He is a national leader within the Sons of the American Revolution. His family has a remarkable history of military service to the country dating from the Revolutionary War.

"Cobra King", C Co., 4th Armd. Div., commanded by Lt. Boggess, was the first tank to break through the German outer defenses to relieve the 101st Airborne Division, surrounded in Bastogne, at 1645 hours, Dec. 26th, 1944. Tank is now a monument in the main square of Bastogne. Photo by Mark Miller, 1995, from collection of Col. Gillis.

30

Relief of Bastogne

Colonel Thomas D. Gillis, USA-Ret.

It was December 18, 1944, the third day of the German drive into the Ardennes. General Eisenhower had summoned his senior commanders to the 12th Army Group's rear headquarters in Verdun. After a discussion of several plans of attack, the decision was made and Eisenhower asked Patton when he could start. Patton said that he could attack the morning of December 20th with three divisions. This in spite of the fact that Third Army was engaged 150 miles to the southeast. Patton, upon given the go-ahead for the 22nd, reached for the field telephone, cranked the handle, and was connected with LUCKY FORWARD. When one of his staff officers answered all Patton said was, "Put Plan A into effect!" Within the hour the Reserve Command (CC-R) of the 4th Armored Division was on the road northward.

The march of the 4th Armored Division of 151 miles, starting in the southeast from Fenetrange in French Lorraine to Vaux-les-Rosieres in Belgium was made in 19 hours and was the longest made by a division. Third Army moved its front 90 degrees with a speed that astonished the Germans. I was then a LTC, the deputy commander of the CC-R (the reserve command). Efforts of CC-R to contact the 101st Airborne Division by radio had been fruitless, so on December 20 I volunteered to drive into Bastogne to determine the situation first hand and learn what supplies the 101st needed most. Arriving at the C.P. of the 101st I reported in to BG Anthony C. McAuliffe, Asst. Div. Comdr., who was acting commander, and LTC (later Lt. General) Harry W. O. Kinnard, the G-3 of the Division. I also had a reunion with LTC Hank Cherry, C.O. of the 3d Tk. B., 9th Armd. Div., a West Point (1935) classmate of mine. Having determined that the 101st was in dire need of medical supplies and ammunition primarily, I was about to take my leave. I told Gen. McAuliffe that I had to get back to appraise my people of the problems.

In response I was told, "How are you going to do that? We are surrounded!"

I replied, "The same way I got in here. I am going to drive back! As we left the perimeter defenses, I told my jeep driver, Harry Moritz, a gung-ho lad from Chicago, to put the pedal to the metal and not to stop for anything. With my carbine cradled in my arms and our backs bent low in the jeep, the forest was a blur of green as we sped southward. No one fired at us, although I saw some figures vaguely in the background. Apparently the Germans figured we were the point of a larger force and planned on ambushing the main body. They waited for a better target. We later learned that we had gone through the lines of the German 5th Parachute Division. As soon as my report reached the 4th Armored Division headquarters that the 101st had lost its collecting station, along with most of its surgeons and medics, and that it was in dire need of ammunition, the division G-4, LTC Bernie Knestrick, started planning the composition of the relief column for the 101st Abn. Div. At 0600 hours on December 22nd, CC-A and CC-B started the drive to Bastogne, pushing to Burnon and Martelange respectively. It was that day the General Patton issued his Christmas prayer: Miraculously, starting on December 23, and continuing to the 27th, there was a break in the weather. Christmas Eve 1944 was bitterly cold, as the thermometer plunged below zero. The gently rolling hills and snow covered patches of

Creighton Abram's tank, 37th Bn., 4th Armored Div. at the Diekirch Museum.

pine woods just south of Bastogne glistened under a brilliant full moon, and one could imagine the Star of Bethlehem among the myriads of stars gleaming in a cloudless sky. The Reserve Command was ordered at two o'clock Christmas morning to pull out of the line on the east flank of the Fourth Armored Division and march from Bigonville around the division's rear to its west flank at Bercheaux, preparatory to launching a surprise attack north to relieve the beleaguered 101st Airborne Division surrounded in Bastogne. In spite of the beauty of the night and the brilliance of the moon, the 30 miles were torture for the G.I.'s who were poorly equipped for such biting cold. Even though I wore mittens sewn from three thicknesses of a G.I. blanket and fleece lined boots, I could feel my hands and feet getting frostbitten. Every time the column stopped momentarily we would all dismount from our vehicles and double time in place trying to restore the circulation in our feet. But, in spite of this, many of us had our hands and feet frostbitten.

At a sudden stop in the column, Col. Wendell Blanchard, the C.O. of CC-R was projected thorough the windshield of his jeep just in front

Vehicles from the U.S. Army's 4th Armored Division race toward Bastogne, Belgium, while troops along the ditch cover their flank.

of me. With great difficulty because of my stiff fingers, I was able to remove his helmet and work his head back between the shards of glass without his suffering any more cuts. He refused medical attention until 0600 that morning when the command surgeon sewed up his neck and forehead at our new C.P. at Bercheaux, while he issued his verbal attack order up the Bastogne corridor. The last 16 miles into Bastogne were the toughest the 4th A.D. ever fought.

The exploits of LTC Creighton Abrams and his 37th Tank Bn., and his side-kick, LTC "Jigger" Jaques, C.O. of the 53d Armored Infantry Battalion, in blasting their way into Bastogne are well documented by historians. In succession, the Reserve Command captured Vaux-les-Rosieres, Nives, and Remoiville. Chaumont changed hands three times. Remichampagne was cleared by noon. They charged Assennois with all guns firing, and the tankers moved in under the barrage of four friendly artillery battalions. The final attack jumped off early the next morning as tanks and halftracks charged into Clochimont. Our tanks then burst through the outer defenses of the 101st Airborne before the Germans could react. The road was open at 1645 hours December 26th.

At 0200 hours the next morning I led the relief column of doctors, nurses, and some 200 ambulances and trucks into Bastogne. Mission accomplished, the three days and nights without sleep took their toll, and I collapsed in my sleeping bag. When I awoke that afternoon, I glanced out of the window and saw that the large building across the street had been reduced to a pile of rubble while I slept soundly. Harry Kinnard and I were boyhood playmates at the Presidio of Monterey. He wrote to me later, "I was worried as hell about how you would fare dodging *krauts* on the way back to Arlon. But our needs were so desperate that I wouldn't have tried to dissuade you even if I could. I only wish I had seen you to thank you when you arrived with the manna from heaven. But if late is better than never, let me say all these years later—from the bottom of my heart—THANKS FOR YOUR SUPERB DELIVERING OF THE LIFESAVING GOODS! WELL DONE!" (his caps.)

LTC Creighton Abrams, who later became a four star general, commanding the 37th Tank Battalion, of the CC-R, followed through with the initial break through. Major General Maxwell D. Taylor, who also later became a four-star general, commanding the 101st Airborne, didn't get back until the whole thing was over.

31

Battle of the Bulge Airborne Infantry

William W. Brannan, EM, AUS

Nine days before Christmas, 1944, German forces launched a massive last-ditch offensive against American and British forces in the Ardennes. At the cost of the lives of many thousands of young, brave men, the reaction demonstrated, once again, the heights to which men and women of the Allied Command could rise to force the Axis to its knees and bring the German catastrophe to an end. The following is an account of one of the actions that took place in what was to become known as the "Bulge".

On December 23, 1944, the 1st Battalion of my regiment, the 517th Parachute Combat Team, had taken positions near Soy, Belgium, with the mission of stopping, if not, at least slowing that particular point of the German advance. We learned that we were facing elements of the 116th Panzer Division of the 58th Panzer Corps, 5th German Army (the center army of the three German armies advancing westward), and the 560th Volksgrenadier Division. Our first contact with the enemy was late in the evening of the 23rd. Companies B & C, with support from tanks of the 3rd Armored Division, were given the assignment of meeting the 116th and 560th Divisions head-on. A Company, in which I was one of the scouts, was given the mission of relieving beleaguered American forces in Hotten, Belgium.

Unknown to us, during the night the Germans had made a sweep on our right flank and trapped A Company in Hotton. To break out, Colonel Bill Boyle, our battalion commander, decided that we would attack from inside Hotton, and that Major Don Fraser, our battalion executive officer, would lead the attack from the outside.

Part of the plan required my squad to advance behind a line of houses, with the first squad on the street side. I was the lead scout; Don Vaughn was my backup.

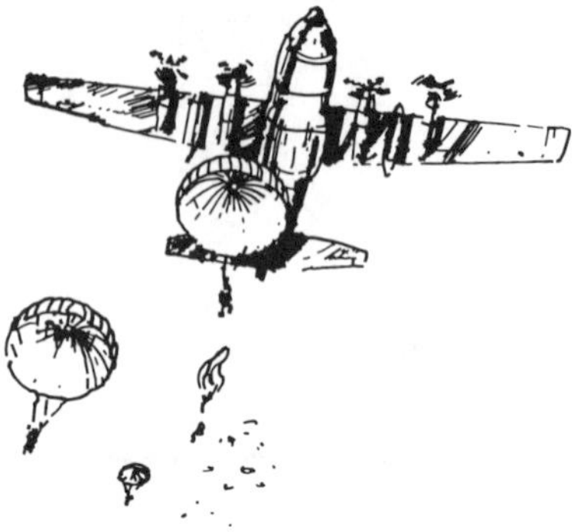

I had moved about fifty yards when, to my utter astonishment, a German officer jumped to his feet and began to run straight away from me. He disappeared around a shed before I could get off a shot.

I continued to move forward until I was stopped by a wire fence and a tall tree. I was between two chicken hutches. I had knelt on one knee so that I could evaluate my position, when two German 42 machine guns opened fire from my left and left front. My instincts were in tune at that moment, for I was already going down when the bullets slammed into the shed to my right. We also had a problem on the other side of the wire fence. A German sniper had dug a hole deep enough to stand in, with complete frontal coverage of anything that moved. I was his primary target at the moment. My concern was for the men in my squad, so I yelled a warning to them to stay back. However, Babe Critchlow, age 20, our squad leader, decided to check out the situation and moved up to the same position as that from which I had first drawn fire. I yelled at him to get down, which he did just as the two machine guns opened fire at him.

Douglas A. Riach (Chapter 22), Milton Anderson (Chapter 34), John H. Roush (Chapter 39), and William W. Brannan (Chapter 31)

I had decided that to continue our advance we would have to knock out the machine guns and then deal with the sniper. I told Critchlow to move back about twenty-five feet, where he could still hear me, so that I could give him the range to the machine guns for our platoon's mortar squads. After registering two or three test rounds, they knocked out both guns.

As for the sniper, it was obvious that to neutralize him, without casualties, we would have to devise an appropriate strategy. Since I could not move to my right or left without drawing fire, I decided to use a grenade. However I had two problems: how to clear the fence to my front and how to time my throw so that the grenade would explode above his hole. There was only one way in which I could accomplish this. I would have to hold the grenade a few seconds after releasing the handle, then spring backward from a prone position in order to loft it over the tree.

Several thoughts coursed through my mind, considering how precarious my situation was. If the grenade did not clear the tree I could have become the casualty. Also, counting to three, after pulling the pin, was cutting it close. Reducing the count to two, I threw the grenade over the tree as hard as I could, but also with as much control as possible. Vaughn told me that it fell short by about ten feet.

Something else would have to be done. Major Fraser's group was meeting stiff resistance, so we had to get on with it and remove the sniper. It occurred to me that a left handed rifleman might get a clear shot from the far corner of the shed without exposing himself to return fire. I called to Critchlow to find someone who shot from the left side,

German Tiger Tank

and, to our surprise, we learned that Lt. Dan Cook, our platoon leader was left-handed. He took out the sniper with his carbine upon the signal of our BAR man, Buck Balleat. We cleared the rest of the houses and linked up with Major Fraser's force. Unfortunately, Critchlow was killed the next day.

I would be remiss if I failed to mention that as Major Fraser's men fought their way into Hotton, several soldiers displayed outstanding heroism. One of the men in B Company, Mel Biddle, engaged in action against a sizable German force, single-handedly destroying two German machine gun nests. Against great odds, armed with an M-1 rifle, he killed nineteen infantrymen of the 560th Volksgrenadier Division. He was causing the Germans so much distress that they mounted a counter-attack which, in that case, was against one man. A following counter-attack by B company facilitated his withdrawal. Subsequently he was awarded the Medal of Honor for his bravery. Earlier, in another incredible feat, Nolan Powell, of C Company, received the Distinguished Service Cross for gallantry in action when he took over leadership after their platoon leader, Lt. Harry Allingham, was killed by attacking forces of the 560th Volksgrenadiers. There were many others that won or deserved to have won decorations, too numerous in number to mention in this space.

A few days after our engagement, the 1st and 3rd American Armies launched an offensive to cut off the "Bulge", marking the end of Hitler's last gasp. Our experiences in Soy and Hotton were only a brief moment in the buildup which led to the Allied attack on January 1st, a period of service of which I will always be proud to have been a part.

Upon deactivation of the 517th in June 1945, we became a part of the 82nd Airborne involved in occupation duty in Berlin.

Bill Brannan was born in San Francisco, drafted in 1943, and volunteered to join a parachute regiment that was being formed. After jump school and tactical training at Camp McCall, North Carolina, his regiment took part in an air assault in Southern France and then fought in the Battle of the Bulge, where they had substantial losses. Of his twelve man squad, six were killed in the two engagements.

Following discharge in January 1946, he completed an BA in Economics at Stanford University. He has been a realtor in San Rafael for many years.

Editor's note: Several separate Parchute Infantry Battalions and Regiments were committed against the nose of the enemy thrust in the Battle of the Bulge, since the Allied front had no other reserves than the two Airborne Divisions and the separate Parachute Infantry Regiments and Battalions. Those small, light infantry units performed incredible feats of courage, for they were only lightly equipped and hardly suitable for combat against Panzer forces with heavy tanks. Nevertheless the brave men of the parachute infantry units accomplished a great deal, but at the same time sustained terrible losses. Of the 745 men in one battalion only 48 emerged. After the action, many of the units had to be disbanded due to losses. One of the men participating recalled it as a montage of misery: "No sleep, frozen feet, trench-foot, knee deep snow, cold food and hallucinations." There were a great many acts of heroism by the light infantrymen who fought in the Bulge, so numerous that it was hardly possible to list them all.

The United States Army suffered more casualties in the Battle of the Bulge in the Ardennes Forest than were sustained during the entire Pacific Campaign. Historians say the Bulge was the greatest pitched battle ever fought by American armies.

The German code name for the bold attack by three armies was HERBSTNEBEL (Autumn Mist).

32

Three Campaigns with the 101st Airborne Division

S/Sgt. Denis M. Parsons, AUS

My wartime service in the 101st Airborne Division extended from 1943 through 1945, as a machine-gunner in "G" Company, 327th Glider Infantry Regiment. Our machine gun section included two squads with five men to a squad. Each had one air-cooled machine-gun. Our guns were used with the bipod for quicker action, but there were times when we mounted the gun with tripod on a hand pulled cart for immediate action. The cart carried plenty of extra ammunition. We used the guns that way during the Holland operation.

I landed in Normandy by boat on D+1, since our 327 Glider Regiment was in reserve. We were ready for action offshore most of the previous day. Artillery fire and clearing the beach were problems, for the action was still intense. But by noon on D+1 we were put ashore and ran and crawled up a raised wooded causeway toward Ste. Marie-du-Mont. I remember coming up the tree-shaded causeway when one fellow called out, "Come on, they won't hurt you." We were crawling up when the Sgt. got up and ran ahead. He took about five steps before he got hit. One learns to be cautious when there is someone shooting back at you. You just can't take chances like that, especially when you are carrying a machine-gun; they visualize you as a more attractive target.

Some of our regiment went in by glider behind Utah Beach. They had it pretty rough, for many crashed against the hedgerows.

Action continued as we advanced forward under heavy fire for the next several days until the division was ready to attack the town of Carentan. We captured that city on the 12th of June 1944 and continued to push forward to secure more ground, while being prepared for a German counter-attack as we struggled ahead.

A new and different kind of fighting came into being when we found ourselves fighting in the hedgerows of Normandy. We could hear the enemy, but couldn't see him, while the Germans had the same

General Eisenhower talking to American paratroops of the 101st US Airborne Division on the eve of D-Day.

problem. Hand grenades were used more often than rifle fire. Tanks were not very successful either, until a clever G.I. designed an attachment to the tanks that allowed them to penetrate the hedgerows. While we had no tanks assigned, they were attached during times of need. The division's main heavy weapons were the 37 mm anti-tank guns, and artillery, while we had bazookas to protect against tank attack.

Normandy was a farming area with many cattle. One cannot describe the pervading smell of dead animals on the roads and in the fields. There were many dead soldiers also. Our last few days in Normandy were spent protecting the Cherbourg Peninsula. The Germans defending the area were cut off and finally surrendered. Our navy needed the port to enable large ships to re-supply the troops.

We were in action in Normandy for 33 days, June 7 to the 10th of July 1944, when we went back to England and had more training. We thought we were going to have another mission right away, but the troops were moving rapidly except in some of the areas around Caen. So they didn't need us until Montgomery wanted to skirt the Rhine and jump into Holland in Operation *Market Garden*. We landed at Son a mile or two from St. Oedenrode on the 17th of September and were there for 72 or 73 days.

Going into Holland, trying to keep that road open was tough. We were the first company to land of our regiment, and we came in pretty good. By midnight we were well established. But The British had it tough, for they landed near the second Panzer Corps northeast of Arnhem. We were keeping one main road open. The British came through us. The fighting was pretty bad. The Germans brought up reinforcements. We were up there too long, over two months. Re-supply was not very effective. The British came up and widened the gap and were fighting on and off around Nijmegen. Both the Brits and Americans took a lot of casualties. We had lost only two men going in, one by small arms. Later we got shot up pretty bad in Veghel. We pulled into a church yard. They had an observation post in one of the church steeples, and they zeroed in, directing fire so that the 88s were coming in almost straight at us.

Following that we came back to a camp near Reims, France, for a rest of two or three weeks and refitting. We heard about a break through, but we didn't realize the magnitude of the counter-attack that was developing. We were loaded into ten ton cattle trucks and driven a hundred miles to Bastogne, Belgium. Our regiment ended up at Marvie, southeast of Bastogne about a mile and a half. Because of its excellent road net Bastogne was one of the prime targets of the German attack. We formed a defense line by the 20th of December and were told to hold firm. The Germans were unable to penetrate our lines, so they went around us. We were then surrounded. That was just before Christmas. The 327 Glider held over a third of the perimeter of Bastogne and that's where the Germans came through us to demand our surrender. While he didn't come through our company area, I saw the envoy with the white flag at a distance. We were outnumbered by five German Divisions.

HEADQUARTERS 101ST AIRBORNE DIVISION
Office of the Division Commander

What's Merry about all this, you ask? We're fighting—it's cold—we aren't home. All true, but what has the proud Eagle Division accomplished with its worthy comrades the 10th Armored Division, the 705th Tank Destroyer Battalion and all the rest? Just this: We have stopped cold everything that has been thrown at us from the North, East, South and West. We have identifications from four German Panzer Divisions, two German Infantry Divisions and one German Parachute Division. These units, spearheading the last desperate German lunge, were headed straight west for key points when the Eagle Division was hurriedly ordered to stem the advance. How effectively this was done will be written in history; not alone in our Division's glorious history but in World history. The Germans actually did surround us, their radio blared our doom. Their Commander demanded our surrender in the following impudent arrogance:

December 22nd, 1944

"To the U.S.A. Commander of the encircled town of Bastogne:

The fortune of war is changing. This time the U.S.A. forces in and near Bastogne have been encircled by strong German armored units. More German armored units have crossed the river Ourthe near Ortheuville, have taken Marche and reached St. Hubert by passing through Homores-Sibret-Tillet. Libramont is in German hands.

There is only one possibility to save the encircled U.S.A. troops from total annihilation: that is the honorable surrender of the encircled town. In order to think it over a term of two hours will be granted beginning with the presentation of this note.

If this proposal should be rejected one German Artillery Corps and six heavy A.A. Battalions are ready to annihilate the U.S.A. troops in and near Bastogne. The order for firing will be given immediately after this two hour's term.

All the serious civilian losses caused by this Artillery fire would not correspond with the well known American humanity.

The German Commander

The German Commander received the following reply:

To the German Commander: 22 December 1944

N U T S!

The American Commander

Allied Troops are counterattacking in force. We continue to hold Bastogne. By holding Bastogne we assure the success of the Allied Armies. We know that our Division Commander, General Taylor, will say: "Well Done!"

We are giving our country and our loved ones at home a worthy Christmas present, and by being privileged to take part in this gallant feat of arms we are truly making for ourselves a Merry Christmas.

A. C. McAuliffe

The Germans must have been dropping bombs by coordinates. They were bombing us night and day. We couldn't see the planes, since the weather was so heavily overcast.

I don't understand how they could have massed such forces without our intelligence people knowing it. The Germans had pulled soldiers in from all over Europe. There is no question but that they had planned the operation for some time, yet they caught us unprepared.

The 106th Div. that the Germans hit first consisted of green troops; they were eaten up by the weight of the attack. Someone must have told them their sector was a piece of cake. They were probably sleeping and got hit hard. That had been a quiet part of the line.

My most vivid recollection, well, the first thing that comes to mind, was seeing people die, to realize that all those bullets kill people. The Germans had such great weapons. That 88 was just a super dual purpose gun; it did everything. And their burp gun could spray more bullets; they didn't believe so much in aimed fire as in a lot of it. That burp gun would run a clip through quickly. Their 88 was far superior to our 75 mm gun. We finally got the 90 mm gun later. Their pistols the Lugers and P-38's were great weapons. We carried carbines, with a folding stock. They are not much good over a hundred yards. The Germans wore white sheets over their uniform, enabling them to blend with the snow. There was plenty of snow then, and it was cold in the hilly, wooded section of the Ardennes. We didn't have trucks, we just carried everything on our back We ate K rations most of the time. We had a lot of bazookas, anti-tanks guns, parachute field artillery, however we didn't have an ample supply of ammunition until our own people could bring it up for us. Soon after we refused the surrender demand the sky cleared and supplies arrived. Much needed ammo, food and medical supplies arrived by glider. Even medical personnel were brought in to attend our wounded, for we had a lot of casualties. We didn't get all of the goods that were dropped; some landed in enemy hands, but we got enough. The Air Force made quick work of the German tanks when clearing weather allowed better visibility.

I recall Lt. Morrison, a platoon leader of our company, seeing him involved in house to house, hand-to hand fighting. He was captured, the fellows got him back, and then he was captured again and spent his time in a PW camp, died a few years ago. It was tough fighting, with snow and rain.

Fortunately I was not wounded; my feet were frozen shortly after we moved forward from Bastogne, soon after the first of the year. I spent a week or ten days in a hospital in France, then returned back to the same outfit. So many of my friends were killed at Bastogne. Three of my very close friends were on the right flank and their bodies have never been found. After I left with frozen feet my section leader was hit; half his hand was blown away.

We didn't have a full complement of 10—we had only eight men in our section when we entered Bastogne and of those 4 were killed and 2 were wounded.

Some of the events you don't recall until someone starts talking about it. Some days were a piece of cake and on others we were involved in fierce combat. I believe the Battle of The Bulge was the most intense battle involving American troops during the war.

I got the Bronze Star, Purple Heart, and the division received the Presidential citation, and the French & Belgian *Croix de Guerre* medals.

I have always considered myself very fortunate to have survived three campaigns. Seeing former comrades on the 50th anniversary of my duty in Normandy during a recent visit there brought back many memories. A Division Reunion is held every year in August, and I look forward to attending those events. Several years ago I was inducted into the 327th Regiment's Wall of Honor.

In civilian life, I was employed by the Blumenfeld Theaters in Marin County for over twenty-five years. Subsequently I had a barber shop on 4th Street in San Rafael until retirement.

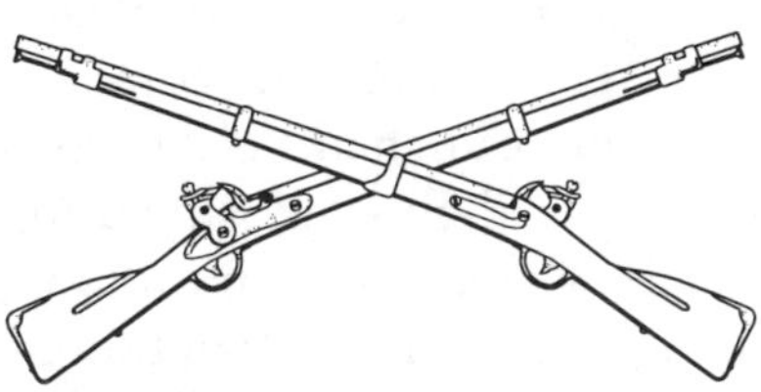

33

Battle of the Bulge

Major General Jack Barnes, USA-Ret.

I was the S3 (Operations Officer) of the 51st Engineer Combat Battalion in World War II. On December 15, 1944 the battalion was supervising the operation of 32 Belgian sawmills in the Ardennes, producing up to 80,000 board feet of lumber a day for bridge timbers and for winter housing for American troops in Europe. The next day the Germans attacked in overwhelming force in the Ardennes, and our mission was changed overnight to combat as infantry.

Company C was ordered to the small town of Trois Ponts at the junction of the Salm and Ambleve Rivers, where the use of three bridges was critical to the advance to the Meuse River by Kampfgruppe Peiper, spearheading the German Sixth SS Panzer Army. Company C was ordered to blow the bridges and hold the town against the advancing tanks and infantry. Road blocks were established on the approach routes into the town and the German tank columns were halted temporarily by tanks in the lead disabled by engineers of the 51st in defiles, allowing the men manning the road blocks to return to Trois Ponts before the bridges were blown.

For the next three days, Company C was able to hold off the Germans by deceiving them into thinking there was a far greater force defending the town. Chains were put on the Company's wheeled vehicles and they and the Company bulldozer were driven continually through the streets of the town behind buildings denying observation by the Germans, leading them to believe that American tanks were reinforcing the defenses of Trois Ponts. The company's wheeled vehicles were then driven blackout without chains out of town at night and then driven back into town with headlights on, simulating motorized reinforcements. Random explosions of ammunition on a burning U.S. weapons carrier, abetted by intentional detonation of individual sticks of dynamite made the Germans believe that artillery had been moved up to reinforce the defenders of Trois Ponts. On December 20th Company C was relieved by the 505th Infantry Regiment of the 82nd Airborne Division.

The result of Company C's defense of the town was to force the German panzer spearhead to detour to the north where it eventually ran out of fuel long before it could achieve its objective of seizing crossings over the Meuse River for the drive on Antwerp to split the Allied Forces.

Meanwhile, Companies A and B had been ordered to defend the Ourthe River from Durbuy to La Roche, a distance of some 20 miles, by defending all river crossings and preparing them for destruction. This involved setting demolition charges on all bridges, mining all fords and preparing obstacles such as *abatis*, heaps of rubble and daisy chains on the roads and trails leading to the crossings. Each of these sites was also covered by 51st engineer teams and squads with their organic weapons, which included 30- and 50- caliber machine guns, rocket launchers and individual small arms. All of these tasks had been completed by the morning of December 19th.

The major crossing and routes in the area were at the town of Hotton, where both civilian refugees and demoralized American troops were streaming in chaos from the shattered front. Our Battalion Commander, Lt. Col. Harvey Fraser, who had taken over the battalion on December 15th, two days before the Germans attacked, had but little success in convincing any of the retreating American units to join us in our defense of the Hotton bridge and the roads that were critical to the successful withdrawal of American troops. However, there were a few exceptions. Volunteering to join us instead of continuing their pell mell retreat to the rear were a squad of armored engineers with its 37-mm antitank gun, two Bofors 40-mm AAA guns with their crews, several bazooka teams and one M4 tank with a 76-mm gun. Together with Company B and an attached platoon from Company A, these newly attached squads and crews were hastily organized into an unorthodox but effective combined arms team by Company B's commander, who was charged by Col. Fraser to defend the Hotton bridge and its surroundings.

Early in the morning of December 21st probing armored patrols of the 2d and 116th Panzer Divisions of the German Fifth Panzer Army approached Hotton from the east and were taken under fire by the 51st Engineers. By 0900 Company B and its attached units had put four of the German Mark VI Tiger tanks out of action. Miraculously, the 37-mm gun, a pea shooter by comparison, accounted for one of the German tanks with two lucky shots, the first hitting the sprocket drive wheel and immobilizing the tank and the second hitting the turret ring and freezing it in place. The German crew was killed as they scrambled from the tank.

By noon elements of the U.S. 3rd Armored and 84th U.S. Infantry Divisions were arriving in the area and the Germans withdrew.

Throughout the 51st Engineer Combat Battalion area many other teams and squads of Company A and Headquarters and Service Company held the Germans at bay with hastily constructed and defended road blocks at critical intersections and defiles. When the tide of battle finally turned and the Allies went on the offensive in early January, the 51st Engineer Combat Battalion had been relieved by units of five divisions: the U.S. 2nd and 3rd Armored, 82nd Airborne, and 84th Infantry Divisions and the British 53rd Division. For its primary role in keeping the German offensive from splitting the Allies and reaching the Meuse River, the 51st Engineers earned the *U.S. Presidential Unit Citation* and the French *Croix de Guerre* with Silver Star.

Following these several accounts of segments of action during the Battle of the Bulge it might be appropriate to add a few quotes from the leaders on the other side.

Colonel General Josef 'Sepp' Dietrich, (1892-1966) commander of the leading element of the attack, the Waffen SS, "I grew big with these plans. I had merely to cross a river, capture Brussels and then go on and take the port of Antwerp. And all this in the worst months of the year, December, January, February, through the countryside where snow was waist deep and there wasn't room to deploy four tanks abreast, let alone six armored divisions; when it didn't get light until eight in the morning and was dark again at four in the afternoon; with divisions that had just been reformed and contained chiefly raw, untried recruits; and at Christmas time." His sarcastic opinion of the German planning for the Battle of the Bulge is contained in Messenger's *Hitler's Gladiator*, 1987.

Field Marshal Gerd von Rundstedt (1875-1953), in charge of German forces on the Western Front, also expressed disapproval:

"My general staff training revolted against an operation of this sort. If old von Moltke thought I had planned this offensive he would turn in his grave."

Hitler was desperately trying to buy time to get his secret weapons into production. Had he gained those extra months we might well have been in greater trouble.

Historians note that the *Wacht am Rhein* offensive was a colossal failure and showed up Hitler as an inadequate military leader, grossly underestimating the abilities of the Allies and vastly overestimating the capacity of his forces.

34

Jungle Campaign

Lieutenant Colonel Milton S. Anderson, AUS-Ret

The Philippine island of Leyte was the last Japanese occupied stronghold blocking General Douglas MacArthur from fulfilling his pledge, "I shall return!" The United States Army was dedicated to that purpose. Leyte would have to be cleared of all Japanese resistance before US forces could build the necessary airfields and supply back-up to mount an invasion of the main island of Luzon, the key to complete victory in the Pacific.

November 1944 found elements of General Walter Krueger's Sixth US Army battling to dislodge the Japanese defenders. It was evident that the four divisions comprising Sixth Army would have to be reinforced in order to completely eliminate the stubborn Japanese units that were dispersed throughout the mountainous island.

It was there that the 11th Airborne Division, nicknamed "The Angels" found itself, after an unopposed amphibious landing. Basically, the entrance of the 11th Airborne could have been called an administrative landing. The only enemy action encountered was by the Japanese Air Force, including attacks by Kamikaze planes. Their brief sorties hastened the unloading of the troops of the 11th Airborne from the nine Navy ships. On November 18, the 9000 men of the Division were established on Bito Beach, a long spit of land with Leyte Gulf on one side and the jungles and swamps of Leyte's lowlands on the other.

The 11th AB Division was much smaller than the normal Infantry or Mechanized Division, however, it had three regiments; the 511th Parachute, the 187th and 188th Glider regiments. These were supported by Airborne Artillery, Engineer, Ordnance, Signal and similar attached units. This Light Division was trained and equipped, however, for mass vertical envelopment, and was little prepared for the type of ground operations it would face on Leyte. We had been trained to jump and land in gliders, but there was little or none of that activity possible or planned for Leyte. Airborne training was helpful, however, in facing the rigors of jungle warfare.

Leyte, a semi-tropical island, not only featured the jungles and swamps of the tropics, but also extremely rugged, densely forested mountain terrain. Passes through the steep slopes were thick with slippery, slimy mud, rocky patches, overhanging tree branches, and intertwined wet, sticky vines.

Thus, significant terrain problems confronted us in our efforts to clear out the Japanese defenders. The monsoon weather conditions, also, were no help; we had nearly 24 inches of rain in November, making the mud omnivorous—it would eat out an infantryman's boots in seven days and cause Jungle Rot, a skin condition affecting the men's feet and legs. That affliction alone caused casualties just as effectively as shells or machine-gun bullets would.

Combat operations were accomplished on foot. Supply and resupply were handled by the local beast of burden, steer-sized Carabao (resembling oxen) which, with their native Filipino handlers provided the main logistical support pipeline for our operations, for they could readily negotiate the jungle and mountain trails.

Christmas season, 1944, found us (elements of the 188th) occupying a tiny airstrip in the mountains of central Leyte. The airstrip was only about the length of a football field, carved out by hand, and barely long enough to allow the Division Artillery spotter planes to bring in needed medical supplies and evacuate the most seriously wounded.

It was not a very festive holiday season for the troopers to celebrate. Some extra rations, such as canned turkey, had been flown in, but K rations, as usual, were the main menu. Was New Years Eve 1944 a

LTC Milton Anderson (left) and Col. John Roush, 1995

time for celebration? It would seem we were winning the war—good news flowed from Europe—we had both the Nazis and the Japanese on the run.

But, locally, our commander, Colonel Robert H. Soule (later Major General and Military Attaché to China) had an intelligence report warning us to be prepared for the possibility of an all-out Banzai attack. The scattered Japanese were starving, in need of medical supplies, and it was thought likely they would take advantage of the possible let-down in security on our part because of the holiday season. We were, indeed, apprehensive of an attack upon our position and were ordered to create a tight perimeter defense around the air strip. All available troops were dug in along a U-shaped line—no one got any sleep that night; we anticipated action—plenty of it! The Japanese had proved to be fierce and determined fighters who would sustain an attack with all available force. Our ammunition, unfortunately, was limited.

It was wet and cold in the foxholes and slit trenches in which we awaited the attack—not the most desirable place in which to spend a New Year's Eve! In the first four hours of darkness everything was still and nothing moved, and it seemed that the warning of a Japanese attack was just another false alarm. Suddenly, the sound of movement was heard coming from the blackness of the jungle outside our perimeter. The reaction was instantaneous!

Every weapon on the line opened up, firing into the black mountain side. The combined fire of Browning Automatic Rifles, M-1 rifles, carbines, machine-guns, and bazookas made the mountain mesa

(left to right) Virginia Roush, Col. Douglas Riach, Eleanor Riach, Col. John Roush, Betty Anderson, LTC Milton Anderson at the CIOR meeting in Oslo, Norway. Aug. 1985

resound as a major battle site. When the Japanese failed to return the fire and no attempt to breach our defenses was made, the firing stopped and the perimeter became quiet again. For the rest of the night the mountain resumed a state of tranquillity.

Next morning, at first light, patrols were sent out to count, "How many Japs were sent to meet their ancestors?" Alas, we found no Japanese—only the splattered remains of our hard-working Carabao scattered throughout the jungle—it was a gory mess! (The animals had been tethered outside the perimeter and apparently had broken loose, wandering into the fire zone.) To make matters worse, none of the meat was salvable to augment our tired K ration fare. It was a night to remember, or, rather, to forget, by sheepish defenders (including the writer)!

A graduate of Infantry OCS at Fort Benning, Georgia, in January of 1943, Lt. Anderson was assigned to the 11th Airborne Division and reported for duty to the 188th Glider Regiment (later designated as Parachute). His various assignments included Platoon Leader, Battalion Supply Officer (S-4), Regimental Ammunition/ Demolition Officer and Company Commander in the battles for New Guinea, Leyte, Luzon, Okinawa, and eventually in occupation duty on Honshu, Japan. He returned to the United States in 1946 and joined the USAR, retiring as Lieutenant Colonel. As a reservist, he was an IMA for many years in the Sixth U.S. Army Headquarters in the Plans and Operations section of the General Staff.

35

Ditching at Sea—South Pacific

Major Richard H. Wright,USAF-Ret.

In the South Pacific, I was flying with the 17th Reconnaissance Squadron, of the 71st Reconnaissance Group. We were stationed on Biak Island, Schouten Island Group, about 25 miles north of New Guinea.

On 13 July 1944, at 0600 hours we took off, a flight of six Mitchell B-25D bombers, to hunt for Japanese shipping. Our B-25D's were equipped with nine .50 cal. machine guns, firing forward. The pilot had use of six .50 cal. fixed guns, two in the nose, and two on either side of the fuselage. I was the navigator and had the use of one flexible .50 cal. machine gun. We had a half bomb bay fuel tank to extend our range and the plane carried four 500 pound bombs.

Our crew included pilot Joe Wise, since promoted to Brigadier General, 2nd Lt. F. Watkins, co-pilot, S/Sgts. Price, Manes and Harold Salerno, gunners.

Our mission required us to fly west about five hundred miles toward Halmahera Island. Around 1100 hours, off the east coast of that island, we sighted a Japanese cargo ship, about the size of a Liberty Ship.

Captain Wise ordered the attack, and we went in at mast height, firing all of our guns. From my position in the nose, I could see the boat firing at us. I was trying to cover the deck of the ship with my flexible .50 cal., while Capt. Wise proceeded to drop the four bombs, striking the target. Going away, the captain came on the intercom to announce, "We have a problem."

Enemy gun fire had shot off the propeller hub of the left engine, and he could not feather the prop. We were told that we were going to ditch the airplane. We landed the B-25 on the ocean about fifteen to twenty miles away from the sinking Japanese ship. Surprisingly, our plane stayed up for quite awhile.

We had been taught, in the case of a ditching, to get away from the plane as fast as possible, for when it sank they believed there would be a suction that might take one down with it. We didn't find that to be true.

The co-pilot jettisoned the cockpit roof before we hit the water. He was supposed to go out first, then the captain, then me. When I stepped out on the left wing, I slipped on oil from the propeller hub and slid into the ocean. Capt. Wise and Watkins rescued me.

Our five man raft had popped out of its storage place and had inflated. Oars were stored in the bottom of the raft. They were in two sections, with a metal fitting to hook them together. Everyone was yelling at S/Sgt Price to get them out so that we could row away from the airplane before it sank. He hastily yanked them out, however the metal fitting ripped a hole in the raft. So instead of six men having a five man raft, six men had to crowd into a 2-man raft. However, we climbed aboard and rowed away. No ukuleles were playing in the background.

Our friends in the five other B-25's had not abandoned us. They began to drop supplies to us in great quantities, gallon thermos jugs, food, water, May West jackets, etc. A Gibson Girl radio went by my head traveling at a frightening 250 miles per hour. Those things were dangerous. We tried to get them to stop the bombardment, but they interpreted our signals as our desire that they drop more.

Finally, as they became low on fuel, they had to leave. We couldn't see any land, and it certainly got lonely fast. We were almost on the Equator, so we were not cold.

We wondered where the air rescue teams were. No ships were in sight. As darkness approached, we knew that rescue that day was out of the question and that we would have to spend the night at sea. With the

B-25D "Little Joe"
The Crew:
(left to right)
Lt. Wright
S/Sgt Manes
Capt. Wise
S/Sgt Price
Lt. Watkins
S/Sgt Salerno

limited space on the raft, all of us had to keep in rhythm. If one of us fell asleep and broke the rhythm, thus falling into the water, we all fell in also. In the night, it got surprisingly cool.

In the morning there were many flyovers by Japanese planes, but they were so high that they did not see us. We didn't know that, however, and would get off, turn the raft upside down to display its blue bottom, rather than the yellow surface. About noon of the second day we saw what we thought to be B-25's, so we dumped an envelope of yellow dye. Our friends were back and brought more supplies, which they dropped, but missed us.

They led a Navy PBY flying boat, and flew fighter cover, since our fighter aircraft could not proceed that far. The PBY landed the plane in very high seas, and, after twenty-six hours on the sea, the take-off was more dangerous than our landing of the disabled B-25. The waves were ten feet high, but, fortunately, we had not seen any sharks.

On the flight back to base, the B-25's had a difficult time staying with the PBY, which flew at half the speed of the B-25's. The PBY had to land on water, so we had to land at the Biak Naval Base. The next day a PT boat ferried us to the docks adjacent to our base. The docks were all full, so we off-landed on the bow of an LST (Landing Ship Tank), through the big front doors, up the stairs onto the deck, which was covered with infantrymen in full battle gear, ready for an imminent landing.

Crew on raft, 14 July 1944

When six Air Force flyers entered, disheveled, with torn shirts, no shoes, sunburned, and no hats, our P.R. Officer told the soldiers, "These men were just shot down and rescued at sea." When we received applause, I think that was the only time that I felt like a hero, for it was a memorable welcome back.

In the late 1970's I received a book about PBY's called *Black Cat Raiders* by Captain Richard C. Knott, USN. On page 162, I found a picture of the scene of our rescue. Capt. Knott provided me with the name of the pilot, Lt. Favorite, of the PBY that picked us up. I was able to contact him in New Jersey and was able to spend a pleasant day with him.

Richard Wright and Captain Wise in their foxhole in New Guinea

36

The Tank

LTC Walker Carlton, AUS-Ret.

As a first lieutenant and Executive Officer of I Company 185th Infantry, 40th Division, I was in the first assault waves to hit the beach at Lingayen, Luzon, Philippine Islands, on January 9, 1945. Soon after, I Company was involved in the heavy fighting, which occurred as the Japanese slowly withdrew into prepared positions in the hills west of Bamban and Clark Field. And it was there during the early hours of February 28th, while I was temporarily in command of I Company, that it and K Company successfully defended the summit of Hill 1400 against a massive Japanese effort to retake this hill which, along with Hill 1700, dominated the area. Dawn revealed 47 dead Japanese lying just outside our perimeter. Less than three weeks later, on March 18, the 185th RCT landed on the island of Panay, near San Nicholas. Encountering only token opposition, the 3rd Battalion turned northeast, and on March 20th was near the barrio of Pavia. It was near there that I was fortunate to survive what is believed to be one of the unique battle experiences of W.W.II:

Following a firefight, the Japanese forces were believed disorganized and fleeing along the Tigon River Valley towards new positions in the mountains northwest of Cabatuan. About 0800 hours I was approached by Capt. Charles S. Dever, my company commander, who told me I was to command a fast moving combat patrol consisting of one of our rifle platoons mounted on the five light tanks of a platoon from an attached tank unit. My mission was to advance some miles beyond our lines in an effort to locate the rear of the retreating Japanese column and, where practical, to destroy dispersed units and stragglers.

Each of the light tanks was armed with a 37 mm cannon and a .30 cal. machine gun in the turret and another .30 cal. MG firing only forward from the seat next to the driver. With six riflemen crouching on the deck behind the turret of each tank, we were soon well beyond our lines and alone on a broad flat plain of previously harvested and now very dry rice paddies. The only live vegetation consisted of the few palms that surrounded an occasional stilt mounted bamboo house and the intermittent groves of bamboo which grew along the banks of a near dry stream which flowed parallel to, and several hundred yards to the right of the road upon which we were traveling. There we encountered several Filipino farmers, who were anxious to make us understand that there were Japanese soldiers and civilians hiding in a particularly large grove of bamboo immediately to our right.

Seeing no way to investigate and, if necessary, destroy whatever forces might be in the bamboo except by crossing the intervening 400 yards of dry rice paddies, the tank lieutenant and I agreed it was best to approach the grove in attack formation, the five tanks in line abreast with the command tank in the center and the riflemen walking close behind the tanks so as to be shielded from gunfire.

The grove seemed unoccupied until we were within 150 yards of it. There, all hell broke loose, and we found ourselves caught in the crossfire of two machine guns, one on each flank of the grove from which now came the popping of rifles. My riflemen either dived for cover behind a rice paddy wall, or crouched behind the tanks, and attempted to return fire. The tanks stopped and opened fire with their 37 mm cannon and machine guns. I recall pulling the telephone out of the box on the back of the command tank so as to be able to talk to the lieutenant inside, and then taking cover by lying on my stomach just behind the right tread. I poked my head out just enough to see if I could locate the machine gun on the right and direct the tank's 37 mm fire on it. Hardly had I put the phone to my ear, when over it came a scream from inside, "We're hit! Back up, let's get out of here!"

Hearing the tank gears shift into reverse, and instantly aware that I had almost no time to escape being crushed, I rolled onto my back and reaching up with both hands, grabbed the rear of the tank's right fender on its outer edge and with, what must have been an adrenaline charged effort, attempted to throw my body out and away. But the oncoming tread rolled over both of my legs between the knees and the ankles. I can vividly remember lying there with my head up, watching my legs being pressed into the burnt grass and baked mud of the rice paddy, and very calmly saying to myself, "You have lost your legs," and then something like, "This is the end of the war and the army for you."

After the tank rolled off of me, feeling pain and believing my legs crushed, I turned onto my stomach, only to see the other four tanks withdrawing, leaving my men and me with no protection from the Japanese fire, except the low rice paddy walls. Exposed there in the open, I knew I had to reach the wall a few yards in front of me. Using my elbows I began to drag myself towards it. Having seen my legs go under the tank, two of the men lying behind the wall began to crawl towards me to help. Seeing the risk they were taking, I yelled that I could make it on my own and for them to stay under cover. It was then that I discovered that I could pull my knees up beside me, frog-like, and use them to propel my body forward. Reaching the bank, I was told that three of our men had been wounded. I quickly determined we had no choice but to attempt an orderly withdrawal. I passed the word

1st Lt. Walker Carlton (left) and Capt. Charles S. Dever, C.O. Company I. 185th Inf. on Guadalcanal in March of 1944 just prior to the 40th Division relieving the Marines on the island of New Britian.

for a few men in each squad to remain behind and continue firing in an effort to keep the heads of Japanese down while the rest of the platoon withdrew by crawling alongside the banks of the rice paddies to another firing position and from there to cover the withdrawal of those who had remained behind.

After staying behind with the covering force long enough to supervise the withdrawal, I began to crawl towards the rear. Fortunately, seeing us pulling out, the Japanese must have felt the need to conserve their remaining ammunition and ceased firing. It was then that I discovered that I could rise up and walk a few steps before falling down again.

Reaching the road, behind which the tanks had reassembled, I approached the tank lieutenant, who had just been told of his tank backing over me, and demanded to know why the tanks had, without warning, abandoned the infantry and withdrawn all the way back to the road. He told me that just after his tank opened fire, a projectile entered the turret, killing the gunner of the 37mm cannon, splashing metal and reverberating around inside the tank. Believing they had been ambushed at short range by a well-concealed weapon capable of penetrating the armor of tanks, he had ordered the pull-out. However, upon reaching the safety of the road and unbuttoning, the tank's crew came to the conclusion that what had happened was a bullet had hit the turret gunner's periscope and somehow ricocheted downward, passing through the gunner's eye and then continuing to ricochet around inside the tank.

It was obvious that the Japanese we had encountered included an organized, well armed military unit. And although two of my riflemen, who had gotten close to the bamboo, told me that they had seen several dead Japanese, I knew that being an isolated patrol we risked more casualties and even our safe return if we made another effort to cross the rice fields and destroy this unit made invisible to us by the bamboo and protected from our flat trajectory weapons by the stream bank. Believing the patrol had accomplished its primary mission by contacting this organized unit of the retreating Japanese column and plotting its probable escape route, I had the riflemen climb back on the tanks and we returned to our lines without further incident.

Lying on a stretcher at the 3rd Battalion aid station, I made an oral report and then, because the doctors could not believe that my legs were not fractured, I was evacuated through several medical units until reaching a field hospital which had a portable X-ray unit. Several hours later the orthopedic doctor who had examined me and read my X-rays came to my bed. After introducing himself, he smiled and told me how amazed he was that, despite the deep abrasions the tank tread had dug into my legs and the obvious pressure and twisting they had been subjected to, the X-rays showed no evidence of fractures. After telling me that I had been most fortunate and that I would be kept in the hospital until I had recovered enough to return to my unit, he started to leave. It was then that he turned and said the words I was never to forget, "But, I have a hunch that in about thirty years you are going to feel all of this." Nine days later, I was back with I Company, 185th RCT and riding an LVT ashore in the initial landing on the island of Negros. Soon after, I was made C.O. of I Company and commanded it until the last days of the Negros campaign.

There is an epilogue to this W.W.II incident in that the doctor's hunch proved correct: After more than thirty years of good health and a successful career as a secondary school teacher and administrator in Los Angeles, I developed a severe case of osteoarthritis in both legs and today have two artificial knee joints and walk with the aid of a cane.

For herioc achievement in this action, first Lieutenant Walker Carlton, 185th Infantry, was awarded the Bronze Star. He received the Purple Heart for the injuries he incurred.

185th Infantry, 40th Division, WWII

37

First and Last — Burma Heartbreak

Colonel James Holland, USA-Ret.

Several of us company grade officers gathered in the "Officers Club" of the 2d Filipino Infantry Regiment (occupying only half of a Quonset Hut) at Camp Cooke, California, on the evening of 17 March 1944, St. Patrick's Day. A Department of the Army notice on the bulletin board read in part: "Volunteers are needed for a one-time classified mission." Another, under the 2d Filipino Regimental letterhead, announced that the unit would be reorganized as a separate battalion effective 1 May 1944.

After much discussion and more than sufficient toasts to St Patrick, our group decided that anything was better than "Repple-Depple" assignments that obviously faced us, particularly for captains, so we volunteered.

Orders came quickly. With but a few days leave we were enroute to Fort Meade, Maryland, designated as shipment GH 770, moving to Camp Patrick Henry, organized (on paper only) as an infantry battalion (separate). We boarded the *USNT Simon B. Buckner*. About a thousand of us soldiers, plus a contingent of Army nurses (off limits, of course), some USAAF types and others who were aboard ship, and, without fanfare, sailed into the Atlantic. Four weeks later we docked at Bombay, India and boarded a little narrow-gauge train for a five day ride through the hills into Chabua, India. There we were transferred to C-47's and flown into Myitkyina, Burma, landing at a shell-pocketed airstrip still under Japanese fire. We were running as we left the planes. The Japanese who had given the field up were still lobbing artillery and mortar shells onto it. We quickly reorganized as LRP battalions to replace the 1st and 3rd battalions of the 5307th C.U.P. (Merrill's Marauders), men who were combat weary, exhausted from almost three months of fighting their way from India to "Mitch."

In Burma, we were again reorganized to permit the evacuation of many sick and wounded original members of the Marauders. We immediately moved out. With my new assignment as communications officer of the newly reorganized 3rd Bn., I was ordered to set up a forward observation post northeast of Charpate, northeast of the airstrip. With Sgt. Dick Bates and another enlisted man, we grabbed some E-8 phones and a couple rolls of wire. With only a compass direction we headed out into our first taste of jungle stink and tropical heat. We had gone only about a quarter of a mile along the narrow jungle trail when we spotted our first enemy sprawled out across it. Our only orientation to battle, conducted at Camp Cooke, informed us that our enemy, the Japanese, were small, bow-legged, buck-toothed little people. This man was over six feet tall, heavy-set, and, even in death, vicious in appearance, especially with that rictus smile on his face. He was unnerving to say the least. We proceeded more slowly and carefully, only to be challenged a short time later by Lt. Norman Berkness and a sergeant.

Berkness asked, "What the hell are you guys doing out here?"

I told him. "Well, Captain," he replied, "we ARE the O.P. and anything beyond here is Jap territory."

Shortly we heard the crack of rifle fire and the more intense noise of bullets (we learned later) going through bamboo. Finding ourselves under attack by a Japanese foot patrol, we formed a small five-man

October 1944, Burma; then Capt. Holland, (on the left, wearing glasses)

perimeter. With two .30 cal. carbines and three M-l rifles we were able, with the help of a couple of grenades, to hold off the Japanese for about an hour. It seemed like at least a day! Hooking an E-8 instrument to the phone line we had deployed, I was able to call for help, and the Japs faded back into the jungle. All five of us later took part in more intense combat actions, but that one small incident, short as it was, and bloodless, registered images of the sights and sounds of battle, recollections of adrenaline flow that remain strong in my memory fifty years afterwards.

Years later, I recall a bright moonlit, warm, clear tropical night in the Mekong Delta just outside the village of Vi Thanh in Chung Thien Province, US. IV Corps area, in South Viet Nam. We had completed a Vietnamese dinner hosted by the ARVN commander. I had returned to my H o o t c h, placed my glasses and .45 cal. weapon on the box next to my cot and settled down to sleep when the first round impacted close by. Somebody yelled, "Incoming!" and two more hit even closer. I dove to the floor, grabbed for and missed my eye glasses, got the .45, and took off for the concrete bunker close by. As senior officer present, I counted heads, came up two short and went back outside the bunker into the trench between it and a five-foot wall surrounding it.

I pulled myself up and peered over the wall, yelling for the missing guys. Mortar rounds were still impacting, and suddenly I felt a sharp, severe pain in my right eye. Reaching up with my hand I felt a wet, sticky, warm mess. A sharper more severe pain hit me. I slumped toward the ground and blacked out. When I came to a few moments later, Sgt. "Doc" Jones was bending over me.

"You got a nasty one Colonel," he said. "We've just called 'Dust Off' and when this crap stops they'll get you out of here."

He gave me a shot of something, bandaged the eye and started some plasma while I lay there. The incoming rounds finally stopped. We heard the chopper almost immediately as it set down in a dry rice paddy next to the bunker. I was gently loaded in and a short time later the aircraft sat down next to a mobile army surgical hospital. Another medic removed Doc's field dressing, re-cleaned the mess, gave me a shot of morphine; and said bluntly, "Jeeze fella, looks like you just lost an eye."

The morphine took hold and the next thing I remember was waking up in a clean bed at the 3rd Field Hospital on the outskirts of Saigon. Two or three hours had elapsed from wound to treatment. The promptness of care and absence of my eye glasses probably saved my life, if not half my sight. Incidentally, the two missing men turned up O.K. After thirty years in retirement, in retrospect, three wars behind me, I am a very lucky man.

Colonel Holland is a well known author and editor of matters pertaining to the Western Pacific Rim countries. After an 18 month contract in Saudi Arabia helping to re-organize the Saudi Arabian National Guard, Holland became associate editor of *The Asia Mail*. He is currently a consultant to the Republic of China, Taiwan Tourism Office in San Francisco. His decorations include: Silver Star w/OLC, Legion of Merit, Bronze Star w/OLC & "V", Purple Heart, Air Medal, Joint Commendation Medal, Burma Star (UK), Order of Chungmu (Korea) & Ulchi (Korea), Order of Yellow Cloud, 2nd Class (ROC).

C.U.P. is Composite Unit Provisional, which as the 5307 was Merrill's Marauders. Deactivated in August, 1944, it was reactivated as the 475th Regt., LRP (Long Range Penetration), deactivated in August, 1945, reactivated as the 75th Inf., during Vietnam.

Col. Holland, November 16, 1993

38

Combat Engineers in the Pacific

Colonel Artis C. Grant, AUS-Ret.

Enlisting in the Army in March of 1943, I was assigned to the Combat Engineers. I was promoted rapidly; while serving as construction supervisor I reached the highest enlisted grade of Master Sergeant in March of 1944 during combat in New Guinea. We had a precarious landing in Finschaven, 36 miles ahead of the existing front lines with the Japanese defenders.

After eight months involvement there, we moved north, landing in the Bay of Tacloban, Leyte, in the Philippine Islands in October of 1944. There we were busy building roads, hospitals, base-ball fields, bridges and other engineering projects. On week-ends, my group did extra work for other units. In return, they furnished us extra field phones, supplied ice and other amenities.

We were close to the action. Our trucks would come in with bullet holes, so we had to provide an additional soldier to ride shotgun. The front lines became fluid. Enemy soldiers would infiltrate our area during the night. The enemy often tried to pass through our area, attempting to reach the mountains that afforded more cover. We took a dim view of this and laid down a heavy fire. By the end of the night, this would drive the Japanese troops back out into the rice paddies, whereupon our infantry would drive them around again. When our firing endangered American infantry units, we set up an agreement: Before 6 p.m. the Infantry would do the fighting. After that anything that moved was deemed enemy and we acted accordingly.

Often, we took fire through our encampment, so we became proficient at digging foxholes. While getting into mine one night, a centipede bit me. Within an hour I had extensive swelling, requiring adrenaline for the heart and morphine for the pain. Contrary to good common sense, I didn't return to my foxhole, crawling, instead, back to my cot.

One night at dusk we were conversing with the AAA unit equipped with 90mm guns next to us. We had observed 14 planes coming across the island who were giving us a friendly signal, wiggling their wings. We recognized them as DC-2's. However, we didn't have any DC-2's in this theater, so the Lieutenant commanding the AAA unit ordered his guns to fire. He was right—those planes were loaded with Japanese paratroopers who commenced jumping. All of the AAA units in the area then commenced firing, bringing down nine of the enemy planes. Some of the paratroopers were caught up in the trees. Silk chutes flapped around in the breeze for days.

During one night the enemy strafed our area. The 50mm machine gun fire traversed through the area. While they were a thousand yards away, the tent pole gave them an aiming point. It was being hit repeatedly as the fire got lower and more threatening. Finally the firing went through a row of tents, including mine. Nine bullets came through my mosquito net while I was still in it. Swinging from right to left and dropping, the bullets got closer and closer, with the last one taking my messkit off the cot next to my head. It was rattling to see the succession of bullets coming ever closer to my head. It seemed a miracle that I was never wounded.

My platoon had several .50 caliber water-cooled machine guns which we had dug in and emplaced to repulse ground action. We found this to be a mistake because we had a hard time getting the guns into action against enemy planes attempting to strafe us.

From Leyte, we went on to Luzon for another eight months. We had additional excitement on the way home when the ship caught fire. Some incompetent was trying to cook doughnuts in a large vat when the flames escaped and caused us much tribulation.

Remaining in the Reserves after the war, Master Sergeant Grant was commissioned Second Lieutenant in 1950 and was promoted to Colonel in 1971, after serving with various troop units for 24 years. Colonel Grant was the California Department President of ROA for one year and held other important positions.

39

Random Thoughts

Col. John H. Roush, Jr., AUS-Ret.

Raucous noise certainly gets your attention, thus I recall vividly the strident racket those thundering V-1 rockets made in passing overhead. You could hear them from a long distance away. Buzz-bombs we called them. The V-1 was used primarily against civilian targets west of us in Belgium, Holland and England. As long as they were roaring you didn't feel jeopardized, but when their loud engine stopped one had to worry and seek some shelter.

At one point in the forward movement of my unit, some bright young officer had selected a small schoolhouse on a high knoll as the CP, perhaps unaware that buzz-bombs would frequently barely clear the roof-top. He heard about that, I am certain, from the Colonel.

Subsequently, one of my sergeants became dramatically involved in developing our information regarding those secret weapons. He had a work party out doing some minor task, when he learned that one of the German workers had also been among such a work detail for high-ranking Nazis. The man thought they had buried something extremely important.

My sergeant immediately proceeded to organize an effort to dig up that package, which we found to contain all the plans for secret weapons, the V-1, V-2 and up through V-12, which detailed plans for establishing a space station. A special plane was dispatched with senior technical officers from Washington to collect the Top Secret material. I was able to write up the soft-spoken sergeant from Tennessee for a high decoration for his initiative. Many soldiers did not get the medals they deserved unfortunately; officers were just too busy most of the time for anyone to write up the recommendations, which had to be in precise form.

Some of my memories are indelible even though fifty years have elapsed. Not all of them are repeatable. Jumping into a ditch and

V-1 Buzz Bomb

slathering into the mud was one, as a Messerschmitt 109 strafed the column. How the bullets missed me I will never know, since they struck all around me. I am grateful for the miracle that they missed.

We saw lots of casualties, but the worst memory of all, still vivid in my mind, was the appalling sight of a stack of bodies over a hundred yards long and five feet high as we entered one of the Nazi concentration camps. Nothing I saw during the war was more horrible. The dreadful emaciated bodies with distorted grimaces were so thin and pathetic. The stripped remains resembled a huge log pile. We could only guess that the awful collection contained over a thousand bodies. Fortunately it was cold, there was no odor.

I have never seen men so thin, such wasted souls; they were dreadful visions of tormented skulls. Why this atrocity had been done to so many we couldn't fathom. The bestiality of the enemy ideology, evidenced by those awful deeds, motivated us to do what we could to bring that war to a more rapid conclusion. How men could be so inhumane to others and transgress so far outside the norms of civilized behavior was beyond our comprehension.

One of my most vivid memories, more easily recalled, is of a squad-sized patrol mission. We were sent out on a cold, miserable, moon-less night, not to fight, but to learn what we could. It wasn't an important mission, not of any real consequence, but those night hours became a period of lasting memory to me.

Abruptly encountering a superior force, surprised by the forceful engagement immediately initiated, we were quickly split up. I found myself suddenly alone and surrounded.

I heard a harsh autocratic, resonant voice demand, "Surrender!" Silently refusing, I used some of my woodsmanship to sneak out. Can you imagine the terror of such a desolate condition? Being captured was the worst thing any of us wanted to happen. Each side tried to catch prisoners for intelligence purposes. Patrols were often sent out for that purpose. Just before dawn, I came in long after some of the others had made their way back to our lines.

One winter night of 1944 I had been helping with plans. Tired and groggy, I went up on the roof of the little school house, a different one, we were using as a headquarters. I needed to get some fresh air, for I was becoming sleepy, it being about one a.m. It was a dreary, quiet gray scene, a cold unfriendly atmosphere; there were no lights. Shortly after reaching the top of the building, a low-flying Messerschmitt 109 fighter, obviously on a reconnaissance mission, skimmed the top of the building. He was so close and the moon so bright that I got a good look at the pilot's face, eyeball to eyeball. His expression was one of such utter hatred that I will never forget the vilifying vision of that arrogant Nazi pilot.

He came back, the single plane, and dropped incendiary bombs all night long. We fought the fires and saved the school house, but other buildings adjacent burned to the ground.

Often we didn't comprehend fully what was going on. Those who knew the big picture, the senior officers, are now, for the most part, no longer with us.

Junior officers seldom knew much more than their men.

In the Battle of the Bulge, we were on the northerly fringe. Most of the American combat troops were rapidly pulled out, swinging toward the action, while our thin ranks held the line. That week was dreadful. The remaining U.S. troops (First and Ninth U.S. Armies) were put under British command, yet that didn't affect us much more than cause further apprehension. We thought of Dunkirk. We were concerned that we might be cut off and forced to surrender. We had the depressing impression that suddenly things had changed, that we were losing the war.

The week was awfully cold, with snowy, miserable weather, and we were not fully informed as to what was going on. We didn't get situation reports, but heard dreadful rumors. Those American planes that appeared briefly were quickly shot down by the enemy. Fortunately, the massive enemy mechanized columns to our south ran out of fuel. We heard that their Tiger tanks were devastating, far superior to what our armored forces had.

We heard that the first American major unit hit by the horrendous Panzer assault of three combined armies, the 106th U.S. Army Infantry Division, fresh from the States, was annihilated. We were appalled to have alerts that German infiltrators were wearing American uniforms, thus we didn't know whom we could trust. We heard that many

Col Riach, Col. Roush, Commander Dodge

American prisoners were abruptly executed by the Nazis. It was the worst week of our lives.

In all of that winter of 1944-45 I never saw a bed. I remember vividly the snow and the mud, but I never caught a cold. One evening was remarkably better than the others spent sleeping in muddy fields scented with the excreta of ages. We were warm inside, with sleeping bags on the lanes of a little bowling establishment.

Some of you know me to be a life-time angler. Well, I carried fish hooks and line in one of my pockets throughout the war, and occasionally got to use them. For some reason never explained to us EM, we sat anchored off Omaha Beach for several days before going in. Enterprising perhaps, I scrounged some bacon rind for bait, a bolt for a sinker, and caught a tuna. One of the colonels graciously relieved me of the fish for the officer's mess. I didn't get my commission until later, in France.

One of my most lasting memories occurred later, during the occupation of Austria, when I was a Provost Marshal with an MP unit under my authority. Getting chewed out by a Cardinal, A Prince of the Church, doesn't happen to many Catholics. One evening my MPs brought in three soldiers who had gotten out of line. Expecting to be rotated back to the States the next morning, they had been celebrating with too much of the local beverages and then had beaten up some of the passing civilians. One of the victims happened to be a frail, kindly old priest highly revered in the community.

I went calling upon him in the hospital the next morning to express our profound regrets. The Cardinal from Vienna came in also, and, as I was the first American soldier he encountered after the outrage, he castigated me more thoroughly than any Drill Sergeant might sound-off upon a miscreant recruit. The victim was more forgiving, but the Prince of the Church stood by the bed directing his rage at me with words of fire and brimstone, telling me that the Nazis were never so bad.

It so happened that one of the soldiers claimed innocence. He vigorously asserted that his father was a close personal friend of Harry Truman and assured me arrogantly that I would be demoted and worse. General Mark Clark, the Army Commander, also a Catholic, I believe, was also harangued by the Cardinal, so later that day the General sent down to Linz his own investigating officer, who subsequently confirmed my report and recommendations. The soldier was convicted by a General Courts Martial. The President did not become involved. Needless to say, I share with others a great deal of respect for President Truman.

While on R&R, in my exhuberence at the war's ending in Europe in 1945, I hunted chamois four to five thousand feet above the valley.

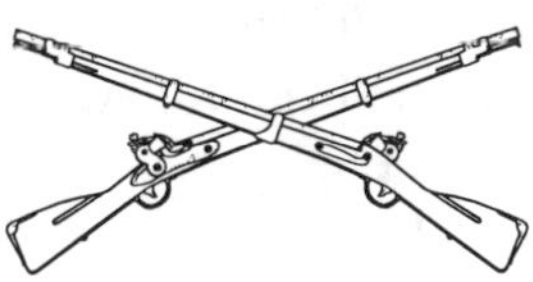

40

Horrors of a Barbaric Enemy

CWO3 Julius E. Bernstein, AUS-Ret.

On Friday 27 April 1945 I was a Special Agent in the U.S. Army Counter Intelligence Corps assigned to the 12th Armored Division. We were a small detachment of nine men, and each of us was trained in a specialized field. My assignment dealt with Counter Espionage and Counter Sabotage. I was the only member of the Detachment with Special Agent status who was American born. The other members of the team were German, Austrian and Polish born.

That morning, the Division was preparing to capture the German city of Landsberg-am-Lech (Landsburg on the Lech River). The city was being defended by both the German Werhrmacht (Regular German Army) and the Waffen SS (the private Army of the Nazi Party). The Germans had been pushed back to the river and the Wehrmacht commander made the decision to withdraw across the Lech River, re-group and establish a defense on the other side of the river. Considering the situation, that was the only rational decision he could have made. The commander of the Waffen SS didn't see it that way. He informed the Wehrmacht commander that the SS would fight house-to-house in order to defend every inch of German soil. The Wehrmacht commander replied that if the SS wanted to fight house-to-house, that was their decision. But he was still ordering the Wehrmacht to withdraw to the other side of the river.

When the civilian population saw the Wehrmacht packing up and pulling across the river, they hung out white sheets, anything white, as a sign of surrender. The sight of the white flags infuriated the Waffen SS, who by then realized the futility and stupidity of house-to-house fighting. In their rage, they went from house to house wherever they saw a white flag of surrender. There they would drag outside whomever they found inside the building and hang them from the nearest tree, lamp post, or whatever was handy. As we rode into Landsburg, we found German civilians hanging from trees like ripe fruit. This was the first and only time that I saw Germans turn against their own, but the grizzly sight was nothing to compare with what we witnessed later that day.

Shortly after noon, we received a message that one of the Division's Armored Infantry Battalions had surrounded a concentration camp on the outskirts of the city, and that the entire camp was on fire. Four C1C agents, including myself, were directed to join the unit and move into the camp as soon as it was taken. We arrived near the camp site as the infantry were preparing to mount an assault on the camp. From a distance, I could see through my binoculars that the camp had been on fire. Except for some smoldering ruins the fire was almost out. I was unable to detect any sign of life inside the barbed wire fence. Black, acrid smoke curling upward obscured the vision. The smell was awful, something I had not experienced before nor since.

When we entered the camp, we found it almost totally deserted. The Waffen SS had made good their escape, leaving behind only a few guards who appeared to be men in their 60's or older, definitely not front line combat troops.

The Camp Commandant, realizing that the fall of the camp was imminent, had ordered that the camp and its remaining four thousand inmates be destroyed. Not having sufficient time to first execute the victims in the gas chambers, and then cremate their bodies, as was their usual procedure, the doors and windows were nailed shut. They had hosed down the buildings with inflammable fluid and were set on fire; thus the inmates were cremated alive! Had we arrived a half hour earlier, we might have prevented the tragedy. We found only a few survivors, 12 out of approximately four thousand. They survived by hiding under a brick building behind a latrine, thereby escaping a fiery, horrible death.

I found one of the guards hiding in the latrine. He surrendered without a word. I escorted him at gun point to an MP truck, to be transported to the POW interrogation point. Meanwhile one of the survivors sneaked up behind me and my prisoner. The inmate struck the guard's head with a timber, and I think the guard was dead before he hit the ground.

Our infantry flushed out two SS medical officers whom we learned had performed weird "medical" experiments on the inmates. We rushed those two out of the camp and turned them over to the War Crimes Commission. I saw those "doctors" a few months later, after they had been tried by a military tribunal for crimes against humanity. They were in the courtyard of Landsberg prison being escorted to the gallows.

You may recall, Landsberg prison is where Hitler wrote *Mein Kampf*, while confined as a criminal for his attempts to incite revolution. I watched the two "doctors" being led through the courtyard with their hands tied behind their backs, marched up the thirteen steps to the waiting hangman. On the gallows, prison guards (American MPs) bound their feet while their Death Warrants were read to them. A black hood was placed over their heads and they were hung.

The day following our entrance to the camp, 28 April 1945, we borrowed a fleet of trucks from the Division Quartermaster and proceeded to round up as many civilians as we could find in the town of Landsburg, including the Burgermeister, and brought them to see the atrocities.

Would you believe that no one admitted any knowledge of the camp? They told us they thought it was a secret war factory, so they didn't ask questions. They all defended Hitler, saying, "The Fuhrer knew nothing of this!" They all blamed Goring, Goebbles and Himmler, but not the Fuhrer. This camp was not the main camp of Dachau, but was known as Vernichtungslager No. 4/Dachau (Annihilation Camp No. 4 Dachau).

There are a few lunatics around today who say that the German concentration camps never existed, that it was only "war-time propaganda" intended to arouse antagonism. However we actually saw the horror of it all.

41

Five Years at Sea Around the World

Commander Elliott G. Dodge, Jr., USNR-Ret

As the war clouds formed over England, I volunteered as an apprentice seaman in 1940 and was commissioned as an Ensign in June 1941. I was assigned to commission the *USS Vulcan* (AR5), a 17,000 ton fleet repair ship with the largest foundry afloat. The last US Navy ship to be built in peacetime, it was built in Camden, New Jersey and named for the Roman God of Fire.

The *Vulcan* was commissioned on June 16, 1941 and had its shake-down cruise in the Caribbean. We relieved the *USS Prairie*, a destroyer tender, due to a fire on board. We moved to anchorage at Argentia Air Force Base, Newfoundland, within sight of two prominent mountains known as "Mae West". It was here in Placentia Bay that President Roosevelt and Prime Minister Churchill signed the Atlantic Charter setting the war aims of the Allies.

German submarines were playing havoc with Allied shipping in the North Atlantic. United States industry was supplying Great Britain with munitions and supplies of all kinds for its fight against Germany. The inevitable happened on October 31, 1941 when two supply convoy destroyers enroute to Iceland were attacked by German U-Boats.

The *USS Ruben James* was sunk and the *USS Kearney* (DD432) was torpedoed in its engine room. It crept slowly 300 miles to the *Vulcan* at Hvalfjordur, Iceland, and tied up alongside. A huge (36 by 17 foot) caisson was installed over the great gaping hole in its starboard side. No.1 engine room was pumped dry and reinforced with welded plates. No.2 engine room was put in operating shape in eight days, and under its own power the ship proceeded at 21 knots to Boston for rebuilding.

I remember with excitement receiving an urgent message, "*USS Vulcan* proceed to Hvalfjordur, Iceland. Serve as part of COMMANDER SERVICE SQUADRON FOUR, COMSERVLANT." After the huge expanse of the North Atlantic, it was a new experience to be in the giant deep-water Fjordur, only 20 nautical miles west of Reykjavik. We were protected from U-Boats by a net tender with its chain across the Fjordur entrance. Mt. Heckla, with its usual cloud bank, rose majestically above our anchorage.

Captain L.S.Fiske distinguished himself as our first Commanding Officer. The *Vulcan* immediately became SOFA (Senior Officer Afloat) with a flag officer and staff aboard. Hvalfjordur became our base for the next two years.

The *Vulcan* was a giant "Floating Navy Yard" whose 1,000 crewmen were split evenly between ship operations and the repair shops. She could repair everything, being 600 feet long and 75 feet wide. Her mission was to service and repair other fighting ships with the 40 shops and repair facilities on board.

After the attack on Pearl Harbor the alerts and "General Quarters" were frequent in anticipation of German air attacks. At times, as many as a hundred combat ships of the US Navy, the Coast Guard, and English and French fleets would be anchored at Hvalfjordur. US Navy PBY's made daily patrols out of Reykjavik against German subs, alert for Allied shipping under attack. Iceland's coastal fogs and mountains made those flights very hazardous, and resulted in the loss of many good Navy pilots.

Later in the war, after Russia had joined the fray, the German pocket-battleships *Graf Spee* and *Scharnhorst* preyed upon Allied convoys enroute to England and Murmansk.

The gulf stream passes close to Iceland, warming the southern coast of this glacier-covered island. As a result, even during winter months the temperature seldom drops below 15 degrees F. However, severe storms, together with heavy tides and currents buffet the coast,

USS Vulcan

making it impossible to return aboard the ship most afternoons. During one hurricane the *Vulcan* was forced to get underway, as did most ships in the fjord, to ease the tension on its two 15-ton anchors and avoid damage to the ship.

Originally, *Vulcan*'s main gun batteries consisted of two single 5-inch, .38 caliber dual purpose turrets, fore and aft, but it had only .50 caliber machine guns as a secondary means of defense. After Pearl Harbor, the *Vulcan* was fitted with twin 40mm guns and 20mm guns at Boston Navy Yard. The *Vulcan* returned to Hvalfjordur to continue its mission of repair work to various U.S. and Allied ships, and even some Soviet submarines. We did work on the radar mast of the French Battleship *Lorraine*, and did a complete overhaul aboard the Hellenic *HMS King George II.*

In April of 1943 the *Vulcan* sailed to Londonderry, Ireland, then to Portugal, and on a westerly course to the Norfolk Navy Yard for ship repairs.

In the Mediterranean on August 4, 1943 we sent a rescue and assistance detail in response to a fire aboard the British ammunition ship *HMS Arrow*. I was in command of one of the motor launches that responded. We were at considerable risk as shells were exploding on deck from the heat of the blaze. There were many casualties, with bodies floating in the water around us. Three of our men, at considerable peril, rescued men from the British ship. They were awarded medals from Britain and from our Navy and Marine Corps for their heroism.

Following the US invasion of North Africa, the *Vulcan* proceeded to that alabaster city of minarets, Algiers. By October 1943 the ship was moored alongside the French Algerian fortress of Mers-el-Kebir at Oran. Our mission was to support the Allied invasion of the Anzio beachhead in Italy, known as "Operation Shingle", which started January 22, 1944. Our work made it possible for more ships to remain "on-line" in support of the major amphibious assaults in Italy and Southern France.

In June, 1944, I was ordered to the *USS Dutchess* (APA 98) being commissioned at Sparrows Point, Maryland. This was a Liberty Ship built to serve as an attack transport in amphibious warfare. Under COMPHIBPAC my first duty as Navigator and Department head was to train our green officers and crew by operating out of Newport, Rhode Island, and this continued through the winter. In April, 1945 we picked up 2,000 marines and cargo at Portland, Oregon and on May 1, 1945 we off-loaded a Battalion Landing Team of the First Marine Division on Orange Beach, Okinawa. During the height of our ground, air and naval attack, for the next eight days, the US forces were subject to constant Japanese dive-bomber attacks at dawn and at twilight. Several ships were damaged, including the cruiser *USS Richmond*, which was hit by a Kamikaze abaft No. 2 turret, killing 40 men and officers.

On June 15 U.S. forces invaded Saipan. Three days later the Japanese were dealt a crushing defeat, losing three carriers in the Battle of the Philippine Sea. The U.S. Navy was then able to cover the Allies' return to the Philippines following the Battle of Leyte Gulf, another devastating defeat to the Japanese. At Manila Bay more than 600 Japanese ships were sunk by our Navy (more than half of the Japanese fleet).

We learned of the Japanese surrender on September 2, 1945 while the Duchess swung at its hook in San Francisco Bay. We then sailed to Japan in Task Unit 54.16, encountering a terrific typhoon enroute, forcing us to reverse course, while other ships were sunk. Later we anchored at Wakayama, Honshu, Japan and went on to Nagoya for the next two months. There we moored alongside a warehouse filled with coins minted for the Japanese occupation of China.

During the months in the Pacific, I navigated 55,574 miles throughout the Pacific area of operations. In all, I counted 61 months of sea duty aboard ships in the Caribbean, the North Atlantic, the Mediterranean and the Pacific waters. On March 5, 1946 I completed my terminal leave and was released from active duty. I continued to serve in the Reserves and retired with the rank of Commander.

Remarkably, in July 1991, I had the opportunity to visit the *USS Vulcan* at Virginia Beach, just after its return from service in "Desert Storm" and was privileged to celebrate, with some of my shipmates, the *Vulcan*'s 50 years of service in the US Navy. One month later the *Vulcan* was decommissioned.

Commander Dodge retired in 1976 from a full 30 year career as an executive in sales and engineering departments of U.S. Steel Corporation. He has been a long-time member of the Reserve Officers Association, serving a term as Nebraska Department President, and served for many years on the National Advisory Council. He has received the National ROA Minuteman Award for distinguished service.

42

Bombing Missions Over Europe

Major Marvin Kraft, USAFR-Ret.

In 1944, I had flown 25 missions with the 487th and 493rd Bombardment Groups of the 8th Air Force. Even though I spent only **six months** in England during the second world war, the scope, scale and intensity of the war was unique in my mind. Looking back, it seems we were on some kind of giant assembly line. We moved to a grand design.

I joined the 487th after second phase operational training, in Almogordo, New Mexico, in January 1944. I had just graduated from aerial navigation school. We went through the third phase OTU, which was the last phase of group training. We had a lot to learn at first, when we got to Europe. Training started immediately. The RAF and 8th AF had served a long apprenticeship. We had to pick up the latest procedures and tactics in that theatre of war. Several of our lead pilots went on a combat mission with another group on a mission to the Ruhr Valley (Happy Valley we called it.) The pilots were sent out to get combat experience. The flak was thick enough to walk on. One of the pilots was hit in the chest by a piece of shrapnel and knocked unconscious. His flak suit, an armoured vest, saved his life. He awoke to find a six inch piece of steel sticking out of his flak suit.

My combat missions began with our bombing railroad marshaling yards and bridges in France and Belgium. I remember taking my racing pulse as we first crossed the French coast in the area that was to become one of the D-day beaches. Our mission was to Troyes, France, where we bombed a bridge. The object of those missions was to isolate the battlefield and to disrupt enemy lines of communication before the invasion commenced. My second mission was to France, and the third to Germany. On my fourth mission, Colonel Lay, our C.O., was shot down over France. He was able to evade capture with the help of the French underground. One of Gen. Patton's units eventually was able to overrun the area where Col. Lay was working on a farm.

Shortly after starting to fly missions in the 487th, we received a message from the Nazi radio broadcasting system. They told us they knew we had arrived, that they knew our tail markings, and that they were going to give us what they gave to the 100th Bomb Group. That group was known to us to have been attacked and almost wiped out several times by the German Air Force. Someone in our group had been listening to the enemy propaganda and spread the word, however it did not frighten us. We calculated that they probably sent a similar message to every new group arriving in the theatre.

Nazi propaganda was not particularly effective. All of the English speakers spoke with heavy German accents. They did not understand us Americans at all. In addition, they devoted an hour to anti-American and pro-English propaganda, alternating with an hour of anti-English and pro-American propaganda. We listened to both, so it became transparent what they were trying to do. However we enjoyed their good music.

For the D-day landings, we had been practicing night takeoffs and landings. On D-day we took off at three or four a.m. and circled until dawn. Our plan was to bomb Caen, so that the German Panzer Divisions could not reach the beaches. Unfortunately, that did not happen. England had been blacked out, as it had been for years. Only coded beacons could be seen flashing below. We had been given the wrong flimsy for the codes. The splasher radio beacons were being meaconed, a type of jamming where the enemy receives your signal and rebroadcasts it after amplifying it a million times. Jamming was intense on all radio signals that night. Bomber groups were assembling all over the sky. We couldn't locate our group, so we joined up with another group and flew over France. The sky had begun to cloud over as we circled. Cloud cover became complete and in several layers below us. We could not drop our bombs. We flew over France for hours trying to find a hole or target of opportunity. Finally, low on gas, we flew back to England. Our plane had to land at a P-38 fighter base on the southern coast, since we were almost out of fuel. Fortunately, the fighter group needed our bombs desperately, and they were immediately loaded on fighters. We watched the P-38"s take off to use the bombs on enemy installations around the beaches.

The P-38 fighters had used up all of their bombs before we arrived. They had been heavily engaged in flying across the channel to France, under the clouds at almost tree top level, in support of the landings. Few bomb groups were able to get below the clouds to drop their bombs on targets. Fighters supplied most of the air support for the morning of the invasion. Many things went wrong that morning. The D-Day landing succeeded through the sheer weight of massed men and material thrown across the channel. That the German armed forces were relatively weak, we think, had something to do with our success.

We in the 8th Air Force had been working hard endeavoring to destroy the German Air Force by bombing their factories. They were forced to use their fighters against us, which we desired, so that our fighter escorts had the opportunity to shoot them down. Since the RAF was bombing at night, RAF fighters were often used in escorting our groups on bombing missions. I recall that the Spitfires approached us cautiously, showing their distinctive wing in silhouette. That was necessary since we fired on fighters if we were not certain they were friendly. If enemy fighters got closer than a thousand feet the probability was that they would destroy us.

By June of 1944, the German Air Force was too weak to attack bomber formations escorted by our fighters. They did attack cripples, bombers separated from the main formation, when not escorted by fighters. Bomber groups without fighter escort would be attacked also, as happened to us on one mission.

After D-day, the 487th became quite effective. We all became more proficient at what we were doing. Bombing accuracy increased, as lead crews were selected with care. Navigation improved. Bombing and navigation were determined by the lead airplane. The bombs of the entire formation were dropped following the lead bombardier's actions. Thus lead crews were most important to the success of any bombing mission.

The tempo of bombing activity increased with good weather. Our targets became railroad marshaling yards, bridges, V-1 launching ramps, German airfields, synthetic oil refineries, aircraft assembly plants, and German army concentrations in Normandy.

We flew on several carpet bombing missions against enemy armor concentrations. From the air the area bombed looked like a carpet on a smooth floor, thus the name. Carpet bombing was effective against enemy armor and troops, totally demoralizing the enemy. These missions were simple for us, since we did not have to contend with flak. There was a danger, however, since wind blew dust over the target and friendly troops were sometimes exposed to the bombing danger. A carpet bombing mission preceded Patton's breakout from Normandy in Operation Cobra. Several other such missions were scheduled but had to be canceled due to the fluid nature of the battlefield.

We were also used effectively against synthetic oil refineries deep inside Germany beyond the range of fighter cover. On one such mission our plane had a serious gasoline leak, filling the bomb bays with gasoline vapor. The pilot ordered us to stand by to jump, and we salvoed our bombs into the North Sea. Standing over the open bomb bay, looking down into the cold North Sea far below, with my parachute on my chest, I was terrified. It hurt to move, and I was numb with fear. Fortunately, we were able to shut off a valve ahead of the leak and were able to land the plane. On such aborts, we did not get credit for a mission.

I remember well my last mission. We had been sent to bomb a jet engine factory near Kiel. We faced an extraordinary amount of flak as we flew north to bomb our target from 25,000 feet. Three planes were lost from our group on that one mission.

Major Kraft served in the 8th AF as a navigation instructor, and as an air transport command navigator in the Pacific in World War II. He served as a troop carrier navigator in Japan and Korea in the Korean War 1950-51. In civilian life he worked as chemist and engineer until retirement.

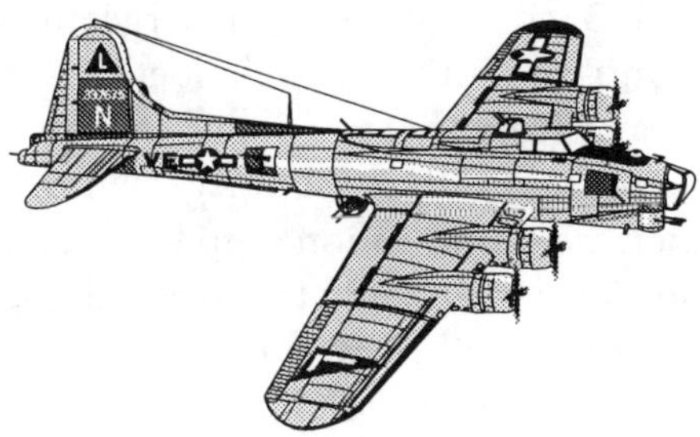

43

How To Get Their Attention

CWO4 Cyril H. Dorsk, AUS-Ret

Drafted in November, 1941, my prior exposure to uniformed training at the Culver Military Academy gave me a considerable advantage. This brought about an early promotion to Corporal, and I found myself in charge of a troop train that took us from basic training in California to Fort Eustis, Virginia. Uniquely, I was allowed a week-end pass for my birthday. Visiting relatives, my leave coincided with the Sunday Pearl Harbor attack. We were suddenly at war, and my uncle drove me back to Richmond, Virginia, to get the train back to camp.

In March of 1943, as a machine-gun sergeant with the 406th AAA Battalion, a 90mm anti-aircraft unit, we landed in Oran, Algeria. Later on we moved to Tunis and from there to Sicily, landing at Palermo, then over the mountains to the south coast at Agrigento. Only a few days later we watched an American ammunition ship blow up.

After four months we returned to North Africa to an airfield just outside of Algiers. One day, while walking in the town, I heard a voice in Yiddish say, "*Mirr doft noch a mensch far a minyon.*" I looked up and saw that I was in front of a synagogue, and as a Jew, I could not refuse him. I met the rest of the members of the synagogue and found that most of them wanted me to come to their homes to meet their daughters. Apparently the elders wanted me in their family so all could come to America!

Later on my unit again boarded ships and landed in Corsica, being taken by trucks to the other side of the island and bivouacked in total blackout. The next morning we were surprised to find we were sleeping in a cemetery that had been the recipient of many artillery shells from the Germans. There were broken caskets and dead bodies scattered all over the area. Needless to say we quickly moved to an open area and set up our guns. We could see the Jerry installations on the island of Elba, a short distance across from Corsica, where their aircraft were taking off and landing; however, they never attacked us.

Dorsk, as a Sgt., early 1945

While on Corsica I was able to attend high holy day services for the first time while overseas. We were on the island eleven months; long enough, we thought, to become citizens!

We again boarded ships bound for Marseille, France, where we turned in our anti-aircraft guns and were redesignated Combat Engineers. Our task was to build Engineer Depot #300, subsequently turned over to French troops.

Next, we were assigned the mission of building fixed bridges, including Bailey bridges, a pre-fabricated set of steel panels of British invention. We continued to build bridges across many rivers in Germany. We were annoyed to find that on some of these, signs were placed "Built by French Engineers".

While in Germany as Combat Engineers we were assigned the task of building a fixed bridge across the Neckar River. We needed a hundred young men, German civilians, to assist by building the approaches to the bridge. Since I spoke German, I was ordered to go to the Mayor and demand a work party of recently discharged German Army personnel who had been prisoners of war. They were to work twelve hour shifts, and we agreed to feed them one meal. However, we gave them additional rations for their families, since food was in short supply.

I and another sergeant who also spoke German were in charge of 50-man crews. One crew worked from noon until midnight, and the other completed the 24 hour cycle. I had the second shift. About 6 AM the next morning one of the Germans placed his shovel over his shoulder and started to walk away. I asked him where he was going and he replied that he had to go home for breakfast or his wife would be angry. I told him that if he left I would be angry. At the same time I took the Thompson gun off my shoulder and cocked it. Then I got a better idea. I unbuttoned my fly and started to pee. When the German crew saw that I had been circumcised, and took a look at my nose, they began to whisper to each other. I heard them say, "A Jew! An American Jew! They started to work like the Devil was after them. They accomplished three times the amount of work in the next six hours that they had accomplished in the first six!

Then, they proceeded to tell the next crew about my being a Jew. The sergeant who ran that crew told me later that his people also worked like demons, afraid that their sergeant might also be Jewish. Neither of us wanted to harm any of them, but they didn't know that nor did we want to reassure them. Needless to say, the bridge approaches were completed in record time and the commanding officer could not understand how we had inspired such industry from these recalcitrants.

With the end of the war in Europe, we prepared to move out to the Far East to fight the Japanese. Fortunately the war ended and we moved to Camp Lucky Strike in southern France to board a troop transport for home.

I joined the Army Reserve and became a Chief Warrant Officer, retiring after 34 years service. Some time later I resumed a military role in the California State Military Reserve, accepting a commission as Major, and retiring as Lieutenant Colonel after 5 years service as the Brigade Engineer.

LTC Dorsk in CSMR uniform, November, 1993

44

We Sank the Tokyo Express!

Commander Warren L. Craig, USNR-Ret

On January 29, 1943, our three ships left from the assembly depot at Noumea, New Caledonia with full loads of 94 Mark VI contact control (sea) mines, on our first offensive mission. My ship was the *USS Montgomery* (DM 17), accompanied by sister ships, *USS Tracy* (DM-19) and *USS Gamble* (DM-15), all old, slow destroyers from World War I.

We were using old mines from WWI, each holding 300 pounds of TNT—enough to break the back of any ship that exploded the mine.

Prior to this time, from April through December of 1942, our ships had laid 2,600 defensive mines in areas at Pago Pago, Samoa, Suva, Fiji, Efate in the New Hebrides, Noumea in New Caledonia, Tonga, Tabu and Dutch Harbor in the Aleutians, in the effort to impede the advance of the Japanese fleet.

Our Marines at Guadalcanal were having a hard time trying to stop the Japanese whose troops were being re-supplied at night by the "Tokyo Express", a task force of ships coming down from north of the Solomon Islands.

It was a moonless night when we steamed alongside Guadalcanal, smelling the pungent sweet odor of land, enroute to the area in which we had been instructed to lay a minefield. Suddenly, gunfire opened up on us from shore; we were then no more than 2,000 yards off shore, proceeding into position to plant our mines. Only the Montgomery was equipped with radar which picked up the beeps of the "Tokyo Express" approaching. We passed the information to the other two ships.

We were closing in on the enemy at 42 knots and had just 15 minutes in which to arm and plant our mines. All three ships inserted their loads of 94 mines and reversed course. Mines were released at 15 knots and we got out of there at flank speed of 26 knots.

This became the first offensive minefield to claim a victory over the Japanese Navy. Our mission became a total success—we lost no personnel in this engagement as the Japanese fleet steamed right over the minefield. They lost a cruiser, a destroyer, and many barges. The enormous explosions in the night sent Japanese destroyers out in force, dropping depth charges in the assumption that their cruiser had been torpedoed. Subsequently, our mines caught a destroyer. By that time an utterly confused Japanese naval commander tried to take his remaining ships out of the area, only to be further crippled by encountering additional mines.

A few days later, a big land-based American airplane swooped low, dipping its wings in salute two times, followed by more planes tipping their wings in salute to our relic mine layer destroyers so obsolete they were not suitable for more important tasks than laying mines. Our three ships received a royal welcome as we steamed back to port. Since we were on radio silence, our skipper was puzzled at the ovations until we found out about the chaos that our minefield had inflicted on the "Tokyo Express". Our work had resulted in many of their ships damaged and dead in the water. There were great oil slicks from sunken ships and hundreds of survivors were clinging to the unbelievable mass of floating wreckage drifting across several miles of ocean.

On the bridge of our newly honored ships we painted four Japanese flags. All three ship crews received the Presidential Unit Citation as well as congratulations from the Commander, South Pacific. Throughout the ranks of the fleet there was created a new appreciation for these old destroyers converted into mine-layers. We had won a great victory for what had been a lowly flotilla.

Commander Warren L. Craig has a twin brother, Wesley Craig, who served on Admiral Nimitz' staff, after his ship was sunk at Pearl Harbor. The brothers had entered the naval service at the same time and wanted to serve together, but regulations prohibited that. Wesley retired as a Captain. (They have another story in this collection).

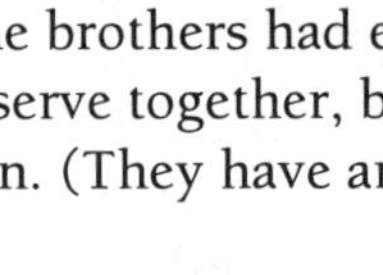

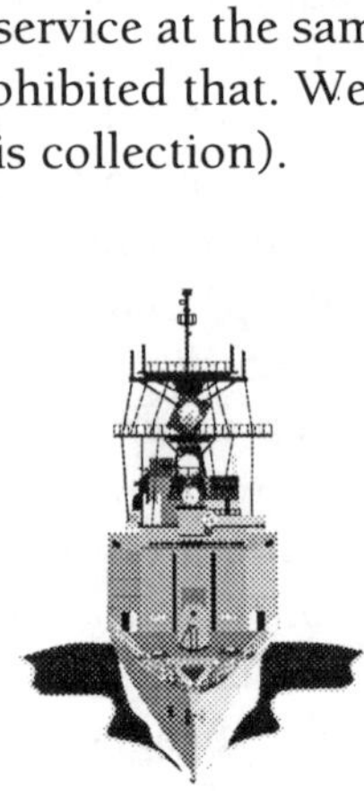

45

Victory Over Zeros

LTC Leonard W. Frame, USAF-Ret.

Lieutenant Colonel Frame was an early volunteer into flight training, entering in March 1941. After going through primary, basic, and then advanced flight training at Stockton, California in AT-6's; he graduated from flight school in October 1941 and was commissioned a Second Lieutenant. He moved on to Hamilton Field, where he was assigned to flying P-40's with the 20th Pursuit Group. Five days later he was assigned to the 70th Squadron, 35th Group, and went overseas with the 70th in January 1942 to Fiji.

Their group received 25 boxed single seat fighter bombers, which their crews assembled on their airstrip. Going on to Guadalcanal as a Captain, he had his first combat in March 1943. He flew his first mission there 11 March 1943.

On April 7th the Coast Watchers radioed that a large group of Japanese planes were headed towards Guadalcanal. I was sent, leading a flight of four P-39's to patrol over the Russel Islands. Since all of the fighters were on the same radio frequency, we heard the big fight going on over Guadalcanal, but nothing came our way in the air. After things settled down, we were ordered back to base. On the way back, my wing man called, 'Bogey, nine o'clock!' (unidentified airplane, off my left wing). It was going in the opposite direction. I whipped around and chased him. I came behind and a little below him. I fired one burst of my guns, and he flamed. The pilot bailed out, while we went on to home base.

One of the most famous missions of W.W.II was flown on April 18, 1943. Navy intelligence had been decoding and translating about 25% of the Japanese radio traffic. One such message was decoded on April 13th and distributed to Pacific Navy Commands. Commander Air, Solomons, was Rear Admiral Marc Mitscher. He received a copy of the message that gave the itinerary of Admiral Yamamoto, Commander In

Chief of the Japanese Navy. He was scheduled to make an inspection tour, leaving Rabaul in New Britain, going to Bougainville, and the message gave times of departure and arrival.

The only planes that had sufficient range to reach Bougainville and return were the P-38 Lightnings. P-38's had arrived in the area in November 1942. Several of my squadron mates had been assigned to fly the P-38's.

The mission was to intercept Admiral Yamamoto's plane just before it landed at Bougainville. Our planes flew within fifty feet of the water, out of sight of land, for about 435 miles, a two hour and 12 minute flight. The last few minutes they started to climb when within sight of land. They soon found two Japanese OB-01 heavy torpedo bombers and their escort of six "Zero" fighters.

Our interceptors included four P-38's for the "killer" attack and twelve for top cover. The "killer" flight attacked the "Bettys" and tangled with some of the "Zeros". One of the "Bettys", the one carrying Yamamoto, burned and crashed into the jungle. The other one was shot to pieces and crashed into the sea.

I was walking on the flight line on Fighter Two strip on Guadalcanal when the mission returned. I met Tom Lanphier, the leader of the "killer" flight as he was walking from his plane to the intelligence dugout for debriefing. I asked, "How did it go, Tom?" He replied, "We got the S.O.B.!" However, there still exists controversy over who shot down which plane.

My first tour of duty on Guadalcanal ended with a flight on April 20, 1943. I was scheduled for R&R in New Zealand, however there were

Captain L.W. Frame, 70th Fighter Squadron, Fiji, 1942, sitting in his P-39 fighter.

eight P-39s at New Hebrides that were to be ferried to Fiji, and I led that flight. Following a C-47, for navigation, we flew to Efate, then, following two B-117s to Fiji. After the ferry trip, I did get a week's leave in New Zealand. Then I returned to Guadalcanal, through Fiji.

I reported to our detachment commander. He told me I was to take a search mission the next morning. I protested that I wanted to get settled, but he insisted. There were three search missions that left at or before dawn every morning, with two P-39s for each mission. I was assigned to lead a mission scheduled to follow a prescribed course,

Painting entitled "First Victory" by artist Skip Rains of Capt. L. W. Frame, pilot off Cape Esperance, Guadalcanal.

Captain L.W. Frame, 70th Fighter Squadron, Fiji, 1942.The tail art depicts "Elsie", the name of his plane.

proceeding north, then west, north again, then east, and back south to base. We were on the westerly leg when a Japanese "Betty" bomber showed up, heading east. We each made three firing passes at it. When I pulled up after my third attack, it was flaming at the left wing root. We watched it land under control in the water 30 or 40 miles from land.

As we returned to base, I motioned with my hands to my wing man that we should do a "victory roll". He motioned that I should do it. I made a low pass over the runway, pulled the nose up a little and did a slow roll, then went on to land. Since there had been no air contact with the enemy for several weeks, this created a little excitement on the field.

On June 16, 1943, the Coast Watchers again reported many Japanese planes heading our way. When the controllers finally scrambled us, it was almost too late. My flight of four P-39s met a flight of six or eight "Zeros" head-on at six or seven thousand feet. We were climbing and they were diving. Although we fired at them, we didn't see any results, however a "Zero" crashed near our camp that ground observers said was shot down by a P-39. After the initial pass, I made about two turns. I couldn't see another plane in the sky. Making a few more turns, then looking over my left shoulder, I saw a "Zero" firing at me. I did a half-roll and dove away. Just as my wing came up in the roll, one of his cannon shells hit my left wing, right next to the fuselage. My dive got me away from that attacker, then I picked up my wing man. We found a group of six or eight planes, P-40s and Wildcats chasing one "Zero" right over the water. We joined in and made two passes. On the second one, the enemy was coming head-on and pulled up near us. We fired and as he went over my head I could see he was flaming. The "Zero" crashed into the water.

As we approached to land, my wheels would not come down; I had to crank them down by hand. When I did land, the left tire was flat. However, I was able to control the plane on the ground and just pulled off to the side of the runway.

The cannon shell that hit the wing sent a splinter through the side of the cockpit that scratched my ankle. I checked into the medical tent where they cleaned my lower leg and put a band-aid on it. I went to camp, took a shower and washed the band-aid off, however I received the Purple Heart.

The last missions I flew from Guadalcanal were on the 12th and 14th of July 1943, providing cover for the taking of Munda. This gave me a (Northern Solomons Campaign) battle star for the Asiatic-Pacific Theatre Campaign ribbon. I was awarded the Distinguished Flying Cross and the Air Medal with six Oak Leaf Clusters for my flying.

Following the completion of my second tour on Guadalcanal I was assigned to Headquarters as Group Operations Officer. Subsequently I was given leave to return home, and then had assignments in the United States and in the Caribbean. Following the Japanese capitulation, I was released from active duty. Continuing in the reserves I was promoted to Lieutenant Colonel in 1955 and retired in 1977. In civilian life I have a dairy farm near Fresno, California.

LTC L.W. Frame, USAF-Ret, 1990

46

Four Pacific Island Campaigns in Thirteen Months

Jack B. Claven

Jack Claven had some exposure to military matters before entering the Marines in October of 1942. His father had been an artillery officer in W.W.I, and had frequently spoken to Jack of his experiences in the artillery.

Ever since I was a kid, all I heard about was the artillery. Consequently, I began to bug my First Sergeant about a transfer to an artillery unit. So much so that one day he came up to me with a Browning Automatic Rifle (BAR) and told me "Claven, this will be your artillery for the duration."

Immediately, I fell in love with my BAR. Although it served me well in battle, the Japanese found it to be disconcerting, to say the least. I fired many hundreds of rounds through it in battle.

My first action was in the landing on Roi-Namur Island, Japanese mandated territory in the Marshall Islands. It was a short campaign, where I contributed to the "Sayonara" of some Japanese at ranges of 100 yards or more.

It is better to recall some of the amusing incidents of our duty. On Roi-Namur one of our guys fell into a "Honey-Hole", (what was left after the outhouse had been blasted away) and had to be dragged back to the beach and thrown into the ocean for cleansing. Another smelly situation happened one night on Saipan when a large Japanese truck (comparable to our 6x6) came roaring toward our lines. When about fifty yards out, we opened fire. The vehicle exploded and burned half the night. We hadn't known that it was a "Honey-Wagon", and with the wind blowing towards us, we suffered what they now call "Undue Stress."

The next landing, on the beach at Sharon Kanoa (Saipan) was more dangerous than Roi-Namur. We were ordered to attack over the sea wall while under extremely heavy artillery and machine gun fire. Upon thrusting my BAR over the parapet, I came face to face with an enemy rifleman only twenty-five yards away. We looked at each other in complete surprise for what seemed like minutes. Probably only a few seconds elapsed before I squeezed the trigger, which separated his head from his shoulders. Over that short distance the barrel of my flash-hider must have been as scary as a 37 mm cannon. Looking back, it was a hairy experience, when you consider that had one more second elapsed, I could have been the victim.

Although we lost a large number of men in various skirmishes on Saipan, an especially bad day for my Company occurred on July 4, 1944. We were suckered into an ambush, wherein we sustained extremely heavy casualties, including myself. I have an indelible memory of the afternoon. Our company commander, Captain Bill Martin led us up a steep open area on Mt. Topoccha. We were suddenly ambushed by a large Japanese force, hidden in the trees and brush. My BAR was almost too hot to touch, when I was hit by a machine gun bullet.

Our Gunnery Sergeant ordered me off the hill to a temporary aid station, where a Corpsman gave me a shot of morphine. While lying there, one Corpsman asked me to put my arm beneath a fellow Marine's head, while he injected him with glucose. The man was shot up badly, bloody from the chest up, so muddy and with a heavy beard that I didn't recognize him for some minutes. A short time later the Corps man came over, pulled the plug, and pronounced him dead. By this time, curiosity got the best of me, so I looked at his dog tags and stared in disbelief. His

Jack Claven with BAR

name was Norman Kajewski, a buddy from the Company, who had enlisted with me at Buffalo, New York.

The worst action that I was in occurred later during the invasion of the volcanic island of Iwo Jima, 660 nautical miles south of Tokyo, in February of 1945. Whenever I think of that God forsaken bit of Hell, I remember it like a nightmare. The Japanese had reworked the eight square miles of volcanic rock and ash into the most impregnable fortress in military history.

Never have I witnessed so many men made casualties in such a short period of time. We were being clobbered from three sides, while we had no protection whatsoever. It was devastating! Out of 250 men in the company that landed on Iwo Jima on February 19, only six were left. The rest were killed or wounded. Much has been written about the Iwo Jima campaign. It was the bloodiest battle in Marine history. I will not elaborate much further, but I pray to God that no American will ever have to face a slaughter like that again. I begrudgingly admit that the 21,000 Japanese on that island were soldiers of the highest caliber and that they defended the island admirably. Their defenses were all but impregnable, and they fought as well as American Marines. However, no enemy force in the world can whip the U.S. Marines on any given day. Yet the taking of the island cost the lives of 6,821 Marines and Navy personnel, plus the loss of about 19,000 wounded men.

A vivid memory of mine revolves around an incident I shared with a close buddy, L. W. "Jo-Jo" Faulkner, who was my assistant BAR gunner. Whenever I made a move, and I made some crazy maneuvers at

Jack Claven with L.W. "Jo-Jo" Faulkner

times, "Jo-Jo" was right behind me and ready to help out. During the third morning on Iwo Jima we had orders to conduct a surprise attack prior to any artillery bombardment. When someone said "Go!", I shot out of my hole in a Gung-Ho charge. Just then we were hit with a hail of rifle, machine gun, and mortar fire. While still charging I looked around to find everyone back in their holes. I suddenly felt like Lady Godiva abandoned without a horse. Shortly I found myself about fifty yards in front of the lines looking for a hole. I soon spotted one, and although it appeared too shallow, it was better than nothing. About ten feet before reaching it, some Jap soldier nailed me with a Nambu (the Japanese version of an automatic rifle, a light machine gun with a bipod attached, a 30 round magazine, similar to our BAR). I rolled into a hole, only to have "Jo-Jo" pile in on top of me. I figured this was a fox hole, therefore I told him to get out. But it wasn't in his creed to leave me without help. He told me later that I got up on one knee and pumped every clip of BAR ammo I had into a trench full of Japanese soldiers, while "Jo-Jo" was trying to bandage my wound. I was so excited that I didn't recall firing all those rounds until he told me later.

Jack Claven (left) and John Harin in khakis, I Co., 3rd Bn, 23rd Marines, 4th Marine Division, 1942, Camp Le Jeune, NC

Soon after I was hit, we heard our tanks approaching, and the artillery barrage commenced hitting the enemy. When one of our tanks was approximately 15 or 20 yards away, "Jo-Jo" shot out of the hole in a mad dash, got on the tank's phone, and asked that they pull over the hole and take me up through the escape hatch. The tank commander refused, but he said he would pull alongside my hole. If "Jo-Jo" would direct the tank's 75 mm gun, he would pin down the enemy's position. This he did, and the next thing I knew, I was on "Jo-Jo's" shoulders while he raced back to our lines. He did not zig-zag, mind you, he ran straight as an arrow. He knew the shortest distance between two points. We must have appeared awfully silly, being the only two men above ground racing down the slot, especially since he was taller than I, and both of us were over six feet tall. In that 150 yard jaunt back neither one of us was hit, but "Jo-Jo" found four bullet holes in his baggy trousers.

The last member of my Company who remembers seeing us racing along was Sgt. Mumm. He called out, "Go, Go, Go!"

It was a happy reunion when, many years later, I met "Jo-Jo" again. He said the only reason he saved me was that it was my turn to buy the beer. Since then we became close friends, and, to my dying day, I will always remember "Jo-Jo" Faulkner, not only because he saved my life, for he exemplified the phrase, "Marines take care of their own." I was very sad to hear of his passing on to the Gates of Heaven.

Upon coming home, after a period of time in the hospital in New Caledonia, following my becoming a casualty on Iwo Jima, I felt it was my duty to call upon the parents of my friend Norman Kajewski. We had written home, speaking about each other. I paced the sidewalk for at least thirty minutes, trying to drum up the courage to knock on the door. Finally I did and when the door opened his dad knew who I was and what I was there for. Although they treated me as if I were their own son, the tears and sadness expressed by his entire family caused me to think that the occasion was more difficult than having been back on Iwo Jima in battle. That sad visit was probably the most difficult task I have ever had to undertake.

In closing, let me add, all Americans should be reminded of Iwo Jima, the Normandy invasion, and other epic battles where America sacrificed so many of her young men in the defense of freedom. *Semper Fi!*

Jack Claven became the National President, 4th Marine Division Association, and contributed several articles to the division history, from which most of this chapter was reassembled.

47

Interrogation Experiences

Major Walter Tanaka, USA-Ret.

After being drafted into the Army on June 2, 1941, I received basic training in infantry heavy weapons at Camp Roberts, California during the summer. On the morning of the Japanese attack on Pearl Harbor, I was on pass visiting cousins, but immediately returned to my unit at Fort Ord.

Some of us spent the night with our unit in the hills of Fort Ord loading ammunition into canvas machine gun belts. The following day, "H" Company departed to the Sonoma County Fair Grounds, and deployed to machine gun positions on the sand dunes of Dillon's Beach in Marin County.

Later as a volunteer I entered Military Intelligence Service Language training. In early March 1943, as a part of an Air Technical Intelligence Team, I embarked on a long voyage to Australia. In Brisbane, my team was assigned to the U. S. Fifth Air Force and attached for duty with the Allied Translator and Interpreter Section (ATIS), Intelligence Section, GHQ, U.S. Army Forces, Southwest Pacific Command, later known as U.S. Army Forces, Pacific.

My duty during the period March 1943 to August 1945 was interpreter of the Japanese language in assisting Allied officers (American, Australian, British and Dutch) in the Interrogation of Japanese air prisoners of war throughout Australia, New Guinea and the Philippine Islands.

During the earlier period of interrogations, in Australia, the morale of the Japanese prisoners was very high and I faced some arrogant prisoners. Some refused to talk. However, nearly all Japanese prisoners finally realized the utter futility of their attitude of non-cooperation. In their minds they had already committed a crime worse than death by allowing themselves to be captured. They felt therefore that they could never again set foot on their homeland. Prisoners were initially shocked to see an interpreter who looked Japanese and also spoke his language.

They then responded favorably to sympathetic and kind treatment. They begged that they never would be required to be returned to their homeland.

Tactical information about enemy aircraft and personnel identifications, strengths and capabilities were obtained. Strategic information regarding critical and important targets in Japan and enemy forward bases were also obtained from the prisoners.

One detailed study was made of enemy aircraft tail markings to identify the unit, the type of aircraft, its capabilities and the training and skill of its pilots. The prisoner drew sketches of the plane and its markings to assist in the identification.

I was involved in another study and research regarding the Kamikaze attacks. While serving with the advance echelon of ATIS at Hollandia, New Guinea, in late 1944 or early 1945, our first knowledge of these was when a Japanese prisoner disclosed information that the Japanese Navy was in the process of shipping "Suicide" torpedoes (the interrogation officer called them "Baka" bombs) to a forward base area. The prisoner believed that the forward base area might be Taiwan or the Philippines but was not certain.

Tokko Tai was the Japanese abbreviation for *Tokubetsu Kogeki Tai* or Special Attack Units, which were units of suicide pilots. The term *Kamikaze* translated into Divine Wind in the English language but was the word used by Americans to refer to Japanese suicide pilots and suicide units.

According to the prisoner's description, the Suicide Torpedo was called *Ohka*. It weighed approximately 2,000 pounds, had a very short wing span or stabilizers, and had rockets with a minimum amount of propulsion. The suicide torpedo was carried aloft by a Japanese Navy bomber and launched approximately 20 miles from American shipping, both transports and warships, and navigated by a pilot who targeted the American shipping. The flight of the torpedo was a one-way suicide mission. The torpedo had only limited maneuverability. The prisoner had only a limited knowledge of the weapon and was not able to provide any additional information. Additional Japanese air prisoners were interrogated for information regarding these human torpedoes, more

commonly known as "Kamikazis" . With the end of the war with Japan I received a direct field commission as a 2d Lieutenant in the Army and was dispatched to G-2, U.S. Eighth Army in Leyte, Philippines, to serve in the occupation of Japan as a linguist officer. In two tours of duty in Japan, I served with the Eighth Army, the 1st Cavalry Division and in the Counter Intelligence Corps. My final tour of duty in the Army was in South Korea. I retired from the Army after twenty years of service, retiring as a major.

Editor's note: The term *Kamikaze*, originated by Vice Admiral Takejiro Onishi, stood for "Devine Wind" and referred only to Navy aircraft, while the army termed theirs *Tokko Tai*. During the later part of the War, the Japanese used 1,228 of these, which sank 34 U.S. ships and damaged many more.

Lt. Walter Tanaka, 1945

48

Fighting the Kamikaze

Major General Sidney S. Novaresi, USAF-Ret.

Flying the Republic P-47 Thunderbolt, considered to be the most versatile fighter of W.W.II, I had to deal with the attacks of the "Kamikaze" against our cargo vessels and combat naval units conducting combat operations against Japanese forces on Okinawa. "Kamikaze" in Japanese means "Divine Wind", and a "Kamikaze Pilot" was a member of the Japanese air attack corps in W.W.II assigned to make a suicidal crash on a target, normally an enemy ship. They were extremely effective, I believe that history records that during the battle for Okinawa they sank 32 Allied ships and damaged four hundred others.

There were two different flying machines used by the Japanese to execute their "Kamikaze" attacks. One was a conventional airplane, normally a fighter type, containing high explosives to be flown in a conventional manner by a pilot in a suicide attack on a target. The other was to carry an "Ohka Bomb" called (Cherry Blossom) in the bomb bay of a modified "Betty Bomber' fly it to the target and release it. The "Ohka" had a tiny cockpit that would accommodate a pilot who would after drop, steer the vehicle to its target crashing onto or into the selected ship. The "Ohka" was a tiny winged vehicle with a 2,646 lb. warhead in its nose, and was flown like a glider since it was not powered. It did have three tiny rockets with 8 to 10 seconds of burn but they did not give it any capability to outrun Allied fighters or any range. It was carried and launched from the bomb bay similar to our X-15 experimental efforts at Edwards AFB, with exception that the X-15 was dropped from a wing pod. It was extremely difficult to defend against either one of the attackers since the pilots of both vehicles were locked into their cockpits. The missions were one way, and the pilot began his journey knowing that there was no turning back. They were treated to a fine meal of rice and fish, washed down with plenty of Sake, and sent on their way.
As a matter of fact the "Kamikaze" that hit the supply ship carrying

the equipment for my fighter group was one of those. The skipper of the ship was standing on the bridge when the Japanese Zero hit the side of his ship just below the bridge. The Captain ended up with the pilots jaw bone in his hand and partly digested rice all over him.

My involvement with the "Kamikaze" occurred while I was assigned to the 413th Fighter Group, 21st Fighter Squadron, flying off Ie Shima just across the water from Okinawa. In order to provide an early warning of imminent Japanese air attacks on Okinawa and surrounding Islands the Navy supplied packages of naval vessels, usually made up of two destroyers and three destroyer escorts, coded "Two DE's and three small boys." These packages were distributed around the Islands in two circles making up two rings, one at 50 miles off shore, and the other ring at two hundred miles. I don't recall the distance between the packages following one another, but probably 200 miles. This effort was called "Picket Patrol", and was the early warning system for that portion of the Ryukus Island chain.

My involvement was that the fighter units on Ie Shima had to fly "Combat Air Patrol" (CAP) over these naval units. The casualty rate of the "Picket Patrols" was extremely high since the Japanese obviously had to take the eyes of the U.S. air defense forces away so that they could execute their air attacks on Okinawa successfully. Therefore, a flight of four fighters had to be over these individual naval packages every second from dawn to dusk. The folks on the ships of the "Picket Patrols" were so nervous about their safety that it became a court martial offense for any flight leader who left his station before his relief flight was in sight. At times this became a problem to the flight leader on station when the relief was late and his flight was running out of fuel. I have been that flight leader. That's when your vision became 5/5 and you could see the specks of your relief flight far far away.

We were successful in shooting down some of the conventional aircraft deliveries, however the "Ohka" proved to be a little trickier. For one, it was very small and hard to hit, number two, in a high powered diving attack to catch up with them before they hit the target, caused a high overshoot problem because of their slow speed, 288 MPH. This meant that an attacking fighter had only seconds to pick them up in the gun sight and fire before he was instantly attempting to avoid a midair collision with a lot of high explosives. I had two occasions to chase them but never caught up in time to keep the pilot from flying the bomb to its selected target. Perhaps we have a "Sailor" in our Department of California ROA who was assigned to "Picket Patrol" duty and could fill in with his experience from the surface point of view.

There were several personal dislikes that I had for (CAP) over "Picket Patrols". One was the monotony of four hours of zigging and zagging over the "Picket Patrols", another was being out of sight of land in a single engine fighter, the engine always sounded rough out there. Because (CAP) was flown below 10,000 feet the heat generated in a bubble canopy of a fighter with the sun beating down dehydrated the pilot excessively. The fact that we did not get credit for a mission while on any (Fighter CAP), unless the enemy was engaged, created a lack of enthusiasm for (CAP's). The only good thing about "Picket Patrol" (CAP) was that when you spotted a "Kamikaze" attack you knew that they were not after you and that you could take some risks in the attack on a "Kamikaze" that a fighter pilot ordinarily would not take in a conventional "Dog Fight", plus you got credit for a mission because the enemy had been engaged.

General Novaresi began his military career in the California National Guard with the 143rd Field Artillery Regiment, of the 40th Division, and reached the rank of Regimental Sergeant Major as a Master Sergeant prior to becoming an Aviation Cadet. He graduated from pilot training October 1, 1943 and after combat crew training at Seymour Johnson Army Airfield, Goldsboro N.C. flew a combat tour in the P-47 Thunderbolt in the South Pacific Theater during WWII. During the Korean and Viet Nam conflicts the General flew fighters and heavy airlift aircraft. During his service he commanded units from squadron up to and including a numbered air force. The General retired June 26, 1982 from the Pentagon.

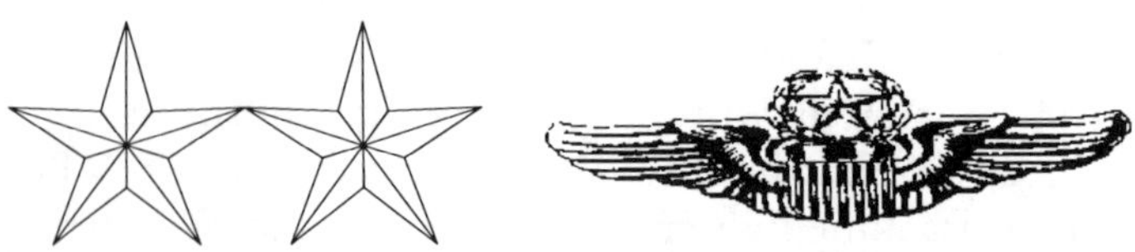

49

Scratch One Battleship

Lt. Comdr. Charles Dickey, USNR-Ret.

This is the thrill-packed story of one of the most successful and fortunate air-strikes of W.W.II, told by an officer who took part.

Every pilot has a beautiful dream stored away in the recesses of his brain-nacelle, and in leisure moments fondly day-dreams it over and over—visions of lightning blows through the ether to strike the enemy a death-blow. The ultimate dream of a carrier pilot is his air group sinking an enemy battleship—that mobile gunnery platform that treaties are broken over, that nations gauge their sea powers by, and wars are lost for lack of; the steel terror that is the scourge of the high seas and the basis of an international naval strategy.

Sometimes dreams come true. For Air Group Twenty, the dream became a reality on the afternoon of October 24, 1944, in the Sibuyan Sea of the Philippine Islands.

On October 20, our task force cruised east of Leyte. For days we had been attacking Japanese air and shipping power in Okinawa, Formosa and the Philippines in advance of the landing operations. Our orders had been to eliminate as much opposition as possible before the invasion. Now our orders were to protect and secure the invasion from any Japanese threat.

The ground troops went ashore under an aerial coverage from our carriers and a barrage from our bombardment forces. No major enemy surface vessels and few planes resisted the landings the first day. But it takes weeks to secure an invasion. Our troops had little more than a beach-head; valuable supplies in helpless transports were waiting to be unloaded; and the Japanese were recovering from their initial surprise. Our cards were on the table, and the stakes were the Philippines. That night the Nipponese wireless operators worked overtime.

The morning of the twenty-second, news of the Japanese fleet having sortied reached our ready-room. And by the night of the twenty-third, word from our scouting submarines and patrol planes assured us the enemy was at sea and up to no good.

Early on the twenty-fourth, carrier based search-planes equipped with extra gas-tanks went roaming through the central and southern Philippines. They and the subs and patrol bombers did a brilliant scouting job. The strategy was now clear. The Japanese did not intend to relinquish the Philippines without a struggle. They were sending all of their available men-of-war to combat our invasion. Their fleet would have complete freedom of movement west of the Islands and through the Islands. Our fleet, steaming east of Leyte, could not possibly intercept with surface vessels unless the Japanese ventured on to our side. We could not risk taking our ships through the narrow, mined waters of San Bernardino or Suriagao straits, the only passages from east to west. Nor, if we penetrated and eluded the mines, could we risk our ships to the attack of enemy planes, who, though rapidly diminishing, were still a potent threat. There was only one way we could attack the approaching Japanese at that time—with carrier-based planes. The strategy was over. Tactics took control.

This is not the story of the Second Battle of the Philippine Sea. It is the story of only one of many strikes made against the enemy fleet by Air Group Twenty. The story of a handful of planes striking capital ships to protect vulnerable ground troops and anchored transports from sixteen-inch rifles. The story of planes made of aluminum against a battleship with fifteen-inch steel armor.

I was in the torpedo ready-room around eleven hundred, when the ticker-tape from air-plot came chattering through, We gathered anxiously by as the words came out one by one, "Stand by to launch 8 VY, 9 VR, 16 VF at 1300. Loading—Avengers torpedoes—Helldivers two 1,000 lb. semi-armor piercing bombs—Hellcats four rockets." This was followed by navigation and weather data. Our squadron flight officer, Lt. Robert McHenry, of Evanston, Illinois, got out his little black book and began making the flight schedule. He walked to the

blackboard and wrote: "Lt. Comdr. Prickett leading Holley, Trowbridge, Schaller; Second division, McHenry, Dickey, Ross, Swint." Then he ducked out the nearest door and ran, as a barrage of pilots descended upon him clamoring for a place on the schedule.

The minutes ticked by as we climbed into our flying suits, checked our Mae Wests, worked our navigation, and talked over tactics. Thirty minutes before launching time, Cmdr. D. F. Smith, Jr., the Air Group Commander, called over the squawk-box from his office: "All right, boys, the Jap fleet is out there today. Anybody that doesn't get a hit may as well keep going. Cmdr. Smith, always known among us as the Commander, is a helluva fighter pilot, and any of us would rather risk the anger of the Lord than incur the wrath of the Commander. There was no alternative. We all had to get hits.

The squawk-box opened up from air-plot. "Pilots, man your planes." We hastily gathered our gear as the other pilots looked enviously on and then gave the usual deep, warm farewells. "Good luck!" and "Give 'em hell!"

Outside on the windy flight deck, eight torpedo pilots under Lt. Comdr. Prickett, nine dive-bomber pilots under Lt. Cooper, and fifteen fighter pilots under Lt. Comdr. Lawler, and Cmdr. Smith as overall commander, climbed into the loaded planes. Plane captains fastened safety belts, and then over the bull-horn came: "Stand by ready to start engines!" An interval; then, "Stand clear of propellers!" and the final, "Start engines!"

The flight-deck roared with the sound of thirty-three engines closely crowded together on the pitching platform. Pilots made last-minute adjustments, checking gas and instruments, as a series of signal flags were hoisted to the island yardarm. The ship started a turn, and as she came gracefully into the wind, the Air Offficer held up a tiny green flag. The first plane, a Hellcat, screamed down the wooden deck. We followed him, one by one, as he headed for the assigned rendezvous sector off the starboard quarter.

The torpedo bombers joined up behind the dive bombers, and with Lt. Cooper leading, we turned westward toward the Island of Samar. The fighters flew above and below us, weaving from beam to beam, a defensive tactic designed to protect bombers from enemy fighters.

The sun shone brightly through the scattered cumulus clouds while below us a fifteen-knot wind blew white spray across the blue swells. It was a beautiful day for an attack. Enough cloud cover to allow protective maneuvering but not so much as to obscure a target. Not enough wind to cause error in the dive-bombing. Enough sun to blind the enemy as we dived from its concealing rays. The elements were with us.

The green coast of Samar appeared in the distance and gradually took shape as we closed, slowly climbing for altitude. As we passed over a cove into enemy territory, our formation tightened while the wary Hellcats continued their ceaseless vigilance. The Commander, like a huge eagle guarding his young, weaved back and forth across us, scouting the horizon for enemy planes. We passed Japanese airfields and entered the Visayan Sea. We were in the middle of invaded land, with scores of air strips around us. But no plane arose to contest our intrusion. The Hellcats had done their jobs too well in the preceding days.

As we neared Masbate Island, we could see native villages and small fishing boats. The shoal water was clear and green and looked inviting, for our engines were running warm, as we had leaned our gas mixtures to conserve fuel, and the enclosed cockpits were heating. But perhaps the bodily heat was from nervous tension as we drew nearer to the Japanese fleet.

Over Masbate, we received a radio transmission giving a later position report on the enemy. We swung farther northward toward the Sibuyan Sea, still climbing for altitude. I was flying wing on Lt. McHenry, which caused me to scan the territory northwestward. Suddenly I saw the Japanese fleet.

In perfect cruising disposition were two task groups three miles apart. This was a moment I had anticipated for hours, dreamed of for months, and trained for, for three years, but it was with difficulty I could bring my senses to the realization of its actuality. It was so overwhelming in its sudden existence that a full comprehension of its imminence could only slowly penetrate my nervous system. An uncontrollable emotional surge of joy, fear, hatred, and anxiety filled my throat crying for a release. I reached for the microphone and called my crew. “Holy hell, there’s the whole Jap fleet!”

Commander Smith’s voice came over the air, cool and reassuring: “There they are, boys. Let’s close with ‘em now.”

We closed on them. As the dim hulls began to emerge into definite shapes, I resolved to remember all of the details of the impending attack for the interrogation I would receive from the Intelligence Officer on returning to our carrier. First, I counted the enemy ships. There were twenty-five. I repeated. There were twenty-seven. In exasperation, I asked my crew for a tally. Cook, my radioman, counted twenty-six. The gunner, McLaughlin, counted twenty-five. They must have been as excited as I.

When we were fifteen miles away, the Japanese opened fire with the main batteries of their larger ships. We could see the initial salvos as the smoke enveloped the turrets. Seconds later the shells burst wide of us. Nothing to worry about as yet.

The ships were a clear silhouette now. I recalled the countless hours I had spent in dull recognition classes. If I were unable to count them accurately, perhaps I could at least identify a few. But my mind had gone blank with excitement. I couldn't remember words like *Haguro, Suzuya* and *Yamashiro* . I could only tell that some were very large. Those would be battleships. The medium-sized would be cruisers, and the smaller ones destroyers. It was not until I returned to our ship that I learned the fleet composition.

The eastern group was composed of two battleships, four cruisers and six destroyers. The western group had two battleships, four cruisers, and eight destroyers. The force was cruising at twenty knots on a course of 090 degrees, headed for the San Bernardino Strait and our invasion troops at Leyte Gulf. Against this armada, Cmdr. Smith had seventeen planes loaded with bombs and torpedoes. We could not hope to knock out more than one ship.

The Commander unhesitatingly made the decision. "Swing to the south of the force, and we'll attack the big bastard in the western group out of the sun!" It was easy to see which ship he meant. Even at fifteen miles, the *Musahi* was much larger than any other ship in the entire force. Other air groups, and later the Seventh Fleet, would not have to contend with the largest ship in the Japanese Navy.

The *Musashi*, sister ship of the *Yamamato* , was designed by the Nipponese to counter our *Iowa* class battleship. In the international construction race the 45,000-ton *Musashi* surpassed anything the British, French or Italians manned, and was equaled only by the German's *Bismarck* . It was the supership of the Imperial Navy, designed to outshoot any but the newest of our battleships. I shuddered to think of its terrific probable armament:

9 – 16 inch triple turret
6 – 6.1 inch triple turrets
24 – 5 inch twin and antiaircraft turrets
16 – 4.7 inch antiaircraft mounts
16 – 25 millimeter quadruple antiaircraft mounts
6 – MG antiaircraft mounts. A veritable floating gun gallery.

To get "up-sun," we swung south of the force and headed westward, still climbing to gain the vital altitude needed for our attack. Added height meant more speed in our dives, and the Japanese gunners would have to swing their guns faster to follow our flight-paths. A few knots might mean the difference between life and death.

The enemy fleet countered our flanking by starting a slow turn to starboard, so that their bows faced us at all times. Their forward batteries were firing faster as the interval had narrowed to twelve miles. The white wakes of the churning screws were outlined in a symmetrical pattern of blue as the enemy Admiral executed his aggressive battle tactics. Suddenly, we noticed the *Musashi*, with a *Mogami* cruiser and *Teratsuki* destroyer, turning to port. This was putting an interval between them and the main body that, however slight, would be to our advantage, because the antiaircraft fire would be a little more dispersed. We needed every advantage.

We couldn't understand the *Musashi's* action. Perhaps the ship's captain had made an error. Or perhaps the arrogant monster had been previously wounded by a scouting submarine, though she showed no outward sign of injury. Whatever the reason, we were glad. When we ran the gauntlet of screening cruisers and destroyers, there would be a few less guns bearing on us.

As the Japanese slowly followed our planes, the antiaircraft shells became more frequent and accurate. The gunners were correcting their mistakes in deflection and range. Huge phosphorus shells would burst near us, throwing discs of shining silver end over end for a hundred yards. Double bursting shells were coming alarmingly close, any one large enough to tear a formation of planes into scrap metal.

Shells would burst above and below, fore and aft. We could see the belching batteries, as they fired, ejecting long streams of flame and volumes of brown smoke. As the agonizing seconds slowly passed, we would suddenly see a tremendous "pouf!" as the time fuse reached its limit, revealing the gunners' aim in a cloud of black smoke and fragments. To aid in spotting, the enemy began using various colored explosives. Great puffs of orange, green, purple, yellow and black encircled us in their irregular death-pattern. As the Commander later said: "It would have been a beautiful sight if we hadn't been on the receiving end." there is something awfully disconcerting about having the ship's main batteries fired at one.

Swinging north and to the west of the angry ships, we gradually maneuvered into the sun. The two task groups had closed and were almost merged into one. The *Musashi,* the cruiser, and can were still a part of the main formation, but were on the north side as a smaller unit within the entirety. No scattering of ships for this Japanese Admiral, as his predecessors had done in other engagements. He was keeping his deadly antiaircraft concentrated. When we reached an altitude of thirteen thousand feet directly west of the enemy, The Commander gave his orders. "Lawler, you and Jamison put your divisions on the cruiser. Verdin, you take the can."

There were no orders for the dive bombers and "torpeckers." All we needed to know was our target, and the Commander had already assigned the "big bastard." We had spent months before making dummy attack after attack on our own ships off the West Coast in an intensive training period. Commander Smith had cursed, praised, threatened and sweated us from a straggling bunch of individual pilots into compact teams of coordinating havoc with split-second timing. It was a familiar story to us. The only difference was that this time there were twenty-six rapid-firing ships.

As the distance narrowed to ten, eight, six miles, the antiaircraft fire increased. Smaller batteries that had been out of range before began an almost rhythmical fire. The bursting shells were coming nearer and nearer. Sixteen, fourteen, eight, six and five-inch rifles began and continued a terrific rate off fire. The horizon was swiftly and surely filling with eddying puffs of smoke as jagged shrapnel went searching for the tender skin of aluminum planes.

A thin cloud appeared ahead of us, and we immediately sought sanctuary behind its protective veil. The fire momentarily slackened. McLaughlin spoke over the intra-communication system. "Check your master arming switch;! Check your torpedo switch! Gun switch on! Don't forget your emergency release! Bomb-bays open!" He didn't want to have to make a second run, either.

Suddenly, we broke through the cloud with the sun at our backs. The enemy came to life with renewed vigor, all guns seeming to begin at once, as if the fire were centrally controlled. The ships actually appeared to leap out of the sea as they lurched at us in their eagerness. The powder-smoke began gently drifting across the water until it almost formed a haze.

The Helldivers and Hellcats jinked for a position directly over the enemy force, while our eight torpedo planes maneuvered behind. We had thirteen thousand feet of altitude to lose in a horizontal distance of three miles. Avengers must go low over the water to drop—to insure a correct entrance angle, and to prevent the delicate mechanism from shattering on impact with the water.

Lt. Cmdr. Prickett gave the breakup signal with his elevators, and our divisions split, Prickett to the *Musashi* ' s starboard and McHenry to port. Our divisions further fanned out into four planes each with different attack angles, all to converge at the battleship's bow. The dive bombers and fighters continued ahead.

Lt. McHenry nosed over, and we wing-men followed, staying parallel with him in surges. I opened my canopy as we started down, in case an emergency jump were required. Cold air rushed in, and I began to feel the air pressure on my eardrums as the altimeter needle rotated. Ten thousand, eight thousand, six thousand. The airspeed indicator swung wildly, and the roar of the wind and engine became almost deafening as the Avenger reached seaward.

The automatic weapons, the most deadly of them all, opened up from all ships. I jinked violently as explosive blemishes came closer and closer. It seemed as though every ship in the task force had singled out my plane for its target. I hunched lower in the cockpit, hopefully trying to look inconspicuous, as I worked the control tabs to neutralize the added stick pressure of increased speed.

The fighters above at thirteen thousand feet rolled into their dives and screamed toward the *Mogami* and *Teratsuki*. Lt. Cooper, the lead dive bomber, peeled off a second later and went vertically for the *Musashi*. One by one the others followed him, some going into dives of one hundred degrees, to counteract the airfoils that would tend to make them overshoot.

Tracers from the quadruple mounts were streaming by as I checked my altitude and began making minute calculations for releasing the two-thousand-pound fish. My shot at the bow would be fifteen degrees, exactly like a dummy attack I had once made on our own *California*. I could see McHenry, Ross and Swint to starboard, and knew we were coming in together, well fanned out for a spread pattern of runs. I glanced to port, and could see Prickett's division, symmetrical with our own, speeding in toward the plowing bow. We would reach the *Musashi* at the same instant.

I noticed smaller tracers, bright balls of orange flame, darting by either beam, above and below, and knew I was inside the twenty-five-millimeter range. I continued to jink, and out of the corner of my eye could see the fighters had reached their targets. Puffs of white smoke beneath their wings indicated they were using their rockets on the cruiser and can. Spurts of flame from the leading edges of wings were fifty-caliber machine guns spitting steel-coated lead into antiaircraft mounts and personnel of the screening ships.

I checked my altitude at a thousand feet, and realized I had to get lower. The pressure on my eardrums had deafened me, but I imagined I heard the exploding guns as the enemy trebled their fire to save the *Musashi*, the backbone of their force. Every mount was smoking, ejecting volumes of armor-piercing, incendiary and tracer rounds.

The *Mogami* broke into flames as five-inch rockets pounded her fantail and fifty-caliber slugs raked her from stern to bow. The *Teratsuki* exploded violently amidship as a salvo of rockets found its mark among torpedo tubes. Smoke poured from her center, and lesser fires broke out to make her an inferno of twisted wreckage. Gun crews, unable to stand the fury of the Hellcats, deserted their recoiling guns and scurried for futile safety.

As I went into the final phase of my run, the first bombs from the Helldivers began hitting the target. Thousand pound semi-armor-piercing bombs descending at terrific speed were battering into the superstructure of the *Musashi*. Great volcanoes of brown smoke rose skyward as powder detonated to crush high-test steel. Flames of yellow and orange seared into the air as bomb after bomb found turrets and towering mainmast.

The bombs were beating a relentless tattoo on the steel main deck, ripping jagged holes to penetrate armor and strike vulnerable fuel and ammunition in vital compartments. The huge monster seemed to slow as bomber after bomber, his sights filled with the bulk of steel, released at point-blank range, to pull out as low as three hundred feet. Fires broke out amidship as explosives compressed against weakening bulkheads. Gigantic volumes of smoke enveloped the ship, until I was afraid the eight-hundred-and-forty-foot target would be completely obscured from my aim.

I checked my angle of attack, estimating the lead, as the long bow emerged through the smoke, and slowly put my thumb on the electric release. The hundred-and-forty-foot pagoda of the battleship loomed through the haze like a three-story building. I forgot about the enemy fire, and almost seemed to freeze to the controls as the ship hypnotically drew me closer. An inner voice screamed at me to release. I pressed the button, and with my left hand jerked hard on the emergency release, feeling a sudden lift as the shackle dropped its load.

I hauled back on the stick in a three quarter left chandelle and headed out. Cook called: “Hot, straight, and true.” I glanced back, and could see the white splash where the missile had entered the water, and the telling track of narrow white bubbles, as the fish sped for the gray mass.

I could see other splashes where planes had closed to almost no range, only allowing enough water travel for the torpedo to arm. Lt. (j.g.) Bill Ross, flying at two hundred feet straight over the battleship, and miraculously escaping the explosions from our own bombs, peering into the smoking wreckage saw a Japanese sailor dragging a wounded comrade by the heels through the twisted superstructure.

The antiaircraft, relentless in its intensity, did not slacken. I maneuvered radically from side to side, gaining and losing altitude low over the water, to throw off the gunners aim.

The Commander's voice broke the air excitedly: "Atta boy, you're blowing hell out of her!"

I looked back to see the last bombs hitting as the converging torpedoes found their marks almost simultaneously. Towering geysers of water went skyward as torpedoes, striking deep below the water-line, went piercing into underwater compartments to shatter supporting bulkheads. Torpedoes below the protective armor belt struck deep into ships' vitals to explode the very structure. Two-thousand-pound cylinders of torpex and watchwork were ripping holes in the steel sides to let in fatal sea water.

Bombs from above and torpedoes from below were coordinating to pulverize the *Musashi* into a flaming scrap-pile. Fuel lines, electrical systems and ammunition stores were feeding fires to burn out the very heart of the monster.

The Commander and his wing-man Woodruff, who had been circling overhead to spot hits and draw fire, dived through the withering flak to strafe and rocket a menacing destroyer that had been shooting uncomfortably near—a parting gesture with steel-coated bullets.

McLaughlin shouted over the mike, "Turn port. Turn port." I skidded violently as a series of puffs broke to starboard. There were twenty-two ships, beside the ones we had attacked, that were still hopefully firing. White splashes of shrapnel were falling like a hail storm around our retiring planes. I shoved the throttle forward and went through every evasive tactic I knew.

Five miles away, I eased off my gun and r.p.m. and sat back to relax. A shell exploded ahead of me. I looked behind, and could see a trail of splashes where guns had been trailing me. I pushed the throttle to the firewall and didn't look back until the shells quit bursting in front of me. Sixteen miles from the *Musashi*, the firing ceased.

A Philippine sampan was sailing lightly on the Sibuyan Sea off Bondoc Point. As I circled around it to rendezvous, natives waved straw hats. I saw Swint, Holley and Trowbridge. Then I began counting the Avengers. There were eight. I counted the Helldivers—nine. In amazement, I counted the fighters—sixteen. All planes accounted for! It was impossible to believe that all our planes had come safely through that inferno of lead and steel. Lt. (JG) Schaller had a slug in his stub flap, and Lt. (JG) Spanagel had only one wing-tip left, but otherwise we were unscathed.

We set course for Burias Island and our carrier. As I leaned back, finally relaxing, and lit up a cigar, the Commander called: "I'm going back to have a look. I'll catch you on the way back."

With one other plane, Commander Smith flew back to the enemy task force. We could barely see the *Musashi*, but the black clouds of smoke and bellowing flames from fires out of control were plainly visible as she settled in her death agony.

Over the southern tip of Luzon, as we passed a native village, I noticed an F-6-F on my wing. It was the Commander. He had a smile on his face from beam to beam. He raised his hands above his head, clasped like a conquering boxer, and shook them. He was flitting from plane to plane, giving each pilot the victory signal.

That night as we sat in the ready-room, wishing for a case of champagne, Lt. Christensen, who led the bombers second division and has a flair for figures, showed us a report he had completed.. Calculating the time we had been exposed to antiaircraft, the numbers of guns that could have been brought to bear, the weight of the ammo expended, and the rate of fire, he estimated that 198,000 rounds had been fired against us, a total tonnage of 399. It seemed to me that all of it had been directed at my plane.

Other statistics were available: The fighters had expended ten thousand rounds of fifty-caliber ammunition and sixty-four rockets. The bombers had dropped eighteen bombs, to score sixteen hits and two near misses. The avengers had released eight torpedoes, all of them exploding against the *Musashi*. We had placed sixteen tons of explosives on the battleship, and had pictures taken by radioman Potter from the rear seat of Lt. (JG) Reed's Helldiver to prove it.

The Commander came in and gave his summary of the action: "*Musashi* left dead in water, smoking profusely from violent explosions, and down at the bow. *Mogami* damaged. *Teratsuki* believed to have sunk. Unidentified destroyer damaged slightly." We felt good, but still a little incomplete about the *Musashi*. We had knocked her out; she would never reach Leyte to shell our troops and transports; but there is no elation like knowing you have sunk an enemy man-of-war. Our high spirits subsided a bit, but we had hopes. Perhaps she would sink during the night.

A few days passed, and as we waited anxiously for news, a message came in: "*Musashi* not seen since October 24." Our submarines were continuing their brilliant scouting work.

Days passed into weeks, and Air Group Twenty went roaming the Pacific on other missions. Then on January 14, we heard the news: CINCPAC, from unimpeachable sources, had learned the fate of the

Musashi. Admiral Nimitz announced that the *Musashi* had sunk late on the afternoon of October 24. On a serene afternoon in the Sibuyan Sea, Air Group Twenty had put the finishing touches to a "super" battleship, killing hundreds of highly trained personnel, wrecking the labor of thousands, and destroying one of the hopes of an empire. A dream had become a reality.

It took nineteen torpedoes and multiple bomb strikes before the *Musashi* sank during the battle of Leyte Gulf in October, 1944.

Lt. Comdr. Dickey now lives in Florida, but lived for a time in California. He is an Outdoor Writer, like myself a member of the Outdoor Writers Association of America, a professional group of well-published writers. He has written four fine books on hunting and fishing. His stories have appeared in a wide variety of magazines.

Lamar Underwood, novelist, former editor of *Outdoor Life,* wrote of him: "Charley Dickey is more than an engaging storyteller; his experience and observation in the outdoors give him credentials few can match in bringing new knowledge to the reader."

He was highly decorated for his service as a naval aviator in World War II. He received the Navy Cross, the Distinguished Flying Cross, the Air Medal, as well as unit and individual citations. At the time of the story he was a Lt. (JG), however he also served during the Korean War during which he was promoted to Lieutenant Commander.

We are pleased to include this story, with his permission, and that of McCall Corporation. It appeared in the old *Blue Book* magazine in August 1945. Many say it is the most exciting of all the chapters.

Active Member

50

Four and a Half Kills in the Pacific

Captain George Shaw-Corthorn, USN-Ret.

At the time of the Pearl Harbor attack I was a newly commissioned Ensign USNR instructing instrument flying at NAS, Corpus Christi, Texas. A graduate of Stanford University, I had entered the Naval Service in December 1940. After the attack I repeatedly requested orders to a Fleet squadron in the Pacific, but was disappointed.

After two years of instructing more than 2,100 hours of flight time, I finally received orders to Fighting Squadron 18 (VF-18). I reported aboard in August 1943. The squadron had been commissioned only a month earlier at NAS Alameda, with LCDR Sam L. Silber, A-V(N) USNR as the C.O.—a real fighter jock and a former All-American lacrosse player at the Univ. of Maryland. Fortunately for me, "Sambo" was a fine leader and an accomplished instructor of fighter tactics. He had been an instructor at NAS Opa-Locka (Miami, Florida) in fighter operational training. He had a prior tour in VGF-27, a Wildcat (F4F) squadron, aboard the *USS Swannee* during operations supporting the invasion of North Africa. with further duty in the South Pacific from the fall of 1942 to the spring of 1943. VF-18 was one of the first 36 plane Hellcat (F6F) squadrons.

During my initial combat tour, our first action was on 11 November 1943 as part of Air Group 17 aboard the *USS Bunker Hill* (CV-17), *Essex* class, involving an air attack on Rabaul. The squadron acquitted themselves like seasoned, experienced combat veterans in spite of the fact that it had the shortest training period of any squadron in naval aviation. The squadron had completed only 55 % of its syllabus.

I can not forget an afternoon during that tour when Japanese dive bombers were diving on our carrier. I was waiting in my F6F on the deck-edge elevator at hanger deck level to go up to the flight deck for take-off, while the carrier under command of Captain John J. Ballentine was taking evasive action. I could look up through my canopy and watch the Japanese planes coming down making their runs on our carrier. I couldn't get out of the F6F to safety. Although I was eager to get into the action, I was never allowed to take-off. The carrier couldn't launch aircraft while under air attack.

After a short stay at Espiritu Santo, in the New Hebrides, VF-18 took part in the Tarawa operation to support the landings there as well as combat air patrols and strikes against ground targets. On 22 November 1943, I made my first carrier night landing. I was part of a dusk CAP of 12 F6Fs to protect our surface formation from Japanese bombers (twin-engined Bettys). At the end of our flight, we received a *CHARLIE* (time to land aboard).

My division broke up and as my turn came to land aboard, the LSO (Landing Signal Officer) gave me frantic come-ons to increase my airspeed. My indicator read a steady 65 to 75 knots—normal approach speed for an F6F. I couldn't understand the come-ons, however I didn't want to receive a wave-off and have to go around again. So I increased my airspeed and received a cut by the LSO—O.K. to land aboard. I zoomed past the LSO like a run away freight train, engaged a late cross-deck wire (pendant), and was arrested just as my propeller engaged the first barrier. The errors were attributable to a lack of proper calibration of the landing attitude light on the leading edge of my plane. At the ready-room Sam told me I was now night qualified, adding that "any landing you can walk away from is a good one."

After Tarawa, we attacked Nauru on the way back to Espiritu Santo. On 25 December and 1 January 1944 we conducted strikes on Kaving. My division shared credit for one Japanese aircraft, a Tony. After that VF-18 took part in the Marshalls invasion—Kwajalein and Eniwetok—in late January and early February. Our next operation included strikes on Truk, Tinian and Saipan in February 1944.

On one of my last carrier landings, I blew a tire. Perhaps this caused our Flight Surgeon to recommend to the Captain it was time for VF-18 to receive orders returning to Pearl Harbor and then to the United States in March 1944. The squadron shot down 78 Japanese planes during that tour; I was awarded the Distinguished flying Cross and four Air Medals.

My second combat tour started with orders to Composite Squadron 84 (VC-84) which had a complement of 12 torpedo bombers (TBMs) and 20 fighters (Wildcats-FMs). It was scheduled to deploy on the *USS Makin* (CVE-93) to the Pacific. I reported aboard in April 1944 as the Senior Fighter Aviator at NAS North Bend, Oregon. We went through training on the West Coast and deployed on 16 October 1944, arriving in the combat zone on 11 November 1944. Our mission was to escort convoys into Leyte Gulf. On 26 November we were relieved and headed for the Admiralty Islands. Our next combat mission commenced 1 January 1945 with assignment to the Luzon area to cover Army landings at Lingayen Gulf from 9 to 18 January. Enroute, while going northward on the west side of Luzon on 4 January, while flying CAP, my division encountered six Japanese fighters (Hamps), which we engaged and shot down one. We also took out an anti-aircraft battery. I received a 20 mm hit on my left aileron, but was able to land safely aboard ship.

From 10 February through 9 March we were involved in operations at Iwo Jima. I was the airborne Air Coordinator for all air strikes (Army, Air Corps and Navy) on the island when the American flag was raised on Mount Suribachi on 23 February 1945. The photographer, Joe Rosenthal (a Californian) captured the event on film and was aboard our carrier developing and printing his work. I was offered one of his prints and gratefully accepted it. The photo hanging in my den reminds me of the terrific battle for Iwo Jima which I observed from the air.

Okinawa was the locale of our next operation, support of the landings through 29 April 1945. My division engaged enemy aircraft and attacked Japanese troops and installations. I recall vividly a Kamikaze pilot flying directly toward me trying to take me out, but I was able to shoot it down. Our division downed two single engine bombers (VALs) and one fighter (ZEKE). Following that we headed back to Guam and then to the United States, where my new assignment was to Fighting Squadron 97 (VF-97) under the command of S.W. Vijtasa, an Ace, at NAS Atlantic City, NJ.

During that second combat tour the fighters of VC-84 accounted for 20 Japanese planes in the air. I felt it most rewarding since I was able to instruct, train, and lead a wonderful group of 28 young fighter pilots, thanks to the training and experience I had received on my first combat tour with VF-18 under Sambo Silber. I was awarded six Air Medals and two Distinguished Flying Crosses for actions in the second combat tour.

51

Ichi Go – A Flying Tiger Tale

Maj. Hal Geer, USAF Ret.

Along the railroad between Canton and Hankow in south-east China there were four airfields during W.W.II. Two hundred miles farther east were four satellite fields used for staging the planes that attacked Japanese shipping along the China Coast.

Flying out of these fields was a motley array of B-24 and B-25 bombers, along with P-40 and P-51 fighters. These small units were collectively know as the 68th Composite Wing of the 14th Air Force. Their commander was Brigadier General "Casey" Vincent, the second youngest general in the U.S. Army since the Civil War. He was better known in the U.S. as the real life counterpart of Milton Caniff's "Colonel Vince Casey" in the newspaper cartoon strip "Terry and the Pirates."

From the beginning of W.W.II, these *Flying Tigers* gave the Japanese a "rough time" as they attacked shipping off the Coast and supported half a million Chinese troops. In the first six months of 1944 the Tigers sank a ton of Japanese shipping for every gallon and a half of gasoline they burned. They also "tied down" over half a million enemy troops that could not be used to resist the American island-hopping campaigns. With American Forces driving westward across the Pacific, the enemy knew they had to eliminate the Flying Tigers, separate south-east China from the interior, and fortify the coast against impending American invasion.

As a Tech/Sgt. I was the leader of a little combat camera unit whose assignment during most of 1944 was to make documentary motion pictures of the 14th Air Force's action in Eastern China. Our headquarters was in Kweilin (now called Guilin). From there, and adjacent satellite fields, we flew as photo gunners on all kinds of missions. And on the ground we often lived with the Chinese troops as a part of small O.S.S. Detachments.

In the spring of 1944, the Japanese, after seven years of war in China, launched their great East China Offensive—code name "Ichi Go."

A rough translation is "number one." Two hundred thousand troops poured down from Tunting Lake in the north and fifty thousand drove up from Canton in the south. The Chinese tried to hold them back, but they were no match for the better equipped Japanese troops. One after another we destroyed our airfields that the Chinese had clawed out of their precious rice paddies by hand.

As the enemy neared Kweilin the "Tigers" fought back with every thing in its arsenal. Fighters, with their shark mouths glaring, dive bombed, skip bombed and strafed. Mitchell bombers and even lumbering Liberators came in "on the deck" to bomb railroad marshaling yards and enemy troop encampments. Despite bad weather, some crews flew three or four missions a day. All this cost many American lives, as well as gas, bombs, and sweat. The toll was heavy.

Within our little combat camera unit, Sgt. Dick Arbogast was aboard a Liberator that flew into a mountain while returning from a sea sweep. Sgt. Kenneth Cox was trapped in a Mitchell that crashed off the end of the runway and exploded in flames. The Squadron commander shot him

T/Sgt. Hal Geer at the controls of an L-5 liaison plane

to end his agony. Sgt. Carl Cannon was the only survivor of a Mitchell crash behind Japanese lines and spent the rest of the war in prison camp. He came home so psychologically deranged that he committed suicide. Lt. Allen, flying on a routine supply drop, was sucked out of a C-47 "Gooney Bird." Taken prisoner by the Japanese he was being hauled to prison on a train that, in violation of the "rules of war", was carrying ammunition. Our fighters strafed the train, blowing it to fragments. Sgt. Lou Gendler, who was limited service because of his eyesight, talked his way on to flying status. On his first mission a dozen B-24s attacked a Japanese convoy, and I photographed his plane as it crashed in flames.

Then the 14th ran out of gas. Chinese troops were routed and escaped into the mountains. Civilians were in panic as they fled the savage onslaught of the Japanese. All personnel but a few engineers and our little combat camera unit were flown out, with what meager supplies they could salvage.

Chinese planted 500 pound bombs in the runway, and we lived in hostels stocked with drums of gasoline, not knowing when the order to blow the runway and torch the hostels and warehouses would come. The Japanese paused about twenty miles north of the city and waited for three weeks to regroup. Then they were ready to advance again.

We all knew our jobs. All night long the buildings on the base burned like a funeral pyre. In the early morning twilight there was nothing left of a great American Airbase but ashes and the taste of bitter smoke in the air. With the coming of daylight we blew giant craters in the runway. Ehr Tong Airbase was a pile of rubble.

The Chinese who lived in the city near the river set fire to their homes and shops and fled on foot with a few meager belongings and

Chinese planting a bomb in the runway of Kweilin Air Force Base

scraps of food slung over their shoulders. They left broken walls and streets full of ashes. When the City was destroyed they blew up the bridge behind. Although there were Japanese "fifth column agents" all around us, I stayed to photograph the demolition of the bridge. Then our little three-man camera unit, with three Chinese house boys who had remained with us to feed us and be our interpreters, loaded on our jeep and headed south to Luichow, the last American Airbase in south-east China. We were a part of a homeless hoard who were fleeing certain death from the enemy. Suffering defied description.

Those scenes were repeated many times during that cold rainy fall of 1944. Finally on November 7th, 1944, I photographed the flag being hauled down at Luichow. Again the Japanese were only twenty miles away.

We lived through three more weeks of hell—out of contact with any Americans—as we wound our way over a muddy dirt road to the headquarters of the 14th Air Force in Kunming. Finally, on Thanksgiving, with a badly damaged jeep and our trailer down on its axle with a broken spring, we arrived late at night to "dine" on water buffalo and turnips. At last we could take off our shoes.

Famous author and Time correspondent, Theodore White transposed our experiences—and stories of Chinese refugees—into a novel entitled *The Mountain Road.*

Our pictures were edited into a film called "China Crisis." And General Chennault gave me a direct "battle field" commission. I write these words through tear-strained eyes as a memorial to those cameramen in our unit who "didn't make it back."

Bridge destroyed to "slow down" the Japanese Ichi Go offensive, summer 1944, near Ling Ling in southeast China

52

Remagen

Major General Jack Barnes, USA-Ret.

On 7 March 1945 Brigadier General William M. Hoge's Combat Command B of the 9th Armored Division reached the Rhine River at Remagen and found the Ludendorff Railroad bridge still standing. Acting on his own initiative, the 9th Armd. seized the bridge and started crossing their command over it to establish a bridgehead on the far shore. Their action was flash reported through channels to General Eisenhower, who immediately supported the initiative by ordering the concentration of engineer units and resources in the vicinity to prepare additional crossing sites for a major offensive into Germany.

The 51st Engineer Combat Battalion received orders on 8 March to construct a 25-ton heavy ponton bridge with equipment provided by the 181st and 552nd Engineer Heavy Ponton Battalions. As the S3 (Operations Officer) of the 51st, I was responsible for planning, preparing the orders and instructions to accomplish the task, and staff supervision of the construction activity. The site selected for the bridge was from Kripp to Linz, two small towns opposite each other on the Rhine, about 1-1/2 miles upstream (south) of the Ludendorff Bridge. This was the closest site available with good approach roads on each bank of the Rhine to support concentration of engineer resources and the traffic of major U.S. units which would use the ponton bridge.

By the morning of 10 March the 51st had moved 40 miles from its previous location to the site and all the resources needed were on hand. Construction began at 1600 with preparation of approach ramps on both shores, interrupted periodically by enemy artillery and sporadic small arms fire until smoke pots were found and used to prevent enemy observation of activity at the site. However, all during construction and until an expanded bridgehead had been established on the far shore, sporadic unobserved enemy artillery fire continued to harass the bridge site. Several engineers were wounded, and six were killed during construction of the ponton bridge, the latter including the commander of the 552nd Heavy Ponton Battalion. The Germans even fired several V-2 rockets from launchers in Holland, the only time they ever fired on German soil. They caused no damage.

Construction continued on into the night and the next day. The bridge was built in parts, with four groups working simultaneously on 4-boat rafts, mostly by feel in the dark. By 0400 the next morning, 11 March, fourteen 4-boat rafts had been completed and were ready to be assembled together as a bridge. When the rafts were in place they were reinforced with pneumatic floats between the steel pontons so the bridge could take the weight of 36-ton Sherman tanks. A total of 60 pontons and 57 pneumatic rubber floats were used.

As the 4-boat rafts were maneuvered into position, they constantly extended the bridge from the near shore, increasing the pull on the anchors holding them in place. Triple anchors were then used but as the bridge extended further out into midstream they too started to fail, and the engineer power boats were not strong enough to hold the bridge in place while anchors were being set. At about this time we discovered that the Navy had some LCVPs (Landing Craft, Vehicles and Personnel) in the area and we requested their assistance. 10 LCVPs came to the rescue and were able to hold the bridge against the current until we could install a 1" steel cable across the Rhine immediately upstream of the bridge, to which the anchors for each ponton were attached. This solved the problem of holding the bridge against the current, estimated to be nearly 10 feet per second. The remaining 4-boat rafts were connected to the anchor cable, eased into position and connected to the ever extending bridge until the far shore was reached.

The Ludendorff Bridge

Finally, at 1900 March 11, 27 hours after starting construction, the 969-ft heavy ponton bridge was completed. It was the longest floating bridge ever constructed by the Corps of Engineers under fire. Traffic started at 2300, with 1 vehicle crossing every 2 minutes during daylight hours. During the first 7 days 2,500 vehicles, including tanks, crossed the bridge.

At the same time we were building our bridge, one of the other battalions in our Engineer Combat Group constructed an M2 steel treadway bridge for lighter vehicles immediately downstream from the Ludendorff Bridge. The two bridges provided two-way traffic across the Rhine, with heavier vehicles crossing our 51st heavy ponton bridge on the way to the front and returning lighter vehicles crossing the 291st treadway bridge. This enabled closing the Ludendorff Bridge for repairs, which were not completed before it collapsed from fatigue 10 days after its capture. It had been weakened by earlier German demolition charges. It collapsed while Army engineers were working on it, trying to strengthen its tired, damaged framework. With a sickening crash, it took down with it a number of soldiers into the icy, fast-rushing waters.

Many of the American soldiers who had captured and held the bridge were decorated for their bravery. The book *The Bridge at Remagen*, by Ken Hechman, tells the story in greater detail.

Gen. Barnes graduated from West Point in 1942, when he was commissioned in the Corps of Engineers. He served though W.W.II with the 51st Engr. Combat Bn., however transferred to Infantry branch in Korea in 1954, and from command of an Engr. Bn. to command of an Infantry Bn. He served three tours in the Pentagon in Army R&D, the last as a Major General, Director of Plans, Programs & Budget and Deputy Chief of R&D for International Programs. Retiring in 1974 from the military he became a program manager at Boeing for several years.

53

Air Ace in the Pacific

Lt. Colonel John Zarlengo, USAF-Ret.

John Zarlengo, a distinguished flier is also a close friend of my good friend, George Goertz, with whom we both have had many enjoyable days afield hunting game. Since John is quite ill he has allowed me to write up a brief account of some of his experiences.

He grew up in Colorado in a ranching environment, but from the time he was a small boy he was fascinated with airplanes and looked forward to becoming a pilot. Early on in our mobilization he enlisted in the Army and went through flight training.

He has been asked many times to write his war memories but has never done so, even though he tells us that they were very interesting and exciting events.

He was flying the first aircraft to make contact with the enemy in the Battle of Midway, a Flying Fortress carrying the name *The Yankee Doodle*. When it was destroyed, having been shot down, he flew the *Yankee Doodle Jr.*, until it was also destroyed in December of 1942 at Espiritu Santo, an island in the New Hebrides about 75 miles long. While flying that second plane he shot down 14 enemy aircraft, sunk a troop transport carrying five hundred enemy soldiers, and scored direct hits on aircraft carriers and cruisers. He was shot down twice, landing on friendly ground in each case.

John received twenty-five decorations, including the Silver Star, the Distinguished Flying Cross, Air Medal, etc.

He continued on in a full career in the U.S. Air Force, flying both fighters and bombers, but most of his service was in fighters. He is a honorary member of the Korean Air Force, having led a squadron of Korean pilots in P-51's and a squadron of Mosquitoes in that conflict.

Zarlengo is mentioned in several books: *Gray Goose Calling,* by William Cleveland; *Heroes of the War in the Air* by Mengos; *Korean Mosquitoes* by William Cleveland. In *Guadalcanal Diary* by Richard Tregaskis, mention is made of the action in which John Zarlengo was involved. Tregaskis wrote graphically of watching from the ground the many aerial gunfights that took place as the Japanese heavily contested the control of the air. Air raids would often come in at noon and Tregaskis would go out to a vantage point to watch them. He had a wonderful window of opportunity to see the exciting dogfights of American and Japanese planes dodging in and out of the towering cumulus clouds, sometimes diving at maximum speed toward the water.

Col. Zarlengo tells us he was among those aerial combatants. I saw several brief dogfights in the air overhead in Europe, but inclement weather afforded little opportunity to see the action. Tregaskis had a better view. He had a good look at the attacking Japanese Zeros and was impressed that they were very maneuverable planes. They didn't carry the armor that protected our fliers. He spoke of the whole area of the sky resounding with the rattling of machine-guns, a sound rivaling the noise of a thunder storm.

Col. Zarlengo says, "I am now so old I can hardly reflect or recall ever doing such reckless things, but I am proud to have fought for our country." He is a modest man, a humorous companion, and one of the outstanding heroes of W.W.II.

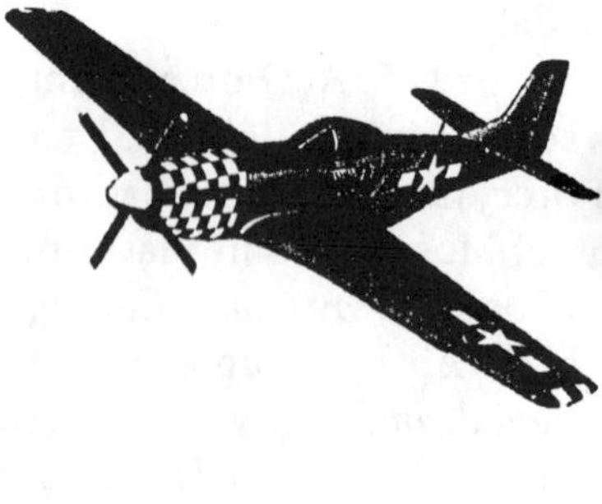

54

Flying in Thick Soup Weather — Aleutians

Major Leo J. Miller USAFR-Ret.

I enlisted in the Army Air Corps technical school at Chanute Field 1 December 1937. In 1938 I was an enlisted bombardier-gunner. Four years later, just prior to the attack upon Pearl Harbor, I entered flight school.

I had been trained in B-24's and was at Geiger Field, Washington, when a B-17 test pilot came through who needed a co-pilot, since his assistant was hospitalized with a bad appendix. So I volunteered, getting out of the ugly B-24's into the beautiful B-17 Flying Fortresses. During World War II our squadron, the 36th Bomb (H) B-17's, flew with the 11th Air Force up in the "Aleutian Pollutions—the String of Black Pearls", as our flight commander, Captain Bob Madison, laughingly called that abominable chain of rocks.

All of our highly skilled crews had a mighty fine navigator assigned to them. They were the best in the world, and it is fortunate that they were. While feeling our way around inside that thick gray garbage the Aleutians are infamous for, our navigators made certain we didn't crack our skulls on those awful hard clouds lined with immovable rock.'

The first air base the Army Engineers and Navy Sea Bees built for us out on the chain was on Umnak Island. I believe they completed the perforated metal runway in only nine days. The men of those two outfits accomplished a great deal in a short time.

Flying a bombing mission to Kiska, where those tough little Nips were holed up, and back to Umnak was a long haul. The fighter squadrons with the limitations of their shorter range, couldn't accompany "the arm chair pilots", as they laughingly dubbed us box car drivers.

As quickly as they could, the Engineers and Sea Bees built a second air base for us on Adak Island. With that field, we were a lot closer to Kiska to unload our 500 pound Dixies on the heads of those "claim jumpers" from the Land of the Rising Sun. The attack on Dutch Harbor in the Aleutians in 1942 was meant as a diversion by the Japanese, while their main attack was directed toward Midway Island. The Emperor's troops certainly wore out their welcome in the Bering Sea and North Pacific. They were very unfriendly neighbors during the year they were with us.

The "round robin" flight from Adak to Kiska and return became much shorter, and the fighters could go with us for a free-for-all over at Kiska. We felt reassured with the fighter lads whipping in and out with guns blazing.

No fighter pilot could possibly navigate himself out to Kiska and back in thick soup weather flying at "periscope depth" which was our usual altitude. Frequently spray off the white caps would wet the round glass of the ball turrets in the belly of the plane. The gunners would then scramble up inside the skin. However, our "cool as a cucumber" ball gunner Benson stayed at his post. One day he drawled over the inter phone, "Hey! Send me down some oars and I'll help you row this big barge!"

Cadet Miller, June 1942 (left); recent photo (above right)

"Peck's Bad Boys", as our C.O. called our crew, were a mighty fine bunch of combat men. Pritchard F. Miller had a devilish sense of humor. He was the top gunner in the power turret, behind the flight deck. When it came time to warm the guns, he used to slyly observe below the bottom rim of the turret and wait for his moment. When Sam and I in the pilot seats were gawking out through the windshield and side windows Pritchard, with his .50 cal. guns level a few feet over our heads, would hit his firing button. He never failed to catch us unawares, making us jump like marionettes on strings. Jack Jafee, our flight engineer, always knew when Pritchard was getting ready to warm up and left the flight deck.

The fighters were last to take off, and, when airborne, scurried over to our formation. A pilot would choose one of us to be his mother MacCree as he slipped in close under a wing tip. Looking around the formation during flight to the target our planes had the appearance of hens in the barnyard with baby chicks under their protective wings.

One day, after bombing our assigned targets, we left the harbor area in wild dives to "get fer home" and away from the flak off North and South Heads. At Semisipochnoi, the rendezvous island, Major "Pappy" Speer, our C.O., was flying a slow circle waiting for us to join up. He was already down to a fifty foot altitude because the ceiling had fallen out. It had been 6,000 feet during the short time we had made the bomb run from the extinct volcano on the northern tip of Kiska Island.

When we were in formation Pappy turned his B-24 into a heading for Adak. (A month or so earlier they had taken away our beautiful B-17's , so now we flew slab-sided B-24's, as did the 21st and 404th Bomb Squadrons.) Just then a P-38 whistled over and latched onto our left wing. The pilot had his goggles up on his forehead, and he gave us a wide grin and the merry wave of a hand. The left propeller of the fighter was feathered, since that engine had been shot out.

On our flight back to Adak we kept throwing questioning looks at the Lockheed "Lightning" cruising along on one boiler. One time Sam shouted to me, "I wonder if we are going too fast for him?" Hitting the MIC button on his control wheel he asked the fighter jockey, "Are you having trouble keeping up?"

There was no answer, but the "Lightning", flying on one engine, moved out ahead of us for two or three plane lengths.

Allowing his fighter to drop back into formation again, the pilot answered on his VHF with a smile, "Does that answer your question?"

Our llth Air Force had code names for all combat aircraft. The single and twin engine fighters were "Toms". The twin engine medium bombers were "Dicks" and the four engine heavies were "Harrys".

Since the fighters, being Toms, carried the least amount of gas they were always first to land. We worried that the Toms sometimes landed merely on gas fumes.

The Dicks, the medium bombers, carried more fuel, thus they had second priority to land. Our squadron flew Harrys, the big hay wagons with the most gas. we were always last to touch down, unless severe damage to the plane gave us priority.

On the day we escorted the P-38 home on his one engine, when the squadron got close to the runway, Sam flicked our left wing tip twice to signal the Lightning to break away. The pilot threw us a grin and showed us the belly of his fighter as he went in to land.

Our tiny 11th AF would bomb the Japanese positions on the islands of Kiska and Attu whenever weather permitted, and that weather was some of the worst in the world.

Our great crew flew together from July 1942 until August 1943. We were one of six B-24 crews who made the first long range raid to Paramushiro, the northern most island in the Japanese archipelago.

If the 11th Bomber Command was able to field 20 or 25 heavy bombers for a raid they were happy. A small force, compared to the one thousand plane raids of the mighty 8th Air Force in Europe. But then, they were the professionals, the Big Leaguers.

The 11th was called, with good-natured contempt, "The Bush Leaguers." One of our veteran pilots once said, "Maybe we're not the best, but—we're as good as the best!" In my opinion, the Bush Leaguers were second to none!

Following his tour of duty in the Aleutians, Major Miller served as a flight instructor in the B-29 training command at Clovis, New Mexico for the duration of the war. His repeated requests for combat assignments were denied.

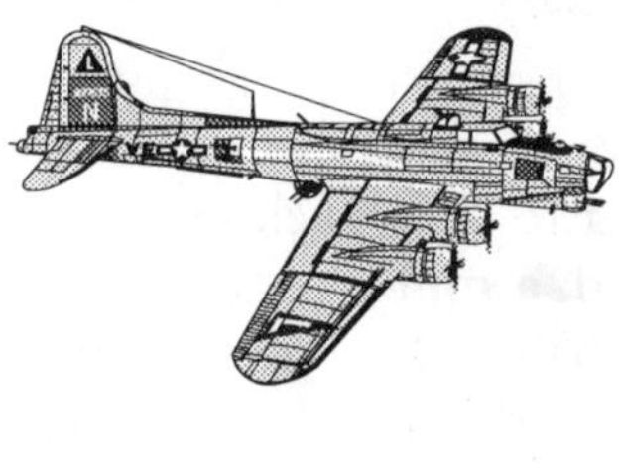

55

Bombing Nazi Germany

Major Philip Rose, USAF-Ret

A unique story is presented by Major Rose, (who narrated for the editor a video illustrated with photos taken during missions, pages of a diary and other memorabilia) describing his crew's 35 missions flying a B-24 Liberator Bomber. His particular airplane was built in Fort Worth, Texas, in January 1943, flown across to North Africa and used in flights against Rommel's troops before being brought to England.

When Major Rose and his crew got the plane it already had 35 to 40 missions, and they flew it for another 25 before being rotated on 14 April 1945. Originally, they had a crew of 10 in those planes, but that number was reduced to 9 with the removal of the ball turret during the Battle of the Bulge in December 1944, when German fighter aircraft were much scarcer in the skies.

Four of the crew were officers—the pilot, co-pilot, navigator, and bombardier. The enlisted men were all quickly promoted to Staff Sergeant or Technical Sergeant when it was learned that Prisoners of War of senior sergeant ratings were treated far better than those of lesser grades. (As many as half of the crews of some squadrons ended up as POWs!)

The B-24 carried ten .50 caliber machine-guns; it had 4 engines of 1,200 horse-power, was 65 feet long and 110 feet wide (wing span). Major Rose was serving in the 578th Bomb Squadron which normally flew in close formation, carrying about three tons of 500-pound bombs. Their flights over Germany took 5½ to 6½ hours from their base in Wendling, England.

For the first 7 missions they were lucky to receive only three flak holes, but the enemy became far more accurate during later flights. On one mission they took 121 hits, 52 of them in the nose of the aircraft. Lieutenant Pratt, the co-pilot, was hit in the leg by shrapnel, and the navigator was also hit in the chest, knocking him flat. Fortunately, he

Bomber squadron in air over Germany

Air Crew
(from left, back row) Lt. Rose, Pilot; Lt. Pratt, Co-pilot; Lt Harnden, Bombardier Nose Gunner; Lt Rohde, Navigator
(front row) S/Sgt Davidson, Top Turret Gunner; T/Sgt Croy, Radio; S/Sgt Manelick, Ballturret Waist Gunner; T/Sgt Scott, Crew Chief Waist Gunner; S/Sgt Bean, Tail Gunner

was wearing a flak jacket and was not hurt. The airplane, however, was seriously disabled.

Lt. Pratt said, "I didn't think we would make it back." Major Rose related, "We were unable to keep up with the other planes. No.3 engine was leaking oil and No.1 engine was shot up and cut out. We didn't have much gas. Our radios were shot out; the instruments were gone. We barely made it back after a flight of 7 hours and 35 minutes. We had been at 21,000 feet on a mission against airfields east of Frankfurt. Fortunately, three P-51 fighters escorted us to the French border. One of the sergeants dressed Jerry Pratt's wound (which even now gives him a little difficulty). Lt. Pratt flew again on the next mission—he didn't want to spend time in the hospital."

It had to be a marvelous bit of flying skill on Major (then First Lieutenant) Rose's part to be able to bring that disabled aircraft back to base!

Major Rose told of carrying an escape kit, a rather minimum collection of essentials: a compass, a map (shot full of holes during the attack described above), high energy food, band-aids and a tourniquet. Often their missions were against marshalling yards, endeavoring to hinder the movement of German combat divisions. At other times they hit refineries and airfields.

There were many close calls in those days of tight-formation flying in dense flak patterns—often in unfavorable weather, and pursued by adroit enemy fighters. Even training flights were hazardous and resulted in fatal accidents. On one occasion, a flight of aircraft had to separate and rise above the clouds. Nazi fighters, cleverly hanging above, shot down each plane as it emerged!

T/Sgt Wayne Scott, left seat, pilot seat
T/Sgt Oatis Croy, co-pilot seat, right seat

Major Rose didn't approve of buzzing, but on one occasion the crew begged to show their presence to a large assembly watching a football match not far from their base in England. The plane passed over the game so low that had not the players hit the dirt they would have become fatalities. There were trees ahead, and Major Rose took the controls from the co-pilot and pulled them out just in time! As the responsible aircraft commander, Major Rose was raked over the coals, took a 105th Article of War censure and a $50 fine; but the stunt boosted his crew's morale. (Air crews were prone to show off a bit at times.)

Another pilot, completing his tour of duty, had access to a fighter aircraft, and buzzed the airfield. Unknown to him, a flagpole had been erected in front of the Officer's quarters in a series of quonset huts.

As he pulled up, the horizontal stabilizer of his plane clipped the flagpole and as he lost control he bailed out. He was court-martialed for wrecking the plane and was fined $630.

On the serious side, Major Rose developed a competent crew and got credit for hitting targets more often that most others. Once, a bomb got hung up in the bomb-bay, and a crew member tried to release it, but was not wearing an oxygen mask. He lost consciousness and could have fallen out had not another crewman come to his rescue.

While some missions were "milk-runs", one could never be certain that they might suddenly turn disastrous. Many were long, tiring missions with great danger never far off. Major Rose developed the skills of his crewmen by teaching them how to assume the duties of all positions so that if any one of the crew were disabled others could assume his duties. He even taught two senior sergeants to fly the aircraft so that the plane could be brought in should the pilots be killed.

Keeping a diary was a court-martial offense, a serious breach of intelligence security, but Major Rose's little notebook provided the basis for this remarkably detailed story of the hazards of flying over Nazi Germany.

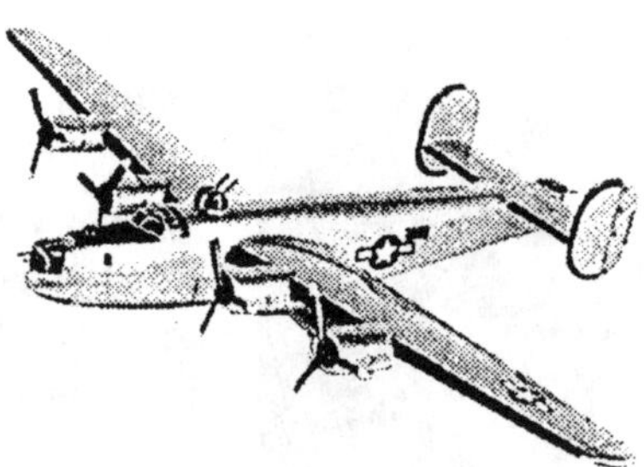

56

Fifty Missions Over Eastern Europe

1st Lt. Edward Schulman, USAFR-Ret.

As a part of the 15th Air Force, based at Foggia, in southeastern Italy, opposite Naples on the Adriatic Coast, I flew as a navigator on B-24 Liberators and later on B-17 Flying Fortresses. The latter was a safer plane, for it could withstand a great deal more damage yet be capable of returning to base. We had a crew of ten, including four officers—two pilots, navigator and bombardier. The engineer and gunners were enlisted men, sergeants. While I received credit for 50 missions, actually we flew 32, for if the mission extended beyond six hundred miles it counted for two.

Our work assignment would start in a theater. Sleepy men who stumbled down the ramp of the Group theater were not coming to laugh at a light comedy in the darkness of 0500 hours. We took our seats on the empty bomb boxes and waited for the show to begin. A drama would follow wherein each of us would take part before the sun was high. The audience, of which I was one, would turn, as a single word was put up on the board. If it was Ploesti we became quiet and apprehensive. The oil fields there were our most difficult and dangerous targets. There was none of the gaiety and chatter usually found whenever young men got together. Pilots, navigators and bombardiers made a lot of notes. The climax came first in those pre-dawn briefings at this B-17 bombardment group. I was one of 50 or 100 officers attending briefings wearing flying gear, 15 or 20 crews. The EM of our crews were briefed later by their officers.

We would bomb factories marshaling yards, airfields, bridges, harbor installations, oil refineries, as well as the oil fields. On one unusual one-time assignment we flew a strategic mission with targets selected by the Russian High Command. We bombed a key German airport at Galatz, Rumania on the Danube River 120 miles below Jasay, where the main Soviet—German land battle was taking place. Our attack

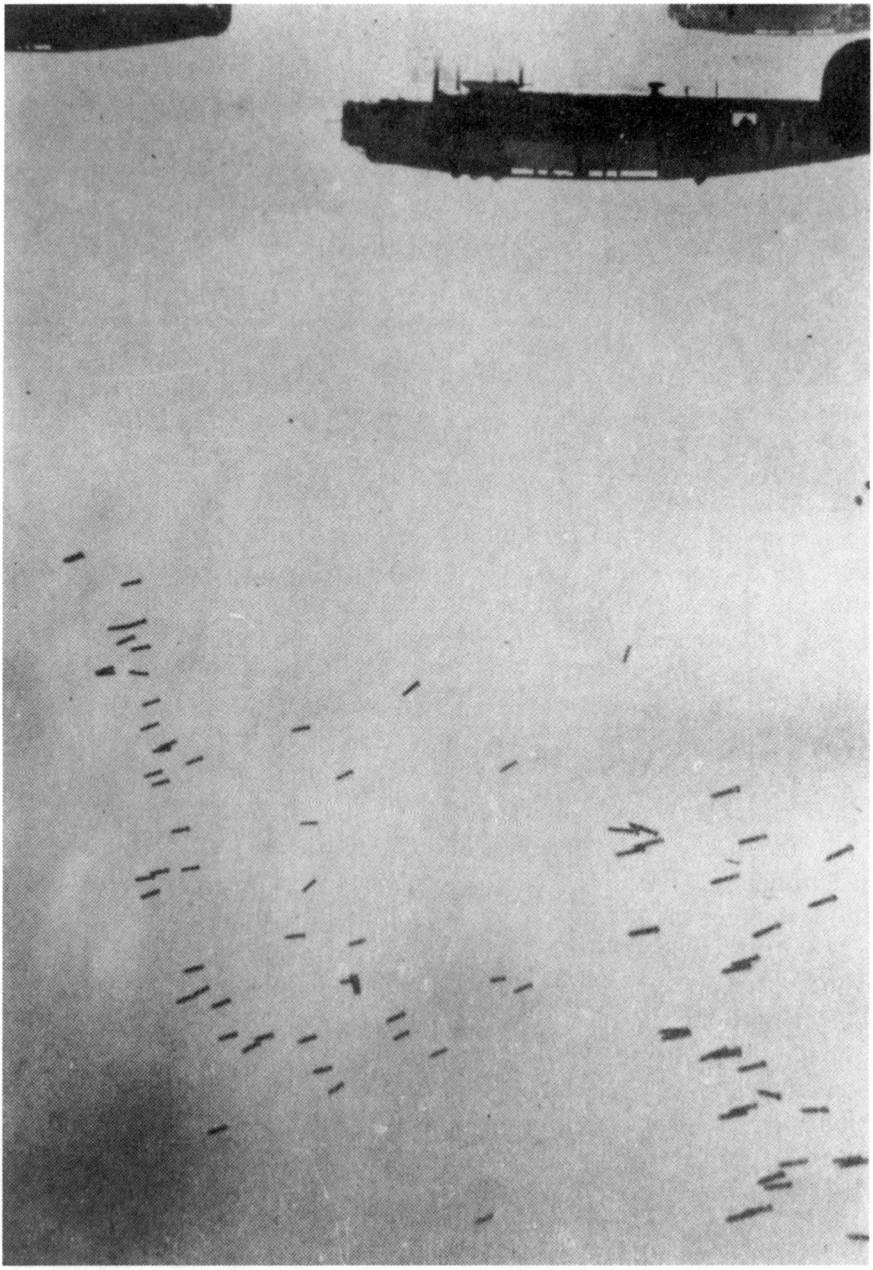

Bombs away!

Lt. Edward Schulman

pulverized fifteen German planes on the ground. Due to the distance of the mission we were unable to return to our base in Foggia, but as pre-arranged, headed to Russia. All of our planes landed safely 60 miles southeast of Stalingrad. We spent two weeks there, were treated well, and returned to our base without any losses. We saw an enormous amount of supplies furnished to the Soviets by America.

We also made long runs to bomb the oil fields at Ploesti in S.E. Central Rumania. To make that run we had to pass between parallel hills of the Transylvanian Alps, on which the Germans had emplaced a great number of anti-aircraft guns. Many planes were lost during those runs.

Our plane was hit many times, however, we were fortunate in that none of the men on my plane were ever hit. We stayed in formation as much as possible, where we had the reinforcing fire of adjoining planes. If we fell behind we were vulnerable. Once, when our engine was disabled, we were attacked by Messerschmitt fighters, but they veered away when P-51 Lightnings came to our aid. Earlier in the war we had only limited fighter protection by P-38s, which had shorter range. When the P-51's came in general use, with longer range, we had protection almost to the target and back.

As we approached above the target, we had to maintain a straight and level course. Our fighters would hold back until we cleared to resume our protection. Often the enemy fighters would hold off, just outside the range of our .50 cal. guns, and lob rockets at us. Our planes were hit many times by flak or by bullets or cannon shells from enemy fighters. Once our landing gear was shot out, but we were fortunate to belly land safely. We would have to wear oxygen masks above 10,000 feet, for the aircraft were not pressurized. After a few missions all the notions of glamour went out of our tasks.

Interestingly, some fliers would have premonitions. I recall one officer who had the premonition that he would die when flying with a pilot named Green, so he had his position shifted to another plane. His premonition of death was correct, but it was him not the pilot. The nose of his ship suffered a direct hit, taking the whole front off the plane.

It is easier to recall the happier moments of our service. A pleasant time was the week of R&R (Rest and Rehabilitation) on the Isle of Capri. The Italians there treated us very well.

We were a part of the 97th Bomb Group, 15th AF, which completed more than three hundred missions, sometimes sending as many as 750 planes against a target, dropping 34 million pounds of bombs, mostly 500 pound bombs, sometimes 1,000. Our group was credited with destroying 375 enemy planes, 204 additional probable, while losing 69 bombers in combat. We couldn't know whether it was our gunners that shot down enemy planes. There was so much fire power extended from our close formations that we couldn't very well claim individual credit. The escorting fighters were mostly responsible for downing enemy planes.

Following the completion of my fifty missions, I returned to the U.S. and had an assignment as a Navigator Instructor at Elington Field, Texas. Soon after the war ended, and I returned to civilian life.

Upon discharge, I returned to San Francisco and attended the University of San Francisco under the G.I. bill. I graduated with a B.S. degree and a teaching credential. The next thirty years were spent in the teaching profession as a teacher and administrator with the San Francisco Unified School District.

57

Philippines Revisited — 50th Anniversary of Battle

California State Senator Milton Marks,
Major AUS-Ret.

The following remarks are extracted from a speech given in the Philippines at commemorative ceremonies for the 50th anniversary of the landings in Leyte.

"The war in the Pacific seems long ago. It was different era. It was a time of immense tragedy and stunning triumph, of human suffering on an unparalleled scale and human courage rarely seen. It was a time when the borders that seemed to divide us came crashing down with the dawn of victory.

"Fifty years ago began the end of an era wrought by conquest, by the power of the sword. With the landing of Allied, American and Filipino forces and men and women on these shores, we began to shape a new world. Today, half a century later, we are beginning to reap the rewards of that new world.

"I landed on these shores as a young man. As with each of us in my generation, World War II is the pivotal event in our lives, shaping us as individuals and as a people, forming our values, inspiring our hopes and our fears. The war marked the end of our innocence, the end of our isolation, the end of the shelter we had felt, safe with our families.

"For me, coming across the world from the pristine waters of San Francisco Bay, I saw a reality I had never known. I saw unimaginable poverty—despairing and wretched. I saw the poverty of human values in a world of dictatorship. I saw the poverty of conquest and exploitation. I saw the poverty of indignity, the poverty of brutality, of hate, of war.

"But in the poverty I found inspiration. It was called hope. It was called courage. It is the dignity of knowledge, the audacity of truth, the clarity of brotherhood, the brilliance of justice. We joined hands in common cause.

"Here in the Pacific, we fought a war of liberation. As Americans, we saw the suffering of the Filipino people under occupation. We saw their dignity and courage. We fought as brothers, side by side, in these great battles for the liberation of a nation. We fought for the same ideals, for freedom, liberty, self-determination. We fought not just against tyranny of dictatorship. We fought against injustice in every form. We fought for President Franklin Roosevelt and for Jose Rizal. We fought for American and Filipino lives lost.

"After the battle, we saw the dawn of a new world. The liberation of Manila was only a beginning. Self-determination for the Filipino nation would be a reality. It was won on these shores by American servicemen, by Filipino soldiers, fighting with Americans and fighting for the Philippines. It was won by the suffering of the Filipino people and by General Mac Arthur's promise that he fulfilled for all of us 50 years ago. When he and we had returned, we would never be the same again.

"These bonds of brotherhood forged in battle have shaped my life. Coming of age, under fire, on these islands, with soldiers who hailed from every corner of America and every island of the Philippines, I learned the real lessons of understanding. I learned the meaning of the words that make up the American creed: *Liberty, Freedom, Democracy*. They are not gifts that we can neglect. They are tangible, made of blood and tears and sand and salt. We must struggle to shape our own destiny. I learned this from my family, but I saw what it meant here, in the Philippines, as the Filipino people fought for their destiny.

"When I came home, these battles, this courage, such hope and compassion and dignity, served as my inspiration. They guided my belief in government, in basic human rights, in equality under the law.

"Thousands of miles away, on the other side of this vast ocean, every day we see the fruits of these battles. Not just in the freedom of America, but in the communities built by Filipino Americans. The Golden Gate is no longer a shelter from the world, but instead a doorway to it. It is welcome reaching across the Pacific.

"I have returned to the Philippines many times, during difficult periods and times of hope. I have shared the joys and sorrows of friends in the Filipino American community and remembered the lessons I learned on these islands. Fifty years ago when we all began a journey, we began our lives, both in battle.

"Today we remember our comrades. We remember why we fought. We remember what we have won. Today, we can see the shape of the world that we saw born so long ago. The world we seek for our children and generations to come.

Senator Marks fought within the 96th Infantry Division, seeing his first combat on the beaches of Leyte, side by side with Filipino scouts within the Allied forces that liberated the Philippines. He later served with the 1st Cavalry Division through the remainder of the fighting, and through Luzon. In the process he was one of those who participated in the liberation of the Santo Tomas prison. He enlisted in the Army early on during the war and rose through the ranks to the grade of Major.

Senator Milton Marks has served in the California Senate since August, 1967. He is Chair of the Senate Majority Caucus and many committees, and represents the third District, with offices in Sacramento, San Francisco and San Rafael.

58

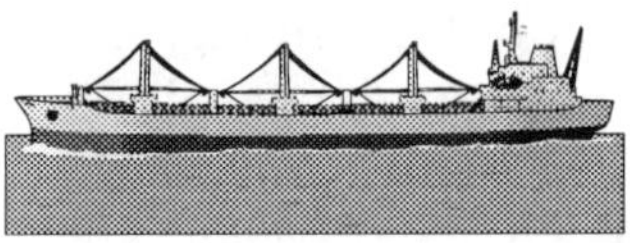

Time at Sea
Merchant Marine in Combat

Joseph S. Rychetnik

Having run away from home during W.W.II at age 16 to join the Marines and fight the Japanese, I was keenly disappointed to learn that they didn't need a skinny kid from the suburbs of Chicago. They didn't care for someone who had not finished high school and had produced a faked birth certificate. After the staffs of a dozen recruiting stations turned me down, when I had run out of geography, a kindly Gunnery Sergeant in Houston, Texas told me that I could get into another Marine outfit—the Merchant Marine. He wrote down the address of the U.S. Maritime Service recruiting office nearby, the agency that supplied the War Shipping Administration with crews to sail ships during the war.

I was accepted without question and was sent immediately to a training camp in Florida. I was told that this would be my springboard into a cargo ship destined for the Murmansk Run, an icy way to die, since few ships got through to Arctic Russian ports. Just as our "draft" was about to be sent to New York to fill vacancies, there developed a temporary glut of Merchant Mariners on the East Coast. We were sent, a whole trainload, to San Francisco. My first assignment was to a Liberty Ship named the *Samuel K. Barlow*. It chugged around the outposts of New Guinea moving supplies wherever needed, and became a slow-moving target for various Japanese bombers. The top speed of the ship was about ten knots. Someone told me the ship paid for itself if it made one successful trip anywhere.

With that experience under my dungaree belt, I was shipped aboard a C-2 that had the great fortune to load large steel pontoon sections for the Sea Bees, transporting them from their home base of Port Hueneme, California. It seemed every westbound ship stopped at Pearl Harbor for re-assignment. The war was moving quickly up the Gilbert and Marshall Islands and towards the Carolines. All the cargo was marked FRAY, which was the code for Hawaii.

We were pointed in a new direction, toward the Eniwetok invasion. I recall the name of the ship I was on. The *Flying Mist* was proceeding on course when stopped in its tracks by a Japanese submarine. The torpedo blasted a large hole in the port bow. We were about to abandon ship, as we had been drilled, and were making an effort to leave the sinking vessel. However, it dawned upon our officers that we were not going to sink, since the steel pontoons were like so many ping pong balls that transoceanic aviators used to fill their wings. We floated but listed slightly, port heavy. Getting back aboard was much more difficult than getting off the ship. We sailed back to Pearl Harbor, were patched up and tried to complete the voyage again.

Other invasions followed, wherein we carried food and ammo to the invasion of Kwajalein, and later to the relatively quiet invasion of the Ulithi Atoll.

During my last trip of the Pacific War our C-1 cargo ship was loaded with barrels of motor fuel, the juice that kept tanks and trucks going. The holds were full, and the deck had a top layer of barrels covered with 6" x 2" timbers that were supposed to afford protection against strafing Japanese aircraft.

We had been at Ulithi, an atoll in the Caroline Islands, in the Western Pacific, where the Navy had a great assembly area, a so-called safe anchorage for its fleets of warships and supply vessels. When just a day or so out, our main steam gland ruptured and the ship came to a halt. We were bobbing up and down in the calm Pacific, dead in the water. Submarine bait, everyone said. The engineers found the steam gland packed with the Oakland Tribune Sunday comics. Various explanations were suggested: either sabotage or sloppy workmanship, but we never found out the reason.

A tug was sent from Ulithi, to tow us in. It wasn't long before the Navy experts and the Merchant Marine engineers had us

Rychetnik in the Alaska State Police, 1960

ready to go—two days too late to make our appointment with history—the invasion of Iwo Jima. We sat on the hook in Ulithi for 61 days waiting for new orders. We sailed an hour after they arrived.

In the meantime we had one day off the ship to sip warm beer and play games on the recreation island of Mog Mog, within the Ulithi Atoll. I pitched horse shoes with Admiral Nimitz. He won easily. The beer was "green" Brew 102.

Orders arrived and we were off with our cargo of gasoline and a hundred Marines who slept on deck, destined for the invasion of Okinawa. We picked up four Navy DE's to shepherd our four merchant ships to Nakagasuku Wan, which soon became Buckner Bay. We arrived there on D+3 and became a part of the dangerous cargo anchorage. Two of our cargo ships were lost to enemy action, both carrying artillery shells, and all four of our Navy DE's, to Kamikaze attacks.

Our ships' Navy gun crew knocked one Jap out of the sky a few seconds before it would have crashed upon our forward deck. A Destroyer Escort just a few hundred yards from our starboard side sank before our eyes with all guns blazing, its stern blown off by a Kamikaze, following which all the depth charges began blowing up around us.

We were bombed or attacked by Kamikaze suicide pilots about six times a day during the six weeks we were unloading barreled gas. In the course of defending ourselves we knocked down three more Japanese. A Kamikaze ripped his wing off when it struck our main mast and bounced off the deck boards into the sea alongside.

I went ashore with the Marines to see the real war and got up forward, toward the action, as far as Naha. I was glad to call as my home the *S.S. Cape Constance*, despite the fact we were carrying a cargo of instant death if struck.

Dumping the barrels into the sea proved to be a better system than off loading into DUKW's and LCVP's, of which two were sunk by us accidentally. The wind and tide carried most of the barrels of gas to the beach, where they were collected and trucked off to the troops.

My two days ashore were remarkable, for all the flags came down on the hundreds of ships in the bay. The Marines I was with thought of no explanation other than that the war was over. I thought that unlikely. A Marine officer in a radio equipped jeep sent a call to the *USS West Virginia*, engaged in shelling enemy strong points. The President had died! Everyone wondered who was President now. None of us had been home recently enough to remember who were the political folks in Washington. The radio operator of the *West Virginia* responded that Harry S. Truman was now President. Several Marines irreverently yelled back at the radio operator, "Who the hell is Hairy Ass Truman?" We soon found out. As you can surmise, we were poorly informed of news and failed to recognize the courage of the new President who efficiently ended the war. I agree with the editor that President Truman saved our lives, for the Operation Olympic (Invasion of Japan) would have cost the lives of many Americans.

I sailed with the Merchant Marine as crew on UNRRA (United Nations Relief and Rehabilitation Administration) supply ships enroute to Europe and the Middle East until 1947. They channeled food and medicines to all the war torn countries of Europe and the Middle East. We shuttled for a year between Montreal with loads of wheat to Denmark, Marseille, and fifteen ports in the Eastern Mediterranean. The Jewish refugees were pouring out of USSR and Romania for Palestine, and that part of the Med was a "shoot-em-up" place, almost a war zone. When I found myself involved in the five-sided war raging in Palestine, I finally decided to come home, get married, have kids, and settle down. My love for the Marines prompted me to join a local Marine Reserve unit. Ensuing events resulted in my spending three years involved in combat during the Korean conflict.

Joe Rychetnik had a career in the Alaska State Police and wrote a fascinating book of his experiences entitled "Bush Cop". He is now a semi-retired writer, magazine columnist and professional photographer. He is an Emeritus Fellow of the Explorers Club. He recently wrote *Alaska's Sky Follies, the Funny Side of Flying in the Far North*, published by Epicenter Press, Kenmore, WA.

Recently Congress extended Veteran status to those members of the Merchant Marine who sailed in the war zone in such dangerous situations as Joe was involved in. They suffered the most casualties in relation to the total number of men of any of the U.S. armed forces in World War II.

59

The Role of Technical Intelligence in Warfare

Colonel John H. Roscoe, USMCR-Ret

This account may vary from others, for while it involves combat and enemy fire, I never served in a tactical unit.

Before we entered the war, a senior Army Air Force officer appeared at Syracuse University where I was teaching to inquire about my research on the use of air photos. He was interested in the quality, quantity and depth of information obtainable. He seemed impressed that not only could one identify land forms, land-use, crop types, industrial production and a myriad of minute other details from the images, but even the year and sometimes the day the photos were taken. As a result, in 1941, when I was teaching at UCLA, the War Department urged me to go to Washington to become the first civilian specialist in military airphoto intelligence.

My first assignment, other than creating my own job description, was with Air Corps Intelligence (A-2), which had only two rooms located in the old Munitions Building. (The National Reconnaissance Office, whose very name was classified until 1993, is now completing a four-tower building complex to carry out its missions.)

Early in the war, the Americans were playing catch-up because the Germans had already drafted the entire Hansa Lufbild, G.M.B.H., an airphoto corporation, into the Luftwaffe, and along with similar efforts by the Royal Air Force, had been engaged in wartime airphoto intelligence operations since 1939. A few US officers were in the United Kingdom for training, and an intensive search began for US citizens who used airphotos in related skills. The Germans picked up civilian teams as well, including one Professor Doctor Otto Schultz-Kampfhinkel, an SS officer and his Forschungstaffel, a special team of pilots, aerial photographers, cartographers, biologists, soils experts, other scientists, engineers and printers, who could and did produce and publish high quality, innovative, special maps from airphotos for the Wehrmacht, on order and from scratch within as little as two weeks. They concentrated on the North African and Russian fronts making maps, for example, showing tank track trafficability through swampy areas.

In addition to finding skilled personnel, my initial responsibilities were to teach officers how to analyze airphotos for strategic information, to determine industrial production, operations of railroad marshaling yards, order of battle, etc., and for tactical purposes such as identifying camouflage, weapons and emplacements, defenses, and similar battlefield information.

My first text for instructional purposes was a captured German manual, but subsequently I prepared Field Manuals and other instructional materials for ground, naval and air forces. It fell to my lot to prepare syllabi for, and teach, special courses in the new Army and Navy Schools established for this purpose.

The first operational experiences began shortly after the Pearl Harbor attack, when I analyzed the airphotos taken by the Japanese at Pearl Harbor to determine what the enemy could have learned about the extent of damage they had done to our fleet, as well as the degree to which and when our ships might be able to inhibit their Pacific

(from left) Col. John H. Roscoe, USMCR-Ret. (Ch 59)
Captain George Shaw-Corthorn USN-Ret. (Ch 50)
Col. Douglas A. Riach, AUS-Ret. (Ch 22)
Commander Elliott G. Dodge, USNR-Ret. (Ch 41)
Col. John H. Roush, Jr. AUS-Ret. (Ch 39)

operations. (How those photos came into my possession is most interesting, but may still be classified.)

At the same time I was assessing our airphotos of Wake Island and elsewhere to determine how our forces were faring, and the tactics and weapons used by the Japanese. Later, I was assigned the task of determining what was happening in certain ports and cities of North Africa, very early in the planning for potential operations there. The RAF supplied photos of the areas three times a week. After a while, the scenes became familiar and one could quickly determine even minor changes in activities. Also, I began to develop and standardize improved photo-interpretation equipment, some for use in various headquarters and others for use in the field.

Very early in 1943 I was informed that to keep the same position I held I would have to be commissioned. While this severely reduced my income, it waived my 4-F status and offered me a choice of services. Naturally, I became a Marine! (Illustrative of the ever growing importance of aerial photography, a colleague and student of mine, who later became an Associate Director of the CIA, was the only one who handed President Kennedy hard evidence of Russian missiles in Cuba detected by enlarged and annotated aerial photographs.)

When our forces began planning amphibious operations, I became involved in producing flexible, rubber, three-dimensional models of landing zones shown on airphotos. Accurate relief was determined by stereo photo alidades and surface information from the actual images.

Col. Douglas A. Riach, Col. John H. Roscoe, Col. John H. Roush, Jr.

The work was done by service personnel who had no idea of the purpose or of the area concerned. In some situations the personnel were confined for security reasons to the areas where they worked.

Because the rubber plantations were mostly in territory occupied by the Japanese, procurement of latex was rigidly restricted by the War Production Board. I had to obtain aircraft engine heaters to keep the latex from freezing in the winter, and a giant refrigerator to keep it from spoiling in the heat of summer! Refrigerators were very scarce, and it became necessary to “steal” one by talking the manufacturer into shorting his one-a-month delivery to the Army. Other ‘requisitioning’ actions had to be taken in moments of severe need, including a two-story office building, a hangar, a fleet of vehicles and maintenance services for them.

In the last year of the war, I was permitted, finally, to go to Europe. Since I was a Marine, the orders were cut to report to the Commander, Naval Forces Europe, and thence to such places as required by verbal orders (which were classified SECRET). This included assignments with British Intelligence, HQ 8th AAF, the Combined and Joint US-UK photo-intelligence operations, and the American Embassy in London. Then I went to France and Germany, obtaining intelligence from German officials and later serving with the US Strategic Bombing Survey in Germany, including Thuringia, which later was turned over to Russian occupation.

The work with the Strategic Bombing Survey involved determining the effectiveness of our bombing by comparing our previous airphoto damage assessment reports with the actual damage found after we captured the installations.

For proper analysis it was essential to get to the scene before the Germans had a chance to destroy the evidence, and before advancing Allied troops liberated and disturbed the area. Survey teams were divided into jeep-loads of four, each operating independently. The personnel were technically competent individuals of all ranks and grades, and some were civilians. We had to ‘forage’ for temporary quarters and food from whatever military units were handy.

One Jewish American civilian of German descent who led one team was captured. He had been told that a town was to be taken on a certain date, but the advance had been held up and when his team drove up the Germans killed the two team members in the front seats of the jeep and captured the other two, one of whom was this team leader. He demanded to be taken to the German General in command, whom he convinced that he should surrender to the Americans before the Russians arrived from the east. The General, perhaps knowing that all was lost, gave the team leader his sword, which he took back to an American Infantry Division commander. The latter became indignant, demanded that the sword be returned to the German General, making clear in no uncertain terms that he (the American General) was going to take the surrender in appropriate military fashion! His staff smoothed over the situation and arranged a proper ceremony.

One memory I'll never forget was seeing the concentration camp at Buchenwald, with its emaciated prisoners, the piles and piles of bodies awaiting cremation, and the torture room below the ovens. It was appalling, later, to have to stand naked in the cold wind picking body lice out of my clothing.

Equally repulsive was the disinterment of American soldiers who had been killed in action. These were removed by black troops wearing gas masks so that the bodies could be reinterred back in the United States. Congress had decreed that American soldiers could not be buried in enemy soil. While politically correct, the desecration of the bodies and parts by bulldozers and unwilling workers with sharp shovels was deplorable. Visitors became sick within minutes!

After the war, I began teaching at the University of Georgia, but not for long. Within two months I received telegraphic orders to join, immediately, Task Force 68, already at sea and en route to the South Pole. My work involved briefing, flying with and debriefing the aerial photo crews taking 160,000 trimetrogon horizon-to-horizon airphotos of Antarctica terrain, much of which had never been seen before by man.

I served on two such expeditions, nearly circumnavigating the ice-covered seas of Antarctica. Later I wrote a dissertation on the new coastline I had discovered, and served as Scientific Advisor to Admiral Byrd until two months before his death. Then I helped develop the large imaging payloads for the first 'spy-in-the-sky' satellites and related projects. These experiences proved useful during my service in Vietnam.

John H. Roscoe, Ph.D., served eventually in three wars—W.W.II, Korea, and Vietnam (in which he was wounded carrying out his duties). The importance of his work is emphasized by the fact that during the Korean War he was given travel privileges accorded 4-star Generals. He is a Fellow of the Explorers Club and a distinguished scholar. For his important work in the Antarctic a glacier and a peninsula on opposite sides of that continent were named for him.

60

Bail-Out and Barbed Wire

Lieutenant Colonel Dale J. Stephens, USAF-Ret.

Contrails blazed a path in the sky for miles behind us. The heavy bomber formation was on its way to Brunswick, a tough, heavily defended target deep into Germany. I was a S/Sgt. Flight Engineer-Gunner on a B-24 Liberator air crew, 392 Bomb Group, 577th Squadron, 8th Air Force, based in England. It was 8 April 1944, and this was a maximum effort mission! Our altitude was 22,000 feet, and the IP at Salzwedel where we would begin our bomb run was in sight. Suddenly we were attacked by an estimated 75 single and twin engine fighters, in single, two and three aircraft head-on passes. In that furious air battle, the 8th Air Force lost 34 bombers shot down. Our B-24 received extreme battle damage from three enemy ME-109 fighters. It shuddered and shook from the recoil of our guns. We fought valiantly but were on fire and in imminent danger of exploding. With only one good engine left we lost altitude rapidly. Under heavy fighter attack we dropped our bombs, then at 15,000 feet were forced to bail out. When my parachute was near the ground, I saw I was to be greeted by the local Gestapo with a pistol in hand. As workers in the potato field surrounded me, the Gestapo man ordered me to gather up my chute and flying gear and head for the road. There was a small canal next to where I came down. In a last defiant gesture, I turned and threw everything into the canal. He exploded with rage! The bore of the 9 mm pistol in front of my face looked like a 105 mm cannon. I was never any closer to being killed than at that moment.

Captured airmen shot down that day, including myself, were picked up by military trucks and taken to a nearby Luftwaffe base where we were placed in solitary confinement. Following an interrogation designed to "soften us up", we were transported by train to the Luftwaffe Intelligence Evaluation Center, about 12 kilometers northwest of Frankfurt/Main, Germany. There we were interrogated by real professionals before being shipped by box car to POW camps.

Several months later in Stalag XVII-B, wounds had healed and we had made the difficult adjustment to slow starvation and survival as prisoners off war. The dreary routine in this prison camp included roll-call formations, rain and mud, dust, vermin, dysentery, heat in the summer, freezing cold and snow in the winter, and poor sanitation. We dreamed of food, girls and escape—all on about 600 calories a day. We planned and evaluated ideas and discussed scenarios that might enable us to escape.

It was a warm, sunny afternoon. The German soldiers in the guard towers daydreamed as they gazed over the POW compounds below. Charley Bennett, radio man on our crew, and I were engaged in walking and jogging around and around our compound. This was an effort to maintain endurance, which would be needed if we ever had an opportunity to escape. While walking, we watched a detail of Russian POWs carrying some bodies to the burial ground. Russian and Serbian POWs died at an alarming rate from typhus, malnutrition, and brutal treatment. The bodies were always rolled in brown paper and two prisoners carried each one, outside the main fences, past our American compound to a tree covered area about 300 yards distant for burial. In front and behind the detail were the usual accompanying guards. Americans had been inoculated against typhus, which was transmitted by bites from the fleas carried by the ever present rats.

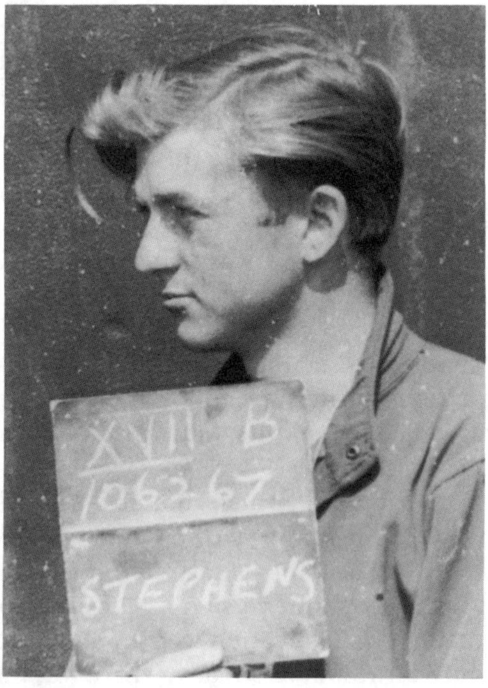

POW photo taken by Germans, April 1944

Further in our walk, I noticed three Russian prisoners in their ragged coats working on the fence which divided our compound from the next. Russian POWs were commonly used on maintenance work details.

Stalag XVIIB was an old and overcrowded camp with 4,250 American airmen, 56 British, 500 French and Serbians, some Polish and Italian partisans, and about fifteen thousand Russian prisoners. It held prisoners during World War I and was used as a concentration camp from 1938 until 1942. Living conditions were appalling.

Charley and I began to jog. As we approached the Russian work detail, I was shocked when I recognized one of the three men. "Charley," I blurted, then reducing my voice to a whisper, "They aren't Russians; they're our guys! What are they up to?"

The men picked up their ladder and carrying it between them moved toward the warning wire and main outside fences, working and hammering staples all the while.

"No doubt about it," Charley replied under his breath, "It's an escape! Keep jogging, but let's be sure we're not in the line of fire!"

In the last attempted escape, two American POWs planned to cut their way through the fences at night, avoiding the search lights while covered by white cloth to camouflage themselves against the snow covered ground. They were detected. Both walking guards and tower guards opened fire and cut them down. While they lay there wounded, calling out, "Don't shoot, *Kamerade*," one of the guards shot them several more times with his pistol. Another POW sleeping in his bunk was severely wounded when a tower guard fired through the barracks. Eight more men in that barracks were savagely beaten by guards. Consequently, most escape attempts were by tunneling.

The warning wire was posted with signs reading, "Anyone touching or crossing the warning wire will be shot without warning." One man crossed the twenty foot space to the first main fence, where he proceeded to hammer, while two other men also crossed.

Prisoners in the open area of the compound area seemed unaware of what was transpiring. Most were in the barracks area. Two of the men picked up the ladder and positioned it against a post to enable them to work on the top wires of the first fence. Soon they had all climbed

In full dress uniform, 1990

over and were working in between the two main fences. They hammered staples and repositioned the tin cans piled along the bottom of the fences as noise makers, should anyone try to cut their way through the barbed wire.

Slowly they worked their way along the fence to where they were almost under the corner guard tower. Placing the ladder against the second main fence, they climbed over. All three men were now outside! They had finished their work.

Hoping the tower guard had been lulled into disregarding them, they shouldered the ladder and carrying the tools walked single file down the path from the corner guard tower toward the shelter of the trees surrounding the burial ground.

Still no challenge from the tower guard. I started to mentally pray, "God, please help them." They were now about one hundred feet from the camp when an ear-piercing blast from the guard's whistle shattered the tranquillity. The three men froze.

The German in the tower yelled at them "Where is your guard?" I prayed again, "Please God, don't let him shoot!" Three other guards came running and took them into custody.

As they were taken away, I started to breathe normally again. "Well, it was a nice try," Charley commented. "They'll probably get thirty days in the 'cooler' on bread and water."

I replied, "I hope that's all. That was really one clever idea, but it took real guts to carry it out."

"Time for roll call and then that rotten rutabaga soup again. God, how I hate that stuff. I can smell it from here."

Our escape attempt came much later when we were force marched west 287 miles ahead of a Russian advance that over-ran Stalag XVIIB. The march ended in a forest compound where we were held without food or shelter near Braunau, Austria. There we came close to death from starvation, dysentery, and exposure until we were discovered and liberated by advance elements of the 13th Armored Division, 3rd Army. I was a POW for 13 months.

Transferred to Intelligence, my unit interrogated ex-POWs from both European and the South Pacific Theaters of war and compiled information for the War Crimes Tribunal. I received a direct commission as an Air Combat Intelligence Officer. With continued service in the Air Force Reserve I retired as a Lieutenant Colonel.

POW Medal

61

Ending the War

Brigadier General Robert D. Upp,
AUS-Ret.

In July, 1944, somebody finally decided that the Aleutians would no longer be attacked by the Japanese, nor be the base from which an invasion of Japan would be launched. Most of us who had weathered a miserable winter in snow covered huts on Adak and Umnak were now rotated back to the United States.

My unit, 138th Infantry, of the Missouri National Guard, was shipped from Umnak to Camp Shelby, Mississippi, where I was eventually assigned to the 259th Infantry of the 65th Division. This was the last Division created during World War II. It departed for Europe aboard the converted Italian luxury liner *Rex* on 1 January 1945 after a happy New Year's eve celebration in New York City's Times Square.

While the Division was at sea, the Germans launched their attack through the Ardennes known as the "Battle of the Bulge." Instead of continuing to England where supplies had been shipped, the units were diverted to France and landed at Le Havre in the snow. Pup tents were pitched at Camp Lucky Strike while we waited for our equipment.

The Division was soon tested under fire as a part of General Patton's Third Army and went into action on the Saar River line. On 17-18 March, the 259th broke through the Siegfried line and continued its advance to the Rhine River.

Our advance party crossed the Rhine in rubber boats under a smoke screen using captured German barrels of chemicals made to hide targets from bombers. With a bridgehead established on the east bank of the river, Third Army engineers put a bridge across at Hersfeld, stopping halfway so that General Patton could relieve himself in the Rhine, something that he said he had waited a long time to do.

On April 1, the balance of the regiment crossed the river on the bridge, reorganized at Neunkirchen and prepared for the drive to end the war. As commander of the heavy weapons Company "M", I was told to mechanize the unit on its own equipment. Heavy casualties had reduced our manpower so this was an easy task. Our equipment table called for 19 jeeps and trailers, plus a 3/4 ton truck. When we first got into action, both the first sergeant and the supply sergeant told me that they needed an extra jeep, so I authorized them to borrow two as long as the acquisitions were not from the 65th Division. Those extras were soon added to our motor pool. We were now able to move swiftly, so were used as the point of the Third Army in our sector. By April 7, "M" Company had passed Muhlhausen without opposition and we were only about 60 miles from Berlin, expecting to be the first unit to reach that goal. But then we received orders to stop, turn around, and head south. Later, we discovered that since the Yalta agreement gave this mission to the Russians, General Eisenhower decided not to risk any American casualties taking the German capitol.

Our battalion then moved down to the Nuremberg area where the strongest pocket of German resistance remained. We were stopped at the town of Newmarkt, a walled fortress of narrow streets. Young German troops were barricaded in basements with machine guns covering all open areas. They also had several self-propelled 88 MM guns, the most feared German weapon, which they were using like rifles in the canyon-like alleyways. We were stopped cold and our popular regimental commander was relieved of command. The new Colonel held a meeting of all company C.O.'s and asked for ideas to break the impasse. I suggested that I had 81 mm mortars and two trailers full of unused phosphorous shells. If he would let me lob them down the roofs of the buildings sheltering weapons, we could burn them out. The method was approved, the firing was accurate, and after the fires cooled down, we passed through without opposition. Since the war, I have visited Newmarkt several times. It is now a well planned, modern German city.

Company "M" then raced on to the Danube River near Kelheim, crossed it in ferries, and moved eastward along the right bank of the river into Austria.

Operating as the "point" of a military campaign has its interesting moments. For the non-military, the "point" means that you are leading the advance and there are no other friendly troops between you and the enemy. As we were in a column of vehicles moving from Newmarkt to the Danube River, we were strafed by a German jet plane. None of us had ever heard of such an aircraft and the speed of its pass was awesome. Fortunately, the pilot's aim was bad and he missed us, perhaps intentionally. Early in our combat experiences, someone started a rumor that the only weapon we had that scared the Germans was our Browning Automatic Rifle. As a result, many of the more experienced men had "found" such a weapon and again substantially increased our equipment tables. When I saw the plane make a bank for a return shot at us, it didn't take much urging to get them all to fire their automatics into the air, along with our mounted machine guns. The pilot missed again and never returned for another try. Perhaps we could claim a spot in history as having shot down the first jet fighter.

While we were advancing across Austria, we smelled a terrible stench and came upon the notorious Nazi death camp at Mauthausen. The SS guards had fled and the inmates were wandering around in a daze. Unburied corpses, unwashed bodies, human excrement, and living skeletons all contributed to the awful odor. I remembered seeing a truck load of newly harvested small potatoes in a field we had passed and sent the motor sergeant back to bring it in. As he drove through the compound gates, those living who still had any energy scrambled all over the truck devouring the potatoes, dirt and all. We left the truck and I explained to the freed prisoners that we had to continue our march to end the war but that others coming behind us would feed and care for them.

Our orders were to continue until we reached the Enns River and to stop there, build a defense line on the west bank in case the Germans tried to attack, and wait for the Russian army.

The last enemy resistance came at Scharding, Austria, where we crossed the Inns River in rubber boats, under fire.

However, once the crossing was completed and the high ground on the east bank was secured, the war for us was over.

When we reached the Enns River, Company "M" had a sector on the west bank south of the town of Enns. I placed my machine guns and mortars in a defensive position along the river bank, and the men not actively manning the weapons were housed in defile farm buildings behind some small hills. There was one bridge in our area, a farm footbridge that could accommodate small wagons but not motor vehicles.

On May 6, after we had been on the river bank for two days, my command post field telephone rang and I heard my First Sergeant on the line. He said, "Captain, you'd better get your butt down here, because there are a million Germans with white flags who want to cross the bridge and surrender."

When I got to the bridge, the horde on the other side looked like a million. Division records later put the number at 18,000. They had opted to surrender to us rather than to the Russians. I asked a German soldier to bring me a senior officer who spoke English. When their Oberst arrived, I told him to have his soldiers stack their weapons after they crossed the bridge and then to organize them in the adjacent fields until

I found out what to do with them. He promised to do so and I was amazed at the efficiency with which they bivouacked. As a parting query, I asked him where he had learned to speak such good English. His answer was, "At the University of Illinois." That also happened to be my *Alma Mater* and he wanted to talk. I reminded him that the war was over, he was a prisoner, and that we had a non-fraternization policy.

Company "M" remained in the farmhouses and foxholes along the Enns River for a couple of weeks after the war and then we got a break. The City of Linz, Austria, was the last to fall between the two Allied forces. As a result, it was crowded with women and girls who had been fleeing from both armies because of propaganda that they would be raped. Instead, they started bartering with the occupying troops and venereal disease became endemic in the city. The Division commander then ordered that the company with the lowest VD rate would be moved in to police the city. Living in the boondocks, "M" Company had no case reported. So we got to move into nice apartment buildings in the City of Linz and take over the cushy job of maintaining order.

General Upp went from Linz, Austria to Marseilles and flew home with a group of veterans aboard a B-29 bomber by an indirect route. They had pleasant days in southern France; Casablanca, Morocco; Senegal; Natal, Brazil, then Georgetown, British Guinea (now Guyana), thence to Port of Spain, Trinidad, where a hurricane interrupted their passage. Arriving in Miami, the war ended before scheduled rotation to the Pacific.

Brigadier General Upp served as National President of ROA for the term 1972-73 and has continued to be active in leadership of the Association at national and state levels.

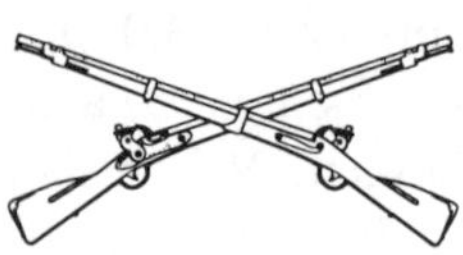

62

Forward Observer in the Bulge

Lieutenant Colonel Alexander A. Terris, USA-Ret.

At the time I was a Captain, a part of the 180th Field Artillery Battalion, 26th Infantry Division. We were part of General Patton's Third Army. Our division had landed in Normandy in August and moved forward rapidly until we got bogged down as we approached the Siegfried Line.

I recall the circumstances of the Battle of the Bulge very well. I was a Liaison Officer, under the S-3 of the DivArty, coordinating the efforts of the forward observers. My battalion of 155 howitzers was in general support, since DivArty consisted of four artillery battalions, one supporting each regiment and the 180th in general support. Each regiment also had a cannon company with their forward observers. We often used their OP to direct fire.

Our division was coming north from Metz against the southern flank of the Bulge, following the 11th and 4th Armored Divisions. But our cleaning up was more like the main effort, since the armored divisions went through so rapidly.

We fired a lot of defensive fire. Actually we fired about six times as much ammunition as the Germans. Many times the artillery fire requested was for non-profitable targets. My job was to screen out some of those requests and establish some sense of priority.

We positioned in front of the town of Wiltz and fired on German concentrations that took some of the pressure off the 101st Airborne Division in Bastogne. We also helped the 4th Armored Division in their breaking through to relieve the surrounded 101st.

Following the Battle of The Bulge we crossed over the Rhine River following the llth Armored and moved into pockets of Germany that had been bypassed. Since I spoke the language, I was able to talk many Germans into surrendering. At one time I was actually captured by them, but was able to convince them of the futility of their position and into

capitulating to my little group: a radio operator, driver and myself. We would merely disarm them and direct them as to which way to walk. It was a bit dangerous, for we ran into cleverly concealed machine-gun positions.

In March and April of 1945 the Germans were retreating rapidly and we linked up with the Russians in Czechoslovakia. Since I also spoke their language, the DivArty Commander, Gen. Ross had me make contact with the Russians near the town of Budweis. At the beginning we got along fine, but shortly after the Russians brought up border guard divisions and they were aloof, uncooperative and unfriendly. The Russians soon became paranoid about the possibility of spies, and they didn't seem to want any contact with us. One job I had was to return to Russian control some of their deserters. Those that had been pillaging I didn't mind, but I regretted having to return some of the others.

We had a general feeling of euphoria that the war was ending. I also recall the Germans often asking when we would get together to fight the Russians. I was not wounded fortunately. I retired as a Lieutenant Colonel, receiving the Legion of Merit, the Bronze Star and other awards.

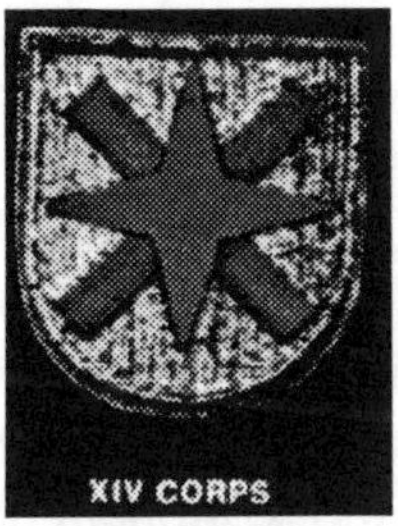

63

Inside Information

LTC Roy T. Uyehata, AUS-Ret.

In early March of 1944, both the U.S. 37th Infantry Division of Ohio and the Americal Division, under XIV Corps, were engaged in heavy combat operations against the Japanese 6th Division from Kumamoto Prefecture, on Bougainville Island, the northernmost island of the Solomons Group. I was a Technician 3rd Grade, POW Interrogator, and a member of the 165th MIS Language Team, attached to XIV Corps Headquarters.

We had captured an unusually great number of Japanese prisoners of war during that campaign.

On the morning of March 8, as I was interrogating a 1st Class Private POW, the POW interrupted my interrogation by asking, "How can I get off this island?" This question from the POW surprised me. I knew that most POWs lied in giving me their surnames, and I also knew, through experience, that none of the POWs wanted to be recaptured by Japanese units. I told him that it would take another three or four days to cut orders for him to become part of a POW shipment to the rear area. Moreover, it would take several more days to assemble enough POWs to warrant their shipment to the rear area.

He was worried that he might be caught in a dilemma, so he remarked, "I guess you know that you are going to be attacked at dawn of March 23rd." March 23rd is a special holiday of the Japanese Emperor known as "Shunki Koreisai."

I knew that this Top Secret information had not been given to our Army Commanders, so I lied and told the POW that this was not new information and that other POWs had also provided me with the plans.

I continued the interrogation for approximately thirty minutes, feigned a headache and told the POW that my headache was so bad that I wanted to return to my office to get some aspirin.

I returned to my office and relayed the warning information to my commanding officer, Captain William Fisher. He was astounded and replied, "A Japanese soldier would not say such a thing." I insisted that the warning information which was given to me by the POW was reliable information, that if he did not believe me, he should send someone to the POW compound to verify or reject the warning message.

Shortly after supper, T/Sgt. Hiroshi Matsuda went to the POW compound and returned, after confirming the warning message by speaking with a Sergeant POW.

Captain Fisher then passed this Top Secret information to Colonel Edgar Treacy, Asst. Chief of Staff, G-2 Section, who in turn passed the important warning information to General Oscar Griswold, commander of XIV Corps.

That evening General Griswold cancelled the showing of all movies by Army units on Bougainville Island until further notice in order to prepare for the anticipated Japanese attack on March 23rd.

During January and February, Japanese forces had laboriously prepared artillery gun positions near the summit of each hill overlooking the American perimeter defense area, a section approximately five miles wide by ten miles long on the north-south axis. The enemy had also distributed hundreds of morale booster leaflets exhorting each soldier to do his utmost for the emperor in order to avenge the defeat they had suffered on Guadalcanal.

Several probing attacks were made by

Bougainville Island, July 26, 1944

Japanese front-line units during the period from March 8 to 20, but they were not taken seriously, since we knew their main attack was scheduled for March 23rd.

In order to launch their main attack at dawn of March 23rd, all Japanese units cautiously approached the American defense perimeter on March 22nd, concentrating their forces along three main avenues of approach, Piva Trail and Numa Numa Trail in the 37th Division sector and an unnamed trail in the Americal Division sector.

All American aircraft which were based on the three airstrips near the south end of the defense perimeter were evacuated to rear areas.

At precisely 7:45 p.m. of March 22nd, we launched a pre-emptive strike using the division artillery of both Divisions and naval gunfire of six destroyers anchored in Empress Augusta Bay. The combined artillery barrage and naval gunfire was so intense that the ground under the XIV Corps Headquarters, which was located approximately 2½ miles from the front lines, shook with the rolling motion similar to that of an earthquake. The front-line was brightly lit with thousands of illuminating flares. While standing in the clearing just south of XIV Corps Headquarters, I heard the muffled "vacuum" sound which was generated by the naval gunfire shells passing overhead with only a few seconds interval. The artillery—naval gunfire barrage was continued for approximately one hour.

Our victory was decisive, as the Japanese soldiers were totally unprepared for the barrage which caught them without the protection of foxholes, trenches or the cover of underground bunkers.

When enemy casualties were counted after the battle action, there were more than five thousand dead and nearly four thousand wounded. Some of the enemy wounded were captured and brought to the 37th Division Mobile Army Surgical Hospital, where I conducted the POW interrogation. U.S. casualties were reported to be 263. The battle action was known as the Second Battle of Bougainville.

Hiroshi Matsuda and I received Bronze Star Medals for providing the fifteen day warning information that saved more than one thousand American lives.

Several weeks later, Colonel Rasmussen, Commandant of Military Intelligence Service

Language School at Camp Savage, Minnesota, came to Bougainville Island to congratulate me for developing the warning information. I was the only MIS Language School graduate to have ever been honored with a personal visit by Colonel Rasmussen. Captain Fisher sent his parents to the Poston Relocation Camp in Arizona, where my parents were confined, to tell my parents that I had performed a very patriotic deed for our country, even though the delegates were not permitted to state the nature of my meritorious service.

LTC Uyehata was recalled for the service in the Korean War from April 1951 to April of 1954. In the Army Reserve he served as a Mobilization Designee in the office of the DCS for Intelligence, Sixth U.S. Army, Presidio of San Francisco, CA. He worked as a Quality/Reliability Engineer, at Applied Technology, Memorex, Sperry Univac and Seagate Technology from 1967 to December 1992, when he retired.

64

Mopping Up On Leyte

Lieutenant Robert L. Mooney,
1st Lt. Inf, AUS

Two weeks into the Leyte Campaign, our 2nd Battalion, 383rd Infantry Regiment, 96th Infantry Division, took the next major objective, a hill stripped of beautiful trees that we had admired only the day prior. Our artillery and heavy mortars had accomplished their work. We met little resistance due to a devastating barrage of firepower. Enemy soldiers were routed from spider holes and caves with hand grenades and small arms fire.

E Company set up a perimeter along the hill covering the valley below. We dug fox holes 20 to 50 feet apart, manned by two or three men. Every man shared in the excavation work, for all of us, officers and enlisted men, carried an entrenching tool or pick mattock.

We had discarded our packs, carrying a poncho and jungle sweater on our cartridge belt, plus a canteen of water kept filled from streams and rice paddies. We purified the water with halazone tablets and took Atabrin regularly which turned our skin yellow. We had discarded our mess kit; a large canteen cup sufficed. A fork, spoon and razor-sharp trench knife were constantly with us.

A fox hole gas stove was available to each squad. White gas in five gallon cans were packed up the trail with rations. I had a turn at carrying one and realized that no pack was heavier. The only extra clothing we had was one pair of socks, which we used also as a wash cloth. We shaved daily and endeavored to keep clean, which was conducive to keeping up morale.

Our E Company sent out patrols as far forward as White Chalk Cliff, where the Japanese prepared positions blocked further movement up the trail. We were also troubled by enemy patrols infiltrating behind us. Outposts had to be maintained at various spots between the forward units and the Battalion base.

It took a party of eighty men every other day to hand-carry enough supplies to maintain the one forward Company with rations and ammunition. Every officer and enlisted man accepted his fair share of packing these up the slippery two mile mountain trail. Any detail that carried a stretcher out returned with supplies. In early December several air drops of rations were made to our battalion dump, reducing some of the long supply haul.

Our E Company set out from the 2nd Battalion base to follow the Benahan River endeavoring to establish a route to Lake Danao. The company was out five days, and I remained three additional days leading a small patrol. We found the rough country was impenetrable. Out of food we had to return.

In jungle warfare no one moved outside his hole after dark, for he risked being shot by his own comrades, a tragedy that did occur. An example of the general confusion of battle was the instance of a lone Japanese soldier strolling calmly into our platoon perimeter one evening believing it to be a Japanese position. One of my men who was busy excavating his fox hole dispatched the visitor with his shovel and went back to his digging.

During the early days on Leyte, a squad leader in my platoon, Sgt. Drummond, stepped on a land mine and was evacuated. He called to me before leaving and presented me with his treasured hunting knife, saying, "Lt. Mooney, this will serve as a trench knife for your protection. Just remember me when you use it." He must have had an intuition that the razor sharp instrument would be needed, for a few days later I was obliged to protect myself at close range, killing two of the enemy.

I developed the habit of holding the knife in the ready position while sleeping in a fox hole. While our battalion was on a mission, I remained in charge of the two remaining platoons while required to defend our strategic stronghold atop a hill overlooking a large clearing. We were dug in with machine guns placed at the outer edge to crossfire the entire front. We thought the danger was largely eliminated, so we had set up a few pup tents.

While fully prepared, we fought an unexpected battle. At midnight, 150 Japanese, drunk on Saki, suddenly attempted to overrun our defenses with a *Banzai* attack. They yelled while charging our positions, firing their rifles and tossing grenades.

We opened fire with everything we had. Our machine-guns blazed away continuously. A few of the enemy penetrated our perimeter and showered grenades into our fox holes. One rolled into my hole, causing us to leave rapidly. I had just expended a third clip of eight .30 cal. rounds through my Garand M-1 rifle. While fumbling to reload, I looked up in time to see several Japanese charging me and my fox hole companion. I rammed the butt of my rifle into the head of one and jabbed my trench knife into his jugular vein, with blood spurting onto my arm. The other "Nip", who had been wounded, was on top of my buddy. I turned and stuck my knife into the man's breast. Fortunately for me, he received a shot to the head from another soldier, for I had difficulty in extracting my knife.

The battle resembled a nightmare. After its conclusion we went on double alert the rest of that night. A number of shots broke the silence during those few hours before dawn. Every time a wounded "Nip" moved or started running he was shot.

Our seven wounded were given first aid and evacuated to a field hospital. The 50 or so enemy dead were buried by mid-morning. We were back to normal by noon and prepared for another attack by the Japanese.

For the balance of December we patrolled the hills, eliminating what few Japanese remained. The enemy action was purely defensive. They showed little desire for combat, but declined inducements to surrender.

Our December patrols were not as debilitating from fighting as from hard marches up and down steep trails, together with the miserable nature of leeches, mosquitoes by the thousands, dysentery, dengue fever, and jungle rot. We suffered untold miseries and fatigue from packing supplies.

On the day after Christmas I led a small patrol behind the enemy lines to where we set up an ambush while enduring torrents of rain. We sat quietly in selected positions for most of the day, ultimately capturing eight severely wounded Japanese of a fifteen man patrol; the other seven were killed.

Although wounded, many of the Japanese tried to escape in the jungle. PFC Ray Webb, my BAR man, found a wounded Japanese in a prone position and thought he could take the man prisoner. But the Japanese rolled over and tossed a grenade. Webb was furious and emptied his magazine into the enemy soldier. Shrapnel from the grenade caught Webb in the stomach, and we had to carry him back.

Mopping up of pockets of enemy continued through January and February, long after the island was strategically secure.

I spent all of February in a tent hospital where I was treated for a nasty infected neck wound from a sliver of shrapnel. The respite allowed me much needed rest. While convalescing, I soaked my feet for an hour three times a day in a purple solution to cure a case of jungle rot.

Our Division, under MG Bradley dispatched some 7,700 of the enemy under awful conditions. Despite the difficulties we accomplished every mission assigned. Our losses, not including the mopping up after

Christmas, were 376 officers and EM killed, four missing, and 1,289 wounded. Another 2,500 were victims of illness or injury.

Gen. Hodge, our 24th Corps Commander, complimented our division, remarking that the 96th had emblazoned on its banners a brilliant and enviable record in its first combat assignment.

Lt. Mooney was wounded twice, was promoted and decorated for heroic leadership in combat. He went on to take part in the invasion of Okinawa on the East China Sea beaches in April 1945. As an acting Company Commander, he was engaged in fierce combat against the Japanese Imperial Army when wounded by several bullets from a machine-gun. Earlier that morning he had been hit by shrapnel but continued in action. Despite all of this, he carried back a more severely wounded officer. Both were hit again by machine-gun bullets. Nevertheless Lt. Mooney got up again and carried Lt. Hill back to the aid station. Despite severe wounds with complications, due to the shortage of officers, Mooney returned again to duty toward the end of the fighting on Okinawa.

He ended his story with these words: "Throughout the long and trying ordeal on Leyte and Okinawa, my faith in God grew. My source of inspiration was Philippians 4:13, 'I can do all things through Christ which strengthened me.' Those words presented new meaning for my life.

"I am thankful to be alive. Each day, rain or shine, I awaken to a beautiful day. I only need to recall those many frightening days in 1944 and 1945 when each morning began with a prayer that this might be my final day.

"I was an Infantry 2nd Lieutenant engaged in fierce combat against the Japanese in a most inhumane warfare. We sustained the loss of many and much suffering. We had little sleep or rest in fox holes so cramped that one could seldom lie in a prone position.

"After five times wounded in action, I am thankful that the Good Lord spared me to contribute in a meaningful way to family, church and community."

Lt. Mooney was recalled to active duty during the Korean Police Action and served nearly a year as a Company Commander, training recruits at Camp Roberts, California. Following that duty he held an assignment as Regimental Trial Counsel and Asst. Regt. Adjutant.

In civilian life, Bob Mooney was a boy Scout Executive, Los Angeles Area Council, retiring in 1977 after 31 years in the profession.

65

From RAF to Army Military Intelligence

Colonel Charles E. Hayden, AUS-Ret.

In August of 1941, before we entered the war, I enlisted in the Canadian Air Force, was trained as a bombardier/navigator and went on to England for advanced and operational training. I flew in bombing missions over Germany in Wellington twin engine bombers, but soon we converted over to Halifax four engine bombers.

Night missions were not flown in formation. Our planes carried .30 caliber machine guns, for our range of engagement was 400 yards or closer, when we were attacked by fighters. Our crew did down two fighters one night. Flak had knocked off the metal cover which prevented the red hot exhaust illuminating us as a target. So we were attacked by a succession of German planes, FW 190's and ME 190's.

We would receive a briefing in a Nissen Hut about dusk or later and would leave just before dusk or after nightfall so that we would arrive over the target during darkness, and, more important, be out of enemy airspace by daylight. Our briefings would cover the route, the force involved, timing and altitude to be flown, as well as identification of targets. We had a tight schedule as to altitude and timing, for the planes would drop their load of bombs within a short time frame. Normally we carried six to eight thousand pounds of bombs, sometimes carrying a single four thousand pounder plus incendiary clusters.

We did not fly as high as the American bombers, usually at 18 to 20 thousand feet altitude. The turbo chargers on the B-17 and B-24 planes allowed those heavy bombers to fly at a higher altitude. We carried a crew of seven men in the Halifax.

While I was the bombardier/navigator, I trained in all of the jobs aboard. We did not have a co-pilot, and cross-training was mandatory so that a casualty could be replaced instantly.

Although not wounded seriously, I was hit by flak several times. Once a two inch piece struck the parachute release buckle, knocking me down and giving me a large bruise. It was fortunate that it hit metal, for otherwise it would have killed me. On another occasion a splinter of flak protruded through my boot cutting my leg slightly. Several times flak hit the plexiglass, shattering it, with the shards cutting my hands slightly.

We had close calls. Once we felt a big explosion under the left wing, but we continued on our mission, dropped our bombs on target and returned. Upon inspecting the aircraft, after it was parked, we found a hole in the underside of the wing but none to the upper surface. It developed that we had a dud 88 mm shell lodged in a gas tank within the wing. The bomb disposal crew found within the shell a ragged piece of paper with the words: "Made in Czechoslovakia". Apparently the forced laborer had not filled the shell with explosives. Had it been so filled we would surely have exploded and all been killed.

Another remarkable instance occurred when we were flying over the North Sea. We iced up quickly when we passed through a cloud and couldn't gain elevation. When we tried to use more power we nearly stalled out. We had to jettison everything. At the time we were carrying a single 4,000 pound bomb that had not yet been fused. (We did not fuse them until over enemy territory.) We were cautioned that we should have 4,000 feet altitude over such an exploding bomb, but we were at 2,000 and could not gain altitude. When the bomb hit the water it exploded, with a huge shock wave like a giant hand slapping us upward. That shock broke off the ice from our plane and we had no further problem, but having no bomb load, abandoned the mission and returned to base. On one mission we had a 20% casualty rate, with three aircraft of the squadron shot down with all aboard killed.

I did not see a German ME 262 jet fighter nor the ME 363 rocket plane in action. But my best friend, a Mosquito pilot on a photo mission was killed by one of the German jet planes. While they could not stay up very long they were incredibly fast. In September of 1943 I was released from the Canadian RAF to join the U.S. Army Air Force, but was assigned back to my original squadron and flew with them for a time. Subsequently I got into aerial intelligence, photo intelligence, and briefing and debriefing returning crews. I did fly a couple of "milk runs" in the B-17 bombers of the 8th AF.

I was recalled to AD during the Korean War for three years but served in Europe as the G-2 Air for 7th Corps. I remained in the reserves, Army Military Intelligence Branch, with a mobilization assignment in the office of the Assistant Chief of Staff, Intelligence, Sixth U. S. Army, until retiring as a Colonel after thirty years American commissioned service.

In retirement, I do volunteer work with Hospice of Marin and with the Twin Cities Police Department. My intelligence background and civilian career in security and safety engineering has been helpful in the tasks I do for the police department.

66

Letters to His Wife from Combat

CWO4 Sidney Bowen, AUS-Ret.

Then T-4 Bowen wrote frequently. While most of the material in his letters was personal and not pertinent to the fighting of the war, there are bits in his book of interest regarding his assignment and combat within an anti-aircraft artillery battalion that shipped to England, and then deployed to France and Belgium.

In his account, he writes: "I can tell you of our first enemy encounter here in France. We were in a ready state, and around midnight a slow-moving and high flying aircraft approached our position and circled about. Suddenly, the surrounding area was awash with the light from several flares dropped from the plane. All of the Battalion gun crews cut loose, and on the Radar scope we could trace the paths of the many projectiles racing toward the target on the PPI screen (Planned Position Indicator). The target on our scope disintegrated into fragments. We traced the fall of the largest fragment. Our CO raced into the set to view the Radar screen and note the azimuth of the falling debris. He was joined by the Range Officer, and they tore off in a jeep hastily endeavoring to find the wreckage. That couldn't be located, for it had fallen into a marshy area which could not be traversed by a vehicle."

On another day, "We have many hostile targets that appear on the Radar screen but none have come within our firing sector. The blips kept the Radar and Director crews on duty around the clock. The gun crews are on stand-by alert and are only called to action with an actual alert. That makes for easy duty for the gun crews. However, some nights are filled with alert after alert, and the gun crews have to take up their posts and abandon card games or whatever."

September 21, 1944: "We had a bit of excitement early tonight. We were seated at chow when WHOOM! A mine went off about 300 yards away, set off by a big, lumbering cow in the pasture next door. We knew there were land mines in the field, as the fences were posted. The field provided a detour around a German roadblock, a concrete emplacement pinching off a road inbound from the beach. A burned-out American tank gave proof to the ruse. A fence had been erected to isolate the area, but cows got in and set off Teller land mines, several in succession."

Thanksgiving, November 23, 1944: "We knew it was Belgium by the water all about us. For three days the downpours have been more than the soil could absorb or could be handled by the drainage canal. Battery trucks were lined up side by side, and food was dished out of the back of the trucks as we sloshed past in overshoes through water ankle deep. We had no place to sit down and ate awkwardly, standing and balancing mess kits. Everyone was pretty well disgusted, need I say."

January 25, 1945: "As you know, I am in a Radar unit on the same identical equipment I trained on at Camp Edwards. The Radar set and the Director unit have to be in sync at all times to insure sending accurate information for firing the big guns. When they are fired the vibrations set up within the ground eventually alter the synchronization between the Radar and the Director. Then we have a daily chore in which we 'orient and synchronize'.

"On Jan. first, New Years Day, I was on the roof of the Radar chassis with head-set on lining up the telescope with the point of reference. Suddenly, to my left, over Battery B, I saw a string of German ME-109 fighters flying low and hedgehopping to prevent our Radar pick-up. I shouted the information over the intercom, and I was answered over the line with a dogmatic voice saying, 'Bull shit!'

"I counted at least forty planes, each carrying a large underslung bomb beneath the fuselage. I insisted the raiders were ME-109s, but another joker came on the line to refute my report with, 'I saw them, they were our own P-47s and 51s.' The planes had flown by so quickly in stealth that no one would confirm my sighting. Within five minutes, we had a report over the Brigade line that a large formation of hostile planes were in the area and that we should open fire without hesitation, using our multiple-mount .50 caliber machine guns. Then there was a great flurry of activity to man the guns, and all other personnel were ordered to take cover. We could not use the big guns because of the low altitude of the planes. The Germans dumped their bombs on the Port of Antwerp. Within 20 minutes of my first sighting, the raiders came back over the same flight course strafing Ack-Ack units with machine gun fire. One of our machine-gunners brought down a plane that crashed a few miles away. The Canadian outfit next door got into the act and dispatched a man on a motorcycle to check the crashed plane. He returned with a naked man secured to the handle bars of the cycle. He turned the prisoner over to his Canadian security section. The Canadian told me: 'I caught the son-of-a-bitch changing from his uniform to civilian clothes. I told him if he didn't like his uniform I was taking him in without it. He about froze his ass on the ride back on the handle bars.'"

After they were out of action Bowen was able to tell, "We landed on Utah Beach on July 16, 1944, moving to Cherbourg and remaining there until August 21, then to Maisy, Normandy, where we were operational in the defense of Omaha Beach. We went on to defend Antwerp and Liege in succession, and from April 12, 1945, were reassigned as a unit to guard POWs."

A total of 45,296 rounds of 90 mm ammo were fired by the 494th Battalion, with a total of 901 kills (270 targets destroyed in air, 631 targets diverted from landing). Bowen's A Battery was credited with an equal share of the kills.

Sidney Bowen continued to serve within the California National Guard and Army Reserve to complete twenty years of service, retiring as a Chief Warrant Officer grade four. His book, *Dearest Isabel*, is a collection of letters to his wife, published by Sunflower University Press, Box 1009, Manhattan, KS 66502. Bowen's civilian career was with the U.S. Postal Service.

67

Landing with an Angel

First Lieutenant Edward J. Scheffelin, USAFR

First Lt. Edward J. Scheffelin joined the 72nd Squadron as a Bombardier in B24s in November 1943, about four months after the Coral Sea battle. He was part of the 5th Bomber Group, 13th AF. At the time of this story he was stationed on Munda.

On the return from one mission against Rabaul, the weather was particularly stormy. It was pitch black except when thunderclouds 60,000 feet high were lit up like Christmas trees from lightning. They were too high to fly over, and it was too dangerous to try to fly under them. Too often those clouds blended with the ocean. Visibility was zero, and the area was dotted with tiny islands and tall mountains. Flying at about 20,000 feet, the pilot, Captain Tom Shearin, had to lace the plane around the menacing clouds. Because they could only use dead reckoning, those maneuvers caused their navigator to lose his position; they were lost.

With only a half hour's worth of fuel left, the crew began to get concerned. All had craned necks at windows, looking for something in the soup. Finally First Lt. Scheffelin saw some anti-aircraft shells exploding in front of them. The navigator determined that the shells had to be coming from Rendova Island, where the US had a small fighter base. Radio silence forbade any contact, but it gave them a position, and the plane made a beeline for Munda, home, about a half hour away. Captain Shearin had all four engines leaned out as much as he dared.

They entered the Munda traffic pattern. On downwind, one engine sputtered and quit. On final, a second engine fizzled out. A B24 lands very heavily on normal landings due to the short chord length of their Davis wings. Good landings required a touchdown speed of 90-100 mph, which also dictates that all four engines are operating. Somehow Shearin made it down in one piece on only two engines. As the plane taxied to the revetment area, a third engine gave up. Shearin parked it with only one engine running, and it had less than five minutes worth of fuel left.

Had it not been for the anti-aircraft fired at them, the crew would not have known where they were in time. They would have gone down. Maybe on an island, maybe on the ocean. Unfriendly land, and unforgiving water. The angel that flew with that crew did not relinquish her duty.

Background Information:

Rabaul Harbor on New Britain Island was the Japanese southernmost stronghold and Navy port. It had a large, well protected lagoon, and it boasted five airstrips complete with fighters and anti-aircraft.

For the push against Rabaul, the Allies would choose an island with at least one airstrip. The Navy would shell the beach, then B25s would drop bombs all along the runway. Last came the landing boats with the invading ground troops, which forced the Japanese deep into the jungle, far enough that they were unable to damage Allied planes and personnel.

August 21, 1943, with sister and father

Often with the ground fighting still going on, the Seabees would repair the airstrip by crushing coral, strewing it over the runway and parking aprons, and compacting it. As soon as the airstrip was ready, the heavy bombers (B24s) arrived, frequently only 3-4 days after the troops hit the beach.

Medium and light bombers would attack Rabaul during the day, and the Heavies would continue throughout the night. Every ten minutes or so, a B24 would take off. From the island of Munda, each mission was expected to take nine hours. In order to maximize their bomb payload, each plane carried only enough fuel for a ten hour mission.

Radio silence had to be upheld. The crew had no radar, no lights, and often no moon to help guide them. Flying at 20,000 feet, they were on their own.

Edward Joseph Scheffelin was born on August 5, 1920 in New Kensington, Pennsylvania. He was living in Coshocton, Ohio when World War II broke out in Europe. He joined the Army Air Corps and was commissioned as a Bombardier in April 1943. Lt Scheffelin flew 44 combat missions during 1943 and 1944 in the Southwest Pacific in B-24s, also known as the Liberator.

He married the former Margaret Ann Merrick in August 1947. Since 1974 they have lived in a house nestled within a floral paradise that covers more than an acre in Carmichael, California. They have eight children, four of whom have served their country in the military service.

Gardening in 1994

68

Naval Intelligence
Tracking the Japanese Fleet

Lieutenant Commander Robert Danforth Ogg, USN-Ret.

Before we were involved in the war, I entered Naval Intelligence in March 1941 as a seaman first class, soon becoming a Chief Petty Officer, and was subsequently commissioned as an officer. I became a specialist in wire tapping of Japanese conferences, set up a censorship station in May of 1941 until replaced by a reserve censorship unit that was mobilized.

My tasks became electronic intelligence gathering, wherein we recorded Japanese radio traffic. We were able to track the Japanese fleet by means of their transmissions. We developed the expertise to distinguish the individual operator's particular manner of transmitting, for every person transmits slightly differently. Thus, by cataloging those slight differences, we could identify the particular ship from which the message was sent. We developed the ability to distinguish the particular differences of sounds created by individual ships of the Japanese fleet by the use of Sofar, underwater listening to propeller sounds. In each case there are subtle differences in propeller sounds and other vibrations of various ships. By tracking these we could place the locations of ships.

You could pick up the sounds as far away as six thousand miles. We found, on November 28, 1941, prior to the Pearl Harbor attack, that the Japanese had put in substitute stations to make us believe that their ships were still in port.

We alerted all the various transpacific communications systems to watch for stray Japanese signals on all radio frequencies.

We picked up the Japanese ships just east of the international date line—half way between Japan and Honolulu—and continued to track them. We found that the Japanese fleet was moving easterly. We monitored and recorded Japanese messages and referred them to linguistic teams for translation.

For the period December 2 through 7, 1941, we tracked the Japanese fleet, and on the night of the sixth we knew the fleet was 500 miles north of Honolulu. We could recognize the ships by their harmonic transmissions, much like distinct fingerprints. This intelligence went forward, thus I am of the belief that high officials were aware of the impending attack.

In civilian life, Bob Ogg was involved in oceanography, geophysics and electronics. He invented the famous Danforth anchor used by ships of all sizes throughout the world. He is a Life Fellow of the Explorers Club; his wife Nancy is also a member.

What Commander Ogg tells us confirms the stories I have heard for many years, attributed to a high level naval officer closely acquainted with the family, namely, that naval intelligence did have advance information of the impending attack. For more detailed discussion of this, see page 359 of Appendix K.

Battleships USS Nevada (foreground) and USS Texas

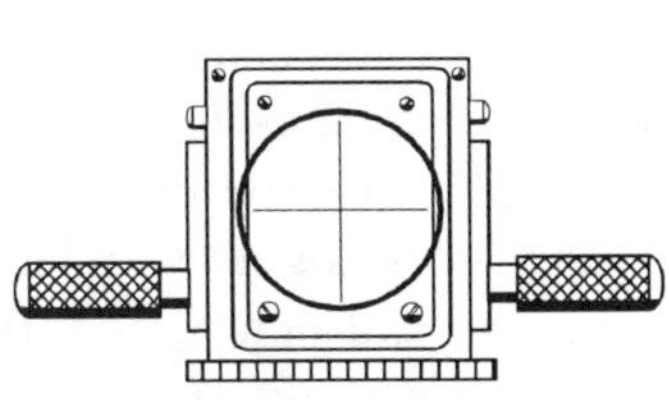

69

Air Offensive Against Japan

Lieutenant Colonel Richard Barclay Vogenitz, USAF-Ret.

The B-29 "Superfortress" was designed to drop bombs from high altitudes and for long-range flights that precluded the accompaniment of friendly fighter cover. They were engineered to be self-defending by installing machine-gun turrets along the top and bottom areas of the aircraft, as well as in the tail.

Being propeller driven, the torque of a clock-wise-turning propeller made it natural for enemy fighters to approach from "Nine-O-Clock-High". Their reasoning was, undoubtedly, that it gave the enemy fighter pilots a split second edge when they dropped the right wing for the initial move against the bomber formation. That approach, in turn, made the left side of each bomber vulnerable. One of the German Luftwaffe fighter techniques was to employ "head-on" attacks. All of these tactics plus Japanese Kamikaze mentality caused us much concern. The "Tail-end Charlie" position in any bomber formation was not a welcome assignment.

The 11 crew members each had different vantage points and all had to work together to fend off attacks, particularly when Japanese planes would penetrate formations and would be likely to attack from almost any angle. In fact, American bombardiers rarely thought, in training, that they would be called upon to use the forward nose gun turrets as much as they did in combat. Forward, of course, the officers had the best view of what was building up. The Central Fire Control non-commissioned officer, Tech. Sgt. C.B. Wall of Texas, was quite often heard on the intercom turning over direct control of some of the six .50 caliber machine-guns to the bombardier. There were four guns topside forward and two mounted just behind the nose-wheel opening below.

The B-29's involved in the great Air Offensive—Japan of November 1944 and until 6 August 1945 were pressurized, since we flew at high altitudes. Oxygen masks were standard equipment. Our pilot and aircraft commander (Capt. Gordon A. Anderson) and co-pilot (1st Lt. Herbert R. Snow) never liked to enter a target area while pressurized. We were told that if flak, bullets or phosphorous bombs penetrated the thin aluminum aircraft skin, the sudden change in pressure would throw us around the plane badly if it did not eject us. Thus we often were on oxygen masks while de-pressurized at high altitudes.

The left and right side waist gunner plastic viewing bubbles were notoriously weak, so we would tie a strong rope around an ankle, especially when pressurizing, for the danger of being blown out of the aircraft was a real possibility. The guns for the left and right waist of the plane were electronically controlled from the gunner's sighting device. This device had a variable circle of light in which we constantly framed the enemy fighter and then fired by pressing a large firing button.

Our supply of .50 caliber ammunition was stored in a large, round, light-weight metal container in the Radar Officer's compartment. We gunners loaded our ammunition barrels ourselves with great care before each mission. For daylight missions every 5th round in the lengthy belt was a tracer bullet.

Sergeant John Gerbig was our tail gunner on "Liberty Belle II." At age 19 he was the youngest of our crew. The enemy attacks toward the nose and tail of the aircraft were quite distinct from side attacks. The side attack was called the "Fighter Pilot's Pursuit Curve". The fighter would come up and position himself slightly higher than our altitude and about 2000 yards or less to the side. Then he would enter a set

B-29 "Liberty Belle II" in revetment on Guam after night mission on Japan, summer 1945

sequence of dropping the wing nearest the bomber and begin to turn in, maneuvering for his gun-bearing position, and then begin firing. Then he would break away. As many of the bomber's guns as could track him would be firing throughout this sequence. The opposite waist gunner had the best chance of picking up the enemy during this 'break-away'. Control was transferred by a switch on a wall circuit box. It was said that it took the Japanese fighters about 45 seconds to get into position to try again after they fired and broke away.

Gunners did not have cameras to record possible 'kills' and policy was unclear as to which gunner or set of gunners should get proper credit. At times, if we were cut off from our squadron formation such as occurred in the boiling, debris-filled 40,000 foot high smoke cloud after bombing Osaka, Japan, on June 1, 1945, we would be firing our 'twin-fifties' on a one-to-one basis. When we could rejoin formations to evacuate the target area we had more safety in numbers against fighter attacks. On one occasion I was firing at a Zero coming from 9 o'clock high, who came so close that I could see the white scarf he was wearing. Although some other crew members were also firing I was given credit for half of that kill.

The courage it must have taken for Japanese pilots to face our concentrated fire-power was admired by many. Inside our bomber, I recall hearing on the intercom about suicide pilots flying rocket bombs (Baca Bombs) trying to collide head-on with our USAAF bombers. Our pilots dodged those with violent maneuvers!

Sgt. Richard B. Vogenitz guarding B-29 aircraft on Iwo Jima (refueling), April or May 1945

One memorable incident involved me walking a narrow catwalk to try to release a bomb that was stuck, swinging on one shackle, and had not fallen with the rest of the load. I wore a chest parachute as I walked over the open belly of the plane. Fortunately, one kick managed to dislodge the bomb. Being a totally black night, I was allowed only one flick of the flashlight to locate this 500 pounder.

Our crews were picked as "Select Crews" with General Curtis E. LeMay's 20th US Army Air Force. The General believed in 'measured force' and we were told the staff calculated only enough to cause a surrender of Japan. On our flights, our views of the damage on the ground convinced me that Japan's surrender would come from air power alone. I was then only 23 years old, and on the first mission I was appalled at the damage I saw, even though I was kept busy lining up my "cross-hairs" on an attacking fighter element.

The dangerous flights over Japan were worrisome, but one morale booster was the fact that the Navy had established a submarine picket system off the Japanese coast so that any B-29's which were shot down or disabled could be rescued (provided they were five miles or more offshore). The submarines knew our probable return routes from bombing runs and if our pilots could manage to get the aircraft out past the five-mile zone, and beyond the mine-fields, there was a very good chance that the crew could be rescued if downed or forced to bail out.

The difficulty of finding downed crews, however, was made clear to us on one occasion when we were called upon to lead a two-plane, two-day search for a downed plane near Iwo Jima. We flew from dawn to dusk for two days but were never able to find the downed airmen. (After the war, I received a call from the mother of one of those downed crewmen. She couldn't understand why we could not have seen their life rafts (one-man rafts). I tried to explain that at the 500 to 700 foot altitudes that we had to fly above the water, those small rafts would look as big as a postage stamp, especially in the stormy seas we had searched.)

Friction among bomber crewmen was rare—most of it was weeded out in our corn and wheat belt training period in Kansas and Nebraska. The friction shown in the Hollywood movie about the "Memphis Belle" was not typical in our crews in the 61st Bomb Squadron (VH).

We were totally prepared, mentally, spiritually and physically, to cover the proposed invasion of Japan in November 1945. There were one-thousand B-29's in the force. The dropping of the atomic bomb and the surrender of Japan which followed came as a surprise to us, as well as some relief. I can only guess what might have happened if we had had to face the estimated 12,000 Japanese aircraft that had been prepared by Japan to repel the invasion forces.

When the bomb was dropped I happened to be on rest leave at an Air Force Camp on Oahu, Hawaii, and most of our combat air crews never returned to our Marianas Islands bases. While at the rest camp we received permission to purchase low-cut Army shoes at the Hickam Field officer's clothing store to replace our somewhat heavy ankle-length "Brogans". As a group of us were waiting in line near the entrance, we had the opportunity to see General Jonathan Wainwright, the hero of Corregidor, being driven up to the store entrance. He had just been flown out from a Japanese Prisoner of War camp in Manchuria and needed new presentable uniforms for the forthcoming surrender ceremonies on the *USS Missouri*, which occurred a few days later. We were impressed with his dignity. He returned our salutes with a smile as he passed by.

The name for our aircraft, "Liberty Belle II", was chosen by us in honor of our aircraft commander's missing brother, who was lost when the original "Liberty Belle" (a B-17) was downed in enemy action over Europe. Captain Anderson had courteously asked us for possible names for our then new B-29. When another officer told us about his missing brother we were unanimous in voting for the name "Liberty Belle II".

In discussing our experiences with Capt. Anderson, we agreed on one of our most memorable occasions. After being on Eniwetok Atoll (N.W. Marshall Islands) for nearly a week, awaiting a new engine from Hawaii, our aircraft was given permission to fly over the battleship *USS Iowa* at anchor. A thousand or more faces were turned skyward while waving a send-off to us on our last leg toward Guam.

Looking back over the past 50 years, and at our 1944-45 "Global" 20th USAAF shoulder patch, I can't help feeling that our B-29 "strategic" bombers were truly the forerunners of the post-war "Strategic Air Command" of the USAF. Back then we only lacked air-to-air refueling capability to give us a world-wide reach.

Aerial Gunner's wings

70

Landing Ship Tank

CWO4 David L. Wischemann,
USCGR-Ret.

Eager to get into the service, I enlisted in the Coast Guard immediately after graduating from High School in June, 1943. After completing training I was sent to New Guinea on a troop transport with orders to become part of the crew of a Coast Guard manned Landing Ship Tank LST 18 operating in the South West Pacific.

Catching up with my ship proved more difficult than I ever anticipated. In crossing the Equator, being the lone CG man aboard and just a youngster, the Neptune Party seized me as a Pollywog to give a thorough hazing. Conditions on the Naval Transport Ship *Harry L. Taylor* were grim for 18 days at sea. We landed in Milne Bay the third week of June 1944, but I didn't catch up to my ship until early in September.

The day we left Hollandia for the invasion of Leyte, Humboldt Bay was crammed full of ships of every description. Late in the afternoon whistles and ships horns began to sound, and suddenly all of the ships began a massive, orderly exit from the anchorage. Ours was one of the last ships to leave. As we exited through the harbor mouth, I looked back and was surprised to see that the enormous harbor was devoid of any vessels. I thought of how difficult and extensive the planning must have been to coordinate such a highly complex operation.

We took our position in the last file of ships in the convoy. The only ships following us were a small escort carrier and two destroyer escorts protecting the rear of the armada. Ahead of us, as far as you could see, there was nothing but a vast gray mass of ships of every description. About three days out we were joined by ships of the Third and Fifth Fleets, comprising together about six hundred ships in the invasion force.

We took seven days from Hollandia to Leyte Gulf, which we entered at night, in the dark of the moon, October 19, 1944.

The Army Rangers had taken a small island at the entrance to the Gulf and were signaling instructions to the ships. The mass of 600 ships, in ranks and lines like a platoon of soldiers, passed the small island at the direction of signal lights. At some pre-arranged point each ship blew it's horn and made a 90 degree turn to Port. With all the ruckus, I wondered how much surprise our invasion would be to the enemy. However I learned later that our destroyers had been in Leyte Gulf for the three days preceding engaged in shelling the beach and sweeping mines.

We approached the assigned beach about daybreak, just as the entire assembled navy commenced a massive bombardment. I have never experienced such a tremendous show. For two hours there was nothing but a continual roar of ear splitting explosions and gunsmoke so thick that you could not see the land. I could not visualize how any living thing could survive that shelling.

David Wischemann, age 19, aboard LST 18, USCG

As the bombardment lifted, the first assault infantry waves headed for the beach. Accompanying those troops were Beachmasters, small groups of Navy or Coast Guard officers and enlisted men who set up markers to identify the landing location of each amphibious vessel. Once the markers were set we were given orders to weigh anchor and prepare to beach.

While we were waiting, a lone Japanese bomber overhead slowly approached the center of the fleet. Every ship that could bear a gun on that plane commenced firing. It must have been his lucky day, for no one hit it. He dropped two bombs that exploded in the water, one fore and another aft of a destroyer. Then the plane flew slowly back to wherever it came from.

Our ship proceeded at top speed of six or seven knots toward the designated marker, struck the sandy bottom, shuddered, then moved ahead a short distance.

My assigned position was in a small bullet-proof booth, where I operated electrical switches to open the bow doors and lower the ramp. My booth was on the tank deck, port side, just aft off the ramp. As word passed to me to open the bow doors and lower the ramp, I watched, with much apprehension, through a one inch bullet-proof window. Sunshine gradually began to flood the tank deck, but no enemy fire struck us.

We were finally on the sandy beach of Leyte, but the invasion area was a shambles. Many of the palm trees had been cut off by shellfire. We saw Navy bombers pass overhead then dive out of sight behind trees just back of the beach. This would be followed by a series of explosions. Any enemy there were catching hell.

The first rig out was a bulldozer that the Army Engineers had retrofitted with a steel cab to protect the operator. He built a ramp of sand for our trucks and equipment to leave the ship.

Despite all of the bombardment and all the people and equipment milling around a lone caribou cow and her calf ambled down the beach utterly unconcerned.

We of the crew were glad to see disembarked the 300 barrels of high octane aviation fuel and 300 artillery rounds, for they had been stored against the bulkhead that separated that cargo from the crew's quarters.

Some of the ships drew enemy artillery rounds, so we were ordered to make fog, to cover the unloading operations. None of the rounds hit near us. We unloaded all night. Early the next morning, October 21, our ship retracted from the beach and headed toward the mouth of Leyte Gulf to make up the first convoy going south to pick up more troops and cargo. It was lucky for us to be in the first convoy, for the area got quite HOT the next couple of weeks.

David Wischemann retired from the Coast Guard Reserve in 1985 with 34 years service. Construction has been his civilian occupation, and he retired from the Coast Guard Training Center, Petaluma, California, as an Engineering Technician in 1987.

71

155 Howitzers in Support

Lieutenant Colonel Edward Douglas Doughty, AUS-Ret.

Entering the Army prior to our involvement in the war, I was inducted 22 March 1941, and was among the first soldiers trained at Camp Roberts. From there I went on to Artillery Branch OCS. Returning to Camp Roberts my assignment was to the 947th Artillery Battalion, with which I served throughout the war in the Pacific Theater.

Attached to the 41st Infantry Division, our battalion moved to a staging area at Finschafen 21 March 1944. The next month we boarded ships for Hollandia on the north coast of the western part of New Guinea. After many delays in moving from the beach, my first day of directing fire on the enemy as a First Lieutenant forward observer was 2 May 1944. That was the first time the M-1 howitzer was used against the Japanese in the southwest Pacific. Our work on Hollandia was light, so on 6 May we started staging for Biak Island, an island off New Guinea, largest of the Schouten Islands, which had three airstrips on the south coast.

The battalion's assigned mission was to provide general support, reinforcing the light artillery and firing counter-battery missions. The first day was easy but exciting. From then on it was rough duty. We were attacked by Japanese planes, and their soldiers in coral rock hillside positions and from within caves on the cliffs. They rained devastating fire on us down from the heights. When the enemy had isolated the 3rd infantry battalion, commanded by LTC Paul Hollister, on the narrow coastal strip and was incurring heavy casualties, we had a call for help. They were hard pressed and believed they had to pull back. So I jumped into a boat that had been evacuating wounded and went across to where they were. On the way over the Japanese spotted my boat and opened up with machine-gun fire. But they were poor shots. Despite heavy fire from the Japanese I landed and joined the advance elements. After I got there, I found the 3rd infantry battalion was really in a bad spot, and the troops

(above) Lt. Doughty receiving the DSC from B.G.Chandler, CG of the Division Artillery, 1944

(left) Lt. Col. Edward Doughty taking the Oath of Office, 1994

were getting panicky. Its supporting artillery from the Divarty had been displaced back about four miles. We were able to give them some relief by my directing accurate heavy artillery fire. I climbed on top of the lead tank to better direct artillery fire. However I left the tank and advanced ahead to get better observation. Our artillery fire then broke up the attack. As forward observer with the 3rd battalion, 162nd Infantry, my job was to stop the advance of the enemy counter-attack. With my driver also acting as radio operator we moved forward for observation. Directing the artillery fire down as close as a hundred yards from our troops, we continued fire all night. Before morning battalion fire was cut to battery fire for the lack of sufficient ammunition.

Lt. Doughty in the jungles of Leyte, overlooking Armoc. This wasn't a fancy dress battle. It took place in a hot, steamy jungle where our men displayed enormous courage.

The next morning the situation became acute, and the infantry battalion had to withdraw along the coast. The enemy had isolated the 3rd infantry battalion on a narrow coastal strip and was delivering heavy fire from caves in the cliff above. We had to fight our way back a distance of two miles. I moved back with the rear guard at the end of the column, directing accurate artillery bursts to the battalion's rear and flanks as we proceeded. It was in effect a rolling barrage in reverse. With that fire registered at my direction we were able to complete the withdrawal with minimum casualties.

Japanese patrols tried to reach our gun position to endeavor to take out the guns but failed.

On the night of 4 January 1944, our artillery battalion was notified that a strong Japanese fleet, including battleships, was expected to arrive in an attempt to reinforce the Japanese garrison on the island. We repositioned the guns to face the threat from the sea, but the Japanese fleet had been hit hard by our naval aircraft and fled the area.

On Biak Island we had three months of rough fighting, for the enemy was well established in caves and fortifications. Most of my time was spent observing by plane or up front with the infantry directing artillery fire.

On 1 October 1944 our battalion was attached to X Corps to be part of King 2 Task Force to participate in the Leyte invasion. We returned to Hollandia to regroup with the large convoy, sailed 16 October 1944 and entered San Pedro Bay (Leyte) on the morning of 22 October 1944. A big naval battle was taking place. We landed in heavy rain and faced the problems of heavy mud in moving inland. Those were four hard, tough months on Leyte. I spent seven days and nights with an infantry unit in the mountains above Ormoc Lake watching for the arrival of new Japanese troops moving into the area. In the early dawn and fog I fired on what I thought was a Japanese troop movement but which turned out to be a herd of water buffalo.

We did use the 155 guns in the fight at Ormoc Bay when the Japanese sailed their ships close to land and within our range.

On 28 December 1944 our battalion was attached to the 1st Cavalry Division an arrangement that continued on through the end of the Leyte Campaign.

Subsequently we sailed from Leyte in a convoy headed for Lingayen Gulf, Luzon, to support the artillery of the 1st Cav. Div. We landed on 28 January 1944. While assembled at the town of Guimba the division was visited by General Douglas MacArthur and Lt. Gen. Walter Kreuger. The division was ordered to take the city of Manila seventy miles south. On 5 February 1945 the division commander ordered all available trucks to go to Bilibid Prison to evacuate released American and Philippine POWs. I made this trip in, the prisoners came out, but I stayed in Manila, moving from one house top to another. Continuing on to church towers I directed fires all over Manila at military targets and onto enemy ships in the bay. While moving toward Fort McKinley, I directed the largest artillery concentrations fired during the Luzon Campaign. All guns of the division and our battalion each fired ten rounds against a large target. Moving on easterly to Antipolo I directed Naval aircraft to their target on a bombing mission. After the fall of Manila we moved south to Mt. Olila, San Pablo, doing reinforcing fires.

After 28 June 1945 our battalion remained in rest camp preparing for participation in the invasion of Japan.

I was awarded the Distinguished Service Cross for my activities in the Biak Island campaign 28-29 May 1944 and the Bronze Star for my part in directing artillery east of Manila. I was released from active duty in February 1946 but stayed in the Reserves, retiring as a Lieutenant Colonel 29 March 1974. In civilian life I was in the construction business.

72

Thanksgiving with Royalty

Colonel Robert J. Greenwald, AUS-Ret.

While the trip across the Atlantic remains conspicuous in my recollections, the afternoon tea with royalty was perhaps the most memorable event during my war years.

I was a First Lieutenant with the 326th Ordnance Company aboard the Queen Mary on a full speed transit of six days in December of 1942 in the worst time to cross the ocean. I was sick in my bed after the first day with the ship continuing to roll from end to end and side to side. Later I learned from retiring Cunard Lines Captain Bissett how unusually rough it was on that voyage and of his fears that the mighty Queen might capsize in the huge waves.

On November 20, 1943, I received an invitation from Buckingham Palace inscribed: "The Master of the Household is commanded by Their Majesties to invite Robert J. Greenwald, 1st Lt., U.S. Army to an Afternoon Party on Wednesday the 24th November 1943 at 3:15 p.m."

I was surprised to be included, for most of the guests were high ranking officers from ETO and the African Theater. At least fifty generals were among the guests. We had a briefing as to protocol and were picked up in a large black Daimler limousine and driven to the palace in style.

We entered the great iron gateways and crossed the courtyard to the main entrance. Proceeding up the steps we were greeted by two footmen of the King's household clad in scarlet and gold livery, then entered the great doors of the King's London home.

I recall King George wearing a full naval uniform, a man with a youthful figure, who stood tall with a quiet but dignified bearing, giving me the handshake one would give to a friend. Queen Elizabeth was wearing an afternoon dress and gave everyone a friendly smile and a handshake.

After we passed through the receiving line, we moved into the large hall for a buffet of finger sandwiches and beverages, including some of the best Scotch. While in the dining room the royalty separated into three corners where the guests might have an informal chat. So I visited the King and the Queen in their corners and the two princesses, Elizabeth and Margaret Rose in another. The conversation was primarily of: "What part of the States are you from?" and "How long have you been here?"

A military band played in the background throughout the tea party. We had been advised that when the band played the British national anthem, the party was over. Upon hearing "God Save the King", there was a general movement toward the doorways. After collecting our coats and hats, we exited the main palace door to our waiting limousines, leaving with a lasting memory.

Robert Greenwald's position in Europe during the war was with the Special Staff in Paris and London, writing and researching for historical purposes. He edited the complete edition of the *U.S. Army Order of Battle Divisions–Europe*. He stayed in the reserves and completed thirty years commissioned service, retiring as a Colonel.

Paris, VE Day. Col. Robert J. Greenwald (then Captain) with throngs of celebrators

73

US Navy Duty in Australia

Donn C. Bolthouse, Commander USN-Ret

August 7, 1942: The invasion of Guadalcanal by the First Marine Division was the first significant offensive action of the Allies in the Pacific. A flotilla of ships covering the horizon as far as one could see took the First Marines into Guadalcanal. My cruiser, the *USS Chicago,* along with others, had gone to Wellington, New Zealand, in the first week of July to pick up the First Marines. Other ships joined as we proceeded toward the Guadalcanal assault. Our battleships, including the *USS North Carolina*, and some aircraft carriers escorted the troop transports carrying the Marines.

Guadalcanal was a peaceful landing because it was a complete surprise to the Japanese, but it became the longest-fought land battle in the Pacific, taking about six months. It was a dreadful place to be in combat.

Two days later, after the landings, the Japanese fleet, on August 9, 1942, slipped by Savo Island and the other islands surrounding the Guadalcanal area and managed, partly by accident, to mount a totally devastating assault on our fleet. As they swept through, they sank the American cruisers *Astoria*, *Quincy*, and *Vincennes*, and the Australian cruiser *Canberra*. About 2 O'clock in the morning they shot the bow off my ship, the *Chicago*, with the torpedo fortunately missing the gasoline storage area by a mere 10 feet. Since I was ahead of the gasoline storage by about 15 or 20 feet it was one of those lucky breaks for me, because a hit in that section would have sunk the ship.

I was lucky to come out of that battle (called the Battle of Savo Island), but it cost more than 1000 lives, primarily American; there were some Australians, of course. The Captain of the *Canberra* was killed. (Later, his widow married our Commodore who became head of the Service Force in 1943.)

After the battle, the *Chicago* was sent to Sydney for repairs, and an upshot of that trip was that some of us were transferred ashore to become part of the newly-created Service Force of the South West Pacific.

At that time, the officer in charge of Public Works in Australia, who was in Brisbane with the operational top command, had only one assistant 3000 miles away. When he saw the orders of the three of us going ashore, he went to Admiral Carpender and asked if he could have us. The Admiral said "Yes", so by accident I became the Public Works Officer of the Sydney and outward areas. (After 3 days of indoctrination, my boss went back to Brisbane and didn't come back for two years!) As a result, I had to handle all the headquarters work for the Service Force. It became a fascinating and intensely busy job, requiring creativity to get production projects started to support Navy needs.

Most of the work for the Navy and Army in that area was done by the Australian Department of Interior on Reverse Lend-Lease. There was

a complicated procedure to get a project started and completed. Everything we needed was scarce so everything had to have a priority and approval of the Naval Board for financing, and the approval of an organization called the Works Priorities Sub-committee. This Sub-committee met once a week on Fridays, and if one didn't have the necessary papers in by then the job would be delayed for another week. Usually, it took 42 days to go through the process and get something started. At one time I had copies of correspondence between General MacArthur and the Prime Minister complaining about the length of time it took. Generally, however, it didn't take me that long; in one case I got one project started in one day! That was because they trusted me to follow with the necessary paper-work and approvals. I was also helped by the fact that I was not an engineer so I would not try to tell the Australian Engineers how to do it better. (The US Army, which had qualifying engineers doing this sort of thing would get into time-delaying arguments with the Australians as to the best way to do something.) I would just simply say "It looks great fellows. How fast can we get started and get on to the next thing?" So the fact that I was not an engineer was actually an asset.

Procurement of essential items and materials and machinery was also an important part of my job. Everything was rationed. The civilian population could not get things as small as electric heaters, for example, because the military had first priority. Even so, the problem of scarcities compared to needs was always present.

Our construction projects included a number of warehouses, some of which were built on railway tracks so that trains could come inside to load and unload. One of the significant projects we had was creation of the equivalent of a destroyer-tender on a wharf in Sydney which would free up an actual Navy destroyer-tender or repair ship to go farther north where the action was. We built three of these on Sydney wharves (called, in aboriginal language, *Wooloomooloo*.)

We were responsible, also, for Admiral Barbey's amphibious base training camp at Port Stevens, 126 miles north of Sydney. The one project which gave us great pleasure to cancel in mid-1945 was a knock-down steel pontoon program being developed at Newcastle (the Australian steel center). These pontoons were being built for the planned invasion of Japan. They were to be loaded on Landing Ships and slipped off to become tank and vehicle tracks over the beaches during the invasion.

About six or eight months before the war in Europe ended, part of the British fleet was freed to transfer to the Pacific war to support us. On Christmas Day of 1944 I was standing on a balcony of a house overlooking the harbor when I saw an aircraft carrier coming in through the fog. "That's impossible!", I thought, "We don't have any carriers here." I was then able to turn over most of the facilities the British needed, and became a familiar figure. I was able to visit a number of their ships, including the *King George V*. As just a lowly Lieutenant, traditionally not entitled to the honor, it was a real pleasure to be piped aboard the British ships which extended that courtesy to officers of other navies regardless of rank.

Another interesting project was creating Base Hospital Ten, some 20 miles out of Sydney. I got the hospital from the Army because they were vacating it to go to New Guinea. The transfer was better for us than having to build one (which we had started to do). We upgraded it to Navy standards and enjoyed a wonderful relationship with the hospital people for the balance of the war.

As I mentioned, many of my projects were done by Australia under the Reverse Lend-Lease program. Towards the end of the war (May or June 1945) a small group of three congressmen, an admiral, and a quiet man in a grey suit, came into Sydney. As we made a tour of the area I landed in the station wagon with this gentleman. It turned out that the admiral was working for this civilian who was W.J. McNeal, the Comptroller of the Defense Department (and who later became president of the Grace Lines shipping company). When he heard what I had to say about us getting credits for returning properties, he was very interested. Over a period of three days we developed a paper to get credits for returned properties under the Reverse Lend Lease program. One of the results was that we sold the Hollandia real estate to the Dutch for 6 million dollars.

Arriving back in the United States in the first week of January 1946 I could look back on these three and a half years of invaluable experiences with great satisfaction, even though I was a battleship man grounded by the fortunes of war.

74

Why President Truman Dropped the Bomb

Colonel John H. Roush, Jr., AUS-Ret.

To understand why President Truman dropped the bomb, one must consider "Operation Downfall", once labeled "Top Secret". Few people are aware of the extensive plans prepared for the invasion of Japan in our final efforts to conclude the war in the Pacific.

Many of us, including the writer, and most of the participant servicemen whose stories are included in this volume, would have been directly involved in that action had it not been for the courage of President Harry Truman in ordering delivery of the two atomic bombs.

Some present day critics say it was not necessary, that Japan already could recognize defeat and would have surrendered irrespective. Not so! Top military leaders of the day were in almost unanimous agreement that an invasion would be necessary to end the war.

Although it would have been possible to bomb Japan extensively with conventional explosives and to establish a naval blockade, that would have choked the enemy to some extent but not destroyed his armies nor their will nor that of the people to fight with ferocity for their homeland.

Captured documents and interviews of key military persons disclose the elaborate plans that were being made by the Japanese to defend their home islands.

Information developed later resolved that the Japanese were saving most of their aircraft, fuel and pilots in reserve for the final battle in defense of the home islands. Their plan for the defense of Japan, *Ketsu-Go* included many underground hangers and take-off strips for the launching of massive suicide attacks using improved types of *Kamikaze* craft, as well as conventional aircraft so used. The Japanese had accumulated a total of nearly thirteen thousand planes for the final defense. They were building a more effective model of the German V-1

Buzz-bomb but modified to include a suicide pilot, greatly increasing their chances of striking their target.

The *Ketsu-Go* included methodical means calculated capable of destroying eight hundred Allied ships. Their Air Force of Army and Naval fighters were to fight to the death to control the skies over the southernmost of the principal islands, with as many as 5,000 planes (including the *Kamikaze* craft used in successive waves, which they calculated would be sustained for ten days. The Imperial navy was to also have been totally committed. Some destroyers were to be beached at the last minute to create anti-invasion gun platforms.

The Japanese planners were convinced that they could shatter any invasion force so that the demoralized Americans would back off and they would accept a less than unconditional surrender on face-saving terms.

Even had the Allies gained a foothold on the main islands, the Japanese had plans to mobilize the full population in the fiercest and most fanatical defense that could be conceived.

(from left) Col. Douglas A.Riach, AUS-Ret.; Lt. Gen. Glynn Mallory, CG Sixth U.S. Army; Col. John H. Roush, Jr., AUS-Ret. Both Colonels Riach and Roush served for a number of years as IMA (Individual Mobilization Assignees) in important positions within Sixth Army Headquarters.

The numbers of Japanese land forces facing the planned invasion force were considerably greater than the over half million men planned to constitute our initial commitment. And those defenders would have been hard-core, well trained troops, many the elite of their army. The Japanese had a national slogan—One hundred million will die for the Emperor and nation—and few doubted that they were, as a whole population, prepared to fight to the death. Twenty-eight million had been enrolled in a National Volunteer Combat Force.

"Operation Downfall" included two massive military undertakings: Operation Olympic, the invasion of Kyushu by 6th U.S. Army, consisting of 14 combat divisions of American soldiers, was scheduled for November 1, 1945 (X-Day) and Operation Coronet, the invasion of Honshu by the 8th U.S. Army consisting of at least 22 more American combat divisions, possibly 28, was tentatively scheduled for March 1, 1946 (Y-Day).

Clearly the loss of lives would have been far greater, probably more than twenty fold had the invasion plans been carried out. The bombing of Hiroshima on 6 August and of Nagasaki on the 9th averted the need for the scheduled invasions. Had it taken place the results would have been far worse. Japan as a culture would have been largely destroyed. Very likely the Soviets would have moved in to divide the country such as was done in Korea and Germany.

In the invasion efforts many of those here mentioned in the earlier pages would have become casualties or worse. Young American officers would have had little chances of survival of the sustained fierce battles, nor would many of the enlisted men fare any better. Many of our battle weary divisions were scheduled to rotate directly to the invasion of Japan from German ports. Practically all of the American combat units would

The "Enola Gay", the B-29 that dropped the bomb on Japan

have been required for the two operations. As one of those so scheduled, who would have likely been killed, and speaking for all the rest of us, I am glad that President Truman exercised his wise decision to end the war forthwith.

Over 1.5 million American combat soldiers with millions more in support would have been involved in the two amphibious assaults, a military undertaking that would have been extremely costly in human lives. The Japanese had correctly calculated where the invasion would attempt their landings and had assembled more than twice the defensive force as compared to our calculations of enemy strength.

Few people are aware of the awful typhoon in October 1945 that twice struck the area in which the fleet would have been assembling for the invasion had it not been cancelled. The massive destruction that would have followed would have seriously jeopardized the possibilities of success and given great encouragement to the Japanese to persist.

It is clear from a study of the intelligence available and of the plans our military staffs prepared in light of then available information of the intent and capabilities of the enemy that the battle that was to ensue would have become the most awful blood bath in the history of modern warfare.

For further details reference is made to the article by James Martin Davis, "Operation Olympic—An Invasion not Found in History Books", page 18, *Military* magazine, January 1995, Vol. XI, No. 8. Thousands of documents were prepared by military staffs in the Spring and summer of 1945, and reviewed by the author upon their declassification.

75

Eyes Only

Col. Gene A. Robens, AUS-Ret.

Colonel Robens, as a young Lieutenant Colonel, flew to London in January 1944, five months before D-Day, to become part of General Dwight Eisenhower's staff. As a member of the SHAEF Headquarters, he was assigned to the Adjutant General's Department. While he did not experience actual combat, he was assigned a role in the overall planning of D-Day and the Battle of Normandy.

Prior to being sent to England he served on the Western Defense and Fourth Army Headquarters staff, at the Presidio of San Francisco. It was there that he unwittingly became privy to one of the most important military secrets ever transmitted in our country. It concerned the bombing of Pearl Harbor. No one in responsible military or government circles knew how badly we had suffered, what our losses were, whether we could recover from them. Secretly, Admiral Chester Nimitz was dispatched by President Roosevelt to investigate and report back to him on the damage inflicted to our naval forces.

First Lieutenant Robens had been transferred, the day after the attack upon Pearl Harbor, from the 41st Infantry Division where he had been stationed, to the Headquarters of the Western Defense Command and Fourth Army. He was assigned to the Adjutant General's Department, which is in charge of all Top Secret documents and custodians of the highest military priority information. As a junior officer, he was promptly given, upon reporting in, the graveyard shift. Just two days later, at 3:00 a.m. a Navy Commander was ushered into his office by an armed military police officer, with a briefcase chained to his wrist. The courier insisted: "I have a top secret message from Admiral Chester Nimitz for the eyes of General John DeWitt only."

Sensing the importance of the document, Gene Robens convinced the courier, who expressed great reluctance, that he was authorized to accept it. The message was a bombshell. It was a copy of the message sent to President Roosevelt, and it contained the first official assessment anyone had made of the devastating damage this nation suffered during the Japanese attack that infamous Sunday morning in 1941. The Japanese would have given almost anything to have had that crucial information, for it recited the tragic losses and what possibilities remained for the use of the remainder of the fleet.

It was a sobering study, most disconcerting. Gene never breathed a word of the document's contents until twenty years later when he was appointed by President Kennedy's Administration to be the Special Assistant to the Secretary of the Army in charge of our nation's National Guard, Army Reserve and ROTC Programs.

Colonel Robens is kind to say of the other men in this volume: "You people are the ones I greatly admire. It is men like you who were in combat on land, sea, or in the air that our nation owes a debt of gratitude it can never repay. We need to continue to educate our children and grand-children as to what you people went through to preserve the freedom of our country and of people abroad. We could even reeducate some of our adults who take things for granted that we won, not realizing what sacrifices so many made in our behalf. America honors you and those who did not return."

A speech by Gene A. Robens, then Special Assistant to the Under Secretary of the Army for Reserves, given to the North Carolina ROA Department convention early in 1961, remains cogent and worth reprinting:

"Since this country can never afford to have, in being, all of the military units required for total military effort, it must possess a backup of reserve units and individuals ready for emergency employment. In contrast to World Wars I and II any next conflict of equal proportion would not allow us the luxury of arming deliberately behind the protection of our allies. Well-trained and ready reserves must be available as reinforcements to support our overseas deployment. An enemy's estimate of the quality of our reserve forces, their combat readiness and their rate of deployment abroad will necessarily influence his decisions and courses of action. Thus it is that the Army never ceases in its efforts to improve the quality of its National Guard and Army Reserve."

Col. Robens is the author of a book, *Reserve Forces and the National Defense*, plus many articles and a great many TV, radio, newspaper and magazine interviews. He is the president of an international consulting firm, and has been an advisor to government officials on high levels. Gene has been the recipient of national awards of the American Security Council and of the Coalition for International Security. He presently is serving as a member of the 50th Anniversary Council of the Battle of Normandy Foundation.

Colonel Gene A. Robens, AUS-Ret. Graduation Day, June 1958, U.S. Army War College, Carlisle Barracks, PA.

76

Overwhelming the Enemy with Logistical Support Rapid Movement

Cyril C. Munsch, EM-USAF

During the war in Europe I was a part of the 1585th Quartermaster Group, Aviation, which had as its mission the movement of ammunition, gasoline, supplies of various types, personnel, and tactical and administrative units from rear areas to installations on or near the battlefield. Generally our task was to ensure the mobility of the Tactical Air Force on the continent.

While the assault troops were attacking the Normandy beaches on 6 June 1944 our men were sweating it out aboard landing craft and liberty ships a few miles off shore. Our vehicles were laden down with material for the construction of the first allied airstrip on the continent. Other units of the group were simultaneously moving to or embarking from the various ports of southern England.

Men of our QM truck Companies waded ashore through enemy artillery and small arms fire on Omaha Beach on D plus 1 and 2. We convoyed trucks past the bodies of men who had fallen and equipment that had been damaged in the assault. We were moving rapidly to deliver the matting for airstrip A-1. The balance of our units followed quickly to the shores of France.

Group headquarters assembled on the continent within the first month and closely coordinated troop movements. Early operations in the constricted areas of Normandy consisted largely of movement of supplies from the beaches to the Air Force dumps established a few miles inland and from those dumps to the fighter-bomber strips nearby. Operations went smoothly, and we had ample trucks to make all necessary movements. In many cases the men of the earlier units arriving ashore joined with the infantry in their spare time and engaged in the mopping up operations that followed the expansion of the beachhead.

The group transported an incredible assemblage of supplies using trucks traveling an aggregate of about 5 million miles during the invasion and Normandy campaign. More than thirty thousand tons of material was moved: engineering material for the construction of airfields, ordnance supplies, aircraft parts, belly tanks, various other supplies. We also moved fifteen thousand personnel and almost seven million gallons of fuel.

Following the blasting of St. Lo and the breakthrough at Avranches, and, as the Battle of Northern France developed, the aggregate figures of movements skyrocketed. The statisticians at headquarters were kept busy while truck drivers rolled up endless mileage required to keep the fighter-bombers within tactical range of the fast moving armored divisions. Moving up the necessary ammunition and gasoline was a challenging assignment.

The planes that closed the Falaise Gap before the link-up of the Polish Division of the First Canadian Army with U.S. Forces at

Chambois, northeast of Argentan, did it with bombs, bullets and gasoline hauled by the trucks of our unit. However the destruction of the German Seventh Army in the Falaise pocket was not the only job. Planes supplied by our unit covered the exposed right flank of the Third Army in their dash across France. They blasted obstacles impeding the paths of spearheading tank columns. To do so our trucks rolled ceaselessly on a twenty-four hour schedule. Glassy-eyed with fatigue, the drivers hardly gave the engines of their 6x6's time to cool between runs as the convoy distances rapidly lengthened out in the fast moving situation. As the campaign of Northern France drew to a close, the truck companies were making runs that averaged eight hundred and forty miles in length.

As the armies drew up before the Siegfried Line and paused to regroup and consolidate for the Battle of Germany, the Group settled down to the task of moving the Air Force dumps and depots from Normandy over some two hundred miles of Red Ball Route to new locations in the interior. Before the Red Ball Route finally closed down with relocation of dumps the Group had rolled over five and a half million miles of truck travel. Over fifty-five thousand tons of freight had been moved as well as nine million gallons of gasoline.

With the German offensive in the Ardennes in December, 1944, increased demands came for all sorts of supplies, while five hundred trucks had to be maintained on alert status for possible evacuation of airstrips and depots endangered by the growing German salient. Even so, our Group put on an additional effort to move Fighter Air Groups and

enormous amounts of equipment as air units changed location in order to render more effective tactical support to the ground forces that were hammering in the flanks of the Bulge.

On one mission, a convoy of twelve trucks loaded with high octane fuel was dispatched for a dump near a town. We arrived at dusk along with three other units. They quickly dispersed us and sent us into the town. By the time we were unloading the last two trucks it was getting dark. Groups of four and five drivers were standing around shooting the bull when someone shouted "Air Raid!" The plane proceeded to strafe the trucks. One GI dived under my truck while I was still sitting inside. I could hear the pops of bullets striking. We scrambled to get away from the trucks, but we found that the GI who had dived under my truck had been hit with shrapnel in the posterior, an embarrassing wound. He had to be sent back to the hospital. Fortunately the plane made only one pass and the trucks had already been unloaded.

As the battle lines moved Eastward and the campaign of Central Europe opened, our supply lines once again became extended. Our convoys were making extremely long runs bringing up the necessary supplies and fuel to facilitate the finishing touches to the German war machine.

When Field Marshal Karl Gerd Von Rundstedt, the dean of German militarists, leader of the last ditch gamble in the Ardennes, was captured in 1945 at Bad Tolz he listed four major reasons for the defeat of Germany. The first of these was the tremendous air superiority which hampered German troop movements. That was accomplished by the tactical air power of the Ninth Air Force. Secondly, the lack of fuel for German tanks and planes was brought about by strategic bombing of synthetic oil plants and the loss of the Romanian oil fields. His third item was the systematic destruction of German railways and road communications, in which the Ninth Air Force played a major role. Finally, he mentioned the destruction of Germany's industrial centers. While our Group didn't win the war, the unit's contributions to achieving victory were substantial.

77

Engineer's Top Secret Mission

Colonel William Ashley Chapman, AUS-Ret.

While tossed madly about by the violent sea I sensed that I was in the curl of another huge wave about to break on the steep beach. I gulped air which I knew I had to do to live. In a deadly sequence I was dashed up on the beach only to be helplessly swept back again into the next crashing breaker by the racing backwash.

As I was hurled up the beach again a hand stuck out to grasp mine. With all my remaining strength I grabbed it! That hand was attached to a human lifeline of brave soldiers of the United States Army 38th Engineers who had come to my rescue. A bath in the surf at Long Beach, Ascension Island, had nearly cost my life. That incident occurred a few days after we had landed on Ascension Island, the site of our mission. Ascension is a 34 square mile remote island at 8 degrees South latitude in the South Atlantic. Our top-secret mission was to build an airfield complete with a 6,000 foot paved runway, taxiways, aviation fuel storage and handling facilities, a sea pipeline for tanker unloading and all other requirements for a complete air base facility.

Graduating in 1941 from Auburn University with a commission of 2d Lt., Corps of Engineers, I was ordered to active duty 1 September 1941 with the 38th Engineer Regiment, Combat, at Fort Jackson, South Carolina. We departed Charleston, South Carolina 22 March 1942 for the mission. I was Platoon Leader of "F" Company and was a supervisor of runway construction.

We were tasked to complete the mission in 90 days, which required a maximum effort from all personnel. The work went on day and night, with men working twelve hours a day, seven days a week, until the job was completed. Living conditions were harsh physically and psychologically. Our water supply was extremely limited, with none for hygiene and barely enough to drink. There was no recreation, nothing but a routine of work, and time for eating and sleep. We were completely isolated with no personal communications with the outside world.

With the help of 75 tons of dynamite we blasted the hard rock into shape, and the first plane landed about June 15 on the partially completed runway. It was a British Fairey Swordfish biplane from the British carrier *H.M.S. Archer* cruising over the horizon nearby. When the Swordfish buzzed the settlement the American anti-aircraft battery, part of our Task Force 4612 equipped with 37 mm and .50 cal. AA guns, failed to identify the intruder, therefore opened fire and hit the plane. As it came around the second time the markings were seen to be British, and the plane landed. Out of it a very angry pilot emerged waving a pistol. One of the .50 caliber rounds had clipped the buckle of his parachute harness. We had to apologize for the hostile treatment, yet we had not expected a visit and were apprehensive of activity from a German raider thought to be in the area.

The first American plane, U.S. Army Air Corps B-24 "Kissin' Cousin", landed on the completed runway 10 July 1942, just 101 days after our arrival. We had achieved our goal, a significant accomplishment and an engineering triumph for Col. R. E. Coughlin, TF 4612 Commander.

Wideawake Field, as it was named, became a refueling stop for planes bound for the African Campaign and later served other theaters of war. It also was important as an anti-submarine base.

I remained on Ascension for nearly two years as a Platoon leader of the 898th Engineer Aviation Company. After returning to the states, I was reassigned as the Company Commander of "C" Company of the 1902 Engineer Aviation Battalion, with an assignment to participate in the construction of an airfield in the Pacific Theater.

My unit landed on Ie Shima (near Okinawa) on April 19, 1945, the day after Ernie Pyle was killed there. Along with other EAB's we built runways and all necessary facilities, again on time. We were on Ie Shima about four months and were bombed every day, sometimes more than once, until the time of surrender. We saw kamikazi planes being shot down while others were seen striking ships. An LST was hit by a kamikazi, was beached and abandoned. The hulk was later hit by several more suicide planes. My good friend, Captain Ray Kidd, our Company Commander on Ascension, was killed by a bomb during July of 1945, just a few days before the surrender. He never saw his son who was born while we were on Ie Shima.

Our island was the stop-over for the planes carrying the Japanese surrender delegation flying in "Betty" bombers enroute to meet General Douglas McArthur on Bataan, Philippines. Those planes were the same type of bombers they had used against us on Ie Shima. As you can imagine, we were all at the runway to see the two white painted bombers carrying green crosses and watch the delegation change to a U. S. Army Air Corps C-54 plane. They were greeted with silence from the spectators.

In September of 1945 we were sent to Japan as a part of the occupation force. I visited Nagasaki and was awed by sight of the destruction created by one A-bomb. Japan had been very badly damaged by high explosive and fire bombs. The Japanese people were polite to us and exhibited no fear. The dear little children followed us around asking for "chewding" (sic) gum and candy.

The airbase at Ascension Island is now an active U. S. Air Force facility used for missile and satellite tracking. It was a staging base for the British during the Falkland Island War of 1982. The base has been in operation, with only a brief hiatus since that first landing July 10, 1942. My wife and I were privileged to visit Ascension in 1988 as guests of the USAF to participate in the dedication of a remodeled building my platoon had constructed in 1943. Much has changed, for they now have ample water, air conditioning, paved roads and other amenities. The dust and everlasting wind remain.

I continued my military service in the U. S. Army Reserve with various assignments. My last duty was with the 351st Civil Affairs Area A Command, Mountain View, California, from which I retired as a Colonel in 1973.

I am a California Professional Engineer and retired from the City of Palo Alto in 1986, where I was a Principal Engineer in the Water-Gas-Sewer Division of the Utilities Department.

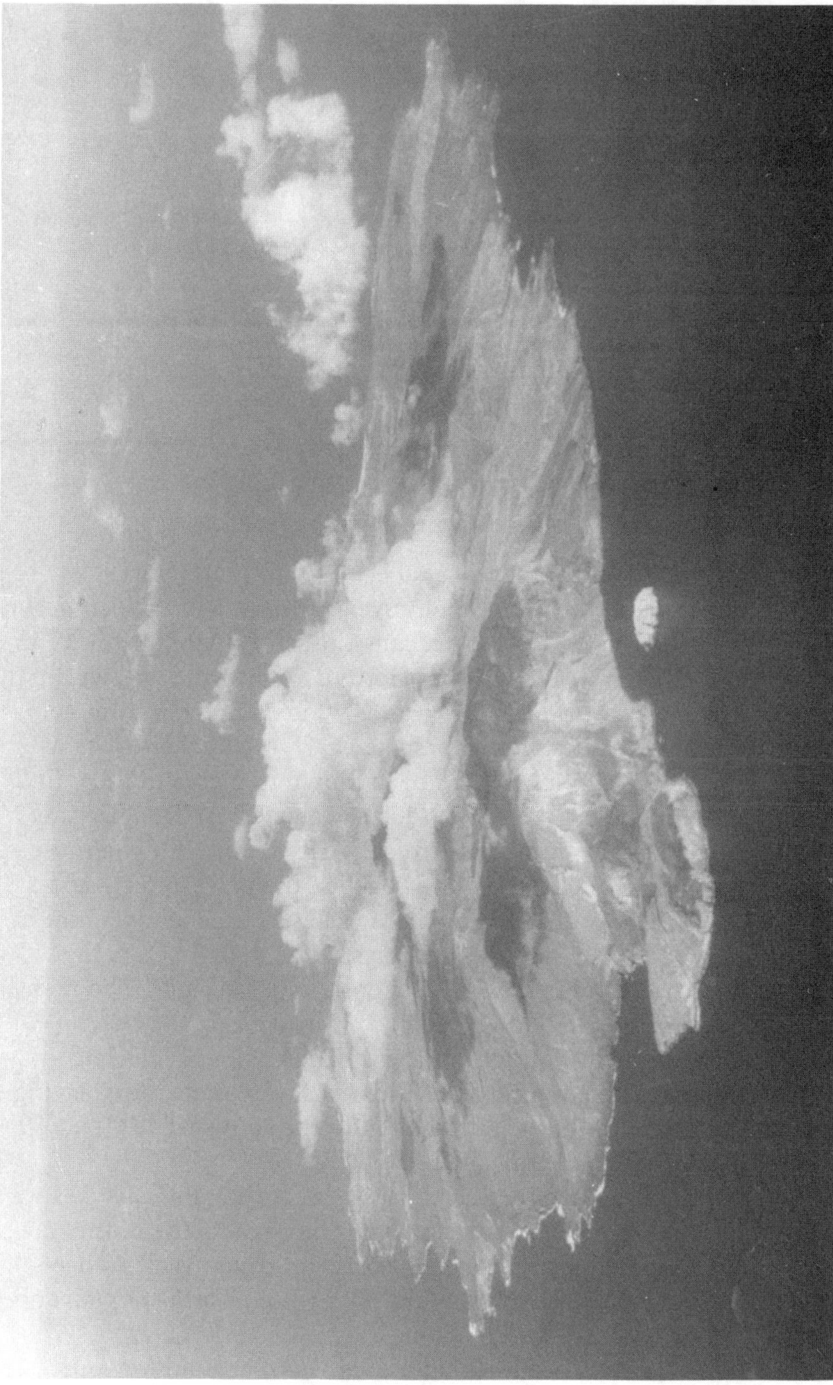

Ascension Island, 34 square miles, far out in the sea from any other land.

78

Watching a Sea Battle from Tulagi

From the Journal of Lt. Commander Tom Larson, USNR-Ret.

November 30, 1942

In the morning our heavy cruisers began to limp into port. The *Northhampton* was sunk, the *Minneapolis, New Orleans,* and the *Pensacola* barely made it into port. We lost no tin cans this time. Our ships were in bad shape but, luckily, still afloat. I met Herb Fairchild who was with me at CINCPAC Staff at Pearl Harbor. He was as white as a ghost from being in the battle on the *New Orleans*. Sailors were carrying buckets of arms and legs and pieces of sailors who had been blown to pieces in the gun turrets of the cruisers. They were taken to the cemetery at Tulagi. I saw the wreckage on Tulagi from the battle of August 7th and 8th when the Marine Raiders landed and the Navy had shelled the place and bombers had thoroughly worked it over good. There was wreckage all over and many shell holes and badly scarred buildings. I saw many men being buried from the battered cruisers. It was a nasty and sad sight. The men were laid out side by side in a long trench. I walked along the beach, looking at the camps. Saw a number of caves where a lot of Japs had hidden, only to be blasted out. Some of the caves were sealed up, leaving the dead Japs in there. In the evening I went to the show called "Texas" which was staged in the ball court.

Later, when I read over the secret messages at the radio shack, I learned that the rumors were all wrong about the naval battle of the night before. The Jap had lost only one measly destroyer. We had been caught completely by surprise again when we lost the *Northhampton* and those three cruisers suffered severe damage.

It was raining off and on at Guadalcanal. I laid around for some time, taking it easy and being as much of a beachcomber as one could be in the middle of a war. I got the word that a big Jap naval force is on the way down to land troops—over 10 warships. Our ship, the *Alchiba*, was just off the beach and burning from a torpedo hit. In the afternoon everyone is getting excited and set for the Jap fleet.

At 5:30 p.m. Baldy, Fearon, and I got on a motor torpedo boat and had a thrilling ride across Lengo Channel to Tulagi. We plowed through the water at a terrific rate. The skipper was named Larson and he was from Minneapolis. At Tulagi we were moved into the Officer's quarters and then had chow. The Navy Chaplain, Father Fitzgerald, woke us up at 11 p.m. We walked with him up a hill where we could get a good look at the drama so soon to take place. At 11:20 we heard a gun shot out in the channel, followed by more shots. You could see the big shells going red hot through the air. Two big ships began really pouring out the lead. It was thrilling to watch. Soon the air was full of flares. The Japs returned the fire, but our ships were really pouring out the lead; at least we thought they were our ships. Two ships were burning savagely, then the other ships caught on fire. Flames were going up a thousand feet into the dark air. Then another puff of flames rose high into the sky. After about twenty minutes of battle the action was over and we went to bed. Things were going to be interesting enough on Tulagi I could see.

79

Someone Was Watching Over Us

Col. Ralph N. Cole, AUS-Ret.

Battery, 340th Field Artillery Battalion, 89th Infantry Division (a part of the Third U.S. Army) was advancing somewhere in central Germany in March, 1945. We were located in a forest area in a ravine.

I had recently returned from my duties as a forward observer and shell hole reporter, and was with some of my associates. We had dug our foxholes, and were inside the foxholes during a shelling that was occurring over our heads.

It is standard policy not to leave the security of one's foxhole during a shelling, and especially, not to dash across an open area at such a time. However, a strong impulse and thought hit me—we simply had to get out of our holes and had to run to another location.

During a brief lull in the firing at us, I told my crew to get out of their foxholes and to follow me across the open area and up the side of a protective ridge. Needless to say, there was some grumbling and there were comments about how stupid it was to leave the security of our holes for another location.

However, the group did as I ordered, and we dashed across the ravine, climbed the protective hill, and again dug in. Firing continued throughout the night.

The next morning, as the firing had stopped, we went back to our former location to check it out prior to mounting trucks for our advancing. To our amazement, the area in which we had been located was totally obliterated!

Yes, someone was watching over us. I shall ever be thankful for that spirit that guided us to safety and saved our lives!

Colonel Ralph N. Cole was awarded the Legion of Merit upon his retirement from the 351st Civil Affairs command, a major command of the U. S. Army Reserve, in Sunnyvale, California, where he served as the Chief of Staff.

CPL Ralph N. Cole, Fire Control Instrument Operator and Forward Observer, age 21, April, 1945, near Zwickau, Germany, north of Czechoslovakia.

In a lull from heavy fighting, the troops got cleaned up and pictures were taken to send to the home front to assure that all was well.

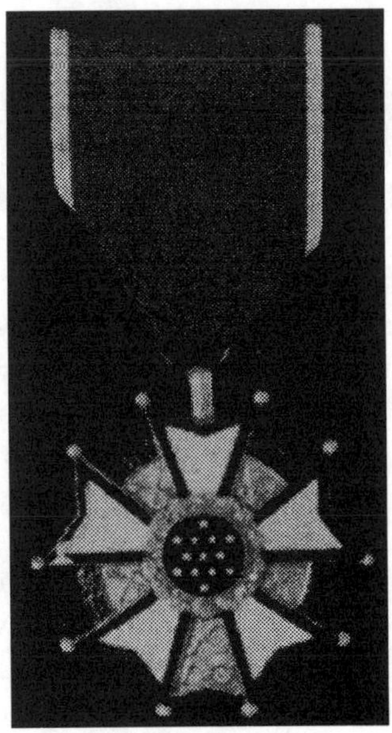

Legion of Merit

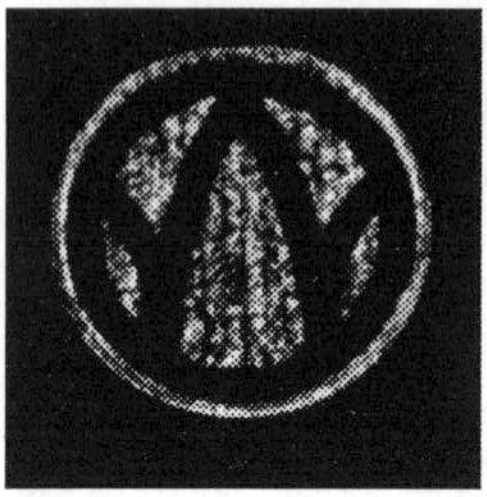

80

Ohrdruf — North Stalag III The Forgotten Death Camp

Colonel Ralph N. Cole. AUS-Ret.

On April 4, 1945, the Fourth Armored Division and the 355th Infantry Regiment of the 89th Infantry Division, part of General George Patton's famed Third U.S. Army, liberated the first death camp, Ohrdruf or North Stalag III, a sub camp of Buchenwald, located near Weimar.

Having moved through France and Luxemburg, and after heavy fighting across the Moselle and the Rhine Rivers, the 89th Infantry Division was at last on German soil. It was there that we fought and took Ohrdruf.

One of the first sights to greet our troops were the bodies of approximately twenty emaciated persons who had just been shot prior to the flight of their Nazi captors. Included in this group was a young American aviator, still dressed in his flight gear. The crematorium was filled with the partially consumed bodies of many people, some still smoldering and smoking. In addition, the Germans had placed iron railroad tracks, interlaced with ties, and had stacked countless corpses on this funeral pyre. Nearby in a warehouse were piles of bodies covered with lye, awaiting cremation. In one locale, a body was still on a roasting type campfire, treated as you might roast a pig.

There were almost no survivors, as the Nazis had killed as many prisoners as possible to prevent anyone from telling what had happened.

Ohrdruf was subsequently visited by Generals Eisenhower, Bradley, and Patton. General Eisenhower stated:

> "I have never been able to describe my emotional reaction when I came face to face with indisputable evidence of Nazi brutality and ruthless disregard to every shred of decency. I visited every nook and cranny of the camp because I felt it my duty to be in a position from then on to testify at first hand about the things in

> case there ever grew up at home the belief or assumption that the stories of Nazi brutality were just propaganda. I want every American unit not actually in the front line to see this place. We are told that the American solider does not know what he is fighting for. Now at least he will know what he is fighting against."

General Patton said:

> "This is one of the most appalling sights I have ever seen. Honestly, words are inadequate to express the horror of these institutions. The scenes witnessed here are beyond the normal mind to believe. No race except a people dominated by an ideology of sadism could have committed such gruesome crimes. Inmates, all in a bad state of starvation, even those who live, in my opinion, will never recover mentally."

General Bradley commented:

> "The smell of death overwhelmed us even before we passed through the stockade. More than 3,200 naked emaciated bodies had been flung into shallow graves. Others lay in the streets where they had fallen. Lice crawled over the yellow skin of their sharp, bony frames. A guard showed us how the blood had congealed in course black scabs where the starving prisoners had torn out the entrails of the dead for food. I was too revolted to speak, for here death had been so fouled by degradation that it both stunned and numbed us."

Having witnessed that holocaust, as long as we live, my comrades and I can so testify!

After inspecting Ohrdruf, the generals flew on to inspect captured artwork and bullion which had been looted by the Nazis. Although their visit had been recorded by the press, that night, April 12 1945, they were notified that President Franklin D. Roosevelt had just died. With that significant news event, Ohrdruf received no coverage!

Ohrdruf remains ever imbedded in the minds of the men of the 4th Armored Division and the 89th Infantry Division. Let us hope that others will learn and remember...

> ***There are times that we must fight for what is right, and in order to accomplish what is right, such as destroying those who caused the Holocaust or who may cause another, we must be strong! With strength, we may further peace!***

Col. & Mrs. Ralph N. Cole, 1995

81

Aleutians to Normandy to Stalag Luft

Major Mozart Kaufman, USAF-Ret.

While flying in the Aleutians, I received the Distinguished Flying Cross for "missions against the Japanese from advance bases against strong enemy positions. Many missions were over long distances over open water under unfavorable weather conditions. On many of those missions, enemy gun positions were strafed from low altitude." I flew 24 combat missions against the Japanese, yet my combat service in Europe remains most vivid in my mind.

From the very first day of the invasion of Normandy I was flying in a P-47 Thunderbolt Squadron affording ground support in mostly bombing and strafing missions. On June 6, we took off at 5:35 a.m. At 7,000 feet we broke through the clouds into sunshine. The entire squadron was in a perfect formation. A few minutes later, arriving on schedule, we viewed the Normandy coastline and the most dramatic sight I had ever seen. Below was the largest armada ever assembled. From the air it looked like a small boy had dumped a box of wooden matches into his bathtub. Within a few miles of shore were battleships, cruisers, destroyers, and landing craft of all shapes and sizes by the thousands. We could only speculate what the crossfire between the Allies and Germans would be.

Some squadrons soon moved to new airstrips established on French soil, however we did so on July 4, at A-4, near the village of Deux-Jumeaux. Of course we flew missions consistently from England before the move.

By July 27, the ground forces were moving ahead with fantastic gains south of St. Lo and Coutances. General Patton was leading his forces in an end run south, in Operation Cobra. Our 48th Fighter-Bomber Group started flying in the morning and sent out five missions during the day. The Germans were fleeing, running barely ahead of CCB of the Third Armored Division. Ground troops had routed the Germans in the area of Cerisy and Canisy, however there were real battles going on all over the sector. One pilot was hit by flak and had to make a crash landing, yet was not injured.

My mission that day, one of the last in the afternoon, included more bombing and strafing of the retreating German forces. As I was heading north to home base, I was flying low looking for anything to shoot at. I was no more than 100 to 150 feet high when I saw a village ahead of me that had been almost completely destroyed. Pushing the nose of my plane down, I flew over the main street between buildings that had been reduced to rubble. Leaving the town I pulled up to about 500 feet and headed north. Suddenly, I ran into a wall of machine gun fire, and I felt my plane shudder from their impact. My engine sputtered, and I fought to keep on course. My windshield became thickly covered with oil streaming from the damaged engine. Shoving my stick forward, I nosed down to get to the level of trees and out of the range of the guns. I knew if I got low enough I could get out of there before they could hit me again. Working just over the trees I tried to reach friendly territory, but realized that I was in real trouble and could not make it back.

On the radio I sent a "May Day" several times and then had a response that they would clear a field for me to come in. I climbed to 500 feet, alert for a possible emergency landing opportunity. My engine was running very rough, but suddenly I spotted the field and made it back just before sunset, a time we were supposed to be on the ground.

I had barely touched the end of the runway when my engine died. My concern then was to get off the runway into the grass to clear the field for other planes.

There was no doubt in my mind then that ground support was the most dangerous form of combat flying. Traveling low as we had to do, we were subjected to AA and became a source of target practice from every German holding a rifle. I had returned to base with my plane shot full of holes from bullets and shrapnel. Only the rugged P-47 could have taken that sort of beating and brought me home. It needed a new engine.

The next day was to be a most exciting mission of close support of the troop line in which we were going to experiment with 45-second delay fuses on our 500 pound bombs against enemy tanks. I bumped another officer and took the lead of the flight of four planes myself. We were of the belief that we could come down on a tank, drop a bomb and have 45 seconds to get away before the explosion. None of us were very experienced in that kind of combat, but we were learning the hard way.

In late afternoon we had no trouble locating the German tanks on the road between Percy and Granville. I alerted my men to keep in close contact for we didn't want to come down on a tank that was about to blow up.

I peeled off and came in low just a few feet above the tank and dropped a bomb right under the treads. Then I pulled up and circled around. But the tank moved ahead before the explosion. My men had the same difficulty, so I told them to hold off while I went down and machine-gunned the treads so that the tank couldn't move.

I came in low with blazing guns wide open firing a long burst. As I pulled up over the tank a bomb went off under my plane. There must

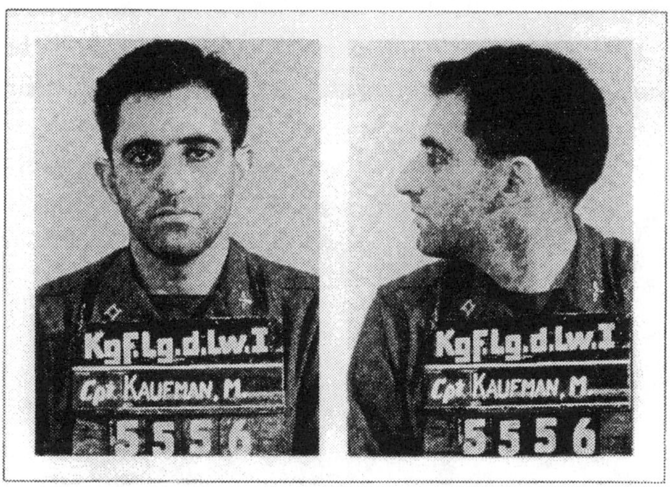

have been a faulty fuse causing a delayed burst. My plane was thrown into the air and oil spattered everywhere. While I immediately believed I was in trouble on my 50th mission the instrument readings appeared in order. My windshield was covered with oil, but I was determined to get that tank. I went into another approach and dropped my bomb right under the tank's tread while firing my machine guns on the approach. However bullets hit my plane when not more than ten feet off the ground. My engine burst into flames and the plane became a flying torch.

I had to reach 500 feet to eject. I opened my canopy and with that the flames swept in and almost enveloped me. I pushed up to get out and then realized I hadn't released my safety belt. I ducked down out of the flames, released the belt and pushed out. The second I was clear of the plane, I pulled my rip cord and felt a jerk. I didn't have time to look to see if my chute opened before my feet hit the ground.

While thinking of escape plans, I unbuckled my parachute and started up a hill. A German soldier came running toward me with a drawn Luger pistol. He was such a pip-squeak of a little fellow with a nervous look that I was tempted to take him on. But the Luger was a compelling neutralizer so that I was taken prisoner and spent the rest of the war in prison camps before being liberated by the Russians.

Continuing his service in the Reserves, Mozart Kaufman retired as a major. His book *Fighter Pilot—Aleutians to Normandy to Stalag Luft 1* is available from the author in San Anselmo, California. It goes into considerable detail of his plight as a POW.

82

Battlefields Revisited

William C. Dillinger, AUS

"Don't go back to visit the old battlefront," Ernest Hemingway warned. "It's like going into the empty gloom of a theater where the charwomen are scrubbing."

Touring France and Germany with a busload of old veterans of the 89th Infantry Division recently, we visited most of the places we had been in during the war and came to the same conclusion—"It's not the same, crossing the Rhine when the only people shooting at you are your buddies with their cameras," a survivor of our bloody Rhine crossing said as we rode across this time on a passenger ferry.

The rock of the Lorelei, on which we planted our battle flag after that terrifying pre-dawn assault, was again just a place to toast the Rhine maiden's golden statue while the tour ship's loudspeaker blared forth the famous song.

The cobbled road winding down to the Moselle, where we suffered our first casualties, is no longer exposed to Nebelwerfer rocket fire from across the river. It is now asphalted, lined with apartment houses where kids were playing in the tiny yards. At Kirn, where we had dashed under fire across a collapsed bridge, we found the stream but not the bridge. Nor could we find the weathered board fence which our young lieutenant thought shielded him. He had stood behind it, shouting in his best Pennsylvania Dutch a demand that the Jerries should surrender. They responded with a bullet through the rotting boards that sent his already high pitched voice into a soul-ripping shriek that we all still hear on bad nights.

We did re-discover the brewery we had liberated at Kirn, where we had merrily loaded kegs and jerycans of beer and huge glass flagons of cider onto every vehicle we could muster of Patton's Third Army.

We didn't see what we thought we had come back to see; not at all. The folks at home had thought of our excursion as a whimsical expedition by a bunch of nostalgic old soldiers; perhaps we thought of the trip in similar terms, but it became an emotional experience far beyond what any of us had expected. It was a genuine catharsis, if you will understand.

Most of hadn't talked about what we had been through. We had all found, early on, that there was no use talking about the war to people who had not been through it. One just couldn't communicate in terms they could understand.

On the bus tour were 30 other guys who had been through everything you had experienced who had the same deep emotional need to unburden themselves to understanding ears. For many of us those thoughts had been bottled up for years. In our travels a place or a name brought out a clotted mix of terrifying memories at times, in other moments a recollection of funny incidents, memories of fool mistakes or crazy happenings.

Time after time, individuals worked their way up to the front of the bus, took the guide's mike, and told their tales.

The Rhine castle at St. Goar reminded Duff Pitcock, who had been a sergeant in our signal company, of the first and only time he saw the legendary General Patton. While taking a little off-duty time to prowl the castle after helping set up Division Headquarters there, Duff had eased open a promising door and found himself eyeball-to-eyeball with the famous general. Patton was vigorously laying down orders to our division commander and a couple of other generals. Duff backed off feeling as awed as Moses glimpsing the backside of God.

A view of the same hilltop castle brought back quite different memories to a quiet member of our group, "Herb" Herbaly, who had been an infantry squad leader whose assault boat was shot to pieces during the bloody night-crossing of the river below. Herb remembered struggling free of his heavy Browning automatic rifle as he was thrown into the dark water and somehow floundering to the relative safety of shore. Very likely the BAR is still on the bottom of the Rhine, Herb remarked, not dwelling on what we also knew—that half the men in his squad were killed that night when they were silhouetted by tracer bullets and flaming debris.

Another veteran of the crossing recalled seeing the last guy left in a shot-up rubber raft trying frantically to get the thing out of the rain of flying bullets using his entrenching tool for a paddle.

Deeper into Germany, the twisting roads of the hilly Thuringerwald reminded someone of the jeep driver who rounded a bend there and came nose-to-nose with a huge Tiger tank. Panicked out of his mind, the driver turned the jeep around right under the tank's fearsome 88 gun, as casually as he might have turned around on a peaceful country road back home. He scooted out of sight before the equally surprised Germans could get their deadly gun directed.

The little town of Crawinkel in the plains of central Germany brought an uncomfortable dilemma to mind for another ex-infantryman. As his company attacked the town he had become pinned down in an open field. Grass-top level machine-gun fire passed over the soldier in the shallow ditch while he desperately realized that he had to pee.

Like old soldiers everywhere we tended to remember the funny incidents. But those who had been in any actual combat also remembered the fear that never left us.

Toward the end of the war we were often walking down a road alert to the possibility of Jerries starting shooting. When we heard the sudden pop of firing and the whish of bullets snapping overhead we often dove for the roadside ditch. Yet we feared that we might be throwing ourselves onto a buried mine. F Company lost a couple of guys that way.

Riding in trucks to the next hot spot, we knew that waiting around any turn, zeroed in on you from anywhere, might be one of those dreaded 88's. Some found the shell coming at them so fast that they never heard the blast of the gun. Others heard the explosion of the shell hitting, but those receiving the hit heard nothing further.

Youngsters, Hitler Jugend, would sometimes pop out of roadside foxholes endeavoring to blow up even our big Sherman tanks with their panzerfausts, simple rocket launchers similar to our own bazookas.

Our best defense against those vicissitudes was a sardonic attitude, a protective shell we developed to ward off the indignities of military life. That became a sort of defense that hardened to preserve your sanity while we kept braced for the inevitable moment when our number might come up.

We all insisted on revisiting the site of the concentration camp at Ohrdruf, which was the first of those ghastly compounds to be discovered by American GI's. Our 89th Division first came upon it in the middle of Germany as we moved forward. About six of us on the bus where among the initial group of the Division that stumbled on the place with its piles of rotting corpses.

Bodies had been thrown in pits and covered with quicklime. Buildings had been set afire with inmates trapped inside. Pervading the entire area was an unbearable stench. All around lay the still-bleeding bodies of scores of inmates hastily slaughtered by the departing Nazis. Bob Chamow remembered emaciated inmates mobbing a belatedly fleeing German guard and beating him to death with a tire iron.

A few of us were present the next day when Generals Eisenhower, Bradley, Patton and others visited the camp. It was at Ohrdruf that Ike said he wanted every soldier in the European Theater to come to see what evil we had been fighting against. We were outraged to find all signs of the camp obliterated without any memorial to all those who had died there.

What we did bring home from the tour was a sense of relief. We sensed something of being more at peace with ourselves having realized that life goes on, that what was the most intense experience of our lives was truly over, ended and could not be relived, nor need be.

Member

owac

OUTDOOR WRITERS ASSOCIATION OF CALIFORNIA

83

Lest We Forget

CWO-4 Alexander T. Coutts, USNR-Ret.

Lt.j.g. Robert Scott Whitman, Jr., a graduate of the Naval Academy, was the command pilot of a PBY Catalina 5A Patrol Bomber, a land-based amphibian flying boat operating in the Pacific in 1942. Whitman had been assigned to Patrol Squadron 44, at the Naval Station, Alameda, California but was quickly deployed to Naval Air Station San Diego following the December 7 attack. His squadron was split, with half going to the Aleutians. Their mission was to locate the Japanese invading forces known to be somewhere in the eastern Pacific.

While the United States had broken some of the Japanese codes, it was known that a large number of their naval ships had dropped out of sight and were operating under radio silence. It was imperative that their location should be determined. The two American carrier task forces in the Pacific urgently need that information. Whitman's section of Patrol Squadron 44 took off from Midway Island on a sector search pattern, and he located the Japanese main invading battle force bearing down on Midway on June 4, 1942.

Japanese Admiral Isorouku Yamamotoa had designated the Plan "I Operation" to knock out the U.S. carrier force by drawing it out from Hawaii and then striking at Midway, 1,136 miles west of Hawaii in early June of 1942. The Doolittle Tokyo raid of April 18, 1942 had brought home to Japanese naval planners the importance of aircraft carriers, and furthermore they wanted revenge for the strike at their heartland.

Whitman broke radio silence, alerting Midway and COMPAC of his position and described the types and numbers of ships in the fleet steaming for Midway. Japanese communications technicians picked up his message, and their fire control vectored fighter cover "Zeros" toward Whitman's much slower plane while he ducked in and out of clouds in evasive action. An enemy fighter pilot making a head-on slant approach opened machine-gun fire which almost cut Whitman in half.

Although mortally wounded, with his plane badly crippled, Lt. Whitman warned his crew of an impending crash landing. He and his co-pilot struggled to bring the aircraft down in a safe landing.

The PBY started taking on water as soon as it hit the surface of the ocean. As command pilot, Whitman gave the order to abandon ship. While his co-pilot tried to help Lt. Whitman leave the aircraft, Whitman ordered all to leave. He knew he was bleeding internally, literally drowning in his own blood. Waist deep in water, the co-pilot struggled through an overhead escape hatch, while Lt. "Scotty" Whitman remained at the controls as his plane slipped into the briny deep. All the crew were rescued due to Lt. Whitman's brave devotion to duty.

A new destroyer escort was launched January 19, 1943, christened the *U.S.S. Whitman BDE-24* by his widow of four months, Josephine P. Whitman, at a ceremony at Mare Island Shipyard, Vallejo, California.

The Whitman's first commanding officer, LCDR Carl E. Bull, USNR, showed a good deal of compassion in two letters that followed:

August 14, 1943

Dear Mrs. Whitman,

May I express my appreciation for the picture of your late husband. It has now been mounted permanently in the wardroom as a continual reminder of the purpose for which this ship was built and named.

It is difficult to phrase my feelings, and sentiment has no place in a navy, or war, but may I promise you that the spirit which imbued your husband in the battles of Midway, the determination to fight, and, if necessary, to die for his country, shall carry on in this vessel. The name Whitman shall stand not for a ship, primarily, to those of us aboard her, but as a symbol of that high devotion to duty which we pledge ourselves to maintain. Your husband is still in the fight, his spirit embodied in the Whitman shall carry on.

Yours Sincerely,

/s/ Carl E. Bull, LCMDR USNR
Commanding, USS Whitman

March 6, 1944

Dear Joie,

I'm back in the states again and sorry to say, have missed you again. The Whitman has a new skipper. I was detached and Lt. Coan, who you will remember as the executive officer, is now in command. Due to the demand for commanding officers for new construction, and as the Whitman was well organized and operating smoothly, I was transferred to a new command, and will now have to do the same thing all over. The Whitman did a good job. We were engaged in attacks on both Makin and Tarawa, and for over a month were the flagship of all destroyers in the Gilberts area. We were in over fifteen Japanese bombing raids, and came out OK. Don't worry about your ship. She is in good hands and a fine ship spirit had developed. I'm sure she will carry on doing a good job.

Sincerely,

/s/ Carl E. Bull

After five years of living alone, Mrs. Whitman agreed to change her name to Mrs. Alex. T. Coutts, and is convinced that some of us care and have high regard for the supreme sacrifice Lt. Whitman gave for his country.

My service in the Navy commenced before the war began. I had at least three incidents which may have been responsible for turning my hair white at an early age. Once in the Caribbean, near Trinidad, while aboard a munitions ship, we were attacked by an enemy submarine. We saw the two torpedoes proceed directly toward the bow of the ship, but fortunately they ran deep so passed underneath without contact. My duty became that of an ordnance officer.

Editors Note: There were only 8 aircraft carriers in the U.S. fleet at the outbreak of WWII, but the U.S. ended the war with over 100 aircraft carriers.

The Japanese fleet at the battle of Midway, one of the greatest naval engagements of all history was superior to that of the United States:

	Carriers	Battleships	Cruisers	Destroyers	Total
Japan	8	11	18	65	102
U.S.A.	3	0	8	15	26

However the imbalance was overcome by the tactical advantage of reading the Japanese coded transmissions and superior flying by our naval pilots.

Surprise was the key to victory, by striking when the enemy carriers were most vulnerable. Their planes had delivered a massive strike against our Marines at Midway. Returning almost out of fuel their fighters were desperate to land aboard the carriers. Other planes were below deck being refitted for a second strike. By attacking the enemy ships then our fighters faced little enemy air opposition, making it possible to quickly sink three Japanese carriers. A fourth carrier, the *Kiryu*, escaped and launched its planes which found and sunk the *U.S.S. Yorktown* (CV-5), while the *Kiryu* was subsequently sunk by planes from the *Yorktown*.

With the defeat of the Japanese fleet the remaining naval forces were equalized, and the U.S. forces were enabled to move from a defensive position to an offensive role in the Pacific. There was no exchange of gunfire between ships; aviation did all of the attacking. Japan lost 4 carriers, all of Pearl Harbor infamy, while the U.S. lost only one.

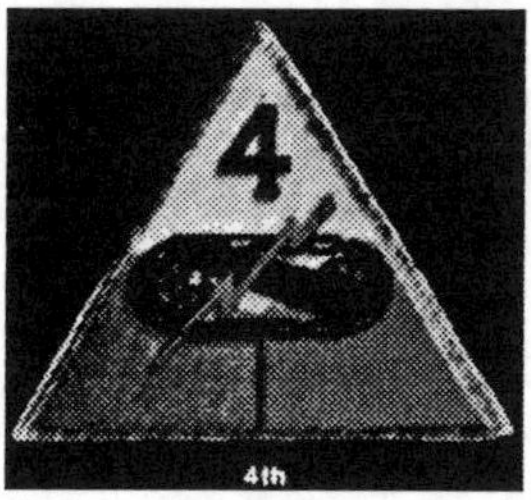

84

Blood and Guts

Colonel Thomas D. Gillis, USA-Ret.

As Christmas 1944 approached, our security became all-consuming.

> "His (Von Rundstedt's) hopped-up soldiers stripped overcoats and combat boots from American dead—and living. Deception, espionage, sabotage were missions of infamous German 'Kommandos' under the German Lieutenant Colonel Skorzeny. English speaking Germans in American uniforms, jeeps and tanks attempted to infiltrate U.S. lines...Behind the lines guards trained tommy guns on their own troops in broad daylight and demanded a whispered password."[1]

One morning I was in our C.P. (CC-R) when I heard a commotion outside. I stepped out just in time to see our sentry with a shock of red hair standing at port arms, blocking the road, and saying, "Sir, I think you're General Patton, but you can't pass through my post unless you give the password."

Seeing me, Patton bellowed, "Gillis, c'mon over here and tell this dumb son-of-a-bitch who'n hell I am." I assured the sentry that it was, indeed, General Patton and that it was all right to let him pass. As he stepped aside and came to present arms, the jeep took off, only to come to a screeching halt in a few yards. Leaning around, General Patton said, "Soldier, wher'in hell is your helmet?" The sentry explained that he had been on patrol the previous night, had somehow lost his helmet, and had

1 Page 105, *The 4 Armored Division from the Beach to Bavaria,* by Captain Kenneth Koyen, P.R.O., Herder-Druck, Munich, Germany, 1946.

been unable since then to find an extra one. With a snappy salute and a "Carry on!", Patton charged up the road toward the front. You always saw Patton going forward. Never to the rear. For he made arrangements with his pilot to be picked up at some pasture or landing strip and flew back to his headquarters in the evening. Late that afternoon General Patton's jeep stopped in front of our C.P. and the driver dismounted. He came up to me and presented me with a shiny, new helmet for our sentry. "Compliments of General Patton," sir, he said. The story, of course, got quickly around the division like wildfire, as only a tale concerning "Old Blood and Guts" could. And another endearment was added to the legend.

85

One Bombing Mission Never to be Forgotten

1st Lieutenant Ben C . Bruce, USAFR

EXETER. It was the 19th of June, 1944 and the invasion troops had secured a line across the neck of the Cherbourg Peninsula. In other words, it appeared that the allies were in a relatively secure position on the coast of Normandy. This was the 26th of my 31 missions.

That day I was flying first pilot or aircraft commander and Capt. Maziarz, now a doctor in Corpus Christi, Texas, was flying Deputy Group Lead. This put us directly below and a little behind the Group Lead. We were behind and a little below the lead ship's tailgun position.

We had had an easy trip south. We were east of the target, Bordeaux, at approximately 22 to 23,000 feet, in clear sunny weather. When flying formation you look at the ship you are flying off of, not the terrain or anything else.

We flew south far enough so that the group, the 91st out of Bassingbourn, located north of London and about 19 miles west southwest of Cambridge, could be safely brought around to a northerly direction for the bomb run. When there are three squadrons of six aircraft each stacked high on one side and low on the other, the turn is a very critical thing. If it's not done correctly you can have the outside six B-17's at full throttle trying to keep their position in the formation and the inside six cutting the power to stay in their position and possibly stalling out. We made our turn and headed north for our target at Bordeaux. We passed our I.P. (Initial Point) and from this point we were committed to the target, normally with little or no evasive action. We were now on the very last part of the bomb run.

Being the Deputy Group Lead, our bombardier, Aldo Viarengo, now living in Gilroy, California, and flying probably his fourth or fifth mission was over his bomb sight and tracking in as if he was the lead. If the lead had been hit the rest of the group would have dropped when he did. A point of clarification—not all of the ships in the group had bombardiers. Each lead ship (6 in a formation) would have a bombardier—the rest had togliers—enlisted men who didn't have bombsights but were taught to arm the bombs, open the bomb bay doors and hit the switch when they saw the bombs drop from the lead ship and then close the doors. No matter who was acting as Bombardier, they all dropped on whichever ship was lead at that time.

As I said, we were on the very final part of our bomb run, Aldo was over the bomb sight, and just at the time the bombs were released, he saw a flak burst through his sight and a reflex action made him jerk his head up and away from the sight. At that moment there had been a burst of flak just in front of our 2 left engines. This was the burst our bombardier saw. He jerked his head up and at that moment a piece of flak came through the glass nose to the left of him, took off the eye piece to the bomb sight, where his eye and forehead had been a split second before. He was sprinkled with shards of glass in the areas of his face not covered by the oxygen mask and helmet. Later he looked like he had a selective case of measles. At the same time the navigator, Lt. Childers, located in the nose behind and to the left of the bombardier, had flak come up through his desk practically wiping out his charts and slightly wounding him.

The number one engine (extreme left) immediately ran away and the number two was on fire and we were in a very sharp spin to the left and losing altitude rapidly. When an engine runs away, you lose all thrust from that prop. It's as if someone had replaced the prop with a solid piece of sheet iron the same diameter and circumference of the prop. Total drag. Captain Maziarz was able to put the fire out in #2 (the second engine from the left) and was helping me add right rudder to try and overcome the spin we were in. I wound in all of the right trim I had and still couldn't gain control. I found out later that neither the Bombardier nor the Navigator, both in the nose, could have escaped from the aircraft. They couldn't have bailed out because the centrifugal force had them pinned to the deck.

Things were happening fast, but it also seemed like we were doing everything in slow motion. Remember, we were hit and went into the spin right at the drop zone. I must get clarification from the Captain because I have a memory (real or imagined) that he tapped me on my shoulder and pointed out to the right wing tip and I saw bombs just sitting out there falling the same speed we were. We were still spinning so we turned away from them. We were fighting the spin and really didn't pay too much attention to altitude. All of a sudden we were starting to recover, we were rounding out, the plane had stopped the spin and dive, I had back pressure on the elevator control and starting the climb, and I was looking at the ground. I could see that we were probably, by then, down to approximately a hundred or two hundred feet above the roof tops. We had spun from our formation altitude (20,000 to 23,000 feet) to roof top level. The houses were all white row houses, and a German soldier was in the middle of the street shooting at us.

To this day I don't think that anything we did caused the aircraft to recover. We took advantage of the forces that were being exerted on the aircraft and helped in the recovery. It was a summer day. It was hot on the ground. We finally spun down into an area that I later presumed to be thermal action rising hot air, and it was strong enough and high enough, probably a thousand to fifteen hundred feet, to where it was able to give us lift and control again. We were able to climb back up to a thousand feet and that was it.

When an airplane engine malfunctions to the point where it becomes "run away", two things can happen. The prop is spinning out of control. The prop shaft becomes hotter and hotter until it either snaps and becomes freewheeling or it freezes up. The alternatives: A. The shaft snaps and it becomes freewheeling. Continuing spinning, the prop is pulled out and away from the engine. It can then spin down and away or up and over the cockpit into the wing or fuel tank or into the cockpit. In that event you have no more drag. B. If the shaft freezes up and you have flat propeller blades a teriffic amount of drag is created. That was what occurred in our case.

We were back to a thousand feet, and every time I tried for a few more feet the plane wanted to fall out from under us. Our indicated airspeed was about 105 MPH, as I remember, just above stalling. I also recall that whenever I tried to add a few more feet of altitude the plane would start vibrating, which is a stall warning. Our worry then was how were we going to get home. First we had to transfer the fuel from the two left tanks to the two right tanks and hope we wouldn't waste any by an overflow. The amount of fuel became very critical. After we found the plane would still fly, such as it was, we would have normally hit the deck and tried for home as close to the ground as we could get. There we were, worrying about being a sitting duck for one of the Luftwaffe fighter types when right in front of us appeared the thickest cloud cover one could ever ask for. It wasn't a choice as to whether we would use it or not, it was dense and it was below us, above us and all around us. We could never have flown home on the deck. We were just above stalling because of the drag exerted by the #l engine and even though #2 was feathered there wasn't any help at all from the left side. We had to lighten the plane.

I don't know how they accomplished it but the engineer and some of the other crew members, with the most basic tools, were able to get rid of the ball turret. I would have said, and I still do, it was impossible with what they had to work with. I was never so proud of a group of men than I was then. They did do the impossible. They also got rid of the tubes, (gun barrels), armor plate and anything and everything that wasn't needed then or wasn't going to be needed for the flight home. Home was about 450 to 500 miles north. The only excess weight they didn't get rid of was the armor plate under my seat. They didn't want to disturb me.

From the time we went into the clouds and until we reached the coast we couldn't see a thing. I know we were being shot at during some part of the way, but we never saw the flak bursts. I did feel the turbulence from the bursts. We were hoping that there wasn't some friendly French family sitting around the table about ready to relax with a glass of wine when our ball turret or any of the other excess weight we had just jettisoned might come crashing through their roof. By getting rid of the ball turret we had sacrificed our ability to ditch in the ocean. It didn't worry us too much, because we had decided to try for the invasion beach, crash land, get ourselves a bunch of souvenirs and go home. This, luckily, was not to be. The navigator gave me the course to the invasion side of the peninsula but I apparently didn't allow enough correction in the course because of the left side drag. We came out on the wrong side of the Cherbourg Peninsula.

I had started to have some misgivings about the beach, for we found there was one hell of a lot of stirred-up Germans compacted into a small area armed with an awful lot of small, medium and large guns, slingshots, rocks—anything that could be launched at our low and slow flying unfriendly bomber. Even though we came out over the ocean on the wrong side of the peninsula, we still would have liked some souvenirs of our trip to France. We thought that we wouldn't face as many unfriendlies as we would have on the other side by crossing over the peninsula from the southwest side, where all our troops had secured an area completely across the peninsula. We were close enough to see the cliffs and decided we might try it on for size. I started a turn to the right and was almost blasted out of the sky. Because of some evasive action I had to take earlier I knew I could make a turn into the dead side and it would turn into a hammerhead stall and we would be heading for the ocean pretty fast.

I did the turn and we headed for the ocean with the flak bursts behind and above most of the way. The anti-aircraft gunners were trying to read my mind as to which way I might turn, and I was trying to read theirs and not do it. I knew that the guns were controlled by radar and that was in my favor because the guns were on the cliff and probably couldn't depress low enough under electronic control to reach us down near the ocean.

This cooled our desire to search for loot on the beach. Before we went out into the ocean and under the control of air/sea rescue we had the misfortune of almost flying over the Isle of Jersey or Guernsey. The navigator was never certain which island we approached. Remember, he was still trying to piece his charts together. I am sure it was Jersey.

We had to do our hammerhead routine again and hope that the anti-aircraft fire wouldn't catch up. By this time, because of the removal of the turret and everything else not needed plus the fuel burn we were finding it easier to hold altitude and even gain some. We gained just enough altitude to allow us to bailout safely if we had to. We were now in touch with Air/Sea Rescue and they were giving us our course to fly. Captain Maziarz had radioed them and given them a long count from which they were able to get a fix on our position.

We finally left Europe behind and were out in the Atlantic wondering just how close we could get to England before we ran out of fuel and had to jump. Just when we were beginning to relax the intercom carried the message—fighter coming in—four o'clock high. We had nothing. We had come this far and now we couldn't even throw rocks at the S.O.B. I couldn't see it, it was on the other side of the plane. We just sat there telling Air/Sea what we were facing but before they could answer, the fighter swung up and over and we could see the elliptical wings of the Spitfire. Just a lad from the R.A.F. out having a good time. I think the pilot enjoyed scaring the hell out of us.

As we were proceeding on the course given us by Air/Sea we looked ahead and there was a destroyer coming toward us as fast as it could go and about a half mile ahead turned back on its own track so it wouldn't be too far behind us after we overflew them. Later there was another speeding our way and it too turned before it reached us.

After that there was a B-24 with a lifeboat hanging from its bomb bay trying to slow down enough to stay with us. It crisscrossed above us for some time and then left. By now, England was on the horizon and we were beginning to think we might make it even though the fuel gauges were being very negative.

We were probably about half a mile off the coast when Air/Sea gave me a course correction which paralleled the coast. I questioned this and told them we didn't have any fuel left. I was told to hold the new course. which I did for a few minutes and he corrected me again into Exeter.

This time we were to fly up a bay and not over land. Exeter was at the very end of this narrow bay.

They had us lined up with the airfield. I didn't fly any pattern. I lined up on the first runway going in the right direction and when we were close enough asked for gear down and found out the tail wheel wouldn't extend, asked for flaps, they worked, and we landed. We touched down at approximately 100 MPH and just as soon as we touched down I found out we had no brakes, the drag on the left side was evident so we cut the two right engines hoping to equalize the drag. There was no control at all.

This was classified as a crash landing. When you touch down at 100 MPH, have no brakes and no engines to control direction, the aircraft does exactly what it wants. You sit there and try to enjoy the fact you are still alive and hope you are going to stay that way. We were already going off the runway to the left and just a short distance off the runway must have been every troop carrying glider in England. A long line of those boxie kites stored there waiting for future use. I couldn't do a thing other than sit there and watch our oblique approach to the first row. At this time we were fortunate to have no tail wheel. If that had been down we would have certainly gone through several of the gliders and possible ruptured a gas line and started to burn. Without the tail wheel the tail section acted as a drag and stopped us about ten feet away from the line. I was looking down into the cockpit of the first one. We were that close.

After we evacuated the aircraft I had the engineer check the fuel tanks. There was no measurable amount of fuel in any of them. I think that everyone who has been in combat feels that they have, during the course of certain battles, had help from the Big Guy upstairs. We did.

1. The initial flak burst should have blown us out of the sky.
2. The Bombardier could have been wounded badly in the head or killed if he hadn't caught a glimpse of the flak burst and reacted as he did.
3. The Navigator, if he had been an inch or two one side or the other would have been wounded badly or killed.
4. Many bombs came close to obliterating us on the way down.
5. The recovery of the aircraft, through what I perceived to be thermal action. At least a force greater than I could exert aided in the recovery from the spin.

6. To have this extremely thick cloud coverage just when and where we needed it. It seemed to appear like a wall immediately ahead of us.
7. To come out on the wrong side of the peninsula with the probable concentration of guns on the other side.
8. To have the fuel last long enough to reach Exeter.
9. To have the tail wheel not extend, thereby creating the drag that kept us from running into the gliders.

I don't doubt that all of the above can be explained, but I still think we had help. This mission was hard on all of us. It was hardest on Capt. Maziarz who had already had to ditch in the ocean returning from a mission over Oschersleben, Germany on Feb. 22, 1944, his 13th mission. The aircraft we flew that day had only three or four missions to its credit. It was new and we were proud of it. It was repaired and flew again, but by that time I had finished my quota of missions and was on my way home.

It is fifty years since that mission was flown that this is being written; however, it is as clear today to me as it was the day of the mission.

On an earlier mission directed towards Brussels, I was looking out the window and saw two radial engine Focke-Wulf 190's (the mainstay of the Luftwaffe fighter squadrons after 1941) flying below the left wing hosing the bomber with machine gun fire. At that moment the German pilot looked up. We two pilots were close enough to see each other's face. I alerted our crew, and the gunners made a confirmed kill.

Ben Bruce was recalled during the Korean War and spent an additional two years on active duty flying B-29s, but that's another story.

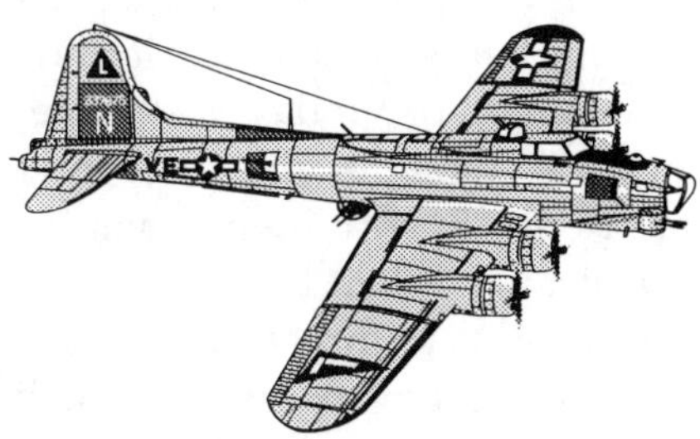

86

War's Familiar Pattern

Ernie Pyle (1900-1945),
War Correspondent

Not long after dark the rifle shots started. There would be a little flurry far ahead, maybe a dozen shots. Then silence for many minutes."

"Then there would be another flurry, way to the left. Then silence. Then the blurt of a machine gun closer, and a few scattered single shots sort of framing it. Then a long silence. Spooky!

"All night it went like that. Flares in the sky overhead, the crack of big guns behind us. Then some passing shells, a few dark figures coming and going in the night, muted voices at the telephones, the rifle shots, the mosquitoes, the stars, the feel of the damp night air under the wide sky—back again at the kind of life I had known so long. The old familiar patterns unchanged by distance or time...A pattern so imbedded in my soul...It seemed I'd never known anything else in my life."

One soldier witness, Capt. Murray Eisman, told of seeing the war correspondent's jeep moving ahead, and heard the stutter of a Japanese sniper's machine gun firing. While soldiers silenced the sniper with a flame-thrower, Ernie Pyle, the highly regarded friend of the troops, was dead on Iwo Jima, an island off Okinawa, April 18, 1945.

In Pyle's pocket they found a draft of a column he was to file on the occasion of VE day, just three weeks hence:

"To the boys who were my friends for so long, my one regret is that I was not with them when it ended...I hope the end of the war will be a gigantic relief, but not an elation. In the joyousness of high spirits, it is easy for us to forget the dead.

"But there are many of the living who have had burned into their brains the unnatural sight of cold dead men, scattered over hillsides and in ditches...Dead men by mass production, month after month, year after year...Dead men in such familiar promiscuity they become monotonous; dead men in such monstrous infinity you grow almost to hate them. To you at home, they are columns of figures, or a near one who went away and didn't come back. We saw him, by multiple thousands. That's the difference."

Pyle wrote of combat soldiers and captured the essence of fear and heroism. His memory lingers on in such compelling words.

He wrote: "I guess it doesn't make any difference, once a man has gone. Medals and speeches and victories are nothing to them anymore. They died and others lived and nobody knows why it is so. When we leave here for the next shore, there is nothing we can do for the ones beneath the wooden crosses, except perhaps to pause and murmur, 'Thanks Pal'."

We in the World War II Commemoration Committee hope that the sacrifices of those brave men are not forgotten and that we do not weaken our defenses so that aggressors might be encouraged to impose their tyranny on free men.

MG James J. Lindsay presenting certificate to Col. John Roush, Infantry OCS Hall of Fame Ceremonies, Fort Benning, GA, February, 1984

Photo: U.S. Photography Dept., Fort Benning, Georgia 31905

Senior-Active Member

Appendix A

About the Editor
Colonel John H. Roush, Jr., AUS-Ret.

One of the first recipients of the Benjamin Franklin Award by National ROA for distinguished journalism in 1985, he was also awarded the Sword & Pen Award for 14 consecutive years. He was given the Minuteman Award, Brigade of Volunteers, by National ROA, and the California Department ROA awarded Colonel Roush the President's Plaque as the most outstanding member of the Department in 1982.

He was given the Freedoms Foundation Medal in 1974 for outstanding writing.

Colonel Roush enlisted in the Army December 19, 1942, while in college, also serving as a Sergeant in the California State Guard, formed after the National Guard was mobilized and federalized. He landed at Omaha Beach as an EM in a combat engineer unit, was commissioned in France as a Second Lieutenant, Infantry, was a platoon leader in combat. He served in the occupation of Germany and Austria, becoming a Provost Marshal. His last assignment before retirement was Assistant U.S. Military Attaché to Norway. He retired from the Army in 1975, however he held an important mobilization assignment for an additional eight years.

He was inducted into the Infantry OCS Hall of Fame, Fort Benning, Georgia in 1989. A graduate of the Army Command & General Staff College, the Industrial College of the Armed Forces, and the Army War College and the Foreign Service Institute, U.S. State Department, he went on to earn a Doctorate in Business Administration and was a management consultant for a number of years.

John Roush is listed in:

Who's Who in the West
Who's Who in California
International Who's Who of Authors
Contemporary Authors

He is the author of eight published books, and has two more manuscripts being considered. His articles have appeared in many different magazines, published in three languages. He has chapters in several other books.

Other books by John H. Roush, Jr., D.B.A.:

Hornets in Our Home: Civil Disturbances and Their Effects on U. S. National Security, 1971
The Problems of Civil Disturbances as They Relate to Public Administration, 1973
Management Audits of National Insurance Companies, 1974
Successfully Fishing Lake Tahoe, 1976
Antlers Afield, Tales of Big Game Hunting, 1987
Enjoying Fishing Lake Tahoe, The Truckee River and Pyramid Lake, 1987

Appendix B

Medal of Honor Recipients

Mel Biddle	Chapter	31
James H. Doolittle (1896-1994)	Chapter	5
Oscar C. Johnson	Chapter	18
Johnathan Wainright (1883-1953)	Chapter	69

213 awarded in European theater of operations
230 awarded in Pacific theater of operations
443 awarded during World War II

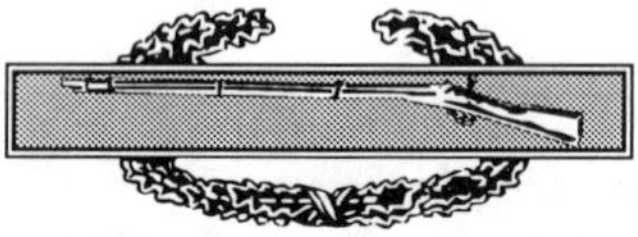

Appendix C

The Combat Infantryman Badge Holders in this Volume

PATTON, George, General, USA (1896-1945)	28	115
PITCOCK, Duff, EM, AUS	82	322
POWELL, Nolan, EM, AUS	31	130
PINNICK, Floyd V., Major, USA	21	88
RIACH, Douglas A., Colonel, AUS-Ret.	22	91
ROUSH, John H., Jr., Colonel, AUS-Ret.	39	160
UPP, Robert D., Brig. General, AUS-Ret.	16	66
VILLARIN, Mariano, LTC, AUS-Ret.	8	27
WOOD, William Stanley, Major, AUS-Ret	21	88

"Iron Mike" statue at Fort Benning, Georgia, home of the U.S. Army Infantry Branch

Appendix D

Members of the Explorers Club Included in this Volume

The Exporers Club is a multidisciplinary society dedicated to scientific exploration and field research.

DOOLITTLE, James Harold	Med	42	Chapter 5
LARSON, Thomas J., Ph.D	E	52	Chapter 3 & 78
OGG, Robert D.**	LF	80	Chapter 68
ROSCOE, John H., Ph.D.	FN	54	Chapter 59
ROUSH, John Huston, Jr., D.B.A.	FN	80	Chapter 39 & 74
RYCHETNIK, Joseph S.	E	67	Chapter 58
SKINNER, Carlton*	FN	62	Chapter 10
CHEATHAM, Nonna E.	MN	90	Assisted in the assembly of this collection

*Former Northern California Chapter Chairman
**Former Vice Chairman, Northern California Chapter
Codes:

E	=	Emeritus
Med	=	Medalist
FN	=	Fellow, National
MN	=	Member, National
LF	=	Life Fellow

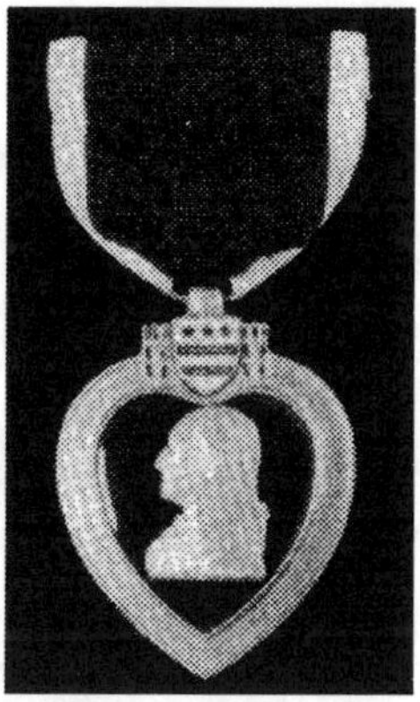

Appendix E

Persons Awarded the Purple Heart Medal for Wounds Received in Combat

Ayers, Lawrence S.
Brannan, William W.
Carlton, Walker
* **Claven**, Jack B.
Dodril, Carl
Dussaq, Rene Alexander
Frame, Leonard W.
Gillis, Thomas D.
Holland, James D.
Kaufman, Mozart
Kuperstein, Abner D.
Lawson, Ted W.
Lay, Kermit R.
* **Mooney**, Robert L.
* **Palassou**, Robert K.
* **Riach**, Douglas A.
Roscoe, John H.
Stephens, Dale J.
Villarin, Mariano
Whitman, Robert S.
Zarlengo, John

*OLC for two or more

Eligible, but did not have papers processed:
Graf, Robert F.
Hayden, Charles D.

"No order taken by me while I was Chief of Staff gave me greater satisfaction than re-establishing the Order of the Purple Heart. It had not been in use for a century and a quarter.

"This decoration is unique in several ways; first, it is the oldest in American history and antedates practically all of the famous military medals of the world; second, it comes from the greatest of all Americans, George Washington, and thereby carries with it something of the reverence which haloes his great name; and third, it is the only decoration which is completely intrinsic in that it does not depend upon approval or favor by anyone. It goes only to those who are wounded in battle, and enemy action alone determines the award. It is a true badge of courage, and every breast that wears it can beat with pride."

General of the Army Douglas MacArthur, "Reminiscences", 1964

Appendix F

Glossary

AAA	Antiaircraft Artillery
Abn	Airborne
ACE	Title given to a fighter pilot who shot down 5 or more aircraft. Less than one percent of pilots achieved this designation
ACR	Armored Cavalry Regiment
AD	Active Duty
ADJ	Adjutant
AEAF	Allied Expeditionary Air Force
AEF	Allied Expeditionary Force
AFB	Air Force Base
AKA	Also known as
ALSOS	Army unit to study German progress toward development of nuclear weapons
AM	Air Medal
ANVIL	Planned Invasion of Southern France
ARVN	Army of Viet Nam
AUS	Army of the United States
AWC	Army War College
BB	Battleship
Bde	Brigade
BG	Brigadier General
Bn	Battalion
Br	British
BSM	Bronze Star Medal
C&GS	Command and General Staff College
CA	Civil Affairs, Heavy Cruiser
CAP	Combat Air Patrol
CAPT	Captain, Navy & Coast Guard

CAS	Close Air Support
CC	Combat Command
CCR	Reserve Combat Command
CCRC	Combat Crew Replacement Center, Air Corps
CMDR	Commander, Naval , title of rank
CG	Coast Guard
CIA	U. S. Central Intelligence Agency
CIB	Combat Infantry Badge *(see Appendix C)*
CIC	Counter Intelligence Corps
CINCPAC	Commander in Chief, Pacific
CIOR	International Congress of Reserve Officers (NATO countries)
CL	Light carrier
CLU	Certified Life Underwriter
CMH	Medal of Honor
CMP	Corp of Military Police
CMTC	Citizen's Military Training Camp
COBRA	Operation to break out of Normandy
COMINT	Communications Intelligence
COMPAC	Commander Pacific
COMSOPAC	Commander, South Pacific
COMZ	Communications Zone
CONUS	Continental United States
CORONET	Second planned invasion of Japan, Honshu
CP	Command Post
CPT	Captain, Army & Air Force
CROSSBOW	German V-1, V-2 ops & countermeasures
CS	Combat Support
CSMR	California State Military Reserve
CV	Aircraft Carrier
CVBG	Carrier Battle Group
CVP	Composite Unit Provisional
DBA	Doctor of Business Administration
DD	Destroyer
DE	Destroyer Escort
Det.	Detachment
DFC	Distinguished Flying Cross *(see Appendix J)*
DIA	Defense Intelligence Agency
Divarty	Division Artillery
DOWNFALL	Overall plans for invasion of Japan
DSC	Distinguished Service Cross
DSM	Distinguished Service Medal

DZ	Drop Zone
EAB	Engineer Aviation Battalion
EM	Enlisted men
Enigma	German Encoding Machine
EPW	Enemy Prisoner of War
ETO	European Theater of Operations
FA	Field Artillery
FLYING TIGERS	American volunteer group of airmen fighting the Japanese, led by MG Claire Chennault
FF	Friendly Fire
FF	Frigate
FLAK	Aerial shrapnel—an acronym from the German language
FM	Field Manual
FMO	Field Artillery Aerial Observer
FORTITUDE	Deception plan for the European invasion, June 1944 *(see page 118)*
FOX HOLE	Deep hole dug by one or two infantrymen for protection
G-1	Personnel Section of Division or higher staff
G-2	Intelligence Section
G-3	Plans & Operations
G-4	Supply Section
G-5	Civil Affairs
GEN	General
Gestapo	*Geheim Stats Polizei*, home security police
GI	Government issue
Gooseberry	Artificial harbors created along Normandy coast
Gp	Group
GS	General Staff
H	Heavy (in the case of bombers B-17s, B-24s)
HERBSTNEBEL	German code name for *Ardennes offinois*, "Battle of the Bulge" *(curtitmon mist)*
Hq	Headquarters
HUSKY	Allied Invasion of Sicily *(see Chapters 13, 14, & 15)*
INFO	Information
Intel	Intelligence
IMA	Individual Mobilization Assignee
IP	Initial Point
JAG	Judge Advocate General
Kamikaze	"Divine Wind"
KIA	Killed in Action

LAV	Light Armored Vehicle
LCI	Landing Craft Infantry
LCMDR	Lieutenant Commander
LCT	Landing Craft Tank
LCVP	Landing Craft Vehicle & Personnel
LD	Line of Departure
LM	Legion of Merit
LRP Bn	Long Range Penetration Battalion (Army)
LSO	Landing Signal Officer
LST	Landing Ship Tank
Lt	Lieutenant
LTC	Lieutenant Colonel
LTG	Lieutenant General
LT (JG)	Lieutenant Junior Grade, Naval rank
LTV	Landing vehicle tracked
LUCKY FORWARD	General Patton's Headquarters
Luftwaffe	German Air Force
M	Mines
MAG	Military Advisory Group
MAGIC	Translations of SIGINT (U.S.)
MAJ	Major
Marquis	Name of the French Resistance forces
MARKET GARDEN	Airborne Operation, Holland
Med Hon	Medal of Honor *(see Appendix B)*
MG	Major General
MI	Military Intelligence
MIA	Missing in Action
MLR	Main Line of Resistance
MP	Military Police
MSC	Medical Service Corps, Army
MSGT	Master Sergeant
NAS	Naval Air Station
NCO	Non-commissioned Officer
NEPTUNE	Naval phase of the Invasion of France
NG	National Guard
NSA	National Security Agency
OB	Order of Battle
OCS	Officer Candiate School, Office of Chief of Staff (U.S. Army)
OFI	Office of Air Force Information
OKHA	Japanese glider bomb, also called BAKA
OLC	Oak Leaf Cluster (indicating add. award)

OLYMPIC	Planned first invasion of Japan, Kyushu
OP	Observation Point
OSS	Office of Strategic Service, predecessor of the CIA
OVERLORD	Plan for invasion of Europe Spring 1944
P	Provisional
PBY	Amphibious Patrol, aircraft (seaplane) (catalina)
PF	Frigate
PH	Purple Heart Medal *(see Appendix E)*, Pearl Harbor
PIR	Parachute Infantry Regiment
Plat.	Platoon
PM	Provost Marshal
POL	Petroleum, oil and lubricants
PPI	Prespositioned Indicator
PR	Public Relations
PT	Torpedo Boat
PURPLE	American nomencalture for Japanese Diplomatic Machine Cipher
QM	Quartermaster
R&D	Research and Development
R&R	Rest and Rehabilitation
RADM	Rear Admiral
RAF	Royal Air Force
RB	Rolling Barrage
RC	Reserve Component
RCAF	Royal Canadian Air Force
RCT	Regimental Combat Team
Recon	Reconnaissance
Rgmt	Regiment
ROA	Reserve Officers Association of the U. S.
ROC	Republic of China
S/Sgt	Staff Sergeant
SAARF	Special Allied Airborne Recon Forces
SACMED	Supreme Commander, Mediterranean Theater
See Bees	Navy Construction Battalions
SAR	Search and Rescue
SCAEF	Supreme Commander, Allied Expeditionary Force
SEAL	Sea, Air and Land
Sen.	Senator
SHAEF	Supreme Headquarters, Allied Expeditionary Force
SIGINT	Signals Intelligence (COMINT)
SM	Soldier's Medal
SMR	State Military Reserve

SO	Special Operation
SOL	Sorry, out of luck
SOP	Standard Operating Procedure
SS	Schutzstaffel (Elite Guard)
T-4	Technician, 4th Grade (Army enlisted rank)
T/Sgt	Tech Sergeant (Army enlisted rank)
TK	Tank
TORCH	Allied Invasion No. Africa 1942
TROA	The Retired Officers Association
UK	United Kingdom
ULTRA	Top Secret (U.S.), Security Classification for SIGINT
USA	United States Army
USAF	United States Air Force
USAR	United States Army Reserve
USCG	United States Coast Guard
USN	United States Navy
USSBS	U. S. Bombing Survey
USSTAF	U. S. Strategic Air Force
V-1	German flying bomb
V-2	German rocket 46' long
VADM	Vice Admiral
VE Day	War ends in Europe
VH	Very Heavy (in the case of bombers, B-29s)
VJ DAY	War ends in Asia
Volkssturm	A people's militia
Wehrmacht	German Armed Forces
WIA	Wounded in Action
WO	Warrant Officer
YP	Yacht Patrol

Appendix G

Minute Man Award of the Reserve Officers Association for Outstanding Service, Brigade of Volunteers

Only a fraction of one percent of the membership of ROA has been awarded this honor by the National Headquarters for their leadership within the organization.

The following participants in this volume have been so honored:

Dodge, Elliott G., Jr., Commander USNR-Ret.

Grant, Artis C., Colonel AUS-Ret.

Riach, Douglas A., Colonel AUS-Ret.

Roscoe, John H., Colonel USMCR-Ret.

Roush, John H., Jr., Colonel AUS-Ret.

Sparks, Bennett S., Rear Admiral USCGR-Ret.

Upp, Robert D., Brigadier General AUS-Ret.

Wahleithener, James C., Major General USAF-Ret.

Appendix H

Where These People Served

*number designates Chapter #

Pacific Theater
- Anderson, 34*
- Birch, 5
- Bolthouse, 73
- Carlton, 36
- Chapman, 77
- Claven, 46
- Coutts, 83
- Craig, 2, 44
- Dickey, 49
- Dodge, 41
- Doolittle, 5
- Doughty, 71
- Frame, 45
- Geer, 51, L
- Graf, 6
- Grant, 38
- Holland, 37
- Holm, 25
- Kappeler, 5
- Kaufman, 81
- Larson, 3
- Lawson, 5
- Lay, 11
- Marks, 57
- Miller, 54
- Mooney, 64
- Munsch, 76
- Novaresi, 4, 48
- Ogg, 68
- Pyle, 86
- Rychetnik, 58
- Scheffelin, 67
- Shaw, 50
- Skinner, 10
- Sparks, 7
- Tanaka, 47
- Uyehata, 63
- Villarin, 8
- Vogenitz, 69
- Walker, 1
- Wamsley, 9
- Wischemann, 70
- Wright, 35
- Zarlengo, 53

Philippines
- Anderson, 34
- Carlton, 36
- Dickey, 49
- Lay, 11
- Marks, 57
- Mooney, 64
- Shaw, 50
- Tanaka, 47
- Villarin, 8

Italy
- Amundsen, 17
- Ayers, 19
- Brannan, 31
- Fox, 12
- Fulton, 20
- Kuperstein, 13, 14, 15
- Palassou, 18
- Patton, 28
- Schulman, 56
- Wood, 21

Alaska
- Kaufman, 81
- Miller, 54
- Skinner, 10
- Upp, 16

North Africa
- Bruce, 85
- Dodge, 41
- Dorsk, 43
- Fox, 12
- Kuperstein, 13, 14, 15
- Patton, 28

European Theater

England/Continental Europe

*number designates Chapter #

Appendix I

Breakdown of Participants

By Branch of Service:

Army	40
Infantry	25
Combat arms	33
Air Force	25
Navy	8
Marines	3
Merchant Marine	1
Coast Guard	3
War correspondent	1
Total	78

(*Note:* some served in two roles during various portions of the war period)

By Rank: (Highest rank achieved)

Flag	8	Generals and Admirals
0-6	14	Colonels and Navy Captains
0-5	16	Lt. Cols., Commanders
0-4	14	Majors, Lt. Commanders
0-1 – 0-3	8	Ensigns, Lieutenants, Captains
Warrant Off.	6	Warrant Officers
EM	10	Enlisted men
Civilian	2	Correspondents/Merchant Marine
Total	78	

Appendix J

Persons Awarded the Distinguished Flying Cross

	Chapter	Page
Birch, William L	5	18
Bruce, Ben	85	331
Dickey, Charles	49	199
Doolittle, James H.	5	15
Frame, Leonard W.	45	183
Geer, Hal	Apx. L	363
Kappeler, Frank A.	5	18
Kraft, Marvin	42	174
Lawson, Ted W.	5	18
Novaresi, Sidney	48	196
Rose, Philip	55	227
Shaw-Corthorn, George	50	211
Vogenitz, Richart Barclay	69	276
Wahleithner, James C.	Foreword	xv
Wamsley, George	9	31
Zarlengo, John	3	221

Appendix K

Additional Information

ADDENDUM TO CHAPTER 68, pages 274-75
"Naval Intelligence/Pearl Harbor Debacle"

Editors Note: For those interested in this topic your attention is invited to a most interesting recent volume, *Days of Infamy – Mac Arthur, Roosevelt, Churchill – The Shocking Truth Revealed – How Their Secret Deals and Strategic Blunders Caused Disasters at Pearl Harbor and the Philippines*, by John Costello, 1994, Pocket Books, a division of Simon & Schuster.

Abundant evidence is cited to show that Hawaiian commands did not receive all available relevant intelligence, including some that was later shown to be of critical consideration, prior to the Pearl Harbor attack. But the Congressional Investigating Committee in 1945 came to the conclusion that Kimball and Short did have enough information needed to order higher levels of war alert. A war warning was sent out to Pacific Commanders on 27 November 1941; they also had an alert on 24 November. However, Washington offices should have shared in the responsibility for the disaster.

Some indicators suggest that British Intelligence in Singapore had learned beforehand of the Japanese plans to attack Pearl Harbor but did not relay those specifics in the belief that the United States had adequate intelligence of their own development. Certainly the Hawaiian commanders could have been better informed of what Washington had learned. The Philippine command was kept better informed with signal intelligence—decoded information—that was not sent to Hawaii, yet they were caught unprepared and suffered appalling losses. On pages 355-356, reference is made to a lengthy deposition of James D. Ogg, then a seaman first class, an electronics expert on the staff of the Naval Intelligence Office in San Francisco. He gave a lengthy interview while identified as "Seaman Z" to COMDR Irwin G. Newman, USNR, Historian of the Naval Security Group Command. He speaks of intercepts of transmissions from an area east of the International Dateline on 2 Dec 1941.

The book contains an extensive bibliography on pages 427-437. Within Appendix 2, this reference to Commander Ogg is included in Special Research History (SIGINT) 355, RG 457 National Archives, Washington, D.C. That volume is described as Naval Security Group History of WWII, prepared by Captain J. S. Hollwick, USN-Ret., June 1971 (464 pages).

Mount Emily, in Southwest Oregon, was the site of the first and only bombing of the contiguous America States during World War II. The Japanese pilot Nobuo Fujita flew from the submarine *I-25*. A forest fire started from the incendiary bomb was quickly put out by forestry personnel. I was camped near by on the Chetco River on a fishing trip on September 9, 1942.

The battleship *U.S.S. California* was sunk at Pearl Harbor on December 7, 1941, but was salvaged to fight the Japanese during the Battle of Leyte Gulf on October 20, 1944, the largest sea battle in history.

Readers of this collection may be interested in other assemblies. Many books have been written about World War II, including a number of recent volumes issued during the last few years commemorating the fiftieth anniversary of the epoch conflict. Few deal with the personal experiences of individual soldiers, sailors and airmen but rather grasp a larger subject matter or deal with sectors of combat.

In *The Officer* magazine, the journal of the Reserve Officers Association of the United States, during the period 1991–1995, Ms. Carol A. Kelly edited a series of brief accounts of members' recollections of their experiences during the war years. These were arranged chronologically as the 50th year unfolded. Some of the participants in that series who live in California are also in this volume, yet their stories included here were edited from their personal accounts and interviews and not from the magazine series.

Operation Memories – Incredible Stories of World War II Veterans, as told to Evelyn I. Gregory, published in 1995, contains 51 stories, primarily those of WWII veterans living in Sonoma County, California. Her collection gives a broader overview of the individuals' war years, while we have confined our chapters of most memorable incidents to cover primarily recollections of combat experiences.

Many of us believe that the experiences of individuals, those remarkable incidents that remain vivid in the person's mind even after fifty years have elapsed, are more interesting than normal histories. Perhaps you will agree after having read this collection.

Most of the men whose stories are included will tell you that those events recited in these pages are indelibly etched into their memories.

A lady of my acquaintance, an altruistic, liberal-minded person, asked, "Well, are you endeavoring to glorify war?" None of the men involved with this volume would answer in the affirmative to that unnecessary question. We are proud to have had a part in quelching the evil ideologies that brought so much suffering to mankind. Collectively we would urge that all reasonable steps be taken to avert possibilities of such a calamity occurring in the future. We agree too that an adequate defense structure is our best guarantee of not becoming engaged in another conflict of the magnitude we were involved in. Perhaps our recollections will give some sense of urgency to the premise of being prepared. This still remains a world of uncertainty, with threats to freedom remaining, some slightly veiled and other bellicose.

In the spirit of Valley Forge,
there have always been some men
in this country who have, like George,
been ready to serve their country often,
or as required to preserve freedom.

Over a million of us have served in the reserves,
of all ranks, of all ages,
endeavoring to raise the preparedness curve,
bearing no animosity, no latent rages
against those who would bury us.

But, instead, feeling that strength brings peace,
has hastened the day when less arms
are needed, yet the threat of war may never cease.
We offer friendship instead of threat of harms.
Strength is the real impetus for peace.

The 50th Anniversary of World War II flag features the World War II Honorable Service Lapel Button. The badge originally designed by Anthony de Francisci for the War Department was issued to all veterans honorably discharged between September 8, 1939, and December 31, 1946.

During the commemorative period, the United States will focus on honoring the World War II veterans and the sacrifices made on the home front by the American people, providing the American public with a clearer understanding and appreciation of the enduring lessons of World War II, acquainting Americans with the reasons why we fought—the values which we strove to defend and protect, and highlighting the advances in technology, science and medicine from military research during World War II. For more information, write: HQDA, SACC; Room 3E524, Pentagon; Washington, D.C. 20310-0101

Appendix L

Additional Photos of Participants

Captain George Shaw-Corthorn , USN, then Chief of Staff COMWESTSEA FRON (Western Sea Frontier Command) at Treasure Island Naval Base, San Francisco, California, June 23, 1972, shortly before retirement from the Navy (Chapter 50)

A-20 being loaded for a night mission in Europe

1st Lieutenant Sidney Novaresi on the island of Ie Shima off Okinawa, July 1945, in front of his P-47 Thunderbolt fighter plane. Ie Shima was used as an advance airfield to provide fighter support for bombers attacking Japan. (Chapter 48)

1st Lt. Milton S. Anderson upon graduation from Jump School, Fort Benning, Georgia, Spring 1944, prior to going overseas. (Chapter 34)

1st Lt. Robert L. Mooney, June 16, 1951, U.S. Army (Chapter 64)

Photos taken on 6 October 1944 on the fourth mission of Major Philip Rose USAF. His plane was flying No. 6 position in the lead squadron. You can see R bar as the second plane in the formation pictures, the plane flown by Major Rose. The pictures were taken from the waist gunner position of plane No. 4. (Chapter 55)

Lieutenant Colonel John Zarlengo, commander of a squadron in the 5th Air Force in Korea, 1952-53. The young pilot during World War II was credited with shooting down four Zero fighters in one engagement when attacked by 20 Zeros while on a bombing mission over Tulagi Harbor. He took part in the battles of Midway, Solomon Islands, and Guadalcanal, as well as those in Korea. The book American Heroes of the War in the Air *by Howard Mingos, published by Lanciar Publishers, 30 Rockefeller Plaza, NY describes his remarkable actions in combat. (Chapter 53)*

Bennett S. Sparks, center, is commissioned Ensign in October of 1957 at Anacostia Naval Air Station. (Chapter 7)

1st Class Aviation electronics Technician Bennett S. Sparks, PBY51 Crewman at MCAS, Cherry Point, N.C. in 1945. (Chapter 7)

Chinese refugees fleeing from Japanese advance with their total world's possessions. (Chapter 51) Photo courtesy of Hal Geer

Hal Geer flew 86 missions in B-24's and B-25's and took part in ground intelligence missions behind enemy lines as a combat photographer. He received the Legion of Merit for his intrepid adventures. His newsreel photography of the Chinese army in action was widely seen in the free world during the war years. The film was smuggled out (containing intelligence information as well) through Japanese lines to Bombay, where it was developed.

Hal Geer retired as Vice President and executive producer of Warner Bros. cartoons. Geer joined Warner Bros. in 1946 as a color technician in the special effects department, was instrumental in keeping the classic WB cartoons, such as Merrie Melodies and Looney Tunes, in children's programming.

In 1985 he helped to organize the Bugs Bunny star on the Hollywood Walk of Fame and was honored along with directors Fritz Freleng and Chuck Jones and voice master Mel Blanc at New York City's Museum of Modern Art during the WB cartoons' Golden Jubilee.

During his career as a filmmaker, Geer worked on 25 feature films, more than 500 television shows, 400 commercials and 100 short subjects.

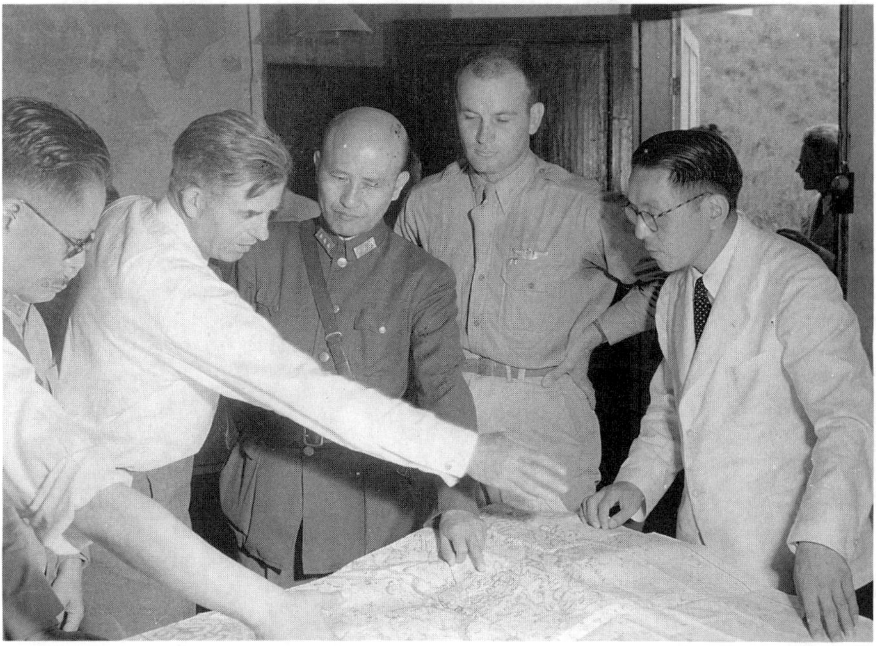

United States Vice President Henry Wallace extending his arm to the map. On his left is the Chinese Minister of Defense and to his left Brigadier General Casey Vincent of the Flying Tigers. At that time it was most important to our strategic plans to keep the Republic of China in the war despite the severe pressure put upon them by Japanese forces. The photo was taken in Kweiling, China, once called the "Paris of China." (photo courtesy of Hal Geer)

A Flying Tiger P-51 fighter of the 16th Fighter Squadron. It is believed the pilot shown was Tex Hill. (photo courtesy of Hal Geer)

A Flying Tiger pilot looking at the briefing board

Seven P-51 fighter planes of the 16th Fighter Squadron lined up on a primitive air strip in China in 1942. (photo by Hal Geer)

The Intelligence Officer Captain Ross Mc Leod of the 435th Bomb Squadron of the Flying Tigers is briefing pilots regarding their next mission. Note the Chinese flag on the back of one pilot's jacket. It was called the "Blood Chit." The letters in the Chinese language printed on the large patch read: "I am an American Flier. My government will reward you handsomely if you help me." The photo was taken by Hal Geer on December 23, 1942.

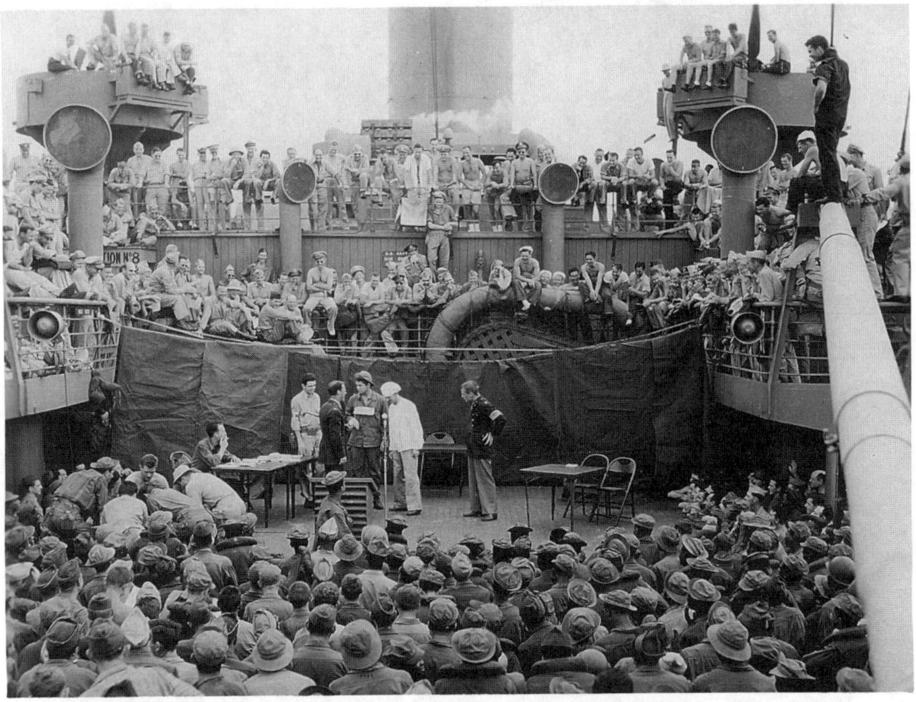

GIs generate an impromptu stage show in the troopship S.S. Brazil, *somewhere south of Australia, in the summer of 1943. Photo by Hal Geer.*

Comedian Joe E. Brown entertains the troops at a 14th Air Force Base in Yunnanyi China. Photo by Hal Geer.

All the airfields in China were built by hand. The rocks were hauled two or three miles from a river bed, then pounded with a hammer to crush them. A binder of water and sand called "slurry" was spread over the rock base. Then the surface was compacted by a large concrete roller, weighing several tons. Over two hundred coolies pulled the roller. For a long day's work their wages were 20 cents and a bowl of rice. Photo by Hal Geer.

In the face of the Japanese advance, Chinese farmers plant bombs in a runway so that the runway can be destroyed. Photo by Hal Geer.

A "Gooney Bird" C-47 lands on a Chinese runway while coolies continue working on an extension. Photo by Hal Geer.